Management Standards for Computer and Numerical Controls

Donald N. Smith
and
Lary Evans

INDUSTRIAL DEVELOPMENT DIVISION
INSTITUTE OF SCIENCE AND TECHNOLOGY
THE UNIVERSITY OF MICHIGAN
1977

Available from
INDUSTRIAL DEVELOPMENT DIVISION
INSTITUTE OF SCIENCE AND TECHNOLOGY
2200 Bonisteel Boulevard
Ann Arbor, Michigan 48109

Printed in the United States of America

Contents

The Industrial Development Division is a unit of the Institute of Science and Technology of The University of Michigan. The Division was established to accomplish two of the purposes of the Institute as stated in the Bylaws of the Board of Regents of the University; namely, "to serve as a center of science and technology," and "to encourage, support, and conduct research in all fields of pure and applied science, engineering, and technology which are potentially important to the future business and industrial development of the State of Michigan . . ." An important phase of the Division's research program has been the study of various Michigan industries, their relation to similar industries elsewhere in the nation and abroad, and the effect of modern science and technology on these industries. Such studies aid in the improvement of the competitive position of Michigan companies as well as contribute to the general industrial development of the State.

In addition to carrying on research and publishing the results of such industrial studies, the Division sponsors seminars and workshops for industry and maintains a liaison service to promote the flow of information between faculty and research groups within the University and industrial firms.

Introduction

A major objective of this book is to present, concisely but thoroughly, the information required by upper level managers when moving into computer-aided manufacturing. The application of computer and numerical controls affects virtually every segment of a manufacturing enterprise. Effective implementation has produced unprecendented gains in organization productivity, but the marginal application has resulted in dramatic examples of failure. To complicate matters further, the decision against implementing computer or numerical controls has been tantamount to forfeiture of certain markets. Yet, in these same markets, the inefficient implementation has meant production stoppages, human relations problems and union strikes, lost sales, and, ultimately, financial losses.

The complexity of computer-aided manufacturing technology has grown to a level such that even managers who progressed through engineering-related departments often do not fully understand the details of computer-aided manufacturing projects their subordinates propose. Because these projects are complex and very costly relative to traditional manufacturing equipment that frequently was introduced a piece at a time and almost always was devoid of the systems implications of computer controls, too few managers had the necessary time required to obtain the knowledge for sound decisions. Managers fortunate enough to have skilled subordinates sometimes saw projects which they approved on faith attain the objectives. Too often, though, results of these projects have been gross underachievement, with the manager's performance and prospects for advancement suffering. Having been victimized once, these managers tend to reject outright future computer-aided manufacturing proposals that could have accelerated organization productivity.

The emphasis in this book is to interpret the technology and its economic implications. In delineating the technological concepts, we have accepted the risk of belaboring the obvious to managers who are relatively more initiated into the computer era than others.

For the advanced, the book will nevertheless serve as a useful reference source that could provide comparative performance criteria against which their organizations and subordinates can be evaluated. For the uninitiated, the book will also provide tutorial information regarding concepts, applications, and future trends.

The book is structured generally into four major sections. They are intended to answer these questions:

1. What are the technological concepts and the theory of design and operation of numerical, computer, programmable, and adaptive controls?

2. What are the financial impacts when these controls are implemented, and how are the direct and indirect savings and penalties evaluated for the financial analysis?

3. What are the programming alternatives, practices and cost relationships; and what are the major programming language developments that influence the evolvement of part-programming systems and concepts now dominant?

4. What are the problems, pitfalls, and profitable practices with respect to maintenance of numerical and computer-controlled equipment?

In addition to all their economic and mechanical attributes, these new controls are more importantly the catalysts that draw together design, manufacturing, and management activities, and the related information networks. While numerical controls were initially applied to a narrow range of general-purpose machines, subsequent electronic controls, such as mini- and microcomputers and programmable controllers, are being adapted to a broad range of processes, including steel and glass making, plastics, rubber, garment making, etc. Once these devices are installed to control such processes, the opportunity of tieing them into integrated information systems becomes obvious.

A characteristic of most computer and numerical control applications is that information related to the execution of the manufacturing function—be it data to control machines, inventories, material movements, accounts receivable and payable, payrolls, or cost records, or other information that makes production operations successful—can be dealt with in an electronic form that is processable in real time. While the immediate and most obvious effect of installing computer or numerical controls is observed at the machine under control, its long-term effect invariably permeates management philosophies, strategies, and techniques up through the organization all the way to the board of directors.

It is a goal, then, of this book to contribute toward the development of management knowledge, skills, and techniques that will effectively move the manager and his organization into the era of computer-aided manufacturing. In the pages that follow, critical distinctions between the controls are described along with performance standards that facilitate the technology's interpretation, application, and economic evaluation.

We would like to express our appreciation for the significant contributions of our colleagues at The University of Michigan, namely Professors Wilbert Steffy, L. V. Colwell and Joseph Martin. Additionally, several research assistants likewise provided important contributions during their student tenures. Chief among these are John McCarroll, James Hardy, Richard Bawol, Jeff Mason, Herman Meilinger, and Teofilo Reyes. We also would like to recognize the patient assistance of Professor Donald Beran of General Motors Institute, James Walter of Lockheed Georgia, Fred King of Ford Motor Company, and Ronald Centner of Bendix, who reviewed sections of the manuscript. Valuable advice and related information were also provided by William Johnson of Rocketdyne, Bob Carlson of McDonnell Douglas and Melvin Monro of Boeing. For all their contributions we are extremely grateful.

Donald N. Smith

Lary Evans

Chapter I

Conventional Numerical Control

Even though the benefits of numerial control are attainable without a thorough understanding of the design details, a working knowledge of functional concepts can be quite helpful. Such knowledge enhances a more effective utilization and maintenance of equipment; it also insures choosing numerical control (NC) systems that are best suited to particular requirements.

A computer or numerically controlled system is composed of two distinct elements: the instructions (program) and the equipment or hardware. Communication between these elements takes place in numerical or symbolic mode—by means of a precise and finite language. The regulation of machine motions occurs when a controller senses and translates the instructions, and then converts them to electronic command pulses for the machine's switches or drives.

The symbolic instructions required by the controller may be either dimensional instructions or management instructions.

Dimensional instructions specify the precise positions of the machine's elements during operations. In the drilling of holes, for example, the dimensional data define the location of the holes, as measured parallel to the machine's slides from an origin point.

Management instructions, on the other hand, control operations such as activating or deactivating a drive spindle, regulating the feeds and speeds, coolant flow, turret and tool changes, etc.

DIGITAL INSTRUCTIONS

Virtually all modern numerical control systems, regardless of the complexity, are designed to operate with digital electronic logic components such as gates, counters, etc. While a detailed knowledge of such devices is not required to understand this chapter, some initial appreciation of the implications of using digital methods for specifying and measuring position is helpful.

Roughly speaking, any measurement system produces either a continuous or a discrete approximation of the measured variable.

A continuous measurement system requires linear analog components for amplification, recording, and comparison. A discrete or digital measurement system, on the other hand, produces discrete approximations of the measured variable and can thus operate with digital logic components such as gates, counters, etc.

For discrete measurement systems, a count or "pulse" is associated with an increment of the measured variable. The size of the increment determines the resolution of the measurement system since it is the smallest discernible value. Magnitudes greater than a single increment are specified as a multiple of the resolution increments. For example, a position measurement system might have a resolution of 0.0001 inch (that is, a digital pulse represents 0.0001 of an inch of motion). Four inches on such a system would be specified as 40,000 increments.

The resolution of the system is the least programmable bit of numerical control information and, correspondingly, the best accuracy that can be achieved. Mechanical factors such as transducer location and performance, backlash, windup, and friction can degrade the resolution with regard to true displacement.

The system shown in Figure 1, while being far too simplified to represent commercial practice, illustrates the use of digital elements for controlling a single axis or slide of a machine.

OPEN-LOOP VERSUS CLOSED-LOOP CONTROL SYSTEMS

Numerical control systems can be divided as to whether they are open-loop or closed-loop control systems.

The example used in Figure 1 is a closed-loop system. The controlled variable, in this case table position, is measured and compared with the command position in a closed circuit.

Open-loop control systems, on the other hand, usually use some form of electric or hydraulic stepping motor that indexes or rotates a fixed angular increment each time a voltage pulse is applied and then holds the position until another pulse is applied. Position is inferred from the number of pulses applied and the motion increment associated with each pulse. For example, a stepping motor built to rotate its shaft 5 degrees for every pulse would rotate 40 degrees after receiving eight pulses. An open-loop position control system is shown schematically in Figure 2.

A fair comparison of open-loop with closed-loop control designs

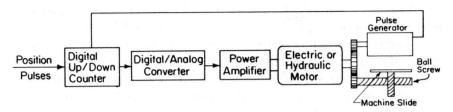

FIGURE 1

Closed-loop, DC motor or hydraulic servo position control.
(Each input pulse causes the digital counter to increase or decrease its content, depending on the desired direction. The resulting error is converted, via the digital to analog converter, to a voltage which excites the drive motor so as to rotate the ball screw. A pulse generator on the drive motor output shaft produces a feedback pulse which nulls the digital counter when the desired motion has occured.)

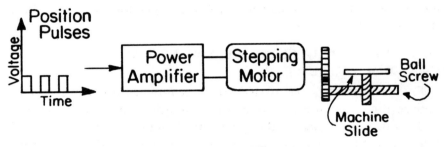

FIGURE 2

Open-loop stepping motor position control.
(Each input pulse causes a known rotation of the stepping motor output shaft and therefore a known displacement of the machine slide.)

can only be made for specific applications. For example, open-loop controls offer certain economic advantages for low-power applications that can be served adequately by electric stepping motors. Electric stepping motors are relatively inexpensive and do not require precise mechanical alignment, inertial problems are not severe, and the electronics can be relatively simple. These characteristics often are well suited to retrofit applications where the original machine design is not adaptable to closed-loop controls.

For medium- and high-power applications, the economic advantage of open-loop controls becomes less convincing. Heavy power requirements seldom have been met economically by electric stepping motors, and frequently the only feasible alternative has been combination electric-hydraulic units. These combination stepping motors are quite expensive compared to DC motors or hydraulic drives of the closed-loop systems. When they are used, this cost differential usually must be compensated for by the resulting electronic circuitry reductions. Electric-hydraulic stepping motor systems may also require additional electronic complexities such as acceleration and deceleration controls.

Because stepping motors move in discrete increments, a trade-off must often be made between resolution and maximum speed. Moreover, there is no absolute assurance that a step will never be missed, and, for some critical applications, additional feedback circuitry is often employed with some sacrifice of simplicity and economy.

Since closed-loop control system principles are fundamental to the understanding of all numerical control applications, the examples cited in the following material will concentrate on closed-loop systems. Further design principles for open-loop systems follow the closed-loop material.

DETAILED OPERATIONS OF NUMERICAL CONTROL SYSTEMS

Five distinct tasks are carried out by a numerical control system: tape reading; data storage; command generation; machine actuation; and position feedback. Although many designs have been used, all must cause the system to carry out the equivalent of these five functions. The first three functions are diagrammed in Figure 3 and the last two in Figure 4.

Tape Reading

Referring to Figure 3, the tape reader decodes information on the tape and transmits it to storage. In the evolution of numerical control, various media have been used to store the instructions until they are entered into the controller. The standard medium is one-inch-wide punched paper or mylar tape. Dials, push buttons, data processing cards, motion picture film, 12-inch-wide perforated paper rolls, and magnetic tape have all been tried. Only dials and magnetic tape are currently used on the relatively few numerical controls that

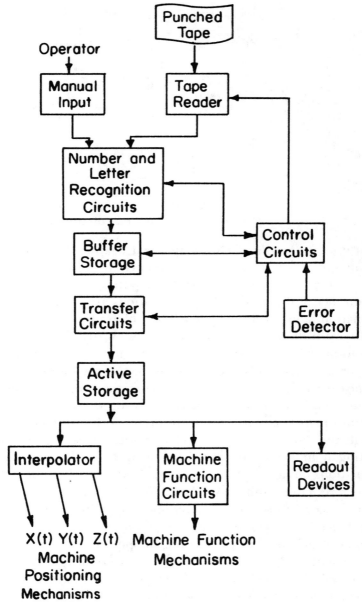

FIGURE 3
Logic section of NC electronic control.

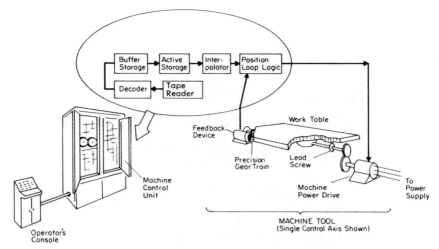

FIGURE 4

General system operation (one axis of control).

do not use punched tape. (Note: the next chapter describes systems wherein the paper tape is also eliminated by directly connecting the controller to a process control computer.)

A number of different coding conventions are used to record the information, and several different types of readers are used by the various controllers. The tape reader best suited for a particular application is determined by the rate at which the controller must generate command pulses and also by cost and reliability.

Some early tape readers were of a pneumatic type; most controllers now use mechanical or photoelectric readers. Pneumatic readers sense information on the tape with mechanical wire fingers passing through the tape holes. Photoelectric readers sense information by detecting light beams as they show through. Both types read the information on a row-by-row basis; however, the photoelectric readers are faster and more reliable. Most mechanical sensing readers process information at rates up to 60 to 100 lines per second. Typical maximum reading rates of photoelectric units are 300 to 500 lines of information per second. In spite of constant reliability improvements and the addition of error detection mechanisms, tape readers and the punched tapes they process are still a source of frustrating malfunctions. These problems have proved serious enough for some users to switch to magnetic tape or to transmit data from a computer by direct wire to the machine control.

Data Storage

The data storage subsystem receives decoded information from the tape reader and stores it until it is called for by the control logic. Storage techniques vary between controls, but they usually contain one group of registers for each axis under control. Storage devices, such as relays, are also used for holding the management information delineated earlier. For high-speed operation and for most contouring functions, two storage registers are used—a buffer storage register and an active storage register. While the control is processing command instructions in the active storage register, the next sequence of data can be simultaneously "loaded" into the buffer register. When the current instructions are completed, a high-speed transfer-in of the next data can then take place without being penalized by the relatively slow (by electronic standards) reader. With both active and buffer storage, a numerical control system can be in continuous high-speed operation even while the machine performs extremely complex maneuvers requiring very high data rates.

COMMAND GENERATION

Command generation—the translation of the tape information into the form required to activate the machine actuation subsystems—is conceptually the most complex function in a numerial control system. Despite the many design stages through which numerical control has progressed, the fundamental command generation principles described below are generally applicable to most controls in the field.

Two basic types of command generation functions should be distinguished:

1. Command generation for controls that reduce the position error between the controlled element and the command position to zero at an *uncontrolled rate*. These are the "point-to-point" controls.
2. Command generation for controls that accurately position the controlled element continuously; this requires constant control of both the velocity and the position. These are the "contouring" or "continuous-path" controls.

Point-to-Point Command Generation

The process of command generation in point-to-point controls is straightforward. Position coordinate dimensions from the tape are converted to an appropriate binary form and then loaded into some form of a computer or storage register much as was shown in Figure 1. Thus, the tape data, with appropriate scaling, serve as the reference input or the command variable for the position control subsystem of the point-to-point machine.

Contouring Command Generation

The command generation function for contouring systems is considerably more complex than for point-to-point systems. In order for a machine to follow a precise path, the data points defining the path must be fed to the position control loops in the proper sequence and at the proper rate.[1] Since it is not uncommon for modern control systems to travel at rates up to 300 inches per minute, a system with 10,000 pulses per inch of travel will require data rates for the position commands that exceed 30,000 data pulses per minute per axis. Clearly, this is far beyond the capability of even the best tape reader, and some other method must be employed.

The standard solution has been to include electronic circuits in the control which are capable of generating intermediate data points for certain path shapes. The circuits that have been developed for generating the intermediate data points are called interpolators and have the functional description:

A device for defining the path and rate of travel of a cutting tool, or some similar machine element or slide, when supplied with a coded mathematical description. It provides the intermediate points between programmed end points to produce smooth curves or straight lines.[2]

Implied in this description are two prominent types of path generation devices—interpolators for straight-line segments or circular arc segments. A third type, the parabolic interpolator, has also been used in special cases. The geometric paths generated by linear, circular, and parabolic interpolation are shown in Figure 5.

There is nothing sacred about these three interpolation alternatives. Virtually any curve that can be defined mathematically can be broken down into the required data points. The popularity of

---

[1] It will be shown later that for a machine element to follow a particular path, the velocity as well as the position must be controlled. Velocity is communicated to the control loop by controlling the rates of arrival of the position command increments.

[2] L. J. Thomas, ed., *N/C Handbook* (Detroit: Bendix Industrial Controls Division, 1971), p. 227.

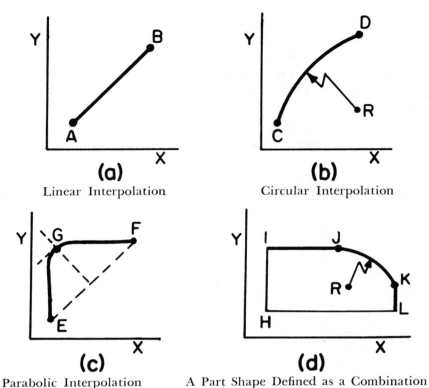

(a)
Linear Interpolation

(b)
Circular Interpolation

(c)
Parabolic Interpolation

(d)
A Part Shape Defined as a Combination
of Linear and Circular Elements

FIGURE 5
Standard interpolation alternatives for numerical control.

the linear and circular interpolators lies in the relative ease of implementing such functions with discrete electronic logic components. The newer minicomputer-based numerical controls can easily provide other shapes such as cubic curves.

On the other side of the coin, there is relatively little need for interpolation capability beyond the linear and circular variety. Complex curves or shapes can easily be developed by piecing together several primitive elements. For example, the part shape shown in Figure 5(d) could be easily generated using four linear segments and one circular segment.

The part shape in Figure 5(d) can also be generated just as well with only linear interpolation. A straight-line segment approxi-

13

mation to the JK portion of Figure 5(d) could have the form shown in Figure 6.

When straight-line segments are used to approximate curves, they must be chosen carefully to insure that the error between the approximate curve and the exact curve never exceeds acceptable limits. Whereas one could envision manually calculating the motions required for the machining sequence of Figure 5(d), the motions for the sequence of Figure 6 would be almost impossible to calculate without a computer. Thus, the advantage of higher-order interpolation lies not so much in the complexity of the shape one can develop but rather in the ease of developing the geometric statements for the control program. When a computer is readily available, the advantages of higher-order interpolation schemes are largely negated.

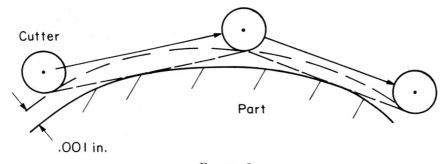

FIGURE 6

The use of straight-line segments to approximate a curved path.

Not surprisingly, many techniques have been used to implement interpolation with digital logic circuits. More recently, the increased use of minicomputers has caused a further proliferation of interpolation techniques. However, since interpolation is such a basic function in a contouring control system, it is well worth the effort to understand the design fundamentals. In this section, the techniques for implementing interpolators with digital logic components will be presented.

Linear Interpolation

The functional concepts of the simplest and most common interpolator, the linear interpolator, are shown in Figure 7. In this example, the linear interpolator inputs are the X and Y departure coordinates of point B with respect to point A; and the velocity to

14

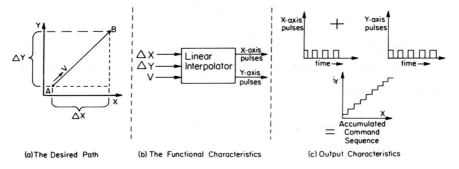

(a) The Desired Path   (b) The Functional Characteristics   (c) Output Characteristics

FIGURE 7

Linear interpolation—a functional description.

be followed along the path. The output of the interpolator is a stream of command pulses to the X- and Y-axis position control systems. Since each pulse represents a position increment, the number of pulses fed to an axis determines the total axis displacement, and the pulse rate determines axis velocity.

The two common electronic circuits for building linear interpolators are the "pulse-rate multipliers" and the "overflow counters" or digital differential analyzers as they are often called. In using either circuit type, a path is defined by simultaneously supplying each axis with properly spaced pulses.

Pulse-Rate Multipliers

An introduction to pulse-rate multipliers can be obtained by studying Figure 8. Here it can be seen that the content of a digital counter is continuously compared with a fixed command input (called "coded" fractional number on the figure). For example, a 0.7 command will pass 7 of each 10 reference pulses to the output by means of gating logic circuitry. As another example, if the number 0.456 is stored as the multiplier command, 456 of each 1,000 reference pulses will be output.

These concepts can be illustrated by the following example. Assume that the path shown in Figure 9 is to be followed by a machine at a velocity of 60 inches per minute. If a pulse weight of 0.0001 is used, the interpolator must output 10,000 pulses for the X-axis servo at a rate of 4,467 pulses per second and 20,000 pulses for the Y-axis servo at a rate of 8,934 pulses per second. The pulse-rate

15

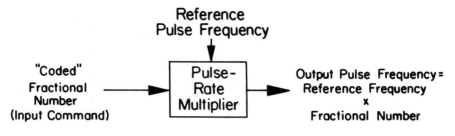

(a) Functional Characteristic

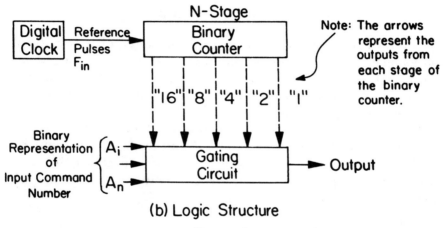

(b) Logic Structure

FIGURE 8
The pulse-rate multiplier.

multiplier and two comparison circuits shown in Figure 10 would generate the properly phased command pulses satisfying the stated parameters.

The pulse-rate multiplier (PRM) is a set of logic elements for varying the rate or frequency of a series of digital pulses. Unfortunately, the name, "pulse-rate multiplier," was a bad choice to describe the function performed. A more appropriate choice is "digital fractional multiplier" as the circuits operate to provide an output pulse train that contains some fractional multiple of a reference pulse train. Reference pulses produced by a digital clock are supplied to an N-stage binary counter. Each successive stage of the binary counter produces pulses that are a binary fraction of the reference pulses; i.e., the first stage produces an output pulse for

16

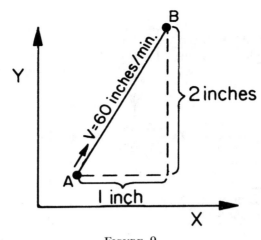

FIGURE 9
A "contouring" tool path along a straight line between two points.

each reference pulse, the second stage for every two reference pulses, the third stage for every four reference pulses, etc. A gating circuit assembles the output pulse train by selectively passing pulses only from the stages specified by the input command number. For example, if the reference frequency is 10,000 pulses per second and the input command binary number calls for passing the third and fourth stage counter pulses, an output frequency of 3,750 pulses per second will be obtained. Assuming a sufficient number of stages is included in the binary counter, virtually any output frequency can be programmed up to the maximum value set by the reference frequency.

The PRM circuit described is typically used to convert a feedrate command number (velocity) into the position servo excitation pulse train. A linear interpolator can be constructed by using a PRM along with circuitry to terminate the pulses when the number generated equals the required departure distance from the point of path origin. The example shown in Figure 10 presented the use of a PRM for linear interpolation.

Upon completion of a move, the X- and Y-axis departure coordinates and axis velocity commands are obtained from the next block of tape data. The departure coordinates, converted into the properly coded form (not shown), serve to preset the distance counters. Concurrently, the velocity command numbers select the axis pulse rates by means of the gating logic circuitry. The output pulses simultaneously command the axis position loops and count

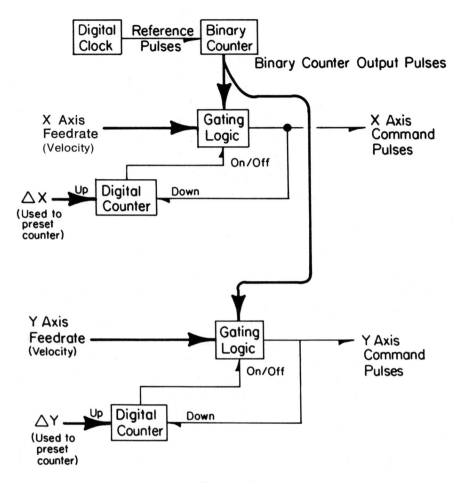

FIGURE 10
Logic circuit schematic for a linear interpolator using a
pulse-rate multiplier design.

down the distance counters. When the distance counters return to
zero, the proper number of pulses has been generated and the gating
logic inhibits any further PRM output pulses from supplying the
position servos. The gating logic also signals the tape reader that
the control is ready for the next block of data (not shown).

This simple explanation of the pulse-rate multiplier approach
for linear path generation ignores many of the practical details that
are required to implement such a system. Nevertheless, the explana-

tion should be sufficient to convey the utility of such a technique for numerical control applications. The reader interested in greater detail is referred to any of the manufacturers' service manuals.

Digital Overflow Counters

Overflow counters, a second technique for using digital logic circuits to implement linear interpolation, are more versatile than the pulse-rate multipliers because they can generate mathematical functions such as linear segments and circular arcs. They are, therefore, particularly useful for numerial control applications.

The basic elements of the overflow counter are two digital registers —an integrand register and a remainder register—and the circuitry for summing their contents. In this context, a register may be any device that can store numerical information. It can be anything from a coded wheel, whose position indicates or stores the number of mechanical inputs to which it has been exposed, to a binary register composed of one or more logic storage elements, such as electronic flip-flops. For the purpose of explanation, consider the simple mechanical equivalent of a numerical control system shown in Figure 11. Each of the two rotating mechanical registers has capacity for the 10 decimal digits, 0 through 9. Initially, a number between 0 and 9 is placed in the integrand register, and the remainder register is set at zero.

The contents of the integrand register are then successively added to the remainder register. When the accumulated sum exceeds the

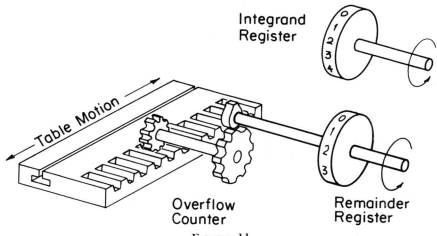

Integrand Register

Table Motion

Overflow Counter

Remainder Register

FIGURE 11
A mechanical analogy of the digital overflow counter concept.

capacity of the remainder register, the machine table will move one increment of motion. If the addition process is repeated "n" times where "n" is the capacity of the remainder register (in this simple case n = 10, since the remainder register can store the 10 digits 0 through 9), then the table will move that number of increments equal to the number originally stored in the integrand register. For example, if the number 4 were originally placed in the integrand wheel, the 10 additions will produce 4 movements:

Addition No.

	0 remainder wheel content
1	+4 integrand wheel
	4 new remainder content
2	+4
	8 new remainder content
3	+4
	2 + 1 table increment
4	+4
	6
5	+4
	0 + 1 table increment
6	+4
	4
7	+4
	8
8	+4
	2 + 1 table increment
9	+4
	6
10	+4
	0 + 1 table increment

This example illustrates the mechanics of the overflow counter technique, but not the advantages. Two valuable results are obtained:

1. The number of motion increments is always equal to the original integrand number.

2. The rate at which motion occurs is determined by the rate at which the addition cycle is processed.

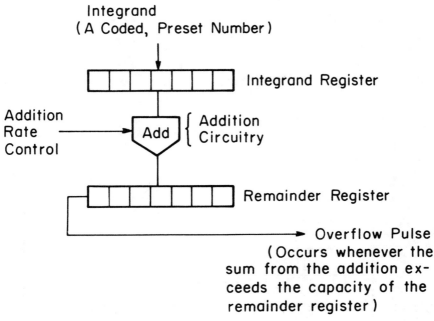

Integrand
(A Coded, Preset Number)

Integrand Register

Addition Rate Control

Add ⟩ Addition Circuitry

Remainder Register

→ Overflow Pulse
(Occurs whenever the sum from the addition exceeds the capacity of the remainder register)

FIGURE 12
An overflow counter.

In numerical controls, the mechanical registers used in this example are replaced by binary logic registers; and the overflow of the remainder register, which is a voltage pulse rather than a mechanical position, commands the axis control system to drive the machine element one increment of displacement. For the remainder of this discussion, the overflow counter will be represented as shown in Figure 12, where the integrand and remainder registers represent assemblies of electronic logic storage elements.

The combination of an integrand register, a remainder register, and an addition rate control—as diagrammed in Figure 12—is called an "overflow counter" and is the heart of most modern numerical control contouring command-generation subsystems. A primitive velocity and position command generator for a single axis can be constructed using such overflow counters and a digital clock, as shown in Figure 13.

Each pulse from the position overflow counter is sent to the axis servo to produce one increment of motion. The number of position command pulses that occurs in one complete cycle is equal to the number initially stored in the position integrand register. The rate

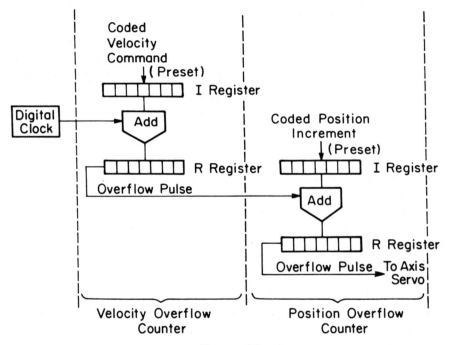

FIGURE 13

The use of coupled overflow counters for producing command pulses for a single-axis contouring control system.

at which position pulses occur (the command velocity) is determined by the rate at which additions are performed in the position overflow counter. These additions are controlled by a second overflow counter whose add rate is in turn controlled by a digital clock. The number in the velocity overflow counter integrand register determines the

22

addition rate as a submultiple of the clock rate so that a judicious selection of the position and the velocity command numbers will produce the proper number of command pulses at the required rate. A pulse-rate multiplier could have been used in place of the velocity overflow counter—a not uncommon control design practice.

Linear interpolation can be implemented by applying two overflow counters operating in a synchronous manner. Suppose the path shown in Figure 9 is to be defined by the interpolator. Three over-

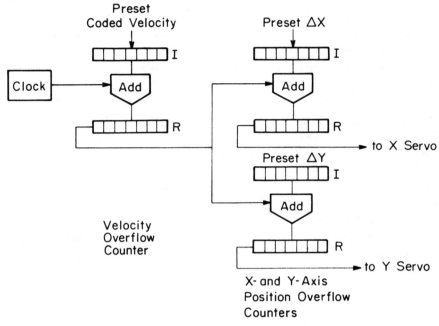

FIGURE 14
The functional arrangement of digital overflow counters
for linear interpolation.

flow counters can be used: one for the X axis, one for the Y axis, and the third for the velocity or feedrate control as shown in Figure 14.

If a properly coded X-axis incremental dimension is placed in the X-axis integrand register and the Y-axis incremental dimension is likewise placed in the Y-axis integrand register, a complete addition cycle will synchronously supply the correct number of pulses to the X and Y axes. As stated earlier, velocity is obtained by controlling the addition rate.

23

Circular Interpolation

Circular interpolation, as the name implies, is the technique of generating commands that will cause machine movements to duplicate a circular path as described in Figure 5(b). As with linear interpolation, the data points required by the axis control subsystem for curved surfaces can easily exceed the data system; therefore they must be generated by internal control logic circuits.

The use of coupled overflow counters is by far the most prevalent approach to generating position command pulses through circular interpolation techniques. It was mentioned earlier that the overflow counter can perform mathematical operations—a property which is used to advantage in circular interpolation.

The overflow counter is in fact a digital integrator. The number of overflow pulses obtained during a complete cycle is directly proportional to the time integral of the number contained in the integrand register—thus, the name "integrand" register. Any mathematical function that can be described by ordinary calculus can conceivably be implemented using the overflow counter principle.

As a case in point, consider the linear interpolator described earlier. A constant was stored in the integrand register, and the output pulses resulted in a linearly increasing motion of the controlled element. (The integral of a constant is a linearly increasing function of time.) Suppose the number contained in the integrand register was not held constant, as was the case for the linear interpolator, but rather increased each time an outflow pulse occurred, as show in Figure 15.

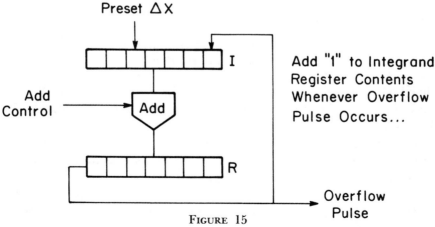

FIGURE 15
A digital overflow counter with logical feedback.

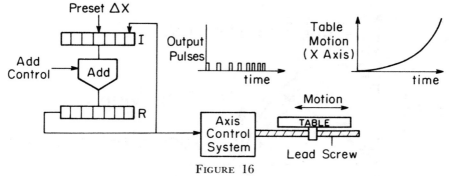

FIGURE 16

The use of overflow feedback to generate an exponentially increasing table motion.

In this case, the integrand number increases linearly with the output number. The overflow pulses for this system will cause the machine element to be controlled according to the exponential time function as shown in Figure 16.

The exponential function has limited practical use. Its primary use is in a velocity command circuit to produce exponentially increasing or decreasing velocity profiles and thus limit the acceleration or deceleration demands.

Circular arcs, or segments of circular arcs, are generated by coupling two overflow counters as shown in Figure 17.

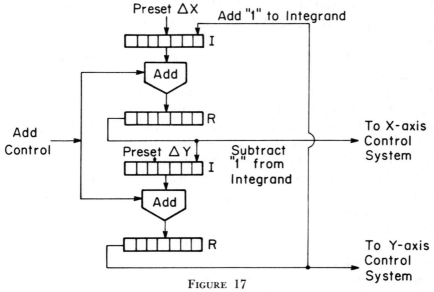

FIGURE 17

The use of coupled overflow counters to generate a circular arc.

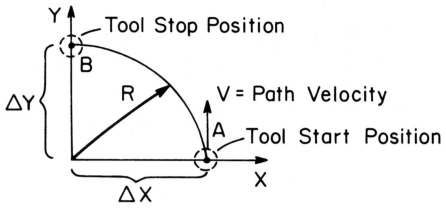

FIGURE 18
Tool motion along a circular path.

In the circular arc interpolator, each Y-axis overflow pulse causes the X-axis integrand register to increase its number by one count, and each X-axis overflow pulse will cause the Y-axis integrand register to decrease its count by one. This sequence might be reversed, depending on where in the coordinate system the circle is started and whether the arc is to be traveled clockwise or counterclockwise. The principles of this operation are best presented by means of a specific example. Consider the circular path shown in Figure 18.

The incremental distance, Y, should be initially loaded in the Y-axis integrand register, while zero is loaded in the X-axis integrand register. When the interpolator is started, the Y overflow counter causes upward (positive) motion to start along the Y axis. Also, each Y overflow pulse causes an increase in the X-axis integrand register. As the X-axis integrand register increases, X overflow pulses occur, which in turn decrease the content of the Y-axis integrand register. As a result, the velocity content (pulse rate) of the Y overflow pulses will start at a maximum value and decrease to zero at a rate proportional to the X-axis displacement at point B.

Likewise, the X-axis velocity content will start at zero and increase to a maximum at a rate proportional to the Y-axis displacement. The result is X and Y command pulses that will cause motion in an almost perfect circular arc. Because the technique presented can only operate in one quadrant, additional logic must be used to change the integrand register contents to allow operation in additional quadrants; it may also be used to allow clockwise travel instead of the counterclockwise travel shown.

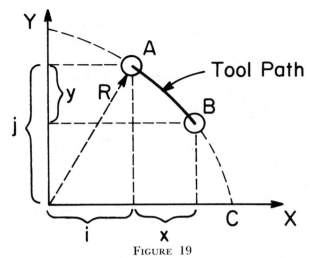

FIGURE 19

Tool motion along an arbitrary segment of a circular path.

Segments of circular arcs can be programmed if additional counters are included. Consider the path shown in Figure 19. Point A is the starting point and point B is the stopping point; i and j are the displacements of A from the arc center and are the values to be initially inserted in the X and Y integrand registers.

If the tool is to be stopped at B rather than at the end point C, the interpolator function must be stopped at B—a condition that cannot be determined by waiting for the contents of the remainder register to return to zero. Thus, the circular interpolator must be modified as shown in Figure 20 by the addition of two position counters.

In Figure 20, the value i is placed in the X-axis integrand register, the value j in the Y-axis integrand register, and the incremental displacements X and Y are preset as the initial values in the X and Y position counters. These counters are then counted down to zero by the X- and Y-axis overflow pulses. The feedrate (add control) pulses to the overflow counters are gated with the position counters so that interpolation ceases when X and Y increments have been generated for the X and Y axes respectively. Thus, the arc segment is programmed by including on the tape the values i, j, X, and Y and the proper feedrate number. Generally, a preparatory function code (G code) must also be furnished to tell the control that circular interpolation is to be performed. The code could also indicate whether clockwise or counterclockwise motion is required.

27

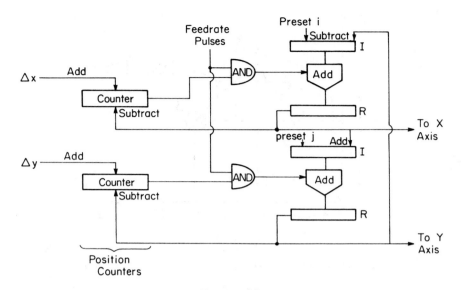

FIGURE 20

A functional schematic of the circuits for generating the circular segment shown in Figure 19.

Parabolic Interpolation

Without too much trouble, the output from a circular interpolator can be modified to produce either parabolic or elliptic path shapes. For example, if the pulses that produced the circle of Figure 21 were modified by adding to or subtracting from the X-axis pulses only, either elliptic or parabolic curves will occur as shown. In the figure, the parabola is centered around the X axis, but by modifying this procedure, it could be centered around any axis.

The parabolic or elliptic shape can be quite helpful for free-form contours where the path accuracy does not warrant a complex combination of linear and circular path segments.

At one time or another, almost all numerical control system manufacturers have offered such an option, and they can be consulted if additional design and function details are needed.

MACHINE DRIVE SYSTEMS

The block diagram of a numerical control system shown in Figure 4 had two major sections for controlling the motion of a machine tool. The first section—the command generation section—

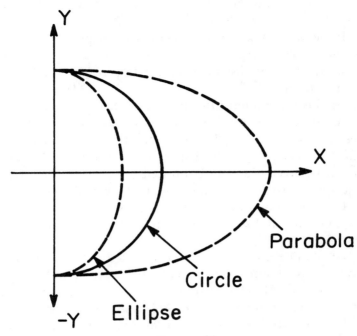

FIGURE 21

The generation of elliptic and parabolic paths by scalar multiplication of one axis of a circular path. The ellipse is obtained by multiplying all X coordinates by a number less than one while the parabola is obtained by multiplying all X coordinates by a number greater than one.

has already been presented. We are now concerned with the second section—the position control section.[3]

The position control section converts the digital pulses from the command generation section into physical motions. This section includes the electronics for loop closure (in the case of closed-loop systems), signal conversion (digital to analog), amplification, and the combination of electrical and mechanical components that make up the machine drive system.

The machine drive system provides the function previously supplied by an operator when he manually positioned the machine's slides. Drive systems are an especially critical design problem as the

---

[3] The practice of conceptually separating the control into two sections is valid for all conventional controls and for all newer minicomputer-based controls that retain hard-wired interpolation and loop closure.

29

high resolution of the electronic control circuits can be quickly wasted by an inferior mechanical drive.

Even on the minicomputer-based controls that provide both interpolation and loop-closure within the software, the separation concept is less accurate but still useful. Chapter II provides further elaboration on this topic.

Drive systems for numerical control must have exceptional static accuracy as there is no human element to compensate for errors. The mechanical structure should move easily and smoothly and ideally have no backlash or deadband. Since virtually all drives use ball screws to convert the rotary motion of an electric or hydraulic motor into the linear slide motions, the ball screw should be of very high quality and consistency. Likewise, the system should have low drift at zero setting and should be capable of uniform speeds at low feedrates.

A good dynamic response for each controlled axis is also required. The drive system should be fast, yet stable, and should be able to change directions and velocity smoothly without excessive dynamic loads on the mechanical structure. For contouring controls, there are additional constraints: the motion and velocity control must be infinitely variable and smoothly reversible and must be synchronized among as many as five separate directions.

While it may not be obvious at this point, static accuracy and smooth dynamic response are conflicting requirements that require compromises by the control system designer.

LOOP GAIN

Static accuracy is obtained by using a very high "gain" in the control loop. Regardless of how well the mechanical components are made, there will always be some friction that must be overcome before motion can occur. When the machine receives a command to move a small increment, the torque is generated by amplifying the error between the commanded position and the measured position to excite the drive motor. Processing this "position error" through a very high gain of amplification between the position error and the drive motor excitation assures that sufficient torque will be developed to overcome the friction, even for very small position changes.

With all modern closed-loop control systems, a more precise definition of system gain is used. If the feedback loop were discon-

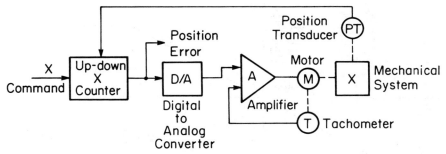

(a) A closed-loop servo system with the feedback loop connected.

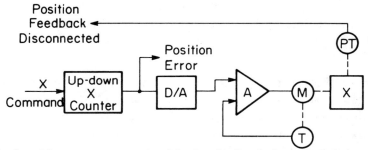

(b) A closed-loop servo system with the feedback loop open.

FIGURE 22

A schematic description of an open-loop arrangement for the
purposes of measuring system gain.

nected, as shown in Figure 22, then the gain can be expressed as
the ratio of the output variable to the input variable. When operated
without feedback, the position error is the position command and
a fixed or constant command will make the table move at a constant
velocity. A typical relationship between position error and slide
velocity obtained in this fashion is shown in Figure 23. The slope
of the linear segment of the curve is the gain. The flattened segments
are caused by amplifier saturation.

The units for the gain are velocity/displacement or one per second.
In the U.S. it is common to express velocity in inches per minute
(ipm) and the error in thousandths of an inch or "mils." The units
of gain for this latter set of parameters are ipm/mil. The numerical
relationship between the two ways to express gain is:

$$1 \text{ ipm/mil} = 16.7 \left(\frac{1}{\text{sec}}\right) .$$

Repeating a previous statement, the higher the "gain," in general

31

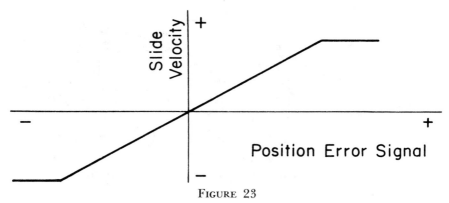

FIGURE 23

The linear relationship between the input or position error signal and the slide velocity. (This relationship exists for almost all numerical control servos.)

the better the static accuracy. A problem arises, however, necessitating some compromise, from the detrimental effect of high gain on dynamic response and stability. The effect of gain on dynamic response and stability requires a knowledge of servo characteristics and is a somewhat more difficult concept than the effect of gain on static accuracy. Elementary servo concepts are needed.

Servo Concepts

The servo concepts applicable to numerical controls are easily developed by relating them to the servos used on tracer milling machines. Figure 24 illustrates the basic arrangement for a tracer servo system. A stylus following a template actuates a servo valve that controls the flow of oil to a hydraulic cylinder. A numerical control system employs an electrical signal rather than a template and stylus to activate the servo valve, but otherwise is quite similar conceptually. The hydraulic cylinder in the diagram could be a ball-nut lead screw, a rack and pinion device, or any other type of numerical control drive mechanism.

As shown in Figure 24, the tracer head or valve contains a spool that moves back and forth as the stylus is deflected by the relative movement. As the template moves relative to the stylus, oil is directed to the cylinder at a flow rate proportional to the linear deflection of the spool. The rate of flow determines the velocity of the machine slide. An open-loop arrangement, in which the feedback arm is removed and a cam replaces the template shown in Figure 24, provides a basic system for studying the dynamic properties.

32

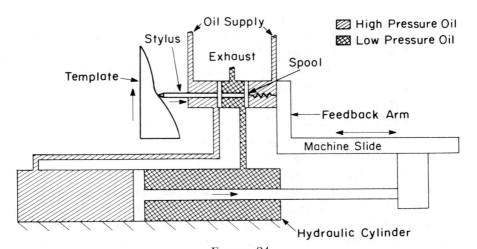

FIGURE 24

A tracer controlled hydraulic servo system for contouring applications.

Rotation of the circular cam, which is mounted eccentrically as shown in Figure 25, provides the stylus of the servo valve with a sinusoidal input of constant amplitude. By varying the speed of the cam shaft the system response may be analyzed for a variety of frequency inputs. A plot of the ratio of the output amplitude to the input or forcing amplitude against the excitation frequency provides the commonly used "frequency response" diagram.

As the cam rotates slowly, the valve is open in each direction for a relatively long period of time, which in turn allows the machine slide to move a relatively long distance. Increasing the rotational speed of the cam will cause the valve to be open a shorter duration

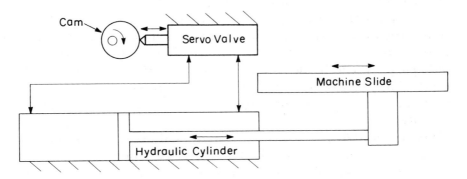

FIGURE 25

The hydraulic tracer servo for Figure 24 with the feedback disconnected and a sinusoidal cam for the input.

33

and the slide to move a shorter distance. Thus, the amplitude of the machine slide travel is inversely proportional to the speed of the cam rotation or input frequency. Also, since the slide velocity is proportional to the valve opening, the slide starts to move in positive direction when the cam passes the zero valve position, attains maximum velocity when the cam is at the maximum valve opening, and attains its maximum positive displacement when the cam reaches the opposite zero valve position. Thus the slide position lags the cam position by one-quarter of a cycle, or 90 degrees, for all frequencies.

Unfortunately, all is not as simple as the above paragraph would imply. The hydraulic fluid is not incompressible and can store potential energy. A spring between the drive piston of the hydraulic cylinder and the machine slide can be used to conceptually represent the compressibility normally found in hydraulic fluids. The system's mass is also important as it can store kinetic energy. The mass can be regarded as lumped at the machine slide.

A plot of the amplitude ratio and the phase shift of mass-motion to cam-motion versus frequency is plotted in Figure 26 to show the amplitude ratio and phase shifts. In this system the resonant frequency is a hypothetical 100 radians per second (Curve 1). Also shown are curves that would result from either decreasing the "gain" (Curve 2) or increasing the resonant frequency to 500 radians per second (Curve 3).

The frequency at which the amplitude ratio becomes "unity" is an important parameter. If the phase shift at this frequency is more than 180 degrees, then a reinforcement of the input would occur when the feedback was connected and instability would result. For example, the system of Curve 1 would be unstable.

What would happen if a smaller valve were used? This would be equivalent to decreasing the gain of the system. Curve 2 of Figure 26 shows that the effect of a decreased gain is to shift the amplitude ratio curves vertically downward but not to change the phase-shift curve. The decrease shown is sufficient to create a stable system. Correspondingly, increasing the gain would only aggravate the instability.

Obviously, the simple solution for dynamic response is to keep the gain below any critical level. However, as was previously pointed out, low gain has a detrimental effect on static accuracy. A second reason for maintaining a reasonable gain is the problem of system bandwidth.

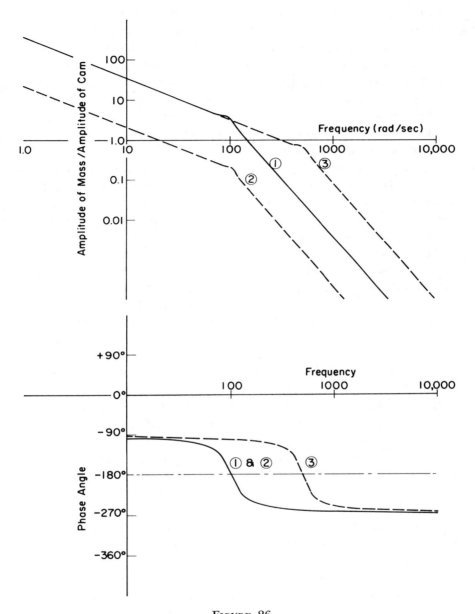

FIGURE 26

The amplitude ratio and phase shift for the
hydraulic tracer system of Figure 25.

System bandwidth is defined as the frequency at which the closed-loop transfer function begins to deviate significantly from the input.

Bandwidth is important in that it is directly related to dynamic response. A system with a high bandwidth can accurately track rapidly changing inputs, whereas a low-bandwidth system can only track slowly changing inputs. Bandwidth is important on many machine functions. For example, the limit on how fast a machine can follow a curved shape, e.g., a circular arc, is virtually dictated by the bandwidth of the machine.

For practical purposes, a system's closed-loop transfer function begins to fall below unity at a somewhat lower frequency than the unity gain crossover frequency of its open-loop response curve (e.g., Figure 26). Thus, one condition for high bandwidth is a high-frequency unity crossover on the open-loop frequency response curve.

The open-loop unity crossover, as explained earlier, is limited primarily by phase shifts occurring as a result of resonance in the individual components of the system. Thus, the one or two lower resonant frequencies in the system determine the maximum frequency response available. The designer can attempt to build a stiffer mechanical structure, in which case he gains as shown by Curve 3 in Figure 26. However, changing the resonance is usually not applicable since it can require massive changes of the mechanical structure—if it can be done at all.

By now, the need for a compromise in selecting "gain" should be apparent. For stability, the gain must be selected so that the amplitude ratio—in this case, output to error—is less than unity when the phase shift between error and output exceeds 180 degrees. Most numerical control equipment manufacturers attain good servo performance by insuring that the phase shift does not exceed 135 to 140 degrees when the amplitude ratio crosses the unity value. Curve 1 fits this criterion with a phase shift of 100 degrees. On the other hand, for accuracy and speed of response, the gain should be kept as high as possible.

Two standard techniques have evolved in the design of numerical control servos to solve the compromise between a low system gain for stability and a high system gain for accuracy. Both techniques are capable of similar accuracy and dynamic response characteristics.
High-Gain Servos

A typical design of a high-gain contouring servo is shown in Figure 27. This system is identical in principle with the tracer servo

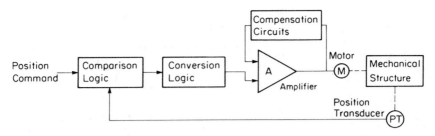

FIGURE 27
A high-gain contouring control servo.

of Figure 24. The input stylus has been replaced by an electrical signal and the feedback arm by a position measurement device. The error is also an electrical signal which, converted and amplified, actuates the drive motor. (It is useful to note that the system gain can be very easily adjusted at the power amplifier.) Carrying this analogy further, the open-loop frequency response for the system in Figure 27 has the form shown in Figure 26. In fact, if the lowest mechanical resonant frequency of the system were 100 cycles per second, Figure 26 would provide close to the exact curve.

The designer can strike a workable compromise between the contradictory requirements of high gain for accuracy and low gain for stability in several ways. As stated earlier, he can attempt to build a stiffer mechanical system with a higher resonant frequency. A higher loop gain can then be used before instability problems arise. In general, however, this solution produces only marginal improvements.

The prevalent method for obtaining a good gain compromise is through the use of compensation circuitry. Compensation circuits, as the name implies, are electronic circuits inserted either in the position loop or as local feedback around the amplifier for the primary purpose of altering the dynamic response. While compensation circuits can be fairly complex, a simple example is sufficient for an understanding of the technique.

A typical compensation circuit and its frequency response are shown in Figure 28. Between frequencies f_1 and f_2, the amplitude ratio decreases to a lower value. The phase shift, on the other hand, varies only slightly from 0 degrees.

If the compensation circuit of Figure 28 were included in the high-gain servo loop, the new amplitude ratio and phase-angle

37

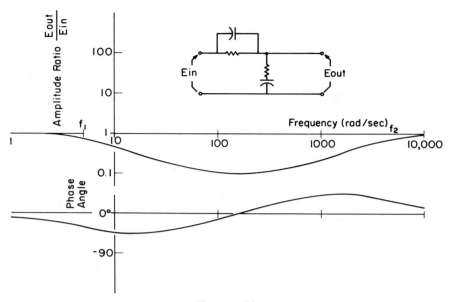

FIGURE 28

Frequency response diagram for a simple lag-lead compensator.

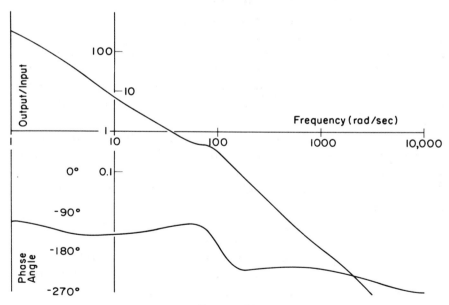

FIGURE 29

Response characteristics for a "high-gain" servo of Curve 2 on Figure 26 with the compensation circuit of Figure 28 included in the control loop.

curves would have the form shown in Figure 29. By carefully selecting the compensation elements, the designer can, within some limits, maintain a very high gain at low frequencies and, at the same time, avoid instability. Note that the system in Figure 29 has the same gain at low frequencies as Curve 2 in Figure 26 but is now stable. The major disadvantage is some reduction in the system bandwidth.

Low-Gain Servos

The low-gain servo uses a completely different approach to achieve the same purpose. As shown in Figure 30, the low-gain servo employs two separate feedback loops, an inner velocity feedback loop and the outer position feedback loop.

A frequency response analysis for this low-gain system is not quite as straightforward because of the two loops. However, some simple verbal arguments can suffice here. The first point is that the inner loop is controlling velocity, not position. Typically, the tachometer is directly coupled to the drive motor output shaft and provides measurement independent of the compliance of the lead screw. As a result, the mechanical resonances of the table and lead screw cannot create an undesirable phase shift within this loop and the velocity-loop gain can be very high. The outer position-loop gain, on the other hand, can be kept well below any value that would cause instability.

Accuracy in the low-gain servo is obtained by achieving a high degree of linearity between the position error and the output speed. An error between the command position and the measured position signals for a motor speed. If the motor does not move as commanded, there will be an incorrect feedback voltage from the tachometer, and the very high gain of the amplifier in the inner velocity control loop will come into play until the position error is corrected.

DYNAMIC RESPONSE

It would appear desirable to have a fast dynamic response—that is, to have the machine able to change speeds rapidly—on all axes. However, rapid changes in speed can mean high accelerating torques on the gears and high forces on the lead screws and other machine components. For large machines particularly, it is possible that these forces can be excessive, and in such cases, it is sometimes necessary to limit them. Thus, like the rest of the control system, the dynamic response is also subject to significant design compromises.

There are two common ways to specify the dynamic response of a servo system—the bandwidth and the time constant. The bandwidth describes the system in terms of the highest excitation frequency for which the system's output amplitude can track the system's input amplitude. (In practice, the maximum input frequency that should be applied would normally be at least an order of magnitude less than the bandwidth to avoid phase-shift errors.)

The bandwidth specification is useful for comparing the relative speed of response of different systems. A high bandwidth system is capable of following a rapidly changing input, whereas a low bandwidth system can follow only slowly changing inputs.

The "time constant" is a second specification for dynamic response. To gain an appreciation for the time constant, consider what happens when the system of Figure 30 receives a velocity change command. The system will respond to the command to change velocity approximately as show in Figure 31. The time constant, "T," is the time that would be required to reach the command value if the initial acceleration were maintained. Because of feedback, the system error—and torque—decreases exponentially and the velocity approaches the desired value exponentially. The system reaches approximately 98 percent of its command value in four time constants.

The time constant is the inverse of the bandwidth. For example, if the system bandwidth were 50 radians per second, then the time constant would be .02 seconds. A fast time constant is equivalent to a high bandwidth, while a slow time constant is equivalent to a low bandwidth. All of the problems of the previous section that pertained to increasing the bandwidth apply here. Also, as the next section will show, the time constant is an important variable in obtaining accurate curve following with a low-gain system design.

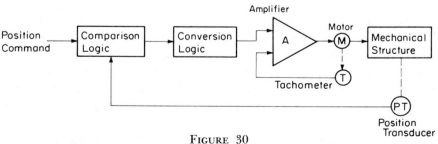

FIGURE 30

A low-gain contouring control servo.

40

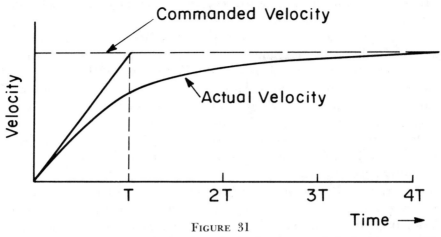

When an instantaneous change in velocity is commanded, the system will
respond exponentially as shown.

Acceleration, Deceleration, and Cornering Characteristics

According to the previous section, for any given servo system, the
maximum acceleration and deceleration levels can be controlled by
judiciously picking the frequency response or bandwidth of the
system. (This assumes, of course, a compromise where the dynamic
loads on the mechanical structure are given equal or greater weight
than the speed of response of the system. There are many applications
where the speed of response is of utmost importance and the
mechanical system is correspondingly designed to withstand the loading. When speed of response is the dominant variable, the designer's
effort is then expended to do whatever possible to extend—rather
than limit—the bandwidth.)

Even if the acceleration and deceleration limits are properly
handled by the designer, there may still be a considerable difference
between the high-gain and the low-gain servo designs with regard
to the way they can be programmed for a velocity change. This
difference has been important enough to shift public opinion in
favor of low-gain servos in recent years, although with the newer
minicomputer-based controls discussed in the next chapter, the programming advantages that accompany the low-gain servo are losing
their favored position.

The response of a servo system to a velocity change was shown
in Figure 31. Of concern here is the way velocity changes can be

programmed for the low-gain servo as compared to the high-gain servo.

With a high-gain servo, accuracy is obtained by insuring a very small error between the commanded position and the actual position. If a large velocity change is required, amplifier saturation can easily cause the allowable position error to be exceeded. On most systems, this would cause an automatic shutdown to occur. In other cases, such as the problem discussed in the next paragraphs of negotiating a sharp corner, the interaction of two high-gain controlled axes can cause undesirable and sometimes dangerous overshooting if it is not properly programmed.

The transient position error during acceleration and deceleration can be controlled on the high-gain system by replacing the desired velocity change with a series of small or incremental velocity changes. Substituting incremental velocity changes for a large velocity change during the acceleration is relatively straightforward and can be done either by the programmer or by electronic hardware. Deceleration, or slowing down, is not quite as straightforward. If the deceleration is not started at precisely the right time, the control either wastes time approaching the final position at a very slow velocity or overshoots the final position.

A major disadvantage of the high-gain system, therefore, is the often considerable length that must be added to the control tape to include the extra blocks of information for acceleration and deceleration. The high-gain system also suffers the disadvantage that torque reversals accompany the velocity overshooting. The torque reversals cause additional loading on the mechanical structure which could cause unneccessary wear.

Because of the above problems, low-gain servos have become the popular choice of most system designers. Nothing in life is absolute—including the distinction between high- and low-gain servos. In practice, hybrid servo designs are often used that utilize a good compromise between the two types. Nevertheless, the concepts being presented are important fundamentals for understanding the various systems. One should remember that the low-gain servo does not require a high gain in the position loop to obtain good static accuracy. The drawback of the low-gain design is that a larger position error is required to maintain the steady-state velocity. (See Figure 32.)

While it has not yet been clearly shown, a system with low-gain servos on each axis can—in spite of a large following error—accurately

42

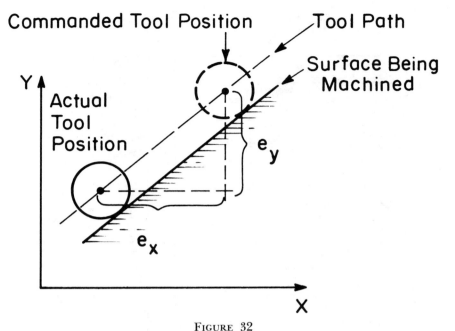

Commanded Tool Position   Tool Path

Actual
Tool
Position

e_y

e_x

Surface Being
Machined

Y

X

FIGURE 32
The effect of following error on tool position for a low-gain servo.

follow any path provided that all controlled axes have identical gains
and identical time constants.

The need for identical gains on all controlled axes can be readily
established with the aid of Figure 32. The figure is a schematic of
a tool moving along a path in the X-Y plane. The dashed circle
depicts the point where the position command says the tool should
be, while the solid circle depicts the actual tool position. The actual
position lags the command position because of the following errors
e_x and e_y on the X and Y axes, respectively. As long as both axes have
identical gains, then e_x and e_y will have the same proportionality
as the velocity components on the two axes, V_x and V_y, and the tool
will be on the correct path even though it lags behind the command
position. At higher speeds, this lag can be substantial—as much as
one-quarter to one-half of an inch or more, and gain matching is
critical. (The following error at any given speed can be easily computed by dividing the velocity by the gain.)

On the low-gain system, the correct proportionality must exist
between all controlled axes during transient conditions as well as
while moving at a constant velocity. In addition to matching the

43

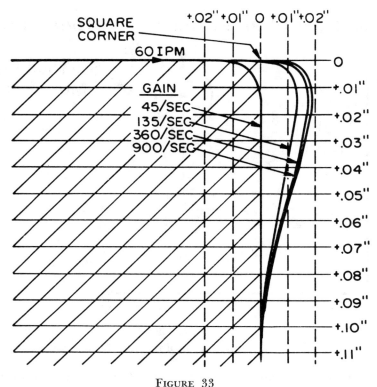

FIGURE 33
How servos would take a right angle corner at 60 ipm.

"loop gains," it is also necessary to insure that all axes have the same dynamic response or time constant. Both during installation and at periodic maintenance intervals, dynamic response measurements must be made and the control loops "tuned" to insure they all have identical time constants. A trained technician can use either frequency response methods or step changes in velocity to adjust the dynamic response. Standard procedures are usually included in the maintenance manuals.

There are many additional situations that can be encountered in the use of numerical control where the dynamic response of the servos can cause serious geometric errors if the command sequence does not properly consider the system's limitations. Typical of these situations are the negotiation of a sharp corner, following a small radius, and coming to a sudden halt. The first of these—negotiating a sharp corner—is clearly the most representative of this class of problem.

44

The curves shown in Figure 33 display the trajectory of a numerical control servo system while negotiating a sharp corner.[4] Four responses are shown, one for a low-gain system and three for high-gain systems. For the sake of comparison, all four systems have the same time constant or response time. Thus, they can all stop from a given velocity in about the same distance. The path velocity for all four cases is 60 inches per minute.

The high-gain servos overshoot the corner before coming back to the desired path. The amount of overshoot is directly proportional to the path speed, and it occurs because the horizontal axis drive cannot decelerate to zero within the displacement limit of the following error.

The low-gain servo does not overshoot because it operates with a large following error. Thus, when the commanded position reaches the coordinates of the corner, the tool is then .02 of an inch short of the corner (60 ipm/2.7 ipm/mil). It, thus, has .02 of an inch in which to decelerate in order to stop without overshooting. Corner rounding occurs because the second feed drive starts to accelerate before the first has come to a full stop. Thus, a low-gain servo will round off a sharp corner.

If an outside corner is being negotiated, a part shape error is avoided because the rounding occurs when the round tool is not in contact with the work; thus, a sharp corner will result. On an inside corner, the low-gain servo may leave a fillet in the corner. The fillet can be eliminated by programming a dwell that causes the second control axis to pause 30 to 50 milliseconds before restarting.

The high-gain servo produces satisfactory outside corners. However, on an inside corner it can gouge the work or consume excessive time negotiating the path. The overshoot can be minimized by programming a series of speed changes as the corner is approached—each step requiring an additional block of tape data. Another approach is the inclusion of logic circuitry that generates gradual rather than stepwise acceleration and decelerations.

Thus, while the dynamic response of the position-error servo systems need not be a severe limitation, there may be inherent performance-related cost penalties. Virtually any critical situation, such as the above cornering example, can be handled by suitably shaping

---

[4] John L. Dutcher, "Servo Drives for Numerically Controlled Machines," *NC: 1971*, ed. by Mary A. DeVries, Proceedings of the Eighth Annual Meeting and Technical Conference of the Numerical Control Society, March 22–24, 1971, Anaheim, Calif. (Princeton, N.J.: Numerical Control Society, Inc., 1971), p. 383.

the command function in the face of the system's dynamic constraints. Whether the effort required to achieve the accuracy is reasonable and economical depends upon the application's requirements.

Understandably, low-gain servos with their inherent acceleration conveniences have emerged as the more popular control design. In the majority of cases, dynamic constraints are not an undue concern for the programmer when his equipment uses low-gain servos. Thus, both manual programming and postprocessor developments for computer-aided programming have been simplified, and tape lengths are considerably shorter. In several cases, machines having high-gain servos have been retrofitted with low-gain servos.

OPEN-LOOP OR STEPPING MOTOR SYSTEMS

While little has been said up to this point on open-loop control systems, their importance in numerical control should not be taken lightly. A very large class of numerical control applications, such as drilling, turning, and light milling do not require heavy, massive machinery. For example, most of the machinery used for electronic fabrication is very light duty compared to classical metalworking standards. Open-loop systems, with their inherent simplicity and low cost, are often a natural for such applications and their numbers are increasing daily.

Open-loop systems were deferred to this section because much of the analysis of the closed-loop system provides a useful basis for comparison and understanding. Open-loop systems need to be separated into two broad categories: the light-duty systems that can be serviced by purely electromechanical stepping motors and the heavy-duty systems that require the added muscle of combination and electrohydraulic stepping motors.

Control systems using electromechanical stepping motors are relatively straightforward. As long as the pulses are fed to the motor at a rate that does not exceed the ability of the motor (and its load) to follow, few problems are encountered. One major constraint is that the maximum pulse rate the motor can follow at a constant velocity is often substantially higher than the pulse rate that can be followed during acceleration or deceleration. To be useful at these higher rates, either the program tape must include acceleration and deceleration blocks—much like the high-gain servos—or the electronic section of the control must include additional acceleration and deceleration circuits or rate-controlling devices that automatically insert a programmed increase (or decrease) whenever a new velocity is commanded.

With stepping motors, there is also the problem that the control will never know if a step is missed by the motor for any reason. On light-duty applications, especially point-to-point work, the assumption of no missed pulses is more than adequate. For occasions like contouring through heavy material, this assumption may be risky, and open-loop systems for such cases will sometimes include a position transducer in the system design. The command position can then be compared with the measured position at periodic intervals to insure that no steps have been missed. This is not a closed-loop system; the amplified error between the command and the measured position is used only for periodic checking and not to excite the drive motor.

When electrohydraulic stepping motors are used, the control system has all of the attributes of a closed-loop control system. To see this requires an understanding of the design characteristics of an electrohydraulic stepping motor.

Contouring Control Using Hydraulic Stepping Motors

Virtually all present hydraulic stepping motor designs employ electric stepping motors to actuate a hydraulic valve and motor. The hydraulic motor shaft is forced to follow precisely the position of the electric stepping motor through the use of a mechanical feedback linkage as shown in Figure 34. A hydraulic valve body is threaded into the output shaft of the electric stepping motor. When the electric stepping motor indexes, the valve advances along the motor shaft thread and opens the hydraulic ports. The resulting flow of hydraulic oil causes the hydraulic motor to rotate and unthread the valve body, thus turning off the oil supply. The motor is then hydraulically "locked" at the new position until another pulse is applied to the stepping motor. The hydraulic motor shaft precisely follows the stepping motor shaft; however, the torque available is much greater, since it is provided by the hydraulic supply pressure and hydraulic motor.

The technique by which the hydraulic stepping motor advances a single step has already been described. However, the typical contouring situation where the slide is required to move at a constant velocity needs further attention. The rotational speed of the motor

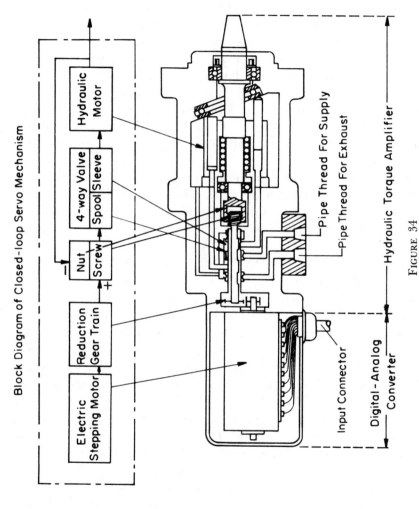

Block Diagram of Closed-loop Servo Mechanism

FIGURE 34

Cross-section of FUJITSU electrohydraulic stepping motor.

48

output shaft is determined by the oil flow rate to the hydraulic motor, while the oil flow rate is determined by the degree of opening of the spool valve. When a velocity change is commanded, the hydraulic motor shaft will mechanically lag behind the electric stepping motor rotation so that the valve can "advance" along the screw thread. This mechanical lag between the electric stepping motor position and the machine slide position is a following error, related to the slide velocity and has a relationship similar to that depicted in Figure 23 for the closed-loop system. The magnitude of the following error is proportional to the magnitude of the required velocity and is inversely related to the "gain" of the hydraulic stepping motor. (The gain of the hydraulic stepping motor is the relationship between the degree of valve opening and the motor velocity.) Hydraulic stepping motors can be designed to behave as either high- or low-gain control systems. Typical practice is to use a low-gain design with the loop gain of approximately 40 1/sec (2.4 ipm/mil). Substantial following errors will occur with this value of gain and all controlled axes must have stepping motors with identical gain values if path accuracy is to be obtained. Other considerations such as maximum velocities and acceleration and deceleration limits are similar to the systems described earlier and will not be repeated here.

MEASUREMENT SYSTEMS

Many techniques have been used for position measurement in numerical control applications. Since the measurement system plays an integral part in the design of a total numerical control system, it is worth discussing the salient features of the more popular types.

The measurement problem in numerical control is very demanding because of somewhat extreme accuracy requirements. For example, a measurement resolution of 0.0001 of an inch on a table length of 50 inches is not an uncommon requirement. The measurement system for such an application must be capable of detecting one part in 500,000. Clearly, simple transducers are not capable of producing this range of accuracy and all measurement systems are complemented with digital processing of some form.

Transducers for numerical control applications can be classified as incremental or absolute. An incremental transducer indicates relative position changes only, whereas absolute transducers output a unique indication for the entire measurement length. More than 95 percent of today's numerical controls use a measurement system based on an incremental transducer.

It is important to distinguish between the measurement transducer and the total measurement system. Absolute position measurement can be provided with either an incremental transducer in association with electronic accumulation, or with an absolute transducer. An incremental position measurement in conjunction with a bidirectional counter (or equivalent position buffer storage) can be used to accumulate a continuous absolute indication of the machine position with respect to a reference coordinate. The only additional requirement with such a system is that care be taken in establishing the reference position; generally, the machine must be started from this reference point since all absolute motions are obtained by accumulating the ensuing incremental motions from the original starting position.

Analog Position Transducers

Analog transducers are represented by two popular types, resolvers and inductosyns. An inductosyn is, unfortunately, a trade name for a linear resolver. Another device of this type is the Accupin. All transducers in this class should be more appropriately called analog incremental transducers as they produce a continuous or analog output for a small distance (typically .1 inch or 2 mm.) For larger distance measurements, the analog measurement cycle is repeated and a count is made of the number of cycles generated.

A resolver, shown in Figure 35, is a rotating mechanical device with two quadrature stator windings and one rotor winding. When the sinusoidal voltages, $V \sin \omega t$ and $V \cos \omega t$, are applied to the

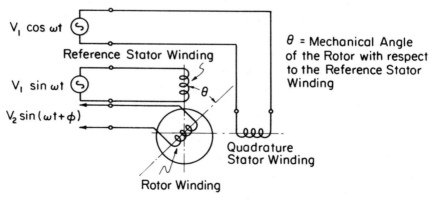

FIGURE 35

A resolver converts a pair of quadrature voltages into a (mechanically) phase-shifted voltage.

stator windings, a sinusoidal voltage is induced in the rotor winding of the same frequency. However, the rotor voltage is phase-shifted with respect to the input reference voltage by an amount equal to the mechanical angle θ between the reference stator winding and the rotor winding. The phase shift—which is a continuous function of rotor position—is used as the position measurement. The electrical phase shift as a function of the mechanical angle of the rotor is shown in Figure 36. The phase angle is a linear function of the

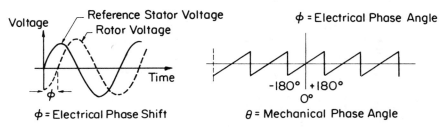

FIGURE 36

The phase relationships between stator and rotor voltages for a resolver.

mechanical angle between -180 and $+180$ degrees and then repeats itself for each additional rotation.

In practice, the resolver is used in conjunction with a measurement system of the type shown in Figure 37. This figure is easier to comprehend if one remembers that it is desirable to have the output in a digital form.

In Figure 37, a reference square wave is generated by counting down from a high-frequency digital clock. This reference wave is shaped in an electronic circuit called a "phase splitter" to produce the sine and cosine stator voltages. The induced rotor wave is fed into a shaping circuit that is little more than a very high-gain amplifier. The position wave, at the output of the shaping circuit, is a square wave of the same frequency as the reference wave but shifted in phase by an amount equal to the angle of rotation of the rotor.

A digital measurement of the rotor position can be readily obtained. Typically, the counting logic produces a square wave for every 1000 clock pulses. If the reference wave has a frequency of 250 cycles per second, then a clock frequency of 250,000 cycles per second is required. One complete mechanical rotation of the motor will produce a position wave phase shift of 360 degrees, which is equivalent to 1000 clock pulses. Thus, one clock pulse is equivalent to 360 degrees per 1000 pulses or .36 mechanical degrees. If the time

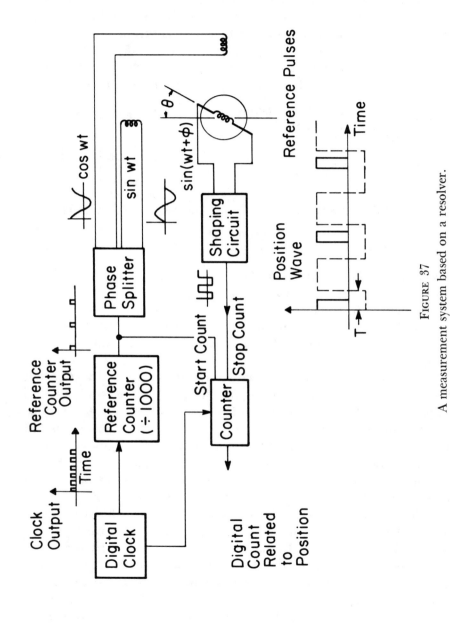

FIGURE 37

A measurement system based on a resolver.

52

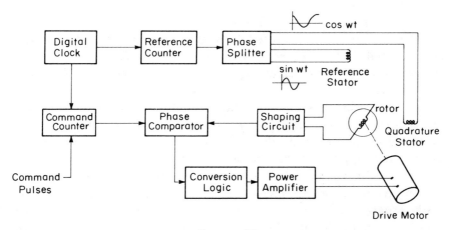

FIGURE 38

An axis servo system using a resolver for position (rotation) feedback.

interval between the on condition of the reference wave and the on condition of the position wave is measured in terms of clock pulses, a digital count is produced with each unit corresponding to .36 degrees of mechanical rotation.

If the resolver is used as part of a feedback control system, it is more common to use the technique displayed in Figure 38. A second counting circuit is used to generate a command wave that has the same frequency as the reference wave. However, the command counter is modified inasmuch as pulses can be added to or subtracted from the clock pulses being counted. If both the command wave generator and the reference wave generator are started at the same time, the two output waveforms will be identical. This is the zero synchronization condition. Then, as command pulses are entered, the command wave will advance or retard the reference wave in time. The command wave is phase-compared with the position wave, and any difference is amplified to command the servo motor. For example, if the system is started at zero and ten additional pulses are added to the command counter, the servo will advance the rotor until the position wave also leads the reference wave by the equivalent of ten counts or 3.6 degrees so as to null the input to the servo.

The above technique works well, provided that the phase difference between the command wave and the position wave never exceeds 360 degrees. Most low-gain servo systems routinely exceed this value.

53

An additional circuit, called an extended phase comparator, contains a reversible binary counter. The counter is up-counted by the command wave and down-counted by the position wave. Thus, if the error exceeds ±180 degrees, a net count is entered in the counter and motion will not cease until both the counter and the phase are returned to zero.

Some commercial systems operate exactly as has been described. Others differ in that the reference wave is sent directly to the phase comparator circuit, while the command pulses are used to modify the voltages applied to the stator windings.

Because the resolver uses a phase measurement principle, these systems are often called "phase-analog" systems. A zero offset can be easily programmed into this system by using an additional hand-set resolver in parallel with the measurement. In such a case, the zero can be offset up to the linear or incremental range of the resolver (one revolution).

Numerical control systems that use resolver feedback often offer position readout as an option. Rather than by direct measurement, the position readout is usually obtained by counting the command pulses and inferring that the control has followed the command. If all command pulses are accumulated after starting from a known position, absolute position display is obtained.

Since resolvers are rotary devices, they provide indirect measurement—the rotation of the lead screw or gear. As such, any inaccuracies of the drive mechanism can result in dimensional errors on the workpiece. Indirect measurement does have the advantage, however, that table resonance with the lead screw is external to the control loop and thus does not cause additional stability problems.

The inductosyn is a linear version of the resolver principle designed to provide direct measurement of the slide position. A schematic of the inductosyn is shown in Figure 39. The primary scale is a single hairpin winding of copper ruggedly bonded to a steel or glass base down the length of travel of a machine tool. The secondary scale, called the "slider" consists of two similar conductors spaced in a two-phase relationship as shown in Figure 39.

The scale and slider are mounted so that the primary and secondary conductors face one another at a small distance. When the slider is fed two alternating currents, which represent $\sin \omega t$ and $\cos \omega t$, a voltage will be induced on the primary scale whose phase is shifted relative to the reference wave by mechanical position. The perform-

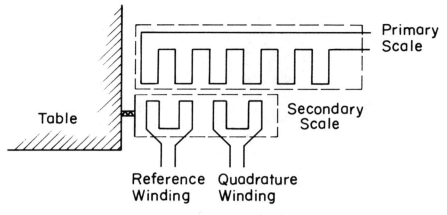

FIGURE 39
An inductosyn.

ance is similar to the resolver, the only difference being that the unit is stretched out and built in a repeating configuration.

A phase-analog control similar to that of Figure 38 can be used for a servo control or for position readout. Note that the analog incremental systems can provide a continuous measurement within a single 360-degree rotation of the transducer (or within a single 360-degree span of the inductosyn scale). This feature can be used to advantage in establishing an accurate zero reference coordinate on the machine table. Mechanical limit switches can be used to stop the slide such that the transducer is known to be within a particular 360-degree cycle. The linear portion of the transducer output can then be used to precisely locate or null the slide at a specific location within the scale. During setup or after an unexpected shutdown, the machine can be quickly returned to the reference position for restarting the measurement sequence.

Digital Pulse Generator

Digital pulse generators are of two types—rotary pulse generators and linear fringe patterns. In either case, the transducer produces a pulse for each increment of distance traveled. Total motion or absolute position is obtained by accumulating or counting the net increments of motion from a reference location.

Several types of rotary pulse generators are available. An optical example will be used to represent the general characteristics.

An optical pulse generator or quantizer consists of a transparent

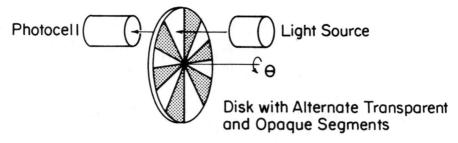

Photocell   Light Source

Disk with Alternate Transparent
and Opaque Segments

FIGURE 40
A pulse generator for converting a mechanical rotation
into an electrical voltage.

rotating disk divided into a number of segments of which alternate segments are opaque. A lamp is placed on one side of the disk and a photocell on the opposite side as shown in Figure 40. As the disk rotates from black to white, the change in light intensity is sensed by the photocell. The output from the photocell is electronically differentiated so that a pulse occurs each time a segment rotation occurs. The distance from the beginning of one black sector to that of the next represents an electrical or pulse cycle of 360 degrees.

In practice, two lamps and two photocells are used. The photocells are situated as shown in Figure 41 so that their outputs are 90 degrees

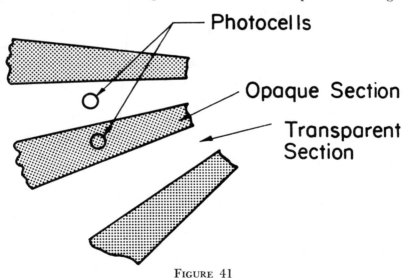

Photocells

Opaque Section

Transparent
Section

FIGURE 41
The arrangement of two photocells in a pulse generator to
determine direction as well as distance.

out of phase. When the disk rotates counterclockwise, the lower cell is illuminated before the upper one. Clockwise rotation causes the opposite to happen. Thus, the system can detect the direction of motion as well as the angle of rotation. The pulse generator is typically mounted on the end of the lead screw. The command generation and comparison techniques for use with pulse generator transducers are similar to the techniques used with stepping motor drives.

One of the problems associated with a pulse generator transducer is the inability to establish a known zero location easily. Modern designs often have two rotating disks with a single opaque segment on the second disk. During installation, the single segment on the second disk is aligned to correspond to a desired location of the slide. A zero reference can be obtained by using mechanical limit switches to position the element within 180 degrees of lead screw rotation of the reference segment and activating the servo system to null at the segment on the second disk. This feature is especially useful for threadcutting.

A typical linear transducer of the pulse generator type can be obtained using optical gratings, or Moire-fringe patterns. The gratings are mounted on the slide rather than on the lead screw and as such form a direct measurement system.

If two similar transparent gratings with equally spaced lines are placed side-by-side with one of the gratings tilted very slightly as shown in Figure 42a, a series of dark and light zones will appear at right angles to the engraved lines when an illuminated source is viewed through the combined grating.[5] (Note: to avoid confusion, the lines on the long grating are omitted.) If one of the gratings is moved longitudinally with respect to the other, the fringes will appear to move upwards or downwards, depending on whether the motion is to the right or left (Figure 42b). As with the pulse generator, motion is detected by two photocells that are arranged to view the fringes through a narrow horizontal slit. The fringes vary approximately sinusoidally so that the photocells can be spaced at 90-degree intervals with respect to the pulse cycles—the same as with the rotary pulse generators. (On commercial versions, four photocells are used to eliminate the effects of variable light intensity, etc. The principle of operation, however, remains the same.)

---

5 O. S. Puckle and J. R. Arrowsmith, *An Introduction to Numerical Control of Machine Tools* (London: Chapman and Hall Ltd., 1964).

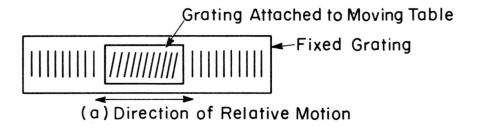

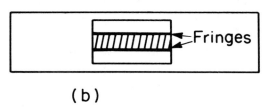

(b)

FIGURE 42
The use of Moire Fringes for incremental position measurement.

Digital Absolute Position Transducers

Digital absolute position transducers—commonly called absolute encoders—are a third class of position measurement transducers. By definition, these encoders present a unique output for any table or slide position. Since these elements represent a very small minority of numerical controls, they will be mentioned only briefly.

The primary advantage of absolute postion measurement occurs during setup and restarting of programs. Since a unique measurement is continuously available, it is not necessary to return to a reference zero each time the measurement sequence is restarted. The major disadvantage is cost. The transducers themselves are quite expensive, and the associated electronics is increased due to the transmission of a digital word rather than a pulse string.

Two types of absolute encoders are available—rotary encoders for the measurement of lead screw rotation and linear encoder scales for direct measurement. A representative rotary encoder disk is shown in Figure 43. In operation, light sources are mounted behind each radial segment and photocells are used to detect the presence or absence of light transmitted through the disk, similar to their use in rotational pulse generators. For the case shown, six light-source, photocell combinations are required, although this number can

FIGURE 43

A disk unit for an absolute position encoder. Each of the radial segments, A, B, C, D, E, and F, would have a combination light source and photocell, as shown in Figure 40, for position readout.

vary considerably, depending on required accuracy. The combination of photocell states provides an absolute measurement, in the form of a digital word, of the rotation of the circular disk. The same principle has been applied to linear encoders where the segments are laid out on a linear track rather than on a circular disk.

These transducer descriptions are, of course, simplified versions of commercial hardware. They are not sufficient to provide the background necessary for engineering applications. The intent has been to acquaint the reader with the different component types available so that he might better understand the complete system.

Chapter II

Computer Controls

Using a computer for machine control is a logical by-product of the exploding application of computers throughout all industry. As this trend matures, a sophisticated machine controller such as a numerical control that is not constructed from a computer module will be a rarity. In addition to the control units themselves, computers will also assume a constantly increasing share of the myriad of tasks that make up the manufacturing effort.

The use of computers today and in the future is limited only by imagination and economics. They are used for process control, part program calculations, and for handling volumes of data for production planning and control, and product fabrication and testing. The computer's power to assimilate, store, and manipulate large masses of information in real-time often allows the performance of all of these tasks simultaneously.

As the transition to computer-aided methods evolves, it is becoming apparent that machine control, of the type described in Chapter I, is but a single element in a much larger concept leading to an integrated computer-aided design and computer-aided manufacturing system. Using a computer as part of the control package offers related advantages such as monitoring, adaptive control, computer-based management information systems, and the easy integration of the total manufacturing capability.

Technological advancements have solidified the transition to computer controls. Constant refinements in computer hardware, software, and telecommunication technologies, and especially the dramatic improvement of performance versus price of small computers, have substantially altered the economical feasibility of computer techniques. In the decade following the advent of numerical control, the cost per computer computation decreased by 50 percent every two and one-half years. During the 1960 decade alone there was a tenfold increase in computer logic circuitry speed; it was accompanied by

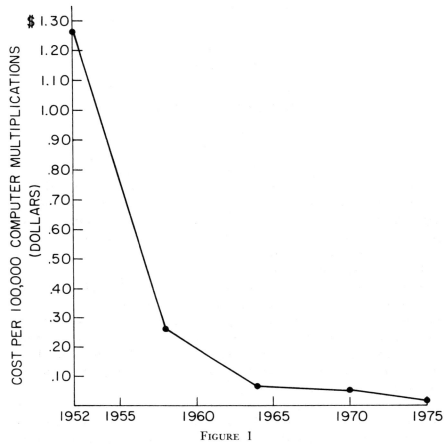

FIGURE 1

Example of dramatic improvement in computer performance versus price.

cost reductions of similar magnitudes. Spectacular reliability and versatility improvements accompanied these price reductions.

Advances in computer technology, both hardware and software, have already made it possible to replace most of the circuits in conventional numerical controls by a highly flexible computer. Eventually, inventory and production management improvements via computers can be expected to close the control loop for total manufacturing systems. (See Figure 1.)

While a complete presentation of computer fundamentals is beyond the scope of this book, some background on this subject is helpful in developing a realistic perspective. Therefore, a brief introduction to computer characteristics is contained in the following section.

COMPUTER CHARACTERISTICS AND CLASSIFICATIONS

Digital computers have four basic subsystems, as shown in Figure 2: input and output, arithmetic and logic, control, and storage. Input and output (I/O) units are used as the interface devices between the human operator or process and the computer itself. They carry the information to and from the computer and have a variety of forms, depending on the applications for which the computer is used. An input device such as a card reader would be analogous to a tape reader on a numerical control system, while output such as the printing actions would correspond to the actual tool movements of a machine.

All of the computing work in the system is done in the arithmetic and logic unit (ALU). This device makes simple logical decisions and carries out rudimentary arithmetic operations at extremely high speeds. It is this unit's ability to operate at fantastic speeds that enables the computer to be such a powerful instrument.

The control unit is the heart of the system. It directs the flow of information throughout the computer.

The storage unit retains all information needed for both control and calculations. It is constantly accepting and giving up bits of in-

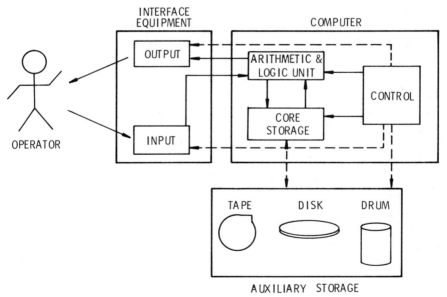

FIGURE 2
The basic computer configuration.

formation while computation is being carried out. Storage units come in different configurations and are referred to as part of the computer's "memory." These devices are classified according to their capacity and "access time"—the time it takes to transfer information from the memory device to the ALU. The main memory—commonly core storage—has the fastest access time, but, because of its relatively high cost per bit, is generally used as a low- to medium-capacity device. Located within the ALU, the core is made up of tiny magnetic rings approximately the diameter of a pinhead. They are threaded together with wire in a three-dimensional array. These rings are in either of two electronic states. When two electronic currents are imparted on the "X" and "Y" wires of an array, they induce a magnetic field on the ring at their intersection. This field induces a current in the "Z" wire through which the state of the ring can be amplified and sensed at any time. An opposite current reverses the magnetic field of the ring and the electronic sense of the third wire. The rings of the core storage are always in one of these two states, making this a binary device.

In recent years, integrated circuit memories have threatened to replace core memories in many systems. However, their increased speed and lower cost advantages are balanced by their susceptibility to power failures and limited availability and, as a result, they are gaining quite slowly on core as the major high-speed storage medium.

Disks and drums and magnetic tapes have access time much slower than the main memory, but are much more economical for large storage capacity. They are located outside the ALU and used for data that are needed only on an intermittent basis. A disk is like a phonograph record that stores information magnetically in circular tracks. The information is written and read by magnetic heads on either side of the disk. A typical disk holds 250,000 computer words, and the number of disks that can be handled by a single computer is limited only by the amount of access time that can be tolerated. With drums the information is stored in tracks around the surface and is read by a series of perpendicular magnetic heads located on opposite sides of the drum. Disks and drums are used to store large files and commonly used programs, operating routines, tables, etc.

Any information requiring only occasional use can be permanently stored on paper or magnetic tape or on punched cards. Whenever these programs or files are needed, they can be read into "active" storage (drums, disks, or core). Information on tapes or cards has relatively long access time, especially if the needed data are fairly randomly distributed along the tape.

There are three fundamental classes of general-purpose computers: business computers, scientific computers, and process control computers.

Business computers perform routine calculations on huge quantities of data. As such, the data input and output characteristics must accommodate high-speed transmission. The working memory of the computer can be relatively small so long as a large bulk memory is utilized. Disks, drums, or magnetic tapes often serve as peripheral bulk memories on business computers. Common input devices include card readers or prepared magnetic tapes, while output is to either a high-speed printer or the equivalent of a graphical display. Business computers are designed to operate in an ideal air-conditioned environment and almost always run asynchronously. That is, a finite number of instructions are sequentially executed until the answer is obtained. Intermediate stops and data insertion are seldom required, and when they are, the timing is not critical.

Typical scientific computers perform very accurate and complex calculations on relatively small amounts of data. Input and output data processing demands are at moderate to slow speeds. Timing is not critical, but high-speed arithmetic is essential. Data are input through card readers, magnetic tape, typewriter terminals, etc. The output is usually printed or graphically displayed. Working memories must be large whereas the bulk memories can be relatively small. As with business computers, the operational environment must be controlled.

The process control computer is designed to perform real-time calculations required for the regulation of a physical operation, for example, of machine tools or other manufacturing equipment. Input data characteristics must allow very high-speed data transmission while the output can be of moderate speed. Process computers operate on an "alarm" or interrupt control basis; calculations are performed synchronously. External inputs can alter or control the program sequence. Timing is very critical and high-speed arithmetic is essential.

Since process computers maintain communication with a process, the input and output data elements must provide both analog and digital transmission to and from the process in addition to the card or tape readers and print-out devices for operator interaction. The capacity of both the working memory and bulk memory can be of a medium size, depending on the application. Many programs must be run simultaneously. Severe plant conditions must be considered part of the process computer's operational environment.

Because of the computer's great flexibility, the foregoing classifications are not absolute. Computers designed for business applications have been imaginatively adapted to control applications and vice versa. Also, special software programs can make a given computer operate in all three of the above categories. Anyone having computer experience is well aware of the myriad of choices and the difficulty of equipment selection.

CONVENTIONAL NUMERICAL CONTROL AND COMPUTER CONTROL

Several distinctive design patterns evolved in the progression from numerical to computer controls. Today, the variations range from using a remote computer system to fully replacing the conventional numerical control system with a minicomputer. Significantly, the traditional numerical control functions are not eliminated by computer-based alternatives; rather these functions are redistributed through a new arrangement of system elements.

Computers that augment or replace conventional numerical controls are often represented as the fourth generation of numerical control. The first three generations are distinguished by the physical attributes of their electronic components—(1) vacuum tube controls, (2) discrete semiconductor controls, and (3) integrated circuit controls. Computer control, on the other hand, implies an entirely new design and management philosophy rather than simply a hardware refinement.

Conventional numerical controls are a combination of digital components and circuits such as electronic flip-flops, gates, counters, registers, etc. These components are inflexibly hard-wired together by back-plane wire-wrapping, and the printed circuit boards are specially interconnected to form circuits that perform specific logical decisions and computational functions. Such hard-wired controls may be viewed as a form of special-purpose computers since they share the same components and fabrication techniques as computers. However, the logic decisions and the calculations that can be performed are determined in the early design stage and implemented with hardware. Once constructed, these hard-wired controls are capable of performing only the original design objectives.

General-purpose computers have evolved from an entirely different design philosophy. They are called "stored program" computers because the instructions that determine the operating sequence are stored in a coded form in the computer memory (and can be changed quite easily). In operation, control instructions are extracted from the memory, decoded with appropriate logic circuits, and then executed. Thus, the computer's general-purpose logic circuits can perform many different functions. In fact, they are limited primarily by the size of the memory, the programmer-specified instructions, and the data placed in memory.

Since the programmed instructions are electronically stored in the computer's memory, they can easily be changed by the programmer. The program, as written by a computer programmer, is referred to as "software" and the computer used to replace a conventional numerical control is sometimes referred to as a "soft-wired" control.

A barrier to grasping the applications of computers in numerical control is the terminology employed. A myriad of terms and acronyms such as DNC (Direct Numerical Control), CNC (Computerized Numerical Control), and SPNC (Stored Program Numerical Control) have been coined and loosely used.

A primary consideration in the dedication of a computer to a single machine is the flexibility to be gained from replacing the hard-wired logic by the stored-program logic of a computer. This principle suggests that a generic descriptor for using a dedicated computer on a single machine is Stored Program Numerical Control (SPNC). An abbreviated term—Computerized Numerical Control (CNC)—has gained wider popular acceptance and will be utilized here.

The fundamental principle of CNC is that a computer is used to replace or augment a conventional numerical control for a single machine. In process terms, the objective of CNC is to improve the conversion of the paper tape information into machine actions.

CNC can be implemented at two fundamental levels. In one configuration, a dedicated computer replaces all of the special-purpose logic of the conventional numerical control system, including path generation (interpolation) and position loop closure. The only discrete elements external to the computer are the electronic elements which match the computer and machine voltage levels.

The second—and presently more popular—CNC level uses a combination of a dedicated computer and special-purpose hard-wired logic. Typically, the path generation functions (interpolation) and the position control loops are implemented with special-purpose logic, and all remaining functions are performed through computer software.

DIRECT NUMERICAL CONTROL (DNC)

A system in which multiple machine control is accomplished by a computer or computers through direct connection in real time—referred to as Direct Numerical Control (DNC)—should be mentioned here. The use of a computer to assist in the control of more than one machine is usually directed toward the methodical organization and administration of the support functions and thus does not strictly qualify as another form of controller. Individual machines can be connected to a DNC system in three ways:

1. *Stand-Alone Control*—A machine connected to a DNC system can be provided with a stand-alone modified conventional controller which is capable of operating off-line from the DNC system—for example, with a tape input—as well as under central computer control. The stand-alone configuration is referred to as a Behind-the-Tape Reader (BTR) system since data from the central computer are supplied to the controller at the terminals normally connected to the paper tape reader.

2. *Hybrid DNC*—A hybrid machine controller in a DNC system implies that the conventional numerical control functions are shared between the central computer and a reduced special-purpose controller dedicated to each machine. For example, the path generation function may be broken up into coarse calculations performed in the central computer and linear interpolation in the special-purpose controller. The special-purpose controller can consist of either hard-wired logic or a small dedicated computer. Since functions are shared with the central computer, stand-alone control of a machine is not possible.

3. *Direct Control from a Central Computer*—With some constraints, all numerical control functions for several machines including path generation (interpolation) and axis control can be performed in a central computer. This technique has been used on some special-purpose machines having stepper motor drives, and it will probably be extended as computer technology advances.

BASIS FOR CNC EVOLUTION

CNC, like its conventional counterpart, is represented by several designs. Confusion arises when a control builder reports that 80 percent of his controller capabilities are in software with the remaining 20 percent in hardware while others indicate that their controller's functions are totally implemented in software. The trade-offs between software and hardware mostly offer subtle variations on a main theme of providing an economic alternative to conventional control's hard-wired logic circuits. Available systems demonstrate that all numerical control functions can be performed either by conventional logic circuitry or by a dedicated computer. The final selection is determined by assessing the economic consequences of each control strategy for the intended job.

With conventional control, once the digital logic components are assembled, alterations to most control operations are relatively expensive. By contrast, with a minicomputer-based controller, the control sequence is determined by a stored set of memory instructions which often may be modified simply by loading a new program. The addition of control functions and features or the adaptation of the software control to many different machines can be relatively simple and inexpensive. Although changes through software are not as easy as is often implied, they indeed are much simpler than rebuilding or extending system hardware.

Control adaptability has been a driving force behind CNC's development because proliferation of designs and options is a major problem in the construction of conventional controls. These controls have been largely "custom" packages consisting of a basic set of standard circuits and a varying mix of optional circuitry. In the early 1970's, one conventional control builder required over 400 unique circuit cards to construct his product line. Out of all these cards, only one or two dozen—the path generation and position loop logic circuit cards—were universal to the bulk of the controls. The remainder were for various options ordered by different users. To combat proliferation, integrated circuitry has helped to standardize some previously optional features. Nevertheless, special features continue to require large card inventories, complex backplane wiring configurations, expensive documentation, and different servicing procedures for the builder and user. Since they found it difficult to standardize their products, it is little wonder that numerical control manufacturers were frustrated in achieving price reductions comparable to those in computers.

Because the primary hardware component for CNC systems can be purchased from a computer manufacturer at a competitive cost, the development and construction costs of such equipment have been shared by others outside the machine control field. Besides sometimes getting a control with a lower price tag, a CNC user finds that he is able to adapt these relatively universal controls to many types of machines. When this happens, his operators, programmers, and especially his maintenance technicians are no longer required to cope with the idiosyncrasies of a different type of numerical control for each machine. This standardization also cuts the inventory requirements for spare parts.

CNC systems initially demonstrated the greatest competitive advantage when used on applications requiring controls of medium to large complexity. The more favorable conditions were where many options were needed, or three or more axes were to be controlled. CNC soon became price competitive on the lower-priced controls as well, and it has increasingly been applied to both point-to-point applications and contouring controls. Because the field is changing so rapidly, managers must expect a continuous penetration into all numerical control application areas.

There are many point-to-point applications where a CNC offers advantages formerly missing, such as on-line program generation and modification, the ability to store special sequences and canned cycles, and, of course, flexibility. Computer controls for punch presses offer an excellent example.

Stretching the nomenclature a bit, an economic advantage of CNC is showing up in another area—multiple machine control. Modern minicomputers sometimes have capacity adequate to control two or three machines simultaneously. When two or more machines are purchased at one time, or if an existing machine is mechanically sound but needs a newer control, there is sometimes a potential for a cost savings by sharing a CNC system.

DESIGN AND OPERATION OF CNC AND CONVENTIONAL NUMERICAL CONTROL

Since most existing CNC systems are contouring controls, the following discussion concentrates on these characteristics. However, relevant principles applicable to point-to-point controls are readily

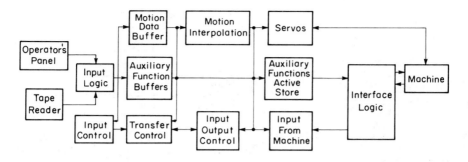

(a) Conventional Numerical Control – Each Block Represents
A Set of Special-Purpose Electronic Circuits

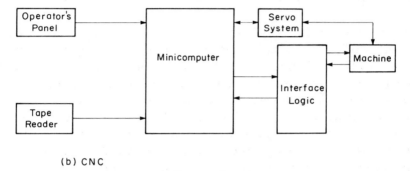

(b) CNC

FIGURE 3

A comparison between conventional and computer numerical control.

inferred. Computer controls are compared with conventional controls in Figure 3.

An effective way to isolate the uniqueness of the CNC design is to distinguish which conventional numerical control functions are typically allocated to the computer. These usually include the following functions:

1. Buffer storage
2. Decoding of tape data
3. Decimal-to-binary conversion
4. Absolute-to-incremental dimension conversion
5. Direct inches per minute (ipm) or inches per revolution (ipr) feedrate programming
6. All functions unique to a given machine
7. Canned cycle sequences
8. Low-volume or special purpose options.

71

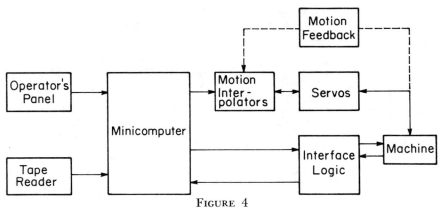

FIGURE 4

A CNC design utilizing conventional interpolators for motion control.

The two principal CNC designs which have dominated the developments of path generation and position control loop functions are shown in Figures 4 and 5. The first, diagrammed in Figure 4, retains, outside the computer, the semi-standardized hard-wired logic circuits universal to conventional contouring controllers. Because these circuits are relatively inexpensive due to larger volume, they are used in the velocity or rate generation cards, the interpolator cards, and the transducer and loop-closure electronics. Another important consideration is that these circuits are flexible and reliable in their hard-wired form and often perform the functions more economically

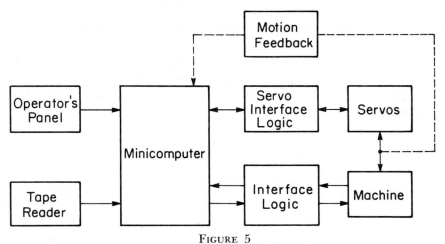

FIGURE 5

A CNC design with motion control provided by software within the minicomputer.

than many minicomputers. Retaining these functions in hard-wired form saves the computer for operations having a greater payoff and also permits the use of a less expensive computer.

The second CNC design, shown in Figure 5, completely eliminates all hard-wired functions except interface electronics. Interpolation functions are implemented through software programs and the position loops are also closed within the computer. The increased demands imposed by assigning axis control to the computer can require that it be larger and faster than needed for the hybrid CNC design. Obviously, the increased cost required for the larger computer must be offset through the elimination of hard-wired components and resulting performance improvements.

CNC ADVANTAGES

In addition to the general economic gains previously cited, several specific benefits are either unique to the CNC technique or offer such substantial improvements that one or a few of these factors often justify the purchase of a CNC system even at premium price. Some of these advantages are discussed below.

The Availability of a Computer

Many companies have considered a CNC system because they are buying not only a control but also a fairly powerful minicomputer. By proper scheduling, the computer may be used for part programming, engineering calculations, cost estimation, etc. when it is not needed for control purposes. On most CNC systems, however, some additional components may be required, such as a memory extension, a teletype, software modules, etc. to use the computer for noncontrol purposes. This initial hardship will certainly disappear as control builders modify their configurations for easier access and multiple uses.

Minicomputers fundamentally are scaled-down versions of large computers having characteristics tailored to scientific and process control requirements. In general, a minicomputer sells for less than $25,000, has a relatively small memory and word size, incorporates flexible input-output structures, and operates at reasonably fast processing rates. As many potential purchasers of numerical control systems quickly recognized, most of these minicomputer characteristics were previously available only on the large and often prohibitively expensive computers.

Axis Calibration and Command Conditioning

Most contouring controls obtain position information by rotational measurement of the axis lead screw. Lead screw inaccuracies, such as pitch variations or backlash, may therefore be reflected in the workpiece. Since many of these errors are repetitive and thus predictable, it is possible to "tune" the total CNC system by storing in memory the results of periodic machine calibrations.

In operation, an accuracy plot can be made periodically for each axis by determining true machine positions relative to those indicated by the system's measurement transducer. The resulting calibration data can be organized into a table of accuracy variations and stored in the computer's memory with an appropriate computer program. As the programmed tape is executed, a computer program looks for these accuracy variation points, and when they are encountered, compensations are used to condition either the axis command or feedback signal.

CNC axis calibration is performed entirely by computer activities, and the added work load and memory requirements are relatively slight. This capability creates the possibility of producing parts that actually demonstrate accuracies greater than that of the machine itself.

Part Program and Tape Editing

Editing or modifying part program tapes through a minicomputer is undoubtedly the most publicized CNC advantage. Machine site tape editing not only speeds tape tryout and debugging, but also encourages program optimization.

CNC on-line tape editing usually has been restricted to changing the tape image data, i.e., the individual characters, groups of characters, or complete blocks on the paper tape. On all but a few CNC systems part programs cannot be modified on the minicomputer at the source level without additional peripheral equipment, such as extra memory, teletypes, etc. Moreover, languages and CNC systems that permit source level program modification usually require the full commitment of the minicomputer, which demands that the machine remain idle for several minutes. Both of these factors create cost penalties that inhibit such applications in a dedicated controller. As minicomputer technology progresses and costs are further reduced, this limitation should subside.

Nevertheless, modification of tape data can be extremely profitable in itself. Many tapes fail because of errors in one or a few characters. Poorly punched holes or parity errors are frequent examples. Others include improper feed and speed commands, characters improperly sequenced, undesirable coolant flows, etc. When the CNC system has a tape punch, several blocks of data can be read into computer memory, the revised characters entered, and a new tape punched without having to dismantle the machine setup and return to a data processing computer.

Program optimization may prove to be the most profitable benefit of CNC tape editing. Many tapes contain "fat" due to conservative programming to avoid failure. For example, a speed change might be desirable while "cutting air," but the part programmer frequently is reluctant to include it until he can observe the actual cutting conditions involving the tool and workpiece clearances; similarly, the machine's table might not need to retract quite so far during tool changing, a chance the part programmer was not willing to take until he could observe actual clearances.

CNC's programming and tape editing aids are especially valuable in punch press operations where so little time is required for each punching operation. Because the bulk of the overall cycle comprises machine movements, these part programs require many blocks of command data. The quick processing of such tapes means that the part programmer is frequently under pressure to resupply a machine with new tapes. To complicate the problem, much of the programming for point-to-point punching operations is handled without computer assistance. A common and costly result of these pressures is that tapes too often are hastily produced without adequate or proper optimization reviews.

CNC controllers not only have the computer to speed programming calculations, but they also allow the storage in memory of the most efficient sequences which interleave paths and changes. These optimized sequences, to be described later in the programming chapter, can be activated by a single program statement. They often generate as many as 50 to 100 ideally ordered operations.

CNC's flexibility in dimensional input modes provides important tape programming and editing advantages. This desirable feature will also be developed in more detail later.

User-Generated Specialized Programs

When CNC systems were introduced, the possibility of users creating special programs adapted to their own conditions was not widely recognized. However, progressive users quickly exploited the computer's flexibility and experimented with new control techniques, strategies, and sequences. The computer's operating program usually was changed slightly to suit particular needs, and if an idea did not turn out as desired, the equipment was easily restored to its initial state by reloading the original program. Thus, programs for special canned cycles or sequences of events that were repeated for a large family of the user's parts could be generated, experimentally tried, and stored in the computer memory. Drilling, tapping, and punching sequences are examples of special programs for repetitive control sequences.

Another example of exploiting the CNC computer for repetitive operations is a variation of part family programming. This concept, especially beneficial for shafts, thread dies, cylindrical surfaces, etc., uses the CNC computer in coding and selecting operations for parts of similar geometrical shapes.

In application, a generalized part program in which the actual part dimensions and machining functions are noted as variables, is stored in the CNC computer memory. Any part meeting the family characteristics can be programmed and machined by calling up the general program and inputting the variables that often are only the descriptive parameters taken directly off the engineering drawing.

The computerized part family programming technique has proven especially valuable in the production of thread dies. Here the part programmer need input only the parameters which define the thread pattern, geometric shape, and the original blank dimensions. All remaining calculations and the control of the machine are automatically performed by the CNC computer. Complete production time for complex die shapes has been reduced from weeks to hours with resultant inventory and manpower savings.

In addition to utilizing the computer for experimentally developing more efficient part-programming methods and control strategies, other specialized CNC programs have been perfected to help in troubleshooting, production management, adapting the controlled operation to changing conditions, etc. Adaptive control software in tandem with appropriate sensors promises substantially improved productivity for metal cutting and other applications.

76

Some special CNC troubleshooting programs have been written to direct the computer to search automatically for malfunctions throughout various system components. The manufacturer of the minicomputer provides as a standard feature the necessary diagnostic routines to troubleshoot the computer. Results of the automatic fault searches will in the near future be displayed on the computer's output device providing printed diagnostics and instructions to the troubleshooter.

The range of specialized programs for performance monitoring and the logging of production management data is limitless. Common factors sensed are: cycle-on, production quantities, elapsed time, rejects, downtime, broken tools, percentage usage of feedrate and spindle speed controls, etc. One highly profitable result of such specialized programs is higher equipment utilization and thus more throughput and profits.

A critical limitation of these special CNC programs is obviously the capacity of the minicomputer. Moreover, many programs tend to be unique and must therefore be written by user personnel. A shortage of trained and qualified personnel needed to generate the computer language for the special programs can restrict the application to the more sophisticated users.

Information Reading and Error Detection

Although CNC systems generally use paper tape for input, several CNC characteristics greatly reduce the tape-related problems. The CNC tape data are loaded directly into the working memory of the minicomputer rather than into a tempoary storage register. Even the minimally configured CNC systems have storage for several blocks of input data, as compared to one block of buffer storage on conventional numerical controls. The greater storage capacity provides several advantages:

a. A large buffer storage increases the reliability of the paper tape reader by reducing mechanical cycling rates. For example, if storage is provided for ten blocks of information, the tape reader will be required to stop and start every tenth block rather than every block.

b. Operations having many short linear tool motion segments such as those commonly found in contour machining can be greatly improved with the extended CNC buffer storage. A double buffer arrangement can be implemented to provide two sets of data, with each set consisting of several blocks of information. While the controller is operating on data from the first set, the tape reader can be loading data into the second. When the first set of data has been used, the control's attention can be transferred to the second set and the tape reader commanded to update the first. Such double-buffering reduces both the required tape reader speed and the start-stop cycles of the reader while assuring that the required data are always available for the interpolators.

c. If sufficient storage is provided in the minicomputer for either an entire program or a subset of the given program, a very low-cost tape reader without character stop capabilities can be used. A high performance tape reader capable of stopping and starting on a specific character can easily cost $2,000 to $3,000, whereas continuous tape readers are available for under $500. The tape search and sequence number detection functions can be implemented with software on the stored data so that flexibility is in no way sacrificed.

The tape reader's work load is significantly reduced on repetitive parts where the computer's memory can store the entire tape. Here the tape is read once, then stored and used as often as necessary during the production of that batch.

d. When the computer storage can accommodate a program or even a program subset, magnetic tape cassettes have proven to be quite valuable. A paper tape program can be loaded in the control and then edited and optimized. When the entire part program can be stored in the computer—the memories of most CNC minicomputers can store programming tapes up to 300 feet in length—the part can immediately be cut from the memory data; even here, it is usually desirable that an updated version of the program be recorded. Rather than tie up the controller with a low-speed paper tape punch, the data can be loaded onto magnetic tape in less than one-fifth of the paper tape punching time. A magnetic tape can alternatively be fed to an off-line paper tape punch or serve as the program storage.

Magnetic tape cassettes become even more valuable when there is not enough storage in the CNC controller for the entire part program. Program segments can be loaded and edited, and then dumped onto the magnetic tape. When editing is complete, the updated program is available much sooner than if a paper tape were punched. The modified program can be run immediately from the magnetic tape and later converted to paper tape.

Magnetic tape cassettes have the disadvantage that they cannot conveniently be read block-by-block; nor is the storage medium as rugged as paper tape. Also, magnetic tape must overcome a questionable reputation before it will be widely accepted in the shop. Many early numerical controls employed magnetic tape and the problems that resulted are painfully fresh in many minds. Still, there is an important distinction between the early attempts at using magnetic tape for control media and the CNC use of cassettes. Here magnetic tape cassettes have been suggested only for temporary storage—at the computer. Permanent records would continue to be of a paper tape form.

e. Sophisticated CNC data transmission and error detection techniques are possible without increasing the purchase price. Software-implemented, high-speed tape checking can lower tape preparation costs by as much as 20 percent.

Data transmission need not be limited to a tape-image data structure as is required by hard-wired numerical control. The minicomputer serves as an efficient data processor, and the flexible, high-speed data input structure adapts to virtually any data link. If present coding systems are replaced or modified by new developments, it is highly probable that the CNC system can be adopted by a program change rather than modified by expensive hardware changes. Finally, because CNC controls offer an excellent vehicle for the systematic progression to a DNC system, tape handling problems can be completely eliminated by a direct link to a central process computer.

Dimensional Input Methods

Historically, several dimensional formats and codes have been variously used in conventional numerical controls. An important CNC advancement allows the processing of a wide range of data codes and formats. Software programs are available that decode both EIA and ASCII codes, detect leading or trailing zeros, and recognize tab sequential or word-related formats, absolute and incremental dimension systems, and metric or inch dimensions. The same flexibility of input characteristics can be built into conventional numerical controls except that future changes may be prohibitive if the selected data structure is ever changed—a likely possibility.

Whether manual or computer programming is used, CNC's flexible input data structure allows the use of conventions most familiar to the programmer. Not only is the part programmer freed of the need to remember several systems of tape codes, it is also unlikely that a new coding system will have to be implemented in order to use the new control.

The flexible input structure has two tape interchangeability advantages. First, if a second or third duplicate of an existing machine is ordered, the CNC system can be specified without a concern that existing tapes will be unusable on the new control. In the past this situation was often not the case if anything but the same machine and the same controller were purchased.

A second tape interchangeability advantage is the use of a CNC system to simulate an existing hard-wired control. CNC's program-proofing and tape-editing powers can be extended to conventional controls by programming the CNC to respond to the hard-wired control's data codes. After completing tape debugging on the CNC system, the tape can be used on the conventional numerical control system for production.

Direct feedrate programming in inches per minute (ipm) is an option that is available on both CNC and conventional controls. However, it is relatively more expensive on the latter, and this premium might easily tip the economic scale in favor of CNC. Direct feedrate programming is especially valuable when manual programming is used.

Direct feedrate programming in inches per revolution (ipr) is also a desirable feature for lathe applications and is essential for numerical control thread cutting. CNC controls and hard-wired controls are equally competent to perform this function; however, the hard-wired control usually requires additional circuitry whereas the CNC system normally requires only an additional software program.

Axis Control Alternatives

Three axes of control are standard on most CNC contouring controls, although additional controlled axes can be purchased. Automatic acceleration and deceleration control, which can be a significant CNC advantage, must be viewed in the proper context before it can be considered a unique CNC advantage. From Chapter I it can be recalled that acceleration control is important during certain transient conditions such as the negotiation of a sharp corner.

Other conditions are also encountered where acceleration control is needed to avoid geometric errors. In general, if both axes are traveling at constant speeds, a path error should not result. However, if a substantial velocity change in either axis is required, dynamic

80

accuracy is not inherent without certain precautions. With conventional numerical control, the programmer or the postprocessor must consider the dynamic constraints of the machine and, if necessary, either program dwells or incremental velocity changes. In achieving these objectives, the dynamic constraint portion of the postprocessor for a conventional hard-wired control can be a fairly extensive program.

With CNC, a more versatile and efficient control of acceleration and deceleration is possible. The computer can "look ahead" to the next block (or blocks) of data on the paper tape and, if acceleration or deceleration is needed (due to a velocity change), the computer can insert a preprogrammed acceleration or deceleration sequence.

The position loop gain can be readily altered in some CNC systems. Low-gain servo characteristics are desirable from the standpoint of reduced acceleration and deceleration loads; however, there are special cases, such as in thread cutting, where a large following error cannot be tolerated. Thread cutting demands that the slide position be accurately synchronized relative to the spindle angle. Since several identical thread-cutting passes must be cut under varying load conditions, it is important that the following error be kept at a very small value for repeatability. Thus, it is desirable for the position loop to behave as a "high-gain" servo during operations of this nature.

The potential of eliminating the geometric constraint portion of the postprocessor by using a dedicated computer suggests that someday it will be possible to eliminate the postprocessor. Since the postprocessor is machine-dependent, the desire to include this program in the CNC minicomputer is quite natural. Several advantages would accrue; the computer that processed the part program would not need to maintain a library of postprocessor functions, and data transmission could be optimized since it would always have a standard form. A discouraging reality is evident, however, in the magnitude of the postprocessor program. For a complex machine it can often approach the size of the source program. At the same time, it is used only to create the control tape, and once the tape is generated, the postprocessor functions are not required until a new part is programmed.

Until further advancements occur in the performance versus price of minicomputers, locating the postprocessor in the CNC system will be practicable only in special cases. The cost of the additional minicomputer capacity that would be required can rarely be justified with present techniques for a function that need be performed only once or twice in the production of a part. Exceptions to this general statement are the special CNC systems such as point-to-point controls for drills and punch presses where the computer can be used for program generation as well as machine control.

Tooling Options

CNC's inherent flexibility simplifies the implementation of tooling-related control functions. Two principal advantages are: (1) the ability to store in the computer multiple offsets and length compensations for machines with automatic tool changes, and (2) the ability to perform calculations for cutter diameter compensation.

Control tape dimensions specify tool geometry and cutter locations relative to the machine and the part. Often, available tools and fixtures vary slightly from programmed parameters. If slightly different tool lengths must be used, on most controls the operator can manually enter a revised dimension and still use the tape. Likewise, tool offsets on turning applications can be revised by inserting dimension adjustments in the control command circuitry.

On conventional numerical controls, storage for these compensation parameters is implemented through operator-activated mechanical switches. One switch assembly is required for each length compensation, and one switch assembly per axis for each tool is required for each offset adjustment. Not only are these extra mechanical devices relatively expensive, they can also occupy considerable space.

With CNC systems, the length and offset compensation factors can be stored in the computer rather than by the switch devices. The compensation values are typically sent to the computer with a single switch assembly or by means of a universal keyboard. Besides the space and cost savings, CNC's reliability is also better.

Cutter diameter compensation, an optional feature on conventional numerical controls for use with rotating tools, involves the generation of a discrete displacement of the progammed cutter path to compensate for the difference between an actual cutter size and the one programmed. Cutter compensation permits the operator to utilize tools of a different size than were programmed and still be able to cut parts to the desired dimensions.

Certain practical difficulties limit the effectiveness of the cutter compensation on hard-wired numerical controls. In theory, these limitations can be overcome by using a dedicated computer to perform geometric calculations and to make decisions when developing an offset path. In practice, however, the demands on the computer, both in time and capacity, sometimes discourage assigning this function to the computer. Nevertheless, the trend to computerize tool length adjustment and cutter compensation will continue and accelerate with computer technology advancements.

Variations between tool changer designs can be accommodated by program changes rather than by expensive special-purpose logic changes. Thus, one control can easily be applied to many different machines with the custom features accommodated by software. Not only are costs reduced by this enhanced standardization, but the software technique has demonstrated reliability and maintainability advantages over the fixed magnetics.

Path Generation Alternatives

Historically, hard-wired contouring numerical controls have been limited to two or three path generation alternatives. A dedicated CNC computer can remove this limitation by making possible path generation alternatives other than the standard linear, circular, and parabolic interpolation. This potential can be valuable when manual programming is used.

Since each system builder tends to offer his own particular interpolation alternatives, the topic does not justify further discussion here. Rather the reader is encouraged to become aware of these efforts and to obtain information on the alternatives from the systems builders.

Protection Against Obsolescence

A vital factor that must be considered when selecting machine controls is minimizing the threat of obsolescence. Typical depreciation accounting schedules amortize a numerical control's investment over 10 to 12 years. Because of advancing technology, a more realistic economic lifespan for a controller is seven to eight years; especially when the decreasing cost of new controls versus the relatively higher maintenance and operating costs of older ones is considered. For example, a third-generation integrated circuit control can provide many additional operating cost-saving options as well as a lower maintenance cost than the second-generation controls;

moreover, it can be purchased at a lower price. In many companies, however, second-generation controls represent an investment which has not yet been fully amortized; as a result, they too often are kept in operation, incurring an operational penalty.

Advanced CNC designs offer an opportunity to avoid such rapid obsolescence. There are no important long-range control technology forecasts that cannot be met with CNC's flexibility. Relative prices might decrease, but it is highly unlikely that the control functions will become obsolete in their lifetime to the point where today's CNC cannot operationally compete with future systems.

CNC'S GROWTH POTENTIAL

CNC is an excellent vehicle for the systematic evolution of a DNC or a total shop floor computerized control and management information system. The flexible, high-speed data input characteristics of most minicomputers can be adapted to most any data link. If present coding systems are modified by new developments, the CNC computer can be adapted by a program change rather than by an expensive retrofit. CNC computers also can be used to structure data into any desired form for transmission back to a central computer. Process monitoring and data collection can be partially processed in the dedicated minicomputer, thus reducing the central computer's work load.

Having a dedicated CNC for each machine in a DNC system provides valuable redundancy. A central computer failure in a DNC system will not cause a machine to be inoperative provided that the correct paper tape or equivalent backup data storage has been maintained.

CNC systems also have many of the desirable features of a total computerized shop floor control system. Part program editing, report generation, and process monitoring are only a few examples. Obviously, these features are usually not as inclusive as they would be on a larger system. Allowing these techniques to be initiated even on a modest scale notably improves efficiency at the outset, but also serves to aid training and development in preparation for a complete multimachine computer control system.

Chapter III

Programmable Controllers

Industrial controls can be divided into classifications that include numerical controls, computer controls, relay logic panels, and solid-state logic modules. Programmable controllers, the subject of this chapter, compete most often with relays and solid-state logic components. Programmable controllers have many of the functional and design characteristics of digital computers, e.g., standard input-output modules, a control unit, and a memory. However, most of them are restricted to performing a fixed but easily programmed set of functions; they lack the computer's ability to perform arithmetic operations. The use of less complex memory and control units and the absence of arithmetic operations have the advantage of lower cost and greatly simplified programming as compared to a computer.

Progammable controllers technically can be applied anywhere digital logic control systems might be used. They produce the greatest economic return, however, when applied to machines or processes utilizing bi-state, input-output devices such as motor starters, solenoids, limit switches, etc. Such machines or processes, traditionally controlled by electromechanical relay panels, operate from signals having ON and OFF conditions, thereby matching the binary characteristic of solid-state digital circuits. Control operations carried out by programmable controllers typically include sequencing, testing, timing, and logical decision making.

EVOLUTION OF PROGRAMMABLE CONTROLLERS

The rapid advancements of the 1950's and 1960's in computer and electronic circuitry technology laid the foundation for the programmable controller. Its birth may have been accelerated at General Motors' Hydramatic Division because of the desire there for a new controller that would reduce the frustrations encountered with electromechanical relays. Maintenance costs from malfunctions mounted as relay contacts and mechanical failure increased in the face of constantly accelerating production speeds and control complexity.

A fundamental relay limitation was caused by high switching voltages necessary to assure that oil or dirt on contacts could be electrically penetrated and yet be low enough to prevent the contacts from welding or pitting. This tenuous voltage-current compromise too often produced contact malfunctions. Failures were also caused by vibrations which loosened relay fasteners and fatigued mechanical components.

Aggravating the reliability problems were the frustrations and delays encountered in troubleshooting a malfunction in a relay controlled system. First, the troubleshooter had to identify the precise point in a cycle where the failure occurred, then locate the troublesome cylinder, valve, relay, or other component to pinpoint the source. A successful troubleshooter required extreme dexterity and expertise to study simultaneously the machine and the operating control relays and then to compare these actions to a circuit or ladder diagram.

Compounding the difficulties of troubleshooting was the reality that electricians, pipe fitters, and millwrights have interrelated maintenance responsibilities, but independent union jurisdictions. Of nearly equal importance was the lack of design standardization for relay controls. Each type providing a different control service was a unique design for the maintenance worker to master. Thus, specially tailored, nonstandard troubleshooting procedures prevailed, which contributed to high levels of downtime.

While advancing solid-state technology provided a natural transition from electromechanical relays to electronic controls, it took the foresight and conviction of the General Motors engineer to turn the potential into a reality. The commercial groundwork was laid in 1969 when General Motors invited bids for a flexible solid-state electronic controller having these characteristics:

1. Easily programmed control sequences
2. Improved reliability in the plant environment
3. Simplified maintainability and repairability—preferably including plug-in assemblies
4. Smaller than a relay control
5. Capable of communicating with computers
6. Cost competitive with relays and solid-state logic modules.

In addition to these general performance and design objectives, the following specifications were established.

1. All inputs must accept 115 volts AC.

2. All outputs must provide 115 volts AC with at least a 2-amp capability adequate for operating solenoid valves, motor starters, etc.
3. The basic unit must be expandable with a minimum of alteration.
4. Each unit must have a programmable memory expandable to a minimum of 4,000 words.

Because industrial controls consisting of conventional relays or printed circuit logic modules were developed with varying levels of capability and complexity, it is logical that a family of competing programmable controllers evolved. The least sophisticated competes with the cheapest control panels having as few as 12 to 15 relays, while a few complex programmable controls may actually be classed as computers since they perform limited arithmetic operations.

The most sophisticated programmable controller has the capability of doing the work of a relay panel control 20 to 30 feet long yet occupies less than 12 cubic feet and weighs less than 100 pounds. Moreover, with its high signal processing capacity compared to relay logic systems, a single programmable controller may handle several machines.

OPERATION

While many programmable controller components are similar to those of a computer, the controller's operation may be more understandable when related to relay controls. A functional diagram of a traditional relay control with typical input-output devices is shown in Figure 1. Here it can be seen that limit switches, push buttons, and other contact-type inputs furnish status information from the operator, the machine, or the process. The control relays implement the decisions programmed by wired-together components—comprising the command source—based on information derived from the sensors. Finally, the output actuators (contactors, solenoids, etc.) execute the desired control sequence. An example of a complex control circuit made up of relays, limit switches, lights, and pushbuttons (a so-called ladder diagram) is shown in Figure 2.

Programmable controllers basically perform the same general functions as the relay control system. In operation, the programmable controller continually monitors each input and compares its status to the required conditions stored in a memory. Control decisions are determined in the control's solid-state logic section as

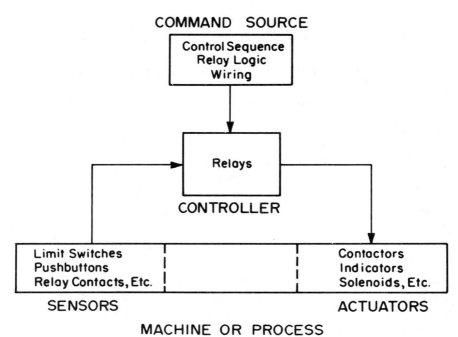

COMMAND SOURCE

FIGURE 1
Relay control system.

indicated by the comparative conditions. If the actual status agrees with the required status, then the programmed sequence stored in memory is allowed to activate appropriate outputs.

Functions of a programmable controller are executed in a way analogous to the rung-by-rung scanning of a relay control ladder diagram shown in Figure 2. Each rung of the ladder represents a specific group of input conditions that must be satisfied to activate a decision output condition. With a programmable controller, instructions are contained in the memory in small groups, with each group analogous to a single rung in the ladder. Also contained in the memory are the sequences for selecting each input specified in a group and testing whether it is ON or OFF. The specified output is selected and set ON or OFF, based on the test results. The controller then repeats this process for the remaining groups of instructions and their associated inputs and outputs. Even though the controller proceeds one instruction at a time, the action occurs so fast that all inputs are checked and outputs properly changed in a thousandth of a second—much faster than the action of only one or two relays.

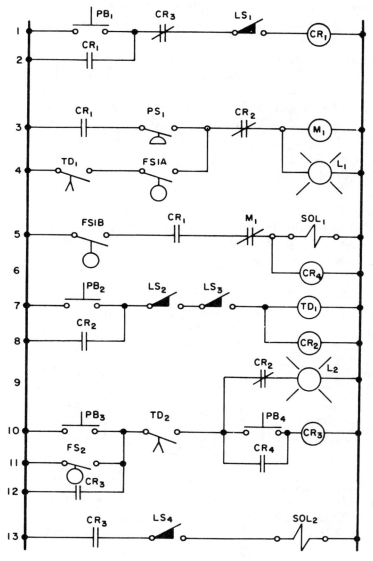

FIGURE 2
Ladder diagram of a complex control circuit.

Although programmable controllers may be the solid-state equivalent of relay controls, they provide the important flexibility, heretofore found only in computers, to meet dynamic manufacturing and operational requirements. Since each input and output is handled independently, thereby eliminating the need for fixed-wired interconnections, the control sequence of a programmable controller with a read-write memory may be altered without changing a single internal wire.

Detailed operations of a representative programmable controller are best reviewed by delineating the functional interrelationships of the major subsystems (see Figure 3). An input subsystem provides standard connections with the various interface devices of the machine or process under control. Each plug-in module, typically accommodating up to 16 units, performs such functions as: termination of the signal source switch, input isolation, AC to DC conversion, filtering, and attenuation of the signal to required logic circuitry levels. Limit switches, push buttons, and other contact-type components are common input devices. Input modules are usually designed to handle 115 to 120 volts AC, incoming signals which are converted into signal levels compatible with solid-state circuits.

The controller's logic circuitry continually scans the inputs and

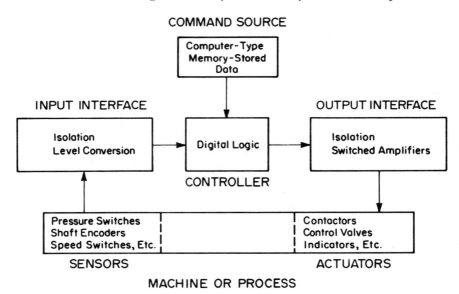

FIGURE 3
The programmable controller.

outputs according to the sequence programmed in memory. The logic subsystem, also known as the control unit, can typically handle up to 256 inputs and 256 outputs, and perform three major tasks: test inputs for ON or OFF status; decide what control function is required; and execute the control decision by setting outputs ON or OFF.

Within the logic subsystem there is usually an instruction sequencer which identifies memory locations where information is to be read. The instruction sequencer compares appropriate memory data with actual input and output conditions, then concludes output decisions based on these comparisons. When selected inputs are in a specified state, the logic causes appropriate output devices to be energized or de-energized.

A timer-counter device is often included to provide signal timing by acting as an internal pacer for the logic or control subsystem. Separate timers, each of which can be included in one programmable controller, have a time interval that can be specified by a programmed instruction. A liberal array of time increments may be programmed, ranging generally from 0.1 of a millisecond to upwards of 99 hours. The timer's input operates as an open contact before timer action is initiated; it closes during the specified time delay and then opens again after the delay. The timer's output acts as an electrically latched relay. When the time delay is initiated, the output is energized and remains energized until cleared by a resetting timer instruction.

The output subsystem receives low-level voltage signals from the controller's logic circuitry and converts these to isolated high-level signals that activate the output devices. Each module, typically consisting of 16 outputs, performs these functions: output signal storage, partial decoding for examining the output signal status, and energizing or de-energizing connected output devices. The last activity is commonly carried out through solid-state AC switches or reed contacts. Connected output devices range from solenoids, motor contactors, and small motors, to lamps and other signal devices.

The remaining programmable controller subsystem is the memory. Serving a function similar to the ladder diagram for relay controls or the punched paper tape of numerical controls, the memory tells the other controller subsystems what to do and when to do it.

Memories of programmable controllers are similar functionally and physically to those of computers. Many programmable controllers with read-write magnetic core memories permit the complete modification of control sequences simply by reading in new instruction codes. The advantage of a read-write memory is that new programs can be speedily entered without rewiring the memory or revising interconnections within the controller. This flexibility, along with the standard input-output modules that afford routine hook-ups, make the programmable controller easily and quickly adaptable to process changes.

The memory, which stores all instructions necessary to define the control sequences, may be likened to a lengthy sheet of ruled paper—each line being numbered to identify the location of an instruction. When the instruction words adequately specify a complete set of control operations, the memory is programmed. One or several words may comprise a complete instruction. Characters forming the instruction words identify the instruction type—such as output instruction, status determination instruction, or an instruction related to an appropriate input or output device. Still other characters identify the memory "line number"—or address—containing the next instruction.

When operating, the logic circuitry sequentially scans the list of memory instructions to see what control operations are to be executed. Starting at the first memory address, scanning occurs "line-by-line" or address-by-address until an instruction is encountered that tells it to do otherwise. For example, when an output command instruction for a typical controller is encountered, the scanning process is interrupted for a split second to determine:

1. Whether the process cycle is such that the machine is ready to perform this output command; and if so,
2. Whether the machine is in the specified state for executing the output command.

If a so-called sequence step character of an output command instruction is a 1, the machine cycle is ready for the command; then, a second condition must be checked to see if the machine status is appropriate for executing the output command. If the sequence step character is a 0, then the second condition need not be checked, and control skips to the memory address of the next specified instruction. The address to which the memory skips is contained in the output command section of the instruction.

The control sequence of even the most complex process thus can be defined through a list of elemental control instructions stored in memory. In totality, a set of instructions comprises a program specifying sequences of relationships between system input and output devices. Its ultimate function is to specify output conditions.

DISTINGUISHING CHARACTERISTICS

Memory design and construction, and programming techniques are the principal distinctions between commercially available programmable controllers. In general, the lower priced models have read-only memories (ROM), while higher priced units have flexible read-write memories. Braided wire and wired-together solid-state components such as diodes are commonly used for ROM's. Ferrite cores similar to those in computers are typically used for read-write memories of programmable controllers. Although read-write memories are more flexible, hard-wired read-only memories demonstrate better resistance to severe electrical interference occasionally present in extreme plant environments.

A popular ROM consists of a braid of wires semipermanently embedded in a potting compound and surrounded by electronic sampling circuits. The arrangement of the wire braid is determined by relatively simple computer-aided programming procedures which create a series of instructions recorded on paper tape to operate an automatic wiring machine. The specially arranged wires of the braided memory represent a unique solution to a specific control problem.

The operation of one ROM is based on the same principle used in the familar current transformer to monitor AC power leads. Fluctuations in the AC current flow produce a varying magnetic field around each wire (Figure 4). The field, induced in an iron core around the wire, produces a small voltage in a "sense" winding. A meter measures both the voltage and current in the AC wire lead. Binary digits comprising a coded instruction are stored in memory by routing the drive line through the iron core if the bit is a 1, or around the transformer core if the bit is a 0. In other words, the presence of a voltage is defined as a binary 1 and its absence as a 0.

Sending a current pulse through each wire typically controls eight individual instructions. Memory read-out occurs in a group of eight instructions. The single desired instruction is selected from these eight, and only the transformers with wires running through their cores will be energized. The pattern of energized transformers is then read as an electronic instruction code.

Wires can be threaded by hand around and through the ROM

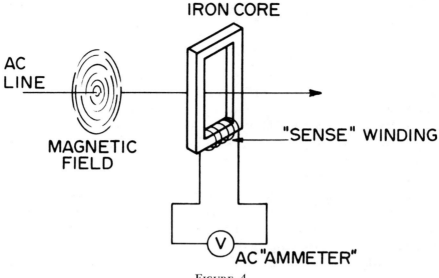

IRON CORE

AC LINE

MAGNETIC FIELD

"SENSE" WINDING

AC "AMMETER"

, FIGURE 4
Current transformer operation.

transformers to produce any instruction code desired. Minor control changes can be made economically by manually cutting out and replacing as many as up to about 20 wires—approximately 15 percent of the ROM.

A major distinction between the read-write and read-only memories is that instructions may be changed in the former simply by reading new information into the ferrite cores. Although limited memory changes can be made by hand, the read-only memory usually is returned to the producer for machine rewiring. The time required for a factory ROM modification is about one week. Delays can be avoided, however, by buying a complete new ROM for $200 to $300. Still another alternative is to substitute temporarily a small computer for the programmable controller's ROM being modified. Some programmable controllers with ROM's also allow the substitution of a flexible read-write memory. Because read-write memories are easily programmed, a single unit can be used to progressively service several ROM programmable controllers being sequentially modified.

PROGRAMMING

The controller's memory type determines the programming techniques that may be employed. As many as three different methods may be used with read-write memories; however, under normal conditions, only a single technique specified by the manufacturer may be used with most read-only units.

Programming Read-Write Memories

Three general programming methods usable for most read-write memories are:

(1) A manual program loader is used to generate the control instructions and to transfer them into the controller's memory.

(2) A computer-aided programming language consisting of special mnemonic codes is used to translate ladder diagram information into properly coded instructions that are read into the programmable controller.

(3) Ladder diagram information or its equivalent is described by a set of Boolean equations; after the equations are computer-translated to programmable controller coded instructions, they are read into memory.

Manual Program Loader

In general, the simplest and often the fastest programming method is to use a manual program loader. Diagnostic facilities of the loader also aid in program analysis and complete system check-out by permitting both the individual execution of programmed instructions and the analysis of the system's step-by-step operation. Undesirable control instructions can be detected immediately and modified to achieve optimum performance. Thus, by means of push buttons, switches, and thumbwheels, all operations necessary to create, test, and amend a program can be performed without any computer language or computer-programming expertise.

An example of the operational characteristics and the instruction building devices of a typical controller will facilitate one's understanding the manual programming feature. The representative program loader shown in Figure 5 and delineated further in Table I will be used. The instruction set for creating a program with this manual loader is shown in Table II.

Program Loading

Although instructions may be generated manually by working directly from a ladder diagram, an initial listing of properly coded instructions promotes greater efficiency. Such a listing affords easier

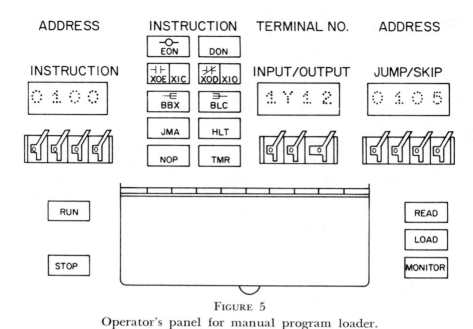

FIGURE 5
Operator's panel for manual program loader.

TABLE I

FUNCTION DEVICES OF REPRESENTATIVE MANUAL PROGRAM LOADER*

Function Device	Operation
STOP	Programmable controller is not cycling through the program in memory
RUN	Programmable controller operates in accordance with the program stored in memory
LOAD	Loads or modifies the contents of memory
READ	Reads contents of memory for program checking or documentation
MONITOR	Actual state of inputs and outputs is displayed
INSTRUCTION BUTTONS	Loads in or reads out a particular instruction in memory
OUTPUT STEP	Exercises all instructions associated with the selected output instructions
INSTRUCTION STEP	Exercises individual instructions one at a time
CONTINUE	Returns the programmable controller to normal cycling mode

* Applicable to manual loader shown in Figure 5.

TABLE II

INSTRUCTION CODES FOR REPRESENTATIVE MANUAL PROGRAM LOADER

Symbolic Code	Instruction Function
EON	Energize Output Non-holding
DON	De-energize Output Non-holding
JMA	Jump Memory Absolute
HLT	HaLT
BBX	Begin Branch eXamine
BLC	Branch List Complete
TMR	TiMeR
NOP	No OPeration

and accurate comparisons between the instructions loaded manually and the control sequences graphically suggested by the ladder diagram. A written record of the instruction set also serves as permanent documentation to supplement the ladder diagram during troubleshooting.

The exact conditions to be satisfied before each output is energized or de-energized also must be defined. For example, to energize Solenoid A (SOL A) in Figure 6, either the Start push button or the M contact and the Stop push button must be closed. Similarly, to energize Solenoid B (SOL B), the contacts M and LS1 must be closed. The condition to be satisfied on each output sequence is recorded

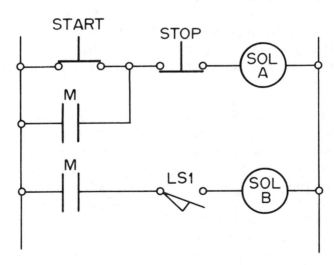

FIGURE 6
Ladder diagram.

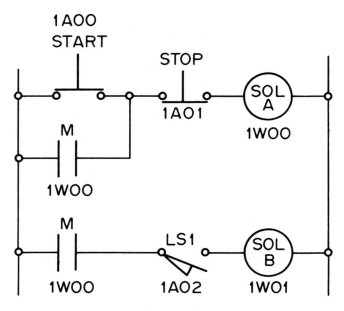

on the ladder diagram or on a separate worksheet such as the initial listing of instructions.

The assignment of terminal numbers to all input and output devices is also required. This can be done by noting both the assigned output terminal numbers near the output devices on the ladder diagram and the input terminal numbers by switches, push buttons, etc., as demonstrated in Figure 7. Each controller manufacturer suggests a set of conventions for numerically coding these input and output devices.

As a first step in manually entering a program with the loader shown in Figure 5, an Instruction Address is set up on the address display. If a new program is being entered, the Instruction Address thumbwheels are normally set at 0000; then the LOAD POWER-UP routines are established by pushing the JMA button; location 0005 is set in the Jump/Skip register, and finally, when the Load button is pushed, the first manually generated instruction is transferred into memory. At the completion of this operation the Instruction Address register will advance automatically.

The foregoing manual process is repeated, instruction by instruction, until all instructions are in memory. When the last output instruction is loaded, the operator, in this example, would manually set up 0005 for the Jump/Skip address. Finally, JMA 0005 is transferred to memory so that the programmable controller will shift back to begin anew the program and the control cycle. The results of employing this process to load an illustrative program manually are shown in Table III.

TABLE III

PROGRAM CREATED BY A MANUAL LOADER

Instruction Address	Instruction*	Terminal**	Jump/Skip
0000	JMA		0005
0002	JMA		0005
0004	HLT		
0005	EON	1WOO	0020
0010	XIC	1AO1	
0011	BBX		
0012	XIC	1AOO	
0014	BBX		
0015	XOE	1WOO	
0017	BLC		
0020	EON	1WO1	0005
0023	XOE	1WOO	
0025	XIC	1AO2	
0026	JMA		0005

* See Table II for function or operation applicable to each instruction code.
** See Figure 7.

If a program is being loaded for the first time, one should anticipate that additional instructions may be needed during program check-out. To provide an expansion potential, a few extra examine instructions can be inserted when the program is created to repetitively sample the same input or output. This space-consuming procedure should be employed judiciously, however, because of the limited memory capacity. Another program amendment technique is to substitute a JMA (JUMP) statement which transfers control to an unoccupied memory area where new program instructions can be added. Following the additional instructions, another JMA instruction must be used to transfer the program back to the proper place in the original program.

Manual Loader Diagnostic Capabilities

Manual program loader diagnostic operations, such as instruction reading, input-output status monitoring, and tape reading or punching, are especially useful during program analysis and system maintenance.

Reading of Instructions

When an instruction address is set up on the manual loader and the READ button is depressed, the complete instruction stored in the programmable controller at the indicated memory address is displayed. The appropriate instruction push button and the Input and Output display will be illuminated on the manual loader, as well as the Jump/Skip display if required. Such a capability is obviously of great value during program testing to determine if it is the source of a malfunction.

Monitoring of Input-Output Status

If the status of an input or output terminal needs to be investigated, the terminal number is set up and the MONITOR push button is depressed. The open or closed status of the selected terminal is displayed on the manual loader's instruction push button lights.

Two other diagnostic operations, Output Step and Instruction Step, may be performed only when the manual loader is connected to a programmable controller that is actually directing a machine or process.

Output Step

When the address of the output instruction to be inspected is entered into the manual loader and the OUTPUT STEP push button is depressed, the complete instruction sequence associated with the selected output will be executed. The resulting energized or de-energized status of the output is displayed on the panel for inspection and comparison to basic documentation such as the ladder diagram.

Instruction Step

Activation of the INSTRUCTION STEP push button initiates the one-by-one execution of an instruction stored in memory. When the address of the instruction to be exercised is entered, depressing the INSTRUCTION STEP push button executes the desired instruction, and the appropriate instruction push button is illuminated to indicate the status. Repeated activation of the INSTRUCTION

STEP push button allows successive instructions to be exercised and their status displayed.

Tape Reading or Punching

Tape punching through the manual loader allows the economical recovery of the programmable controller's memory contents. The tape can be used to produce a detailed listing for inspection of a newly created program when the tape is translated by a computer and then printed. This capability is also very useful when the manual loader is used to amend a program already in memory since valuable up-to-date program documentation can easily be obtained. The tape reading facility is useful for rapidly loading a program previously stored on tape.

COMPUTER-AIDED PROGRAMMING

As in numerical control part programming, a computer may also be used to aid in the preparation of the coded instructions for programmable controllers. First, a description of the control sequence is prepared by using abbreviated English words (mnemonics) to code the appropriate instructions symbolically. Then, a general-purpose computer uses a translator program, generally similar to that used in numerical control, to convert the mnemonic codes into digitally coded instructions acceptable to the programmable controller's memory. Since the translation program is furnished by the controller manufacturer and the complete translation is computer-executed, a user need only concern himself with the simple task of mastering its use.

Unlike the many symbolic words comprising a numerical control computer-aided part-programming language, the repertoire of a typical programmable controller vocabulary needs only a few codes. The 20 mnemonic codes shown in Table IV are for a representative controller.

With computer-aided programming, the programmer first studies the ladder diagram and makes the earlier described terminal assignments for each input and output. Then the series of symbolic command statements is created to describe in words the control operations depicted graphically by the ladder diagram.

The symbolic statements are entered in a computer which contains the translator program to produce the programmable controller's coded instructions. Usually these translator programs also reside in nationally available time-sharing computer systems, and can be

Table IV

Symbolic Instructions for a Representative
Programmable Controller

Type	Code	Description
Output Commands	EON	Energize Output Non-holding
	EOH	Energize Output Holding
	DON	De-energize Output Non-holding
	DOH	De-energize Output Holding
Examines	XIC	eXamine Input Closed
	XIO	eXamine Input Open
	XOE	eXamine Output Energized
	XOD	eXamine Output De-energized
Branches	BBX	Begin Branch eXamine
	BLC	Branch List Complete
Timing Operations	TMR	TiMeR start
	XTE	eXamine Timer Energized
	XTD	eXamine Timer De-energized
	XTO	eXamine Timer Open
	XTC	eXamine Timer Closed
Jumps	JMA	JuMp Absolute
	JMM	JuMp and Mark
Sequence Control	SSA	Sequence Step Activate
	SSD	Sequence Step Deactivate
Control	HLT	HaLT (stop memory cycle)

accessed by the telephone system from any plant location. Alternatively, the translator can be placed in the user's computer for direct in-house access.

Computer processing of the symbolic statements produces instructions coded on punched paper tape, printed documentation listing the instructions, their order, their assigned memory locations, and certain tutorial comments. The computer translator program serves an important edit and error-detection function. Erroneously structured instructions and certain incorrect control sequences cause the translator program to abort the computing process and print out an explanation of the error, resulting in computation stoppage. When the properly coded instructions are on the tape, they are read into the memory, and the programmable controller is ready to operate.

These computer-aided programming concepts are delineated

through the programming of the conditions depicted in the ladder diagram of Figure 8.

After terminal assignments are made, the programmer writes a short sequence of program steps to correspond with each rung of the diagram.

Input and output terminal assignments for this example are:

$$PB1 \quad = \quad 1A0$$
$$PB2 \quad = \quad 1A1$$
$$LS1 \quad = \quad 1A2$$

$$\cdot$$
$$\cdot$$
$$\cdot$$

$$SOL1 \quad = \quad 1WO$$
$$SOL2 \quad = \quad 1W1$$

A complete listing of the program properly coded for the computer follows:

```
A1 EON SOL 1 1 A2
   XIC PB1
   XOE SOL3
A2 EON SOL2 1 A3
   XIC PB2
   BBX
   XIC LS1
   BBX
   XOD SOL1
   XOE SOL2
   BLC
A3 EON SOL3 1 A1
   XOE SOL2
   XIC PS1
   JMA A1
```

The following remarks will facilitate interpretation of the foregoing program statements. Starting with rung A1, the symbolic command

A1 EON SOL1 1 Aw

says, "Energize solenoid 1, non-holding." This command will be placed in readiness for execution, pending examination of the required input (or output) conditions which follow:

XIC PB1

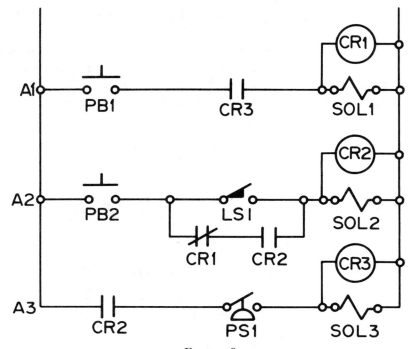

FIGURE 8
Ladder diagram programming.

That is, "Examine input push button 1 for closed condition," and "examine output solenoid 3 for energized condition."

$$\text{XOE SOL 3}$$

If these two conditions are met, the output command is executed— i.e., SOL1 is turned on. If the stated conditions did not exist, then the output command would not be executed, and the program would have transferred control to an address that stored the next instruction. In this example, the next symbolic instruction would be associated with ladder diagram rung A2, and appear as follows:

$$\text{A2 EON SOL2 1 A3}$$
$$\text{XIC PB2}$$

This symbolic statement says, "Energize solenoid CR2, non-holding, if push button 2 is closed." Now, two parallel paths are encountered (see Figure 8): one via limit-switch 1, and the other via control relay 1 (normally closed) and control relay 2 (normally open). This alternate course is handled by the next command BBX, which says, "Begin branch examine" followed by XIC LS1. The next command BBX says, "Begin another branch examine" operation followed by the two examines of solenoids 1 and 2. Finally, the command BLC says, "Branch list complete." The third rung A–3 is programmed similarly.

The final command in the sequence JMA A1 is an unconditional jump back to the beginning of the program so that the program and the control sequence will recycle.

When certain origin and end-statements are added, the program in symbolic form is ready for computer translation into instructions properly coded for the programmable controller. Information from the punched tape may be loaded into this representative programmable controller through either the manual program loader or a special memory loader. In addition to serving as a mechanized loader for the tape information, the diagnostic aids of the manual loader previously described are also valuable for testing and amending programs prepared with the aid of a computer.

PROGRAMMING BY BOOLEAN EQUATIONS

Manufacturers of programmable controllers that are capable of being programmed by Boolean equations supply Boolean translator programs usable on in-house or time-shared computers. These computer translation programs accept a list of coded Boolean equations as input information and produce a paper tape with properly coded instructions for the programmable controller.

The mathematical characteristics of Boolean equations, uniquely compatible with the binary (ON-OFF) logic circuitry of programmable controllers, make it possible to proceed via a mathematical definition from control design concepts directly to properly coded control instructions. Thus, the expense of preparing a ladder diagram (traditionally required to guide electricians in wiring together relay logic controls) is saved.

The concepts involved in using Boolean equations for programming are demonstrated in the following hypothetical control applications.

IF a specified push button is pressed OR a milling machine spindle is turning then the spindle is to be traversed to the left. Also, the operator of the machine may wish to move the spindle left at any point in its automatic cycle by activating a push button. And lastly, the spindle should automatically traverse left whenever it is turning.

105

A Boolean statement defining the operation of a control system for the above application has three functional parts:

If push button is pressed

TEST

OR

spindle is turning (the motor is on)

THEN

EXECUTION   move spindle to the left.

For the purposes of this example, address numbers are arbitrarily assigned as shown below to the input and output terminals wired to the milling machine's input and output devices.

The push button is input 36.
The spindle motor contactor is output 7.
The hydraulic solenoid which causes a ram to actuate the spindle slide to the left is output 142.

The Boolean statements describing the control sequence are:

IF input 36 is ON,
OR
Output 7 is ON,
THEN
turn output 142 ON.

One equation normally is written for each output to be actuated—the left member of the equation is the specified output, and the right member defines the required conditions that must be met. When Boolean equations depict representations of programmable controller functions, they are composed of operators having two conditions ON and OFF, and of variables which are the control inputs. The equation's input and output values determine the ON or OFF condition of the output. For example, the Boolean equation:

$$Y10 = X23 + X21 * Y7$$

is read, "Output is set ON when input 23 is ON, OR when both output 7 and input 21 are ON." The numbers following the X and Y symbols define specific inputs and outputs.

The above equation creates all the instructions necessary to cause one representative programmable controller to test input 23, and if it is ON, output 10 is set ON. If input 23 is OFF, output 7 and

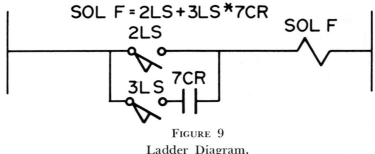

FIGURE 9
Ladder Diagram,
SOL F = 2LS + 3LS*7CR

input 21 are tested. If they are both ON, output 10 is set ON. If neither set of conditions is satisfied, output 10 is set OFF. This equation could be graphically illustrated by the ladder diagram in Figure 9 where SOL F corresponds to Y10; 2LS corresponds to X23; 7CR corresponds to Y7; and 3LS corresponds to X21.

Each group of computed instructions represents the solution of one equation associated with one output that is to be on or off. If a machine control has twenty outputs, there are twenty equations and associated instruction groups in the control program. The last instruction group is terminated with a "jump" to the first instruction group so that the controller's program will recycle the process.

As with the symbolic programming language translator, the Boolean translator program also produces computer-printed documentation listing the detailed instructions, their order and memory address locations, etc. Extensive statement edit and error-detection capabilities are also designed into Boolean computer translator programs. No input statements are computed until the errors are corrected.

The Boolean method has a distinct advantage over ladder-design programming, in that it saves both time and effort because the translator does so much of the programming task. The Boolean translator program virtually does everything to convert the equations into programmable controller machine code instructions. Since a ladder diagram is not required, the design and drafting effort to prepare one is saved.

Programming Read-Only Memories (ROM's)

Read-Only Memories (ROM's) are attractive to use in programmable controllers because of their cost advantages. The major deterrent is, however, that only restricted programming methods may be used. Programming procedures and guidelines for programmable controllers with ROM's are therefore most helpful to users of equipment having the special type of memory being discussed. Nevertheless, a brief delineation of two currently popular ROM techniques demonstrates the essential concepts.

Programming a Diode ROM

Two separate phases are involved in programming a diode ROM. First, any of three techniques described earlier for programming read-write memories may be used to create the properly coded instructions. A paper tape containing the instructions for a programmable controller having a read-write memory is actually the result of Phase 1. Rather than using the tape to transfer the coded instructions into a read-write memory, the tape is used as input to a second ROM programming phase in which a numerical control wire-wrap machine wires together the required pattern of diodes and other solid-state components. When the resulting ROM circuits are activated by the programmable controller's logic circuitry, properly sequenced instructions are produced for the programmed control job.

In actual practice, the punched tape produced during the first programming phase for this diode ROM is used initially to load a read-write memory for program testing. After completion of the check-out procedures, which are described below, the proven tape is then used to direct the wire-wrap machine in manufacturing the diode ROM.

Program check-out is accomplished by connecting the input and output modules of the ROM controller to the machine being controlled, and then temporarily connecting these I–O modules to a programmable controller having a read-write memory or to a minicomputer. The programmed instructions are loaded in the memory from the punched tape in the same manner as described earlier. After the program and the total system's operations have been tested and verified, the tape instructions are used to manufacture the ROM. The ROM programmable controller is then delivered to the control application site where the read-write programmable controller could have continued to operate the machine. Process operation is interrupted only briefly while the input-output modules are removed from the programmable controller with the read-write memory and plugged into the chassis of the ROM programmable controller. The former controller, which is loaned to the user for program check-out, is then returned to the manufacturer.

Programming a Braided-wire ROM

Boolean equations and two computer programs are used to program one braided-wire ROM programmable controller. The programming procedures of the first phase are generally similar to the Boolean equation concepts described earlier. As with diode ROM's, the major distinction occurs during the second phase when the results of computer processing of the equations produce instructions that drive a wiring machine to braid-wire the ROM.

The step-by-step procedures to program one braided-wire ROM follow:

1. Assign appropriate X and Y numbers for each input and output.
2. Set up the Boolean equations for each output or inputs and outputs.
3. Enter the equations into a computer.
4. Use the Boolean computer translator to generate the instructions.
5. Read the calculated instructions into the computer simulation program to verify the instructions for each equation by varying the input and recording the resultant output value.

In addition to the Boolean equation computer translator, a computer simulation program also tests the computer instructions.

PROGRAM SIMULATION

Operation of the programmed instructions for ROM's as well as for read-write memories can be simulated entirely within a computer or with a computer connected through the programmable controller's input-output modules to the machine or process. The latter on-line simulation method is obviously more thorough since the dynamic interaction between the programmed instructions and the machine or process functions is tested. However, the objectives of both simulation methods are identical—i.e., to produce and test various input conditions and output responses so that errors can be detected.

In operation, these manufacturer-furnished computer programs simulate the operation of the input devices—lights, switches, etc.— and record resulting machine actions. By this means the programmer is able to test his work for a nominal cost and assure himself that the control sequence produces the desired results. Computer simulation uncovers programming errors which lead to incorrect machine operation and potential damage. These are control or machine sequence problems rather than program composition errors that are detected by the computer translator program.

In order to use the simulator, a tabulation is prepared of the machine functions expected in response to the prescribed sequential operation of the input devices. This tabulation begins with the exact status of the inputs that exist at cycle initiation. Having prepared the list of expected responses, the user is ready to perform the simulation when the simulation program and the programmable controller's instructions are loaded in the computer. Interconnections between the computer, the machine, and the programmable controller's input-output modules must also be made for on-line simulation.

As simulation proceeds, the simulated machine operation is compared at each step with the expected actions. If simulation shows that program changes are necessary, they can be implemented simply by changing Boolean equations or mnemonic codes in the program input statements. Following each input command change, the simulator recycles through the program, performing the required output changes and continuing until one complete cycle is performed during which no output changes are necessary.

Full documentation of the original program statements, as modified by subsequent changes, should be maintained at all times during simulation—and all in a form consistent with the original program statements. A current and correct program listing and paper tape record of each program in source form, i.e., either Boolean or symbolic statements, are essential for managing future changes.

The on-line simulation technique wherein the computer is interconnected with the total system (less the memory) offers the attractive advantage that when the program and complete system or process is fully verified, the total system or process can immediately be placed in operation. If the programmable controller has a read-write memory, the computer simply transfers the checked-out program to the controller's memory and the system is ready. Even when a ROM must be manufactured, the computer can continue to supply the programmed instructions while the ROM is being produced. The short interruption caused by unplugging the computer from the programmable controller and connecting the ROM may be the only operation interruption from the time the simulation is completed.

ADVANTAGES OF PROGRAMMABLE CONTROLLERS

Greater efficiency is the principal advantage of programmable controller applications. Enhanced reliability, simpler total system engineering, integration and start-up, and lower overall costs are the major contributors to better efficiency. Because programmable controllers are used most frequently where relays previously excelled, consideration of the advantages listed below relate to relay controls; comparisons to computers appear later.

  a. Reliability
  b. Maintainability
  c. Flexibility
  d. System Engineering and Start-up
  e. Cost Economies
    1. floor space
    2. less power
    3. reduced obsolescence
    4. simplified troubleshooting
  f. Computer Compatibility.

RELIABILITY AND MAINTAINABILITY

In the majority of programmable controller applications, maintenance economies and improved system utilization are the most significant advantages. Compared to relay controls, programmable controllers have components with increased reliability that provide greater mean time between failures, are easier to troubleshoot when malfunctions do occur, and afford simpler replacement once the faulty component is identified.

Several design and operational characteristics are responsible for reduced downtime. Built-in troubleshooting aids and improved documentation are especially helpful in bringing about fast and simple fault isolation. As one example, programmable controller indicator lights guide the troubleshooter to the defective circuit or machine component. In addition to signalling the condition of programmable controller elements, these lights indicate whether machine or process devices such as solenoids, limit switches, push buttons, etc. are operating.

The relative miniaturization which makes possible the centralization of control elements also saves maintenance steps. Because the electronic and electrical components are packaged in a more con-

111

densed arrangement, troubleshooters no longer are forced to crawl around and over the machine and several control panels when analyzing the status of dispersely located machine and control components.

Compared to the inadequate troubleshooting documentation customarily available for relay controls, programmable controller schematics, diagrams, and logic tables represent important advancements. With custom-wired functions of relay controls, maintenance costs pyramid because of incomplete or outdated documentation. Too often, relay controls have been modified on the production floor without appropriate documentation changes being made. Obsolete diagrams are not only a source of frustration to the maintenance worker who subsequently tries to trace a circuit malfunction, but they also cause confusion and misunderstandings between plant engineering and production personnel.

By limiting memory access, not only are unauthorized changes prevented, but just as important to the maintenance department, up-to-date documentation is immediately available. Since the control sequence of a flexible programmable controller can be changed only by rewiring or reloading the memory, and because both methods require special instructions, unauthorized and improvised changes cannot be made by shop personnel. Therefore, when control sequences are changed, plant engineers can assure that revised documentation is generated as part of the process.

The plug-in modularity design of programmable controllers also speeds troubleshooting and reduces downtime. When a problem is suspected to emanate from the programmable controller, it is a simple procedure to disconnect any module and plug in a replacement to quickly determine whether the old module was defective. Every module, and there are only five different types in one representative programmable controller, is of the plug-in variety so that a complete change of all system modules can be made within three to five minutes—all without disconnecting any wires.

Economical computer-aided troubleshooting is also made possible by the programmable controller's compatible binary solid-state circuitry. When a low-cost computer is connected to one representative programmable controller and the diagnostic program is executed, the controller is completely tested in just a few minutes. All the controller's circuits are exercised and checked, then statements describing the diagnosis—complete with the identification of the faulty component—are printed. Computerized troubleshooting is even more effective when an on-line central computer is used to continuously monitor one or several programmable controllers.

The computer's ability to sense and analyze changes is particularly helpful in indicating the need for preventive maintenance. Deviations in cycle times are of continual interest since they provide early warnings about performance degradation which often presages breakdowns. During scheduled shutdowns, the developing problems can be investigated and necessary repairs made. With proper programming, the computer can produce a list of factors or elements responsible for the specific problem. For example, in one system the computer indicates:

1. which limit switch failed to trip or release;
2. which solenoid failed to energize or de-energize;
3. which motor starter failed to energize or de-energize;
4. which motor starter overload tripped;
5. which push button failed;
6. the occurrence of a manual override of the switch or solenoid by anyone;
7. the specific ground being detected in an element;
8. the exact point in the machine cycle at which the shutdown occurred; and
9. any element in the wrong position at any time.

Just as important, computer-developed statistical reports of cycle rate changes and malfunctions allow engineers to evaluate equipment performance and make design changes where indicated.

Other costs can be saved through reduced maintenance training requirements made possible by the ability to control many different types of machines with one standard programmable controller. Beyond slight differences in the read-only memories, programmable controllers of a given type differ only in the number of input and output modules. This means that once maintenance personnel are familiar with a given model, they understand all the programmable controllers of that type in the plant, regardless of the type of machine or process they control. Thus, maintenance training time on new machines having different control functions is greatly lessened.

Since the input modules, output modules, and power supplies are similar and interchangeable, it also means that the investment in spare parts inventories is profitably minimized.

The more reliable solid-state circuitry compared to electro-mechanical components contributes significantly to reduced maintenance expenses. Solid-state programmable controllers without any moving parts to wear or stick outlive their electromechanical predecessors by five- to tenfold. As an example, a typical machine relay provides 7 to 10 million machine cycles, while solid-state components have a longevity of up to 100 million cycles.

Solid-state components also are less susceptible to shop environmental hazards that include oil and cutting mist, moisture, dust, and other contaminants known to be troublesome to electromechanical devices. Cooler-operating programmable controllers, generating less than a 12 to 18 degree rise over shop temperatures, more effectively shut out contaminants since they may be enclosed in airtight cabinets.

Better documentation, built-in fault indicators, computer testing and monitoring, and more reliable components all play important roles in cutting maintenance costs in half when programmable controllers rather than relay controls are used. Not only are maintenance expenses cut, but more importantly, the revenue from increased machine or process utilization grows. In one typical application the replacement of relay controls with programmable controllers produces sufficient increases in machine up-time and production that an additional machine originally thought to be required for increased demand actually was not ordered. Consequently, a capital outlay of $200,000 was saved.

SYSTEM ENGINEERING AND START-UP

Although days are required to wire and check out a relay panel, a programmable controller, with its control sequences, can be bolted in a cabinet and its input and output wires connected in a matter of hours. The flexibility, the modularized components, and the ability to simulate and check out control sequences before the programmable controller is connected to the machine or process are primarily responsible for the fast integration and start-up. Typical system integration and start-up time savings approximate 75 percent.

Once the input and output wires are connected, the programmable controller—with its input-output indicators—can aid the installer in checking out all input-output actions. By contrast, total system check-out of relay panels must await final integration—a process which often discloses underlying and frustrating design-manufacturing errors. When programmable controller instruction changes are needed, they are simply implemented by a few commands addressed through the manual program loader. Again, this software change is a pleasant contrast to the extensive wiring changes necessary in relay systems.

As was shown in the programming discussion, the process used to generate a typical programmable control's command sequence includes a number of error-detection aids which reduce the chances for program errors. Simulation programs alone permit the check-out of control sequences which previously were delayed until the relay control was fully integrated with the machine or process.

In addition to the time saved, less money is required for designing and documenting the engineering activities for each programmable control application. Moreover, once the new machine control has been checked out to the designer's satisfaction, it is difficult for unauthorized personnel to modify the control sequence. Hence, the designer retains control over the way in which a machine is actually wired and operated.

COST CHARACTERISTICS

The investment principles for assessing the economic competitiveness of numerical control are adaptable for determining the cost effectiveness of programmable controllers. Investment or acquisition costs and operational costs are the two major types of costs to be considered. Only for the few instances where the programmable controller produces a shorter machine or process cycle will there be a direct operational savings. Operational economies largely will be of an indirect type, since they emanate from such elements as maintenance, floor space, power, and increased revenue from less downtime.

Early programmable controllers demonstrated a lower acquisition cost only for those applications requiring more than 80 to 100 relays. As the technology advanced, low-cost programmable controllers having read-only memories became available and were economically applied to machines or processes using as few as 15 relays. Today, any application that previously would have been controlled by a relay panel of any size is a potential programmable control application.

Even though acquisition cost relationships may weigh in the favor of relays, some of the following operational economies often result in an overall programmable controller cost advantage.

Power

A programmable controller operating in the five-volt range uses approximately 40 to 60 percent less power than that required for a comparable relay control.

Production Floor Space Requirements

The profitable potential of floor space savings is demonstrated by the fact that in a highly mechanized plant, relay panel controls traditionally consume 10 to 15 percent of the production floor area. Each complex relay control may consist of several large cabinets, while a programmable controller contained in one small cabinet of about 12 cubic feet may do a comparable job.

Decreased Rate of Obsolescence

When a new machine is needed, or a cycle change has to be implemented, an existing relay control is sometimes rebuilt, but it is usually scrapped. As service-type labor rates continue to spiral, rewiring and refurbishing an existing control is often more costly than constructing a totally new panel. Moreover, the used panel's components are less reliable due to the wear of several years of service.

In contrast to these costs of wear and obsolescence are the economical alternatives afforded by the flexible programmable controller which may be reused on different machines or processes after reprogramming. Thus, even when the programmable controller's acquisition cost exceeds that of a relay panel, further analysis may indicate that the low obsolescence provides a net long-term saving. Such a relationship is more probable if proliferating product changes are expected to increase the rate of tooling changes.

Maintenance Savings

Because of the factors previously cited, such as the modular design and the programmable controller's capability to signal vital information, repair is as close to instantaneous as is technically possible with today's production equipment. Users find that expenses due to troubleshooting and machine downtime from control failures are reduced by a minimum of 50 percent.

System Design and Start-Up

Installation and check-out of a programmable controlled system, accomplished by connecting the input and output modules to the machine or process, inserting the programmed memory, and verifying the previously simulated program is typically shortened by half to three-fourths. A representative programmable controller was completely integrated and checked out on a transfer-machining system in one day rather than the week formerly required for a relay control.

The quantitative impact of these and other indirect operational economies may in many instances be determined by using adaptations of the computational procedures delineated for ascertaining numerical control's indirect savings. Obviously, the savings percentages and the annual expenses used in the procedures must be consistent with relay control and programmable controller operations.

COMPUTER COMPATIBILITY

Unlike the popular 110 to 220 volt AC relay controls, the programmable controller does not require special interface devices for signal matching with computers normally operating at 5 volts DC. The programmable controller's ability to match the signals of computers as well as those of the machine's power devices represents a valuable and adaptable element in the total control-monitor system. Conventional machine interface and switching instrumentation operates at relatively high-power levels—normally 110, 220, or 440 volts AC. Since programmable controllers are designed to handle inputs and outputs of 115 to 120 volts AC and also to operate at 5 volts DC, they are uniquely fitted for industrial process controls interconnected with machines and on-line 5-volt DC computers.

Thus, for little additional cost, an available computer can be connected to monitor such activities as the status of control inputs, timers, outputs, and storage outputs. The computer can use the information for many of the same interpretative and report-generation operations carried out in a Direct Numerical Control system. As an example, the monitored information allows the computer to:

1. record machine performance,
2. compare performance to an established standard,
3. predict future performance, and
4. signal problems needing attention.

When operating in unison with a central computer, the programmable controller may be used selectively to perform a combination of monitor and control operations. If the programmable controller performs only a monitoring operation, its memory contains instructions to test inputs and outputs, as well as to specify the format and timing of the information forwarded to the computer. In such a role, the programmable controller may operate without a memory if the computer is programmed to make all testing operations and control decisions. In this case, the programmable controller functions largely as a relatively inexpensive and efficient interface device by providing the electrical signal match-ups between the computer and the machine, and also by providing the addressing circuits for the computer.

When both monitoring and control operations are carried out in tandem by the programmable controller, the usual control instructions as well as a group of special monitoring instructions must be stored in its memory. The latter instructions direct the control unit to select specific results for transfer to the computer. Part of the computer program is restricted for emergency operations such as signaling supervision or the computer operator that the controlled device is encountering a problem needing special attention. The computer may be programmed to assume command of the control functions until the emergency passes.

Some programmable controllers are prewired with a connector for the computer monitor interface that may be added in short order and at any time. About fifteen minutes are needed to interconnect a computer and a representative programmable controller. Three cables are installed which carry data signals from the programmable controller to the computer. Return computer control and interrogation signals are also transmitted by the cables. Signals may be transmitted on command from either the computer or the programmable controller's program. The type of control of monitoring operation performed is dictated by the application requirements as defined by the programmed instructions.

In ascertaining the optimum technical and cost-effective division of functions between the programmable controller and the on-line monitoring computer, it is good practice to determine if a computer alone can economically fulfill all the control requirements. In making such a determination, consideration of the relationships delineated below are important.

Compared to computer controls, programmable controllers demonstrate the following characteristics.

1. *Information Storage Capacity.* Computers have considerably greater capacity.

2. *Control Flexibility.* Both devices are comparable.

3. *Programming.* Programmable controllers are much easier to program. System analysis and programming efforts for a computer-controlled system often equal hardware costs.

4. *Interfaces.* Programmable controllers have excellent signal match-up abilities, while an extra cost is involved to interface the electrical signals between most computers and machines.

5. *Recording and Reporting.* Computers can easily generate voluminous reports while programmable controllers can only provide information to computers or produce information for recording on tape.

6. *Multimachine Control.* Control of two or more machines is possible with both programmable controllers and computers. However, the latter obviously have a greater capacity for multimachine control.

7. *Mathematical Capability.* Computers have powerful arithmetic operational capacity, while all but the most sophisticated programmable controllers do not. This restricts the ability of the programmable controller to generate modified commands, but does not affect the ease of changing commands by reprogramming.

8. *Environment.* Programmable controllers do not require a controlled environment as do many computers. Special electrical shielding is not required for "normal" radio-frequency (RF) noise since programmable controllers' circuits withstand electrical interference while computers normally are more susceptible.

The optimum final solution in many applications is arrived at by the selective utilization of programmable controllers that are monitored by report-generating computers. Not only is such a hybrid system lower in cost, but reliability is enhanced because several machines are not dependent upon the central computer for all control instructions. By contrast, if a programmable controller fails, only one or a few connected machines will be inoperable. In a hybrid system a computer failure interrupts the monitoring function, but control of the production equipment continues.

The superior hardware reliability of programmable controllers compared to conventional computer equipment operating in an open-plant environment is now clearly demonstrated. Although quite reliable in a protected environment, computers have proven to be more susceptible than programmable controllers to high levels of RF signals and stray AC electrical noise such as that emanating from conventional relay controls and motor starters. Since on-line computer monitoring of programmable controllers can be accomplished from a remote location, it often is desirable to have programmable controllers carry out the control on the production floor and communicate information to the monitoring computer remotely located in a clean and air-conditioned room.

A system using both programmable controllers and an on-line monitoring computer in effect allows the profitable employment of the respective strengths of each component. By starting with the less complex programmable controller, previously uninitiated maintenance, programming, and operational personnel progressively learn and develop their skills with less pressure. They mature gradually as more complex solid-state, programmable equipment is introduced in a phased progressive schedule. The step-by-step approach contrasts sharply with trauma encountered when an inexperienced work force panics over mass production stoppages caused by software or hardware failures of a central computer controlling several production machines.

When a control system is being sought for jobs traditionally done by relays and where economy and reliability are vital, programmable controllers will often prove equal to, if not superior to, computer controls. As computer programming techniques and hardware developments progress, the decision favoring programmable controllers may become less obvious. Clearly, for most applications, the two devices will continue to be teamed up to provide improved control and monitoring of industrial processes.

Chapter IV

Adaptive Control

Adaptive control facilitates production optimization through automatic manipulation of process variables, which commonly include torque, force, temperature, vibration, and tool wear. Variations in processing conditions are sensed and fed back to the adaptive controller so that necessary adjustments can be calculated and executed. Greater productivity and output of higher quality result, and often at lower costs.

The capabilities of adaptive control are significant extensions of numerical control which introduced automatic closed-loop control of the machine's spindle and slides. In metalworking, as an example, machinability variables are closely monitored in the same automatic, precise, and untiring fashion characteristic of numerical control systems which guide the cutting tool precisely along the part geometry. A new control dimension is added through adaptive control by machining automation that provides continuous, closed-loop optimization of the cutting action.

The roots of adaptive control predate those of numeral control by about a decade. From the early adaptive control experiments evolved a general definition that implies certain useful principles for metalworking applications. In general terms, an adaptive system has these characteristics:

(1) a means for continuously monitoring its own performance in relation to established *performance criteria;* and

(2) a capability to modify its own control variables by closed-loop action in attempting to achieve the optimal condition.

Workpiece size, surface finish and integrity, and minimum cost are ideal *performance criteria* for most metalworking adaptive control applications. Because technological constraints seldom permit sensing the status of these *primary criteria,* adaptive controls monitor *secondary performance criteria,* which commonly include tool forces, vibration, tool wear, tool or workpiece deflection, and cutting temperatures.

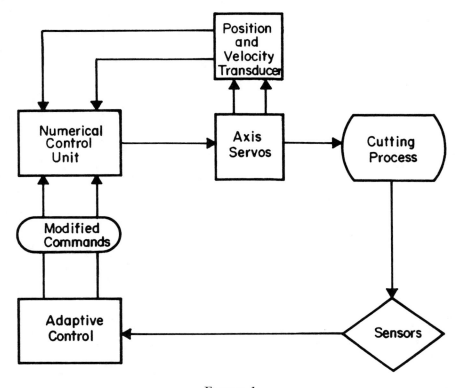

FIGURE 1
Adaptive numerical control system.

TECHNOLOGICAL STATUS OF ADAPTIVE CONTROL

From the introductory concepts it is apparent that adaptive control in metal cutting must automatically modify *input program* elements as the need arises. Typical components of the *input program* are: cutting speed, depth of cut, tool material, tool shape, and coolant flows. *Input programs* are stored in punched tapes, in a series of data processing cards, or in a computer memory. Cams or preset controls also are common *input program* storage media for certain machines.

The heart of adaptive control systems for metalworking machines are the sensors. (See Figure 1.) The extent to which optimal operations can be achieved and sustained is largely determined by the availability of sensors which can successfully monitor appropriate *performance criteria.* Sensors must be perceptive enough to oversee the full operating range of a process and yet be sensitive enough to detect minute variations within relatively broad limits. Added to these requirements are unusual demands of reliability and stability in the presence of hostile conditions.

By repetitively sensing the status of *performance criteria* and making fine adjustments, system performance can be improved within the constraints of existing sensor technology and process knowledge. In practice, these constraints force certain adaptive control compromises. With the exception of the metal-removal rate and minimum cost factors, on-line sensing of all primary *performance criteria* has not been easily achieved on the metalworking production floor. Critical technological and knowledge factors limiting adaptive control are described below.[1]

Size

Various types of sensors and control instrumentation have been developed for automatic, on-line sensing of workpiece size. Attempts, with varying degrees of success, have been made to measure single fixed quantities like length, diameter, etc. However, completely effective on-line, size-measuring devices have seldom been applied successfully in production applications for the more complex shapes producible by numerical control.

Surface Integrity and Finish

Continuous on-line measurement of workpiece surface finish during metal cutting also has been restricted for the most part to laboratory demonstrations. Consequently, in most numerical control applications, surface finish still is largely dependent on the specifications of the *input program*. Surface integrity, which refers to residual stresses, cracks, and other surface characteristics that adversely affect the functional properties of the finished part, is likewise still at the mercy of the *input program*.

Minimum Cost and Metal-Removal Rate

Compared to the vagaries of on-line sensing of workpiece size and surface conditions, considerably more is known and can be done about the dependent relationships between the *input program* and the *performance criteria* of metal-removal rate or minimum cost.

---

[1] For a fuller discussion of the technological status of adaptive control see: L. V. Colwell, *et al., Research in Support of Numerical and Adaptive Control in Manufacturing,* The University of Michigan, 1969.

These relationships have been examined and reasonably well quantified by F. W. Taylor and others. For example, the Taylor equation expresses dependent relationships between the cutting speed, size of cut, and tool life when these relationships can be represented as straight lines on logarithmic coordinates. Taylor's equation has been incorporated into other equations either for determining the unit cost per part or the production rate wherein consideration is given to the fact that cutting tools lose sharpness and must be replaced, thus consuming time and money.

Using calculus, these equations may be differentiated partially with respect to certain *machining variables* including cutting speed, feedrate, and depth of cut. The results make it possible to solve mathematically for the optimal values of these variables.

Theoretically, the mathematically determined efficiency of metal removal increases continuously as both the feedrate and the depth of cut are increased. Because there are no mathematically optimal values for these quantities other than infinity, the feeds and speeds obviously should be as large as is permitted by equipment constraints and application conditions.

Tool Forces and Wear Rates

Because tool forces and cutting temperatures are increased by tool wear, the workpiece dimensions, surface finish and integrity, and the metal-removal rates are all adversely affected. With all *primary performance criteria* so influenced, it would be helpful to be able to monitor, in real time, the rate at which tool dissipation occurs. Current technological barriers, however, have not permitted the on-line, direct measurement of tool wear while machining is taking place, and it is doubtful that any universally effective means will be developed soon. Developmental efforts are being focused on finding the dependent relationships between tool wear and those factors which now can be measured such as tool forces, tool temperature, and vibration.

Present technology does permit relatively efficient measurement of spindle torque and deflection, both of which directly indicate changes in tool forces. Among other advantages, dynamic control of tool forces promises to extend tool life, to upgrade dimension or size standards, and may improve surface finish.

Existing adaptive control systems monitor tool forces by sensing spindle deflection primarily through the use of strain-gage sensors.

The resulting output is used automatically to reduce the feedrate or accelerate the spindle speed when a reduction in tool forces is needed. In at least one adaptive system, x- and y-axis deflection is sensed by four contact-shoes that ride on the spindle. Here, the feedrate is automatically increased until the spindle deflection reaches a preset constraint. When a constraint violation occurs, the feedrate is automatically retarded. In this same adaptive control system, spindle torque is monitored in parallel and equated with deflection as a basis for the coordinated adjustment of the spindle speed as well as the slide feedrate.

In a second adaptive control system, spindle torque is measured by a four-arm strain-gage bridge which is mounted in a small groove around the spindle's periphery. The mechanical and electrical design of the bridge is such that effects of lateral loads and temperature variations are essentially eliminated from the resultant output signal.

Tool and spindle vibrations, a cause as well as an indicator of changes in tool forces and wear, have been measured with reasonable success. The adaptive control system developed by Ronald Centner for the original Air Force experimental project, sensed spindle vibration by two crystal accelerometers mounted on the spindle near the toolholder.[2] An accelerometer was mounted in each of the vertical and horizontal planes.

For systems where tool or spindle vibration has been monitored on-line and adaptively controlled, substantially improved workpiece surface finish and integrity have resulted. A truly economic cutter life also appears more feasible since vibration control reduces tool wear and breakage.

Cutting temperature has received considerable attention as a potentially useful feedback element for adaptive control because of known and suspected relationships that exist between tool wear and cutting temperatures. More so than for the previously described factors that may indicate tool wear, the succesful use of cutting temperatures for adaptive control depends upon the future development of reliable and durable sensing devices, as well as on uncovering technological information describing the dependent relationships between temperature changes, other *machining variables,* and the *primary performance criteria.*

---

[2] Air Force Materials Laboratory Technical Documentary Report No. ML–TDE–64–279, "Final Report on Development of Adaptive Control Techniques for Numerically-Controlled Milling Machines," Wright Patterson Air Force Base, 1964.

Much of the experience with on-line measurement of metal-cutting temperatures has been confined to laboratories where the objectives have been either to develop reliable measurement techniques or to explore dependent relationships between temperature and the rate of tool wear. Unfortunately, most of these efforts have been concentrated on the first objective, although recently an increasing amount of effort has been focused upon the latter goal. Particular emphasis has been placed upon finding fundamental determinants and the nature of tool wear.

Popular laboratory methods used for measuring cutting temperature are:

(1) Tool-work thermocouple
(2) Imbedded or contact thermocouples
(3) Thermal radiation sensors
(4) Thermally sensitive lacquers.

The present inadequate state of knowledge about the role of temperature in metal cutting, and the lack of suitable instrumentation for on-line measurement has restricted the sole incorporation of cutting temperature measurements into an adaptive control system. Although future research may reverse this trend, there is little probability of either economic or technological success without at least supplementary aid from the measurement of cutting forces.

ADAPTIVE CONTROL BENEFITS

Minimizing the risk of equipment or workpiece damage, extending cutter life, simplifying part programming, controlling workpiece size, surface finish and integrity, minimizing cost, and reducing operator intervention are principal adaptive control advantages. The extent to which these advantages can be achieved will be determined by the capabilities of the adaptive control system; the system is directly influenced by technology and by each application's economic and engineering characteristics.

Part Programming

Even relatively modest adaptive controls can significantly ease the part-programming task. Sensing tool forces for automatic on-line adjustments of predetermined cutting rates can free a part programmer from much of the drudgery required for the detailed analysis of all factors likely to affect the cutting process. For example, in order to program feeds and speeds for a milling machine with an early type of adaptive control, only the following relatively simple machinability program information was needed.

(1) Nominal Brinell hardness and horsepower requirements for the material being machined.

(2) Desired workpiece tolerances and tool life.

(3) Width and depth of cut at the maximum part cross section to be encountered by the cutter.

(4) Cutting tool's diameter, flute length, and number of flutes.

(5) Parameters for cutting speed, tool life, and cutter-workpiece deflection constraints.

From this relatively sketchy information, maximum and minimum speed and feed boundaries, and the adaptive control settings were calculated by a computer processing routine during preparation of the control tape. Formulas for computing cutter stiffness and strength, and tables of spindle-machine compliance were used to determine total system stiffness and deflection limits. The adaptive control, by using the information from control settings and sensors, was able to maintain the system performance within the maximum and minimum limits.

Adaptive control's relatively simplified programming requirements contrast sharply with the procedures employed in conventional numerical control where cutting feeds and speeds are ascertained from experience or handbook machinability data. Because of unpredictable metallurgical variations in both the tool and the workpiece and the deviation of handbook feeds and speeds from those preferred by specific shop personnel, such empirical techniques often produce less than ideal results. Conventionally programmed feedrates invariably are conservative estimates of the worst-case conditions the programmer conceives may be encountered in production. Even those companies with machinability research staffs, who can determine their own data for specific tool-workpiece metallurgical combinations being processed by their unique set of machines, rarely apply optimal feeds and speeds.

Numerical control's feedrate override capability is relied upon too frequently to compensate for improperly programmed machinability commands. Feedrate overriding by the operator has two serious drawbacks: (1) there is little assurance that operator modifications are optimal; and (2) permitting operator intervention forfeits management control of production. In actual practice, the operator's adjustments distort even further the conservative tendencies of a part programmer.

Another example of an adaptive control facility that eases part programming is the so-called gap eliminator, a control method that frees the programmer from specifying feedrate changes for the points at which the cutting tool disengages the workpiece sections. As soon as a drop in torque is sensed, the feedrate is automaticaly increased by the adaptive control—up to 36 times in one system design—and maintained there until the tool recontacts the workpiece. Milling an outside corner offers conditions in which the gap eliminator facility is highly useful. Between milling passes at the corner the cutter temporarily clears the workpiece at which time feedrate is greatly increased. When the cutter recontacts the work surface the adaptive control's tight servo loop instantaneously retards the feedrate to safe preset limits.

Another important source of increased programmer effectiveness is the simplified tape debugging for improperly programmed machinability commands. As long as the programmer selects the speeds and feedrates within reasonably liberal limits, adaptive control handles the machining optimization.

Adaptive control's facilities and advantages obviously can result in a more productive part programmer. Of equal importance is the possibility for utilizing a less qualified or experienced programmer for feed and speed selection.

Equipment and Workpiece Protection

The machine, the cutter, and the workpiece can be protected from damage when an adaptive control restricts the buildup of cutting forces. Machine drives can be regulated so that maximum velocities and forces do not exceed damaging limits. Other benefits resulting from avoiding abusive forces are fewer workpiece dimensional errors and quality part surfaces with better integrity and superior finishes. The reduction or elimination of vibrations and cutter chatter, and the assurance of more uniform cutter loads also play important roles in bringing about better part quality.

Equipment motor damage may also be avoided by an adaptive control horsepower sensor on some systems that regulate torque within safe limits. Adjusting the feedrate when required can reduce motor damage and also help to extend tool life. Increasing the number of parts produced from three to four before regrinding a cutter is typical of adaptive control's favorable impact on cutting tool life.

COST AND EFFICIENCY

Production improvements from adaptive control applications have ranged between 15 and 75 percent, with most users experiencing a 20 to 40 percent gain. Greatest economies have occurred where the part configuration presents a variety of cutting conditions throughout the machining operation, and where the material is difficult to machine—e.g., high-strength steels, titanium, and high-temperature alloys. The high-strength materials requiring heavy cuts have been especially attractive applications. Titanium airframe forgings demanding low feedrates over extended machining cycles are typical examples. A 35 percent reduction in processing time was experienced in an application which previously had required 110 machine hours.

Adaptive control cycle time efficiencies were demonstrated in the original Air Force tests which evaluated three different machining modes:

(1) milling a straight constant-depth profile;

(2) milling a variable-depth profile to simulate unpredictable variations in cutter load; and

(3) machining both inside and outside corners, utilizing both linear and circular interpolation.

Tool-workpiece metallurgical combinations used in the majority of the Air Force tests included a carbide-tipped cutting tool with 4140 steel workpiece material, and a high-speed steel tool with AMS 5639A stainless steel workpiece material. Feeds and speeds for the nonadaptive tests were set at the best predetermined values based mainly on trial-and-error experiments and were maintained constant throughout each test. For the adaptive tests, feeds and speeds were selected automatically by the adaptive controller and were dynamically modified as dictated by changing cutting conditions. The Air Force test part is shown in Figure 2.

The test results, summarized by the bar graphs of Figure 3, demonstrate the cost reductions produced by adaptive control. Economies ranged from 5 to 38 percent for the constant-depth cuts, and were about 50 percent for the variable-depth cuts.

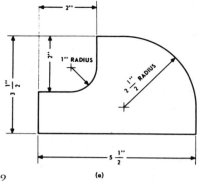

(a)

FIGURE 2
Test part and geometry.

These results indicate that adaptive control's profit potential is closely related to the variability of the machining conditions. For the constant-depth tests, where the smallest improvement was obtained, the primary variation was tool sharpness, since all other conditions were held as constant as possible. Figure 4, illustrating the response of the adaptive controller to changes in tool sharpness, plots average feedrate as a function of volume and metal removed by the tool. Here it can be seen clearly that as the sharp tool dulled,

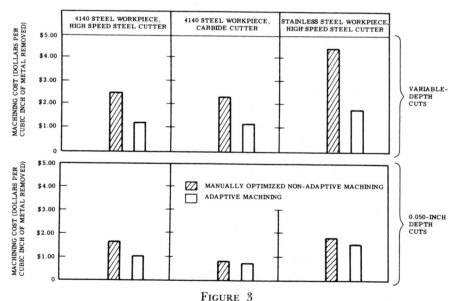

FIGURE 3
Machine cost comparison for adaptive and nonadaptive control.

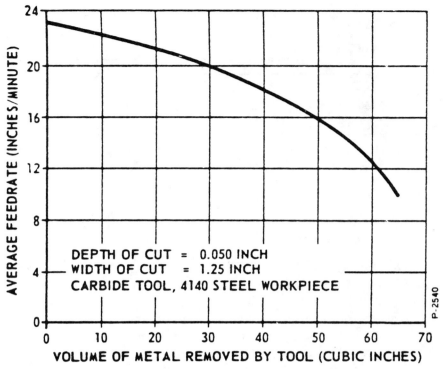

FIGURE 4
Feedrate versus metal removed by tool.

the adaptive controller automatically decreased the feedrate to maintain optimal performance. In a nonadaptive application the feedrate would have been preset for the input program at a constant parameter near the value required for an acceptable operation of a "nonsharp" tool. One obvious effect of conventional practice is to restrict productivity while the tool is sharp .

For the variable-depth tests, the feedrate and speeds were varied dynamically by the adaptive control to compensate for cutter load changes as the depth of cut varied from 0.010 in. to 0.060 in. (See Figure 5.) In the variable-depth tests, these larger differences were added to changes in tool sharpness.

Results of typical variable-depth tests are shown in Figure 6. For the nonadaptive mode, variations of the sensor signals in accordance with the changing depth of cut are illustrated in the left-hand portion of the figure. These conditions were sensed while the feed and speed values were held constant. The right-hand portion of the figure shows

131

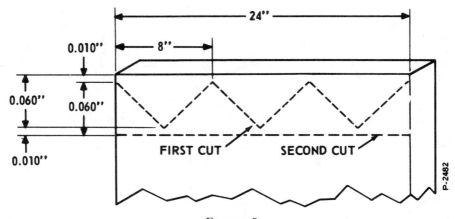

FIGURE 5
Cutter path for variable-depth test.

the effect of adaptive control on these signals. The feedrate and spindle speed varied in accordance with the changing cutter conditions in such a way that the sensor signals were maintained at a relatively constant level. During the experiment, the adaptive controller maintained optimal cutting performance in the face of a dynamically changing cutter load.

Other examples of adaptive control productivity improvements

TABLE I

COMPARISON OF ADAPTIVE AND NUMERICAL CONTROL PRODUCTIVITY

Workpiece Material	Numerical Control Cycle Times* (minutes)	Adaptive Control Cycle Times* (minutes)	Percentage of NC Time Required by A.C.
17–7 PH Stainless (180 BHN) Steel	100	55	55
4330 (250 BHN)	55	30	55
3AI–13V–11Cr Titanium (380 BHN)	198	117	59
AISI 4340 (380 BHN)	82	48	59
7075–T6 Aluminum	55	37	67
Inconel–X (360 BHN)	227	161	71
6AI–6V Titanium (410 BHN)	169	128	75

* Excluding tool change times.

132

have been published, some of which are shown in Table I. Productivity increases are summarized in the table's last column which depicts the percentage of numerical control cycle time required by adaptive control.

The chief cause of shorter adaptive control cycle times is the higher feedrates used by the control. Adaptive control feedrates will be as low as those of nonadaptive control only during the very heaviest cut. When adaptive control's shorter machine cycle times are

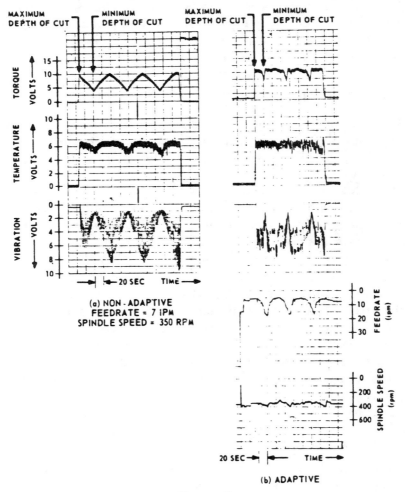

FIGURE 6

Strip-chart recordings obtained for both nonadaptive and adaptive variable-depth tests under identical conditions, stainless steel workpiece material, high-speed steel cutter.

combined with more efficient part programming and cutting tool utilization, better quality and less scrap, and fewer equipment repairs, a substantial improvement can be expected.

Because the Air Force tests covered a relatively limited range of cutting conditions, considerable work was required to permit adaptive machine control to be universally applied. While stubborn technological problems have been solved, many, nevertheless, remain. Encouraging progress has resulted in continued sensor refinements, and new control system designs have been applied to an increasing variety of machines. These multi-company developments have paved the way for the commercial introduction of adaptive machine controls by several machine tool or control manufacturers.

DESIGN AND OPERATION OF AN ADAPTIVE CONTROL

Adaptive control can be provided as an integrated system within an NC controller or as supplemental instrumentation that operates in parallel with a conventional controller. Depending upon the design concept used, adaptive control can be operated either as a second feedback loop outside the numerical control's closed loop, or if a computer is part of the machine control unit, the adaptive control can be tightly integrated with the control loop. In principle, the operational concepts are similar: sensor signals are supplied to an adaptive control subsystem which calculates command modifications that are transmitted to the equivalent of a numerical controller.

Shown in Figure 7 are the principal system components for one of the earliest commercially available control systems; they include the adaptive controller, the milling machine, the control station, and the spindle instrumentation. Their relationships are depicted in Figure 8. Sensor instrumentation, to be described in a later section, supplies measurable parameters to the adaptive controller, which responds to the signals by making adjustments in spindle speeds and slide feedrates.

Adaptive Control Unit

The objective of this early adaptive control system was to maintain maximum metal-removal rates consistent with acceptable quality and tool life standards. The control principle was a constraint violation mode of operation; that is, the adaptive controller was programmed with predetermined limits for the measurable parameters

FIGURE 7
Adaptive control installation.

of the milling machine. Constraint limits used and their ranges of adjustment are shown in Table II.

TABLE II

CONSTRAINT LIMITS

	Constraint	Range of Adjustment
1.	Spindle Speed (Max)	0–2000 rev/min
2.	Chip Load (Max)	0–100 in/rev
3.	Torque (Max)	0–200 in–lbs
4.	Temperature (Max)	0–10 millivolts*
5.	Force X (Max)	0–500 lbs
6.	Force Y (Max)	0–500 lbs
7.	Feedrate (Max)	0–50 in/min
8.	⎧Available Constraints	
9.	⎨Not Used in Present	
10.	⎩Installation	

* Temperature is expressed in millivolts generated by the tool workpiece thermocouple effect.

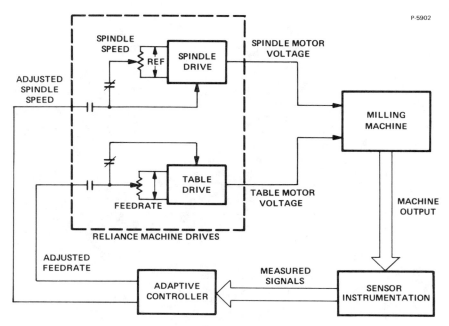

FIGURE 8
Adaptive control system block diagram.

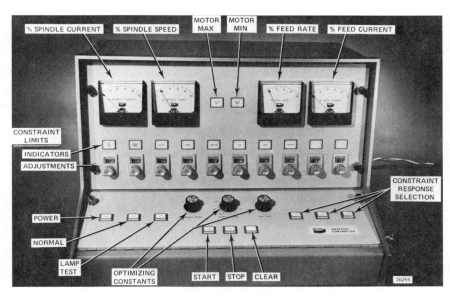

FIGURE 9
Front panel of adaptive controller.

The adaptive control unit shown in Figure 9 regulated ten constraint limits for controlling two output variables. Because this system was used in manufacturing research activities, the constraints were entered manually by setting dials. In a production application, however, these parameters could be part of the input program.

The internal variables used by the adaptive controller were spindle speed (revolutions per minute) and chip load (inches per revolution). Control signals to the milling machine were spindle speed and feedrate.

Feedrate was computed in the output stage of the adaptive controller according to the following equation:

$$\text{Feedrate} = (\text{chip load}) \times (\text{spindle speed}).$$

The adaptive controller used two modes of operation. In the optimization mode, the controller increased the metal-removal rate by increasing both chip load and spindle speed. In the constraint mode, the control responded to a detected constraint violation by an appropriate corrective action.

The adaptive controller's ability to switch automatically between the constraint and optimization modes throughout the machining process is depicted in Figure 10. The set of hypothetical constraint limits illustrated in Figure 10 is a maximum torque of 100 inch-pounds and a maximum temperature signal of 2 millivolts. Two corrective actions were selected: a decrease in chip load for a torque constraint violation, and a decrease in spindle speed for a tempera-

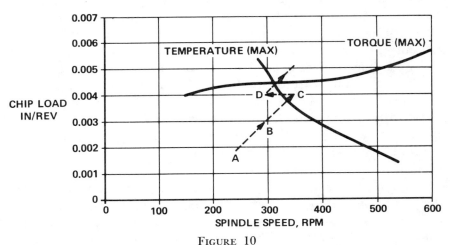

FIGURE 10
Spindle speed, RPM; hypothetical constraint limits.

ture constraint violation. As an example, if the initial operating position was at Point "A," then no constraint violations existed and the adaptive controller automatically placed itself in the optimizing mode.

First, the chip load and spindle speed were increased by one of four preselected increments to Point "B." Remaining in the optimizing mode, the chip load and spindle speed were again increased. This sequence continued to Point "C" where the adaptive controller detected a temperature constraint violation; that is, the incoming signal exceeded the preselected value of 2 millivolts. The adaptive controller then automatically placed itself in the constraint mode and corrected the constraint violation by decreasing spindle speed until the operating point moved to Point "D," where no constraint violation was present and optimization was resumed. This adaptive controller can ultimately reach a limit cycle where the torque limits the chip load and temperature limits the spindle speed.

Sensor Instrumentation

The key components of the sensor instrumentation are depicted in the schematic diagram in Figure 11. The sensors measured spindle torque, spindle vibration, tool-tip temperature, and tool forces. Spindle torque was measured by four strain gages mounted on the spindle. Mounted in two vee patterns and connected to form a bridge circuit, these gages permitted cancellation of compressive and bending forces in the spindle and provided compensation for changes in temperature. Electrical connections to the bridge were made through rotary transformers at the end of the spindle.

Tool-tip temperature was measured by monitoring the thermoelectric voltage generated at the tool-workpiece interface. Since the tool and workpiece are dissimilar metals, a natural thermocouple is formed at their point of contact. The direct current signal developed was transferred from the rotating shaft by means of a garter spring device (see Figure 12). An inner and outer race encompassed a toroid spring which rotated between the two races as would a ball bearing.

Vibration was measured by a crystal accelerometer mounted on the spindle housing. Tool forces in the X and Y directions were measured by a milling dynomometer mounted on the milling machine table. In addition, tachometers on the spindle and table feed motors supplied motor speed data to the controller.

138

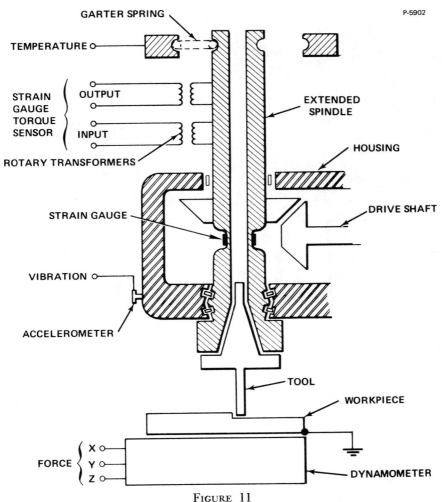

FIGURE 11
Schematic diagram of sensor instrumentation.

Milling Machine

The milling machine employed had the following special features to make it compatible with the adaptive control system:

(1) Spindle drive—10 hp, variable speed, DC motor 3600 rpm to 412 rpm at constant torque with tachometer feedback to maintain speed regulations within ± 1 percent.

(2) Table feed drive—1½ hp, variable speed, DC motor, 2500 rpm to 312 rpm at constant torque, with a tachometer feedback to maintain speed regulation within ± 1 percent.

139

FIGURE 12
Garter spring device.

(3) An electric switch interlock with both spindle speed and feed
    motor mechanical gear change lever to enable the controller
    to determine actual table feed and spindle speed with motor
    tachometers.

System Performance

The benefits produced by the configuration described above can
be gleaned from representative performance data. The results cited
involved profiling with high-speed steel end mills on Ladish D6AC
steel.

Cost per cubic inch of material removed was the criterion used
in the evaluation. This cost criterion was computed by means of
the following procedure:

$$\text{Cost/cubic inch} = \frac{T_c + (TL + TCT)M}{MR}$$

Where:

$$T_c = \text{Tool cost}$$
$$= \left[\text{Regrind cost} + \left(\frac{\text{initial costs}}{\text{no. of grinds}} \right) \right], \text{dollars}$$

140

TL = Tool life, minutes

TCT = Tool change time, minutes

M = Cost of (labor + overhead), dollars per minute

MR = Volume of material removed during cutter life, cubic inches.

The cutter was considered worn out when the average flank wear-land was 0.012 inch. Overhead and labor costs were estimated to be $40 per hour with a tool cost per regrind of $6 and tool change time of 5 minutes. Machinability values were established empirically by recording the torque, forces, and temperature signals during standard machining tests. These tests were performed to establish spindle speed and feed values for the particular milling machine, cutter, workpiece, tolerances, and coolant combination being used. The maximum values recorded during these tests were used as the constraint values in the adaptive controller for the various adaptive tests.

Profiling—Cuts of Constant Depth and Width

A series of fixed-depth and fixed-width cuts twelve inches long were made to compare adaptively controlled profiling to nonadaptive profiling. A one-inch diameter high-speed steel end mill was operated in a climb-milling mode. The principal variable was the changing wear-land on the cutter. All other test conditions were identical except the spindle speed and table feed which were continuously adjusted by the adaptive controller. Two different methods were used to select feeds and speeds for the nonadaptive cases: (1) handbook values, and (2) manually optimized values. The adaptive system reduced the machining costs under the test conditions by approximately 5 to 10 percent (see Table III) from the manually optimized values established from a series of machining tests.

Profiling—Variable Depth of Cut

The ability of the adaptive controller to adjust the operating conditions for changes in depth of cut was demonstrated by making a series of climb-milling cuts twelve inches long, with a one-inch diameter high-speed steel end mill. The depth of cut was varied from 0.020 to 0.080 inch in 0.010-inch increments. The cutter life in minutes and the volume of material removed was recorded to establish the cost per cubic inch for both adaptive machining and non-adaptive machining with manually selected feed and speed. The test

141

TABLE III
CONSTANT DEPTH COMPARATIVE TESTS

	HANDBOOK	MANUALLY OPTIMUM	ADAPTIVE
SPINDLE SPEED	265 rpm	340 rpm	330—415 rpm
FEED RATE	5.2 ipm	6.5 ipm	6.2—8.4 ipm
VOLUME REMOVED	51 in^3	27.5 in^3	22.5 in^3
TOOL LIFE AND TOOL CHANGE	158 min	75 min	54.5 min
MATERIAL REMOVAL RATE	0.322 in^3/min	0.366 in^3/min	0.413 in^3/min
COST PER IN^3	$2.20	$2.04	$1.89

MATERIAL — LADISH D6AC   DEPTH OF CUT — 0.050 INCH

HARDNESS — 262 BN   WIDTH OF CUT — 1.25 INCH

CUTTER — HSS, 1 INCH DIAMETER, 2   MAX. DEFLECTION — 0.005 INCH
INCHES LONG, 4 FLUTE

TABLE IV
VARIABLE DEPTH COMPARATIVE TESTS

	NON-ADAPTIVE	ADAPTIVE
SPINDLE SPEED	420 rpm	325—470 rpm
FEED RATE	2.5 ipm	2.4—11.2 ipm
VOLUME REMOVED	15.75 in^3	20.5 in^3
TOOL LIFE AND TOOL CHANGE TIME	91 min	55.6 min
MATERIAL REMOVAL RATE	0.173 in^3/min	0.369 in^3/min
COST PER IN^3	$4.25	$2.10

MATERIAL — LADISH D6AC   DEPTH OF CUT — 0.020—0.080 INCH

HARDNESS — 262 BN   WIDTH OF CUT — 1.250 INCHES

CUTTER — HSS, 1 INCH DIAMETER, 3   MAX. DEFLECTION — 0.010 INCH
INCHES LONG, 4 FLUTE

results, summarized in Table IV, show that the adaptive system reduced costs by approximately 50 percent. The main reason for the greater efficiency was the system's ability to increase the feedrates

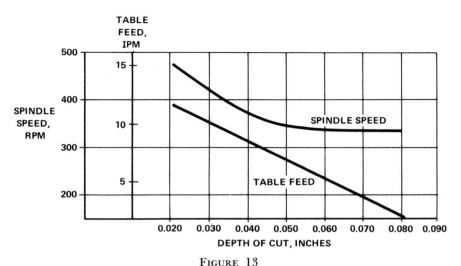

FIGURE 13

Average adaptive spindle speed and table feed versus depth of cut.

for the lighter cuts and slow them down for the heavier cuts without destroying the cutter or causing excessive deflections. The adaptive control system's ability to adjust the spindle speed and table feed as a function of the depth of cut is illustrated in Figure 13.

Profiling—Variable Width of Cut

The adaptive control system's ability to adjust for variations in the width of cut with a single set of constraint limits was investigated for both adaptive machining and nonadaptive machining. The test consisted of a series of climb-milling, fixed-depth cuts twelve inches long, using a one-inch diameter, high-speed end mill with the width of cut (engaged axial length) allowed to vary from 0.25 to 1.25 inches in 0.25-inch increments. The test results summarized in Table V show that the adaptive system reduced machining costs by approximately 25 to 30 percent by responding approximately to variations in the width of cut. The most active on-line constraint in this test was the temperature, since both torque and force are maximum values for full engagement of the cutter. The adjustments made in spindle speed and table feed as a function of the width of cut are illustrated in Figure 14.

The performance data demonstrated that this adaptive system was capable of making proper adjustments for the type of variations typical of many profile milling operations. In each of the cases

143

TABLE V
VARIABLE WIDTH COMPARATIVE TESTS

	NON-ADAPTIVE	ADAPTIVE
SPINDLE SPEED	265 rpm	375—480 rpm
FEED RATE	5.2 ipm	5.0—13.5 ipm
VOLUME REMOVED	35.8 in^3	20.5 in^3
TOOL LIFE AND TOOL CHANGE TIME	190 min	75.5 min
MATERIAL REMOVAL RATE	0.189 in^3/min	0.272 in^3/min
COST PER IN^3	$3.75	$2.75

MATERIAL — LADISH D6AC	DEPTH OF CUT — 0.050 INCH
HARDNESS — 262 BN	WIDTH OF CUT — 1/4 — 1-1/4 INCHES
CUTTER — HSS, 1 INCH DIAMETER, 2 INCHES LONG, 4 FLUTE	MAX. DEFLECTION — 0.005 INCH

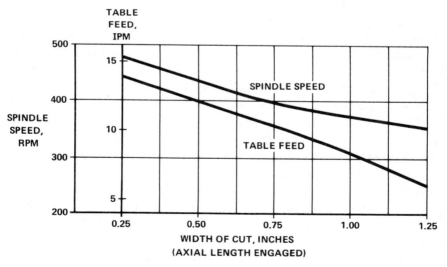

FIGURE 14

Average adaptive spindle speed and table feed versus width of cut.

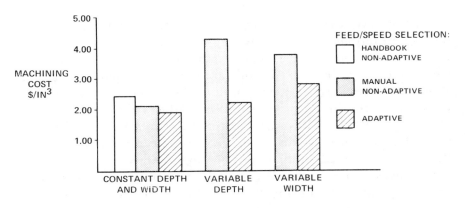

FIGURE 15
Summary of comparative tests.

evaluated, the automatic adjustment of the table feedrate and spindle speed by the adaptive system resulted in a lower machining cost than would occur in a comparable conventional operation. A summary of these results is illustrated in Figure 15.

User acceptance of the early adaptive control designs was impeded by overall complexity, software problems, and relatively high costs. Moreover, the early systems were not easily retrofitted to computer or numerically controlled machines already in user plants. As a result, subsequent developmental efforts in adaptive control have been directed toward a less complex concept that could be simply added to existing equipment.

In one of the more popular simplified systems, the developers experimented by using only a deflection sensing ring mounted on the spindle dust cover and a spindle motor sensing transformer as sensors. The system controlled feedrate only and kept spindle speed constant. Through this approach, the developers were actually using only the feedrate constraint mode of control typically found in the complex adaptive control systems. Test results indicated that the simplified design could obtain 80 to 90 percent of the productivity improvement obtained with the more complex systems.

A LOW-COST RETROFITTABLE
ADAPTIVE CONTROL

The adaptive control concept just described might better be called a "chip-load maximizer." It achieves the maximum chip load and maximum metal-removal rate permitted by cutter load, fixture load, cutter-workpiece deflection, or machine load in end milling and face milling operations. It does so by measuring the force on the cutter in-process and continually comparing this measured force to a reference force prescribed for the operation by a computer program. When measured forces are within 10 or 20 percent of the limiting reference force, the adaptive controller reduces the feedrate command to the machine in proportion to the error between measured and reference force signals. It acts to prevent the reference force from being exceeded. Similarly, by sensing motor current and comparing this signal to a reference value, it prevents the spindle motor's rated horsepower from being exceeded. Controlling force and horsepower in this way permits the system to maintain feedrates in the cut that are two to six times faster than those typically used in a conventional operation.

Elements of the System

The following principal elements constitute the adaptive control system:

(a) Spindle-nose force sensor system (one for each spindle),
(b) Spindle-motor load sensor (one for each spindle motor),
(c) Adaptive control unit,
(d) Numerical control interface,
(e) Machinability computer program.

Force Sensors

Force sensor systems, shown in Figure 16, are mounted on the spindle nose in or near the dust cover on each spindle of the machine. Each system consists of four inductive transducers spaced 90 degrees apart around the spindle. This arrangement produces very accurate measurement of vectoral forces. The individual sensors are physically adjusted to the spindle surface. They are then electronically balanced and "zeroed" to create a unified direction force-sensing system. These transducers are extremely sensitive devices whose design makes use of special core material and unique winding techniques. They can detect spindle displacement from 20 millionths of an inch up to the maximum permitted—when the spindle is subjected to the highest allowable spindle bearing force specified by the machine tool manufacturer.

146

FIGURE 16
Spindle nose force sensor system.
(One for each spindle)

Motor Load Sensors

A horsepower measuring sensor is used to monitor variations in motor load of each spindle during machining operations. On AC spindle motors this sensor is a simple current transformer. A shunt is provided for DC spindle motors. These units are mounted in or near the machine tool magnetic panel enclosure. The purpose of this sensor is to provide overload protection in cases where maximum metal removal is limited by available spindle horsepower. In these cases the feedrate is reduced to maintain a horsepower level which is acceptable. A spindle motor load sensor is shown in Figure 17.

Adaptive Control Unit

The adaptive control unit is a compact electronic cabinet 25 inches wide, 12 inches high, and 10 inches deep. The system constantly surveys all sensor outputs and selects the highest signals with which to control feedrate. The unit's mounting is dependent upon the configuration of the machine and control system to which it is applied. It

FIGURE 17

Spindle motor load sensor. (One for each spindle motor)

may be mounted on the machine column or carrier or on top of the machine control cabinet.

One of the most attractive features of the system concept is that there are no operator devices on the control panel. No operator intervention is necessary. All control parameters are determined by the part programmer and are input into the system via the control media.

Numerical Control Interface

The system operates on the principle of controlling the feedrate override of the numerical control unit on an infinitely variable basis during the cutting process. In order to do this it is necessary to perform only minor modifications within the existing machine control unit. These involve wiring into the feedrate override system and, in effect, operating the feedrate override on a continuous basis from the adaptive control unit.

In addition, in order to allow the unit to be operated without operator intervention, it is necessary to have all input to the adaptive control made through the media of the machine control system. This allows the part programmer to have complete control over all aspects

148

of the machining process and eliminates the possibility of unnecessary feedrate override by the operator.

To control feedrate, a current or voltage level or pulse rate is varied according to the numerical control system involved. This is done by making connections to existing connector pins or terminals in the machine control. It is unnecessary to modify any printed circuit board or other circuitry of the existing control system.

Machinability Computer Program

The computer machinability program is essentially a preprocessor that takes into consideration all known facts about the cutting situation—e.g., cutter size, material type and hardness, type of cut, and machine tool characteristics. This information is inserted in the program in place of the normal "feedrate" and "spindle" program statements. Maximum feedrates, spindle RPM, and force limits are automatically computed by the adaptive control software and inserted onto the tape when the part program is processed. The maximum feedrate obtained in this way will be up to six times the value that would be programmed by conventional numerical control methods using the same information. Adaptive control hardware, however, will reduce the feedrate during the cut as much as is necessary to prevent the force limit or the spindle motor current rating from being violated.

A typical adaptive control software flow diagram is shown in Figure 18. The program has been implemented mainly for the APT language on an IBM 360 computer. Modifications of the program may be required to fit it precisely into the local computer and local APT configurations. The core storage requirement for this program is approximately 2,000 eight-byte words. The program may be run either as an independent computer program with print-out or integrally with the APT computer program to effect a single pass operation.

System Performance and Experience

A relatively large amount of data on the performance of low-cost adaptive controls in the cutting of steel, aluminum, and titanium has been acquired. A representative sampling of the data developed indicates average machining time reductions of approximately 40 percent in the case of steel and titanium, and roughly 30 percent for aluminum from using the adaptive control system. Cutter life has

149

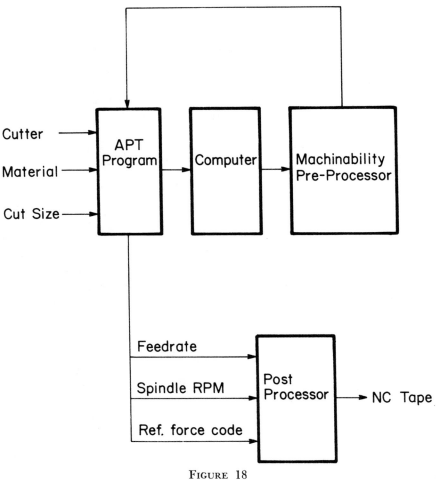

FIGURE 18
Adaptive control software flow diagram.

been measured under controlled conditions to be increased by 50 percent during the machining of steel parts. Some phenomenal increases in metal removal have been achieved in cutting titanium. In at least one case the increase was demonstrated to be as high as 240 percent. In other cases adaptive control was responsible for a 100 percent increase in metal removal. When these orders of magnitude are possible, the limiting factors often become the horsepower available to the spindle and the rigidity of the machine tool.

Attractive cost benefits result from these productivity gains. In spite of higher expenses in such areas as equipment cost and maintenance, the total cost of the adaptive control system usually is considerably less than that of using only numerical control. Due to greater efficiencies and because of reductions in such areas as part scrappage, cutter breakage, and tool tryout time, investment payback often is achieved relatively quickly. According to one company's findings, the cost of adaptive controls for 3-spindle profilers was returned in an average of four months. Several other companies have recovered their adaptive control investment in six to eight months.

One aerospace company conducted extensive research for the Air Force on the use of a low-cost retrofittable adaptive control system.[3] Overall, it reported an average reduction in metalcutting time of 37 percent, as compared to using conventional numerical control. The largest improvements took place in cutting titanium (46 percent), while reductions in cutting aluminum and steel were reported at 35 percent and 33 percent, respectively.

Both surface finish and dimensional factors were considered equivalent in the two systems. With adaptive control there were 23 percent less cutter breaks.

Adaptive control required 7 percent more programming time during the tests. However, it was estimated that after the programmer became well acquainted with the new system, the figure could be reversed to a 5 percent reduction in programming time.

This study also investigated costs and investment payback. A composite program payback of .489 years (about 6 months) was calculated. If the system were used only for cutting titanium, costs could be recovered in .27 years (about 3 months).

Other, less expected benefits can accrue from using adaptive control. Time studies have shown that conventional numerical control machining time on the same part may vary as much as 35 percent between individual machine operators. When adaptive control was used, the variation never exceeded 2 percent. This significant difference indicates an opportunity not only for greater efficiency, but also for better facility scheduling and inventory control, as well as for more meaningful cost estimates.

The faster machining times achievable with adaptive control, however, may create some problems since cutters and machine tools may be pushed to the extreme limits of their capabilities. Users have

---

[3] W. J. Whetham, "Low Cost Adaptive Control Unit Manufacturing Methods," Air Force Materials Laboratory Technical Report No. AFML–TR–73–263, Wright-Patterson Air Force Base, 1973.

found that they must exercise more caution in selecting cutters, which may be the weakest link in the adaptive control system. The best cutters may operate ten times longer than the worst while the cost differential is much less. Improved design of both cutters and machines should minimize the hazard of the cutter's affecting cutting tolerances.

Clearly, recent developments of simplified retrofittable adaptive control systems have transformed both the economic and performance potential of this technology. Coupled with computer and numerical controls, adaptive control promises many long-term benefits to the metalworking industry.

Chapter V

Economic Justification: Defining the Investment

Outlined in this and the next chapter is a methodology for determining whether the acquisition of computer and numerical control equipment is economically justified. The high initial cost of this type of equipment and its pervasive impact upon an assorted array of indirect expenses are a large part of the reason that investment decision making is such a demanding process.

When evaluating proposed investments in conventional machinery, many cost elements can be disregarded since they are equally affected by the competing alternatives. Often, such indirect costs as handling of materials, tooling, inspection, assembly, and inventory-related factors, vary little regardless of which conventional machine is selected. However, once computer or numerical controls are considered as an investment possibility, indirect costs may change drastically, and the many factors previously ignored must be thoroughly examined. To further complicate matters, affected cost elements and their relationships fluctuate greatly, depending upon machine capabilities and the degree of automatic control under consideration.[1]

The computer and numerical control investment dilemma not surprisingly produces two distinct consequences. Many decision makers simply feel overwhelmed by the many facets that must be evaluated and avoid the drudgery of an exhaustive analysis by rejecting outright the proposed investment. Some also pass up profitable cost reductions because their investment analysis was too cursory and overlooked the less obvious, but substantial indirect economies. Secondly, other decision makers have simply authorized the investment on the basis of good faith. When for one of several reasons the faith proved unjustified and the predicted economies failed to mate-

---

[1] For a more complete discussion see: Wilbert Steffy, Donald Smith, and Donald Souter, *Economic Guidelines for Justifying Capital Purchases* (Ann Arbor: The University of Michigan, 1973).

rialize, an embargo against future computer or numerical control investments was ordered. The unfortunate result of all these decisions is that technologically superior equipment is not utilized to the extent that is actually warranted.

Investments in computer and numerical controls are mostly proposed for expansion or the replacement of existing equipment. A comparison of the predicted profitabilities of competing investment alternatives is the basis of decision making for expansion purposes. Replacement decisions, on the other hand, require answers to at least two principal questions: Which alternative is best, and when can the replacement be made most advantageously? The best of the competing alternatives is the one which demonstrates the least annual cost and generally provides the fastest and shortest payback of the investment. The time to replace existing equipment is that time when it is more economical to do so than not, typically at the end of the asset's economic life. The number of years which the equipment must be retained to achieve the least annual cost determines the economic life.

MAJOR EQUIPMENT COSTS

Capital Recovery Costs

Three types of equipment costs must be considered in all investment evaluations: capital recovery, operating, and penalty or opportunity costs. The capital recovery process amortizes the asset's initial cost over the productive life of the equipment. Depreciation accounting is used to record systematically the declining asset value by charging off the depreciated value against revenue as the equipment wears out.

Annual depreciation charges should be computed in order to correspond as nearly as possible with the actual loss in asset value during each accounting period. Often, it is erroneously assumed that assets deteriorate uniformly, and the annual depreciation expenses are therefore computed according to the straight-line method, which equally divides the asset cost, less any estimated salvage value, over the expected service life. This straight-line method has serious drawbacks when the asset's productive capability is not affected uniformly by age and is unable to maintain the same rate of production during later years as it had earlier. To offset such shortcomings more realistic depreciation accounting techniques are used to recognize the higher rate of asset devaluation in the earlier years. The two popular

154

depreciation methods described below more genuinely match capital recovery costs with the asset's true contribution to the revenue flow rate than does the straight-line method.

1. *Fixed percentage applied to a diminishing asset book value.* By this method a depreciation rate is applied to the declining net book value of the asset at the beginning of each year, which results in writing the asset's stated value down to the salvage value during the expected life. Yearly depreciation charges determined by this method diminish as the asset's book value is written down each year.

The depreciation rate "r" is computed by the formula:

$$r = 1 - \sqrt[n]{\frac{\text{Salvage Value}}{\text{Asset Cost}}}$$

$$= 1 - \sqrt[n]{\frac{S}{P}}$$

The fixed percentage "r" is applied to the asset's previous year-end value. A simple example will illustrate the use of "r."

Assume: asset cost "P" = \$100;
salvage value "S" = \$10; and
useful life "n" = 9 years.

Then, $r = 1 - \sqrt[n]{\dfrac{S}{P}} = 1 - \sqrt[9]{\dfrac{10}{100}}$

$r = 22.574\%$ (See Table I.)

On occasion, the salvage value "S" in the above equation may be zero. A convenient technique in the zero salvage situation is to assume a nominally small salvage value, calculate "r" and apply it in the manner described for every year except the final year, in which case a straight-line depreciation charge is assumed in order to arrive at a final book value of zero.

2. *Sum of expected life periods.* The annual depreciation charge is determined by computing a different fraction or percentage for each year. The denominator of this depreciation fraction is the sum of the digits representing each of the years in the estimated service life of the asset. The numerator is the remaining life of

TABLE I

APPLICATION OF FIXED PERCENTAGE METHOD

Year	Depreciation During Year	End of Year Value
1	$22.57	$77.43
2	17.48	59.95
3	13.53	46.42
4	10.48	35.94
5	8.11	27.83
6	6.28	21.55
7	4.86	16.69
8	3.77	12.92
9	2.92	10.00
	$90.00	

the asset at the beginning of each year. Thus, the depreciation fraction for the second year of an asset with a three-year service life is $\frac{2}{6}$. This fraction is applied to the asset cost minus the salvage value to determine the second year's depreciation charge.

As another example, assume that the estimated life of a machine is nine years; the sum of the digits would be:

$$1 + 2 + 3 + 4 + 5 + 6 + 7 + 8 + 9 = 45$$

For long service periods the calculation of the digits' sum can be shortened by using the following formula—where "n" is the number of years in the asset's service life:

$$\frac{n}{2}(n + 1) = \text{sum of digits}$$

Using the data from the fixed percentage example the sum of digits depreciation would be as follows:

$$\text{Sum of digits} = \frac{n}{2}(n + 1)$$

$$= \frac{9}{2}(10) = 45 \qquad \text{(See Table II.)}$$

The effect of these two accelerated depreciation computational procedures is illustrated in Figure 1. A capital recovery pattern of the type shown is consistent with the deterioration rate of most types

TABLE II
APPLICATION OF SUM OF DIGITS METHOD

Year	Fraction	Depreciation During Year	End of Year Value
1	9/45	9/45(90) = 18	82
2	8/45	8/45(90) = 16	66
3	7/45	7/45(90) = 14	52
4	6/45	6/45(90) = 12	40
5	5/45	5/45(90) = 10	30
6	4/45	4/45(90) = 8	22
7	3/45	3/45(90) = 6	16
8	2/45	2/45(90) = 4	12
9	1/45	1/45(90) = 2	10
		90	

of automatic equipment, such as computer or numerical control machines.

The method of computing the depreciation charge significantly affects the after-tax cash inflows because depreciation charges are tax-deductible expenses. The higher the depreciation expense that

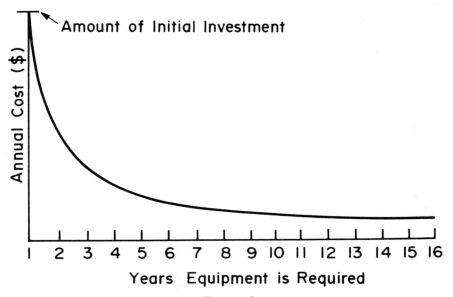

FIGURE 1
Pattern of capital recovery cost component.

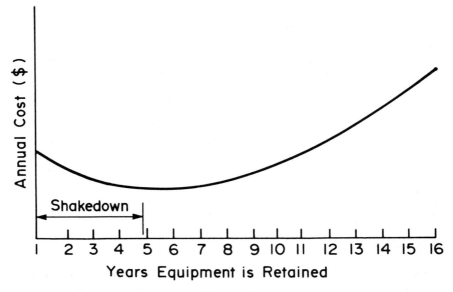

FIGURE 2
Pattern of operating cost component.

is realistically allocated to any given year, the lower the taxable income for that year and the greater the cash flow from the depreciation charge.

Operational Costs

The second component of the annual cost is operating expenses, which include the traditional costs of power, labor, maintenance, scrap, etc. associated with normal operations. As shown in Figure 2, the operating cost cycle begins with the equipment shakedown period, during which costs tend to decrease. As equipment complexity increases, the duration of the orientation period likewise is prolonged. Beyond the shakedown period, operating costs achieve a fairly stable state, then begin to rise because malfunctions increase and the operating cycle lengthens as the condition of the equipment deteriorates.

Penalty or Opportunity Costs

Penalty or opportunity costs are the difference between the value of the results obtained with the existing equipment and the best results which reasonably could be expected from using the most efficient equipment available. These nebulous, but actual cost penalties accrue from the failure to take advantage of improved technology. Some causes of opportunity costs include the need for relatively higher skills, more labor per unit of output, and lower product quality—all of which create higher costs than are possible through the use of advanced equipment. A typical penalty cost pattern is shown in Figure 3.

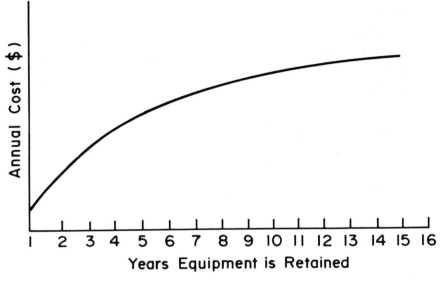

FIGURE 3
Pattern of penalty costs.

Penalty costs, because of their imprecise nature, are commonly the most difficult of the three cost components to evaluate. However, if this component is ignored because of estimation problems or is significantly underestimated by including only very well established costs, then the resultant error produces a misleading decrease in the cost curves other than capital recovery and unrealistically indicates an extension of the economic life.

Since real annual capital recovery costs normally decrease exponentially with the number of years during which the equipment is retained, a serious underestimate in the rate of increasing non-capital recovery costs (which include penalty costs) will cause a marked and erroneous increase in the indicated economic life. While one might, on the other hand, overestimate the penalty cost com-

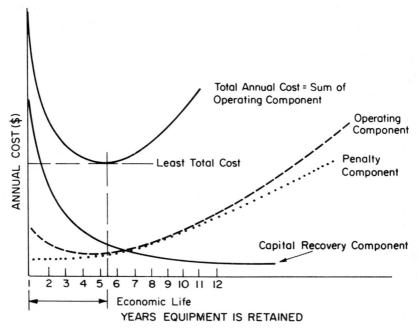

FIGURE 4
Total annual cost pattern due to three additive components.

ponent because it is so hard to evaluate, the attendant decreasing change in economic life is relatively less in magnitude than the life extension resulting from an error of underestimation. Moreover, if the economic life is used to create a signal for periodically bringing up the question of whether or not to replace, then a slightly early signal is obviously less harmful than a late one.

An optimum equipment replacement strategy should normally provide for an overall minimization of the total annual costs. Because capital recovery costs (see Figure 1) decline as the asset ages, it might appear advantageous to postpone the retirement of aging equipment instead of buying expensive new machinery. Minimizing the other annual cost components, however, suggests the opposite policy. Clearly, these tendencies compete, and the result is a total annual cost pattern that is concave upward (see Figure 4).

The total annual cost curve is relatively flat in the region of the least annual cost indicating that a precise determination of the economic life is not crucial. Since the curve tends to rise faster toward

160

early replacement than toward late replacement, errors toward late replacement appear less serious. However, one might replace earlier than the indicated economic life if the prospective cost savings would provide a suitable return on the investment necessary to obtain the economies. One might also postpone replacement beyond the economic life if the best replacement has a higher least annual cost than the cost of the existing equipment.

The difficulty of creating valid and accurate estimates for penalty and operational costs is especially pronounced in the evaluation of proposed investments for computer or numerical controls. If one could reliably estimate future annual costs when such an investment is being considered, the best replacement strategy could easily be determined. Little difficulty would be encountered in either determining the exact time that the existing equipment is at the end of its economic life or in ascertaining that a machine should be replaced with another one that has the least annual cost among several competing machines.

Whether expansion or replacement is the objective and despite the cost estimation difficulties, the investment decision maker must determine if the predicted annual savings from computer or numerical controls will be great enough to warrant the capital investment. Occasionally, other reasons may suffice; e.g., to obtain valuable experience in manufacturing research projects. Normally, the decision to purchase computer or numerical controls, however, must be supported by projections showing that a minimum return on the capital invested will be achieved.

Because computer and numerical control applications affect an unprecedented array of manufacturing and management activities, conventional equipment investment evaluation techniques which do not adequately measure all cost effects throughout the entire organization usually create erroneous conclusions. Few operational costs are left unchanged by computer and numerical controls. Such important savings as less tooling, setup, inventory, and part assembly costs may be greater than the economies originating from the obvious productivity improvements. Because too little attention in conventional investments often has been paid to many indirect operational expenses which previously were considered semifixed and thus often buried in overhead, related cost data frequently are difficult to obtain for computer or numerial control investment evaluations. Since the attendant depreciation and capital use charges for costly computer and numerical controls are relatively large, unless all the direct and indirect operational savings are measured, even the most rigorous analytical evalution process may indicate a poor investment—when in fact an attractive return may be earned.

Recognizing that estimates of indirect savings often represent little more than educated guesses due to the lack of company cost records, financial personnel tend to discount or completely ignore these savings assessments during their evaluation of the investment analysis. Increasingly, however, the utilization of computer and numerical controls is providing a growing body of semi-standard data for reference in estimating savings and expenses in both direct and indirect cost activities. If these preliminary semi-standard data are used with discretion and modified by the relevant conditions of each application, they may provide acceptable quantitative information for this phase of the investment analysis.

PRELIMINARY ANALYSIS

The large capital investment required for computer or numerical controls is in itself ample reason for a careful cost analysis. Many firms, however, are reluctant to commit the labor expenses for an intensive analysis unless there are strong indications of a positive result. Unfortunately, because simple answers are not possible, the evaluation process can be arduous and expensive.

Before extensive effort is committed to performing a detailed investment analysis, an evaluation of the parts to be processed should be made to assess the computer or numerical control prospects. Parts that are profitably produced by computer or numerical controls commonly have some or all of these characteristics: They (1) require lengthy setups on conventional equipment; (2) are complex or are to be manufactured in small-to-medium batch sizes; (3) have a high value, making errors costly; (4) require expensive jigs or fixtures when produced conventionally; (5) involve frequent engineering changes; or (6) require multiple operations such as milling, drilling, tapping, etc.

More specific criteria for screening parts for numerical control have been developed at the English Imperial College of Science and Technology. These guidelines have been especially valuable for evaluating parts to be produced by continuous-path machining.

Some 600 parts were evaluated during one phase of their study, and part complexity showed the strongest correlation with situations where numerical control was the most favorable. Initially, attempts were made to measure complexity in terms of machining time and the volume of metal removed. Statistical analyses, however, eventually demonstrated the following factors to be more accurately indicative of part complexity: (1) the number of machine decelerations; (2) the number of straight lines on the part parallel to an axis; and (3) the number of curves on the part.

Data correlation studies showed that when the above factors are present in definite relationships, numerical control is more likely to produce machine cycle time savings and economic advantages. Favorable relationships of these factors are deemed present when: (1) the number of machine-decelerations for a given part is greater than 25 and the number of straight lines on the part is equal to or less than the number of curves; or (2) the number of straight-line movements is greater than 50.

In a random sample of 36 parts Brewer and Millyard were able to use their procedures to predict successfully the true economic relationship for 30 of these parts.[2] In five of the six failures, the procedure predicted that numerical control would not be the most economical, although it did ultimately prove to have a slight economic superiority. The parts involved in all six unsuccessful predictions had a relatively small number of curves, a circumstance that suggests that these guidelines should be used cautiously in the evaluation of parts having few curves. The results also indicate that a high number of machine decelerations does not alone indicate a complex part that can be more economically produced on computer or numerical controls.

Since the Brewer research group further tested their preliminary procedures with continuing favorable results, these criteria offer a reasonable compromise between an exhaustive or expensive investment analysis and intuitive guesswork. If postaudits follow each application of these criteria, weaknesses should become apparent. The criteria can then be modified to fit the unique production characteristics of each company.

In modifying the criteria it is important to consider all cost elements and not restrict the comparison to machine cycle times. Actual hourly machine costs for conventional and computer or numerical control methods can differ considerably because of variations in

2 P. W. Millyard and R. C. Brewer, "Some Economic Aspects of Numerically Controlled Machine Tools," *The Production Engineer*, **XXXIX**, No. 3, p. 141.

tooling, maintenance, programming, and capital recovery costs. Consideration also must be given to the effort spent in machine setup and finished part inspection and assembly.

Just as there are factors which are favorable for the application of computer or numerical controls, there are also certain part and processing characteristics which are unfavorable. The application of computer or numerical controls tends to be less profitable when: (1) batch sizes are large; (2) part design is simple; (3) parts have non-geometric shapes, thereby making programming difficult; (4) part setup is simple; or (5) the condition of incoming raw materials varies and is difficult or costly to control.

When a majority of these factors is present in a manufacturing situation, a pro forma investment study may be warranted as a next step to determine if a full-fledged analysis appears worth the expense.

INVESTMENT EVALUATION PROCEDURES

If a clear assessment of the profitability of computer or numerical controls cannot be made by comparing the parts to the foregoing criteria, a detailed investment analysis is the recommended alternate route to obtaining reliable conclusions. The advantages and disadvantages of computer or numerical controls listed during the preliminary investigations should now be evaluated and compared with competing alternatives and then expressed in monetary terms.

There are several types of methods currently employed in industry by which the profitability of an investment is measured. In this book the *discounted cash flow method* is suggested. This method calculates the rate of return by taking into consideration the time value of money. It recognizes interest as the cost incurred in the use of money, and therefore is judged to be the most realistic method to use for decisions regarding long-term investments, such as computer or numerical controls.

Because of the many variations among accounting systems and the wide range of computer and numerical control applications, no single procedure will fit all investment situations. However, the discounted cash flow method described below should prove adaptable to virtually any application. In particular, the guidelines and procedures for quantifying the specific impact of a proposed investment on individual operational expenses can be effectively employed in any traditional equipment investment analysis method. As an example, every investment evaluation process requires answers to the following

164

types of questions—answers which can be quantitatively developed by the procedures recommended in the methodology delineated below.

1. What are the individual elements comprised in the total investment?
2. What is the amount required for each investment factor?
3. When will the expenditure of funds be required?
4. What direct operational savings are anticipated from the investment?
5. What indirect operational savings are anticipated from the investment?
6. How much will be saved in each operational savings factor and when will the savings occur?

The discounted cash flow method focuses on both the amounts and timing of cash receipts and disbursements. Other methods might fail to give proper emphasis to the timing of cash flows, thereby incorrectly ranking competing investment alternatives. The significance of the timing of cash flows is illustrated in the following example.

Two competing investments require the same initial disbursement of $300,000. Each has an expected life of ten years and zero salvage value. Option A is expected to yield a total profit of $450,000 over ten years, while a total profit of $500,000 is projected for Option B.

A tabulation of the year-by-year cash flows of both investments is shown in Table III.

By using the discounted cash flow method, the rate of return on Option A is computed to be 20½ percent, compared to a rate of return of 6⅛ percent on Option B[3]. This should not be surprising when one carefully examines the cash flow patterns of both investments shown graphically in Figure 5. A dollar in-hand today has a greater present worth than a future dollar, since it can be reinvested for the coming year at the prevailing interest rate. Consequently, the early profits of Option A weigh more heavily than the late profits of Option B.

PHASE I—Determining the *Total Cost* of the Proposed Investment. Because expenditures are required to implement certain

---

[3] See the illustration of rate of return computations in Appendix A at the end of this chapter.

TABLE III

ANNUAL CASH FLOW TABULATION
(In thousands of dollars)

Year	Option A		Option B	
	Annual Profit	Cumulative Profit	Annual Profit	Cumulative Profit
1	$200	$200	$ 0	$ 0
2	100	300	0	0
3	50	350	10	10
4	30	380	10	20
5	20	400	20	40
6	20	420	20	60
7	20	440	40	100
8	10	450	50	150
9	0	450	125	275
10	0	450	225	500
Total Profit	$450		$500	

operational and organizational modifications and because there is a need for new programming and maintenance skills and for supporting equipment, the "total" cost of an initial machine can be considerably more than just the equipment price. Some of these expenses need not be duplicated when additional equipment is installed.

PHASE II—Estimating the Savings. Computer and numerical control operational savings are evaluated according to direct and indirect classifications. Direct savings (Phase II–A) accrue from the economies of part floor-to-floor production time, i.e., the time it takes to complete jobs on a conventional machine minus the time required to produce the same jobs on computer or numerical controls. The method employed to estimate direct savings differs little from the techniques used for conventional equipment. Direct savings can be converted to dollars by multiplying the time saved by the appropriate labor and overhead rates for the setup and machine operator personnel.

Indirect operational savings (Phase II–B) occur in cost categories other than machine setup and operator expense; some of these are maintenance, tooling, programming, inspection, scrap, inventory, floor space, material handling, etc.

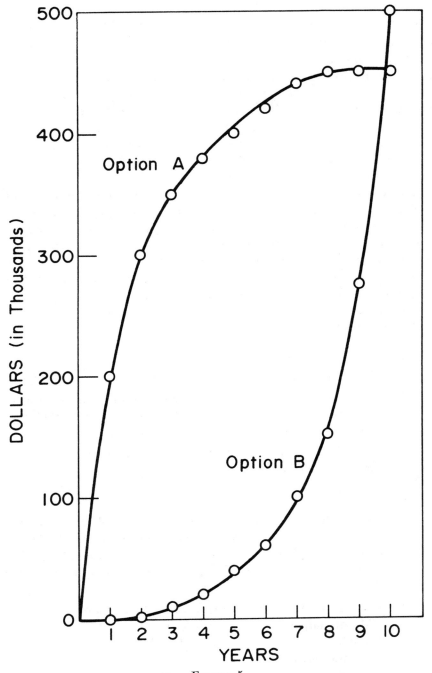

FIGURE 5
Cumulative profits of options A & B.

PHASE III—Computing the Discounted Cash Flows and Determining the Equivalent Rate of Return. Future cash flows anticipated from the investment and the annual savings are discounted where appropriate, and an interest rate representing the rate of return is computed. In investment applications, the resulting rate of return is the compound interest rate at which the predicted savings and revenues are equivalent to the required disbursements. It can also be described as the interest rate at which the total present value of a series of expected annual savings is equivalent to the initial investment.

The resulting rate is then compared with the minimum rate of return that the firm considers acceptable for a capital investment. The minimum rate determined by management is influenced by many factors, including the prevailing cost of capital and the firm's willingness to assume the financial risk.

A simplified example with hypothetical figures will help to illustrate how the discounted cash flow technique is used to compute the rate of return for computer or numerical control investments.

Assume the following conditions:

Investment

1. The equipment costs $20,000.
2. Training cost for maintenance, programming, and operating personnel is $2,000, shipping and installation is $1,000, and additional supporting equipment is $7,000.
3. The initial total investment outflow for Items 1 and 2 is therefore $30,000.

Savings

1. Assume that numerical control makes possible direct operational savings of 1,250 machine hours per year. In a one-man, one-machine situation, if the operator cost including overhead is $4.00 per hour, the direct savings amounts to $5,000 per year.
2. Assume that the indirect operational savings are:

Maintenance	$ (400)*
Tooling	6,000
Programming	(2,500)*
Inspection	1,000
Scrap	900

Inventory Carrying Costs   1,000

     Net Indirect Savings $6,000   per year

   * Negative savings.

3. The total annual direct and indirect savings is then $11,000 per year. If the tax rate is 50 percent, the after-tax savings is $5,500 per year.
4. The net effect of the depreciation charge is an annual cash inflow equal to the depreciation charge multiplied by the tax rate. In this example, assuming a ten-year machine life with a uniform rate of deterioration and a straight-line depreciation method, the after-tax inflow would be $3,000 times .50 or $1,500. Adding this to the net annual savings of $5,500 yields a net annual cash inflow of $7,000.

Computing the Rate of Return

1. The discounted cash flow technique will determine the interest rate at which a cash inflow of $7,000 per year for ten years (the estimated economic life of the equipment) will be provided from the "annuity" investment of $30,000 today.
2. Compound interest tables are used to determine the interest rate that will provide the ten annual payments from the initial investment of $30,000. In other words, the analyst determines the interest rate that will provide ten yearly "annuity" payments of $7,000 from a present investment of $30,000. This interest rate is best calculated by a trial-and-error method. Two interest rates are assumed, then the present worths or equivalent annual payments are calculated, after which the interest rate can be found by interpolation.

     Using this method, the present worth of the savings series of $7,000 for ten years is equal to $30,000 at the rate of 19 percent. The rate of return in this example is therefore 19 percent.[4]

The foregoing has presented an overview of one effective computer or numerical control investment evaluation process. The detailed procedures follow which may be used for quantifying the investment components. The principles of nearly all of these quantification

---

[4] See procedures in Appendix B.

procedures are effective for virtually all investment evaluation methods.

DEFINING THE INVESTMENT

The total initial investment consists of all money to be spent for procuring, installing, and equipping the machine, as well as for training the personnel needed to operate and maintain it. Included are the expenditures for all accessories, parts, and services necessary to ready the new machine for operation. Many of these initial costs will not recur during the life of the machine. At least five initial investment factors must be considered: basic machine cost, training cost, initial tooling cost, shipping and installation cost, and support equipment cost.

Basic Machine Cost

The basic machine cost is the price quoted by the vendor of the machine and the control. All taxes should be included in this cost. To avoid duplicating the cost of various options and accessories, the vendor's quotation must be itemized to determine exactly which machine features and services are included. Little difficulty should be experienced in determining this investment component since the required information can be readily obtained from the machine manufacturer.

Training Cost

The total costs incurred in training personnel for operating, maintaining, and programming the computer or numerical control machine should also be included in the initial investment. If training is to be conducted outside of the acquiring company's plant, this cost should include training program fees, reimbursements for travel and living expenses, and the trainees' wages during the training period. For in-plant training, the cost should include the wages of all company personnel involved in the training program, as well as outside instructor fees if there should be such charges.

Computer or numerical control machine operators commonly are trained in the plant of the acquiring company during or immediately following the equipment installation. Representatives of the machine manufacturer normally handle the training activity.

The training costs of several numerical control users were studied in one University of Michigan survey,[5] and these experiences can provide useful guidelines for companies considering their first acquisition of computer or numerical controls. The average length of the operator training period at the survey firms was 4.2 days, and the average training cost per trainee was $158. A firm usually trained one operator for each shift. Additionally, one supervisor was trained in machine operation. Where specific training costs are not readily obtainable from a company's own experience, these operator training costs (OTC) may be estimated by the following procedure.

$$\begin{aligned}
\text{OTC} &= \$158 \, [(\text{No. of Operators Per Shift}) \, (\text{No. of Shifts}) + 1^*] \\
&= \$158[(1) \, (2) + 1^*] \\
&= \$158[3] = \$474
\end{aligned}$$

* represents a Supervisor Factor

Note: This example assumes one operator per shift, a two-shift operation, and one supervisor.

Computer and numerical control maintenance and programming trainees commonly are sent to the equipment manufacturer's plant for up to two weeks of instruction. Maintenance courses familiarize the trainee with the machine components and the theory of design and operation of the hydraulic and electronic control systems. Programmers are instructed in the detailed part-programming conventions.

The average length of the training programs utilized by the numerical control users in the survey was five days for maintenance personnel and four for programmers. The average cost of the maintenance training programs was $370 per trainee, while the average cost of training each programmer was $340. Most firms dispatched only one trainee to each of these programs for each type of numerical control machine they purchased.

Thus:

Maintenance Training Cost (MTC) = $370

Programmer Training Cost (PTC) = $340

In the absence of in-plant experience, the total training investment for the first piece of computer or numerical control equipment may be estimated from the survey data by adding the three costs just described:

---

[5] Wilbert Steffy, Richard Bawol, Louis LaChance, and David Polacsek, *Numerical Control Justification: A Methodology* (Ann Arbor: The University of Michigan, 1967).

$$\begin{aligned}
\text{TRAINING COST} &= \text{(Operator Training Cost)} + \\
&\quad \text{(Maintenance Training Cost)} + \\
&\quad \text{(Programming Training Cost)} \\
&= (\$474) + (\$370) + (\$340) \\
&= \$1,184
\end{aligned}$$

The cost of training computer or numerical control maintenance and programming personnel is influenced by the complexity of the application and the qualifications of the trainees. The preliminary standards suggested by the survey data should therefore be modified to reflect the additional training required for particularly sophisticated equipment or for trainees that may be marginally qualified. Typical training periods for relatively complex equipment are one to two weeks for machine and hydraulic maintenance and two to three weeks for the electronic control. Programmer training for complex five-axis equipment can last up to a month with on-the-job training continuing for another 6 to 12 months. The average data also should be revised if a firm plans to train at the outset more, or less, than one operator per shift, one maintenance man, or one programmer for the proposed equipment. Training costs are substantially reduced when additional computer or numerical control machines are purchased.

Initial Tooling Cost

Complex jigs and fixtures required for conventional production are commonly replaced by simple computer or numerical control workholding devices. On the average, *standard* workholders were sufficient to tool 92.7 percent of the numerical control jobs done by the survey companies. Obviously, an investment expenditure is incurred in purchasing the inventory of *standard* workholding devices.

To determine the total effect of computer or numerical control on nonperishable tooling costs, annual tooling costs for the comparable conventional and automated machines must be weighed. The method for weighing these costs and ascertaining if there is an annual computer or numerical control *special* tooling savings will be described in the next chapter when the indirect savings are considered. Estimating the *standard* tooling investment for computer or numerical control should be considered, however, in this phase of the investment evaluation.

The *standard* tooling investment is the cost of all nonspecial, non-perishable tools required for the computer or numerical control machine. Nonperishable tools are defined for this purpose as tools with an expected life of one year or more and include such items as universal fixtures, vices, clamps, studs, matchplates, toolholders, and tool presetting equipment. A detailed list of these requirements should be developed and priced item by item, and the total cost should be used for the tooling investment factor.

When such detailed information is not readily available, an approximate cost for the initial standard tooling investment may be estimated from the experience of the numerical control users in the survey. Each survey firm reported its investment in these categories: workholding devices, toolholders, and tool presetting equipment. In Figure 6 their standard tooling investment is plotted as it related to the basic machine cost. The graph's line, the least squares linear regression line for the 33 data points, can be represented by the equation $Y = (.089X) - \$740$, where "Y" is the expected value of the tooling investment in dollars and "X" is the basic machine cost.

By using this relationship, the value of the standard tooling investment can be estimated by either inserting the basic machine cost

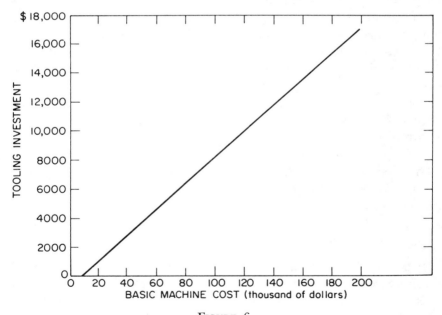

FIGURE 6

Relationship of standard tooling investment to basic machine cost.

into the above formula or by reading the expected value of the tooling investment from Figure 6. This procedure can be illustrated by the following example. If the basic machine cost is $100,000, the expected value of the standard tooling investment is $8,160, i.e., ($100,000 × .089) − ($740).

Since the correlation coefficient of this survey relationship is relatively high at .81, Figure 6 may reliably be used as follows: given a basic machine cost, the expected value of the tooling investment is read at the intersection of the machine cost and the least squares line on the graph.

Shipping and Installation Costs

Shipping costs vary with equipment size and weight, the distance from vendor to buyer, and current freight rates. The vendor should be contacted to determine the exact shipping cost for the machine being considered.

The major cost element of installing a computer or numerical control machine is often the foundation cost. Larger types of computer or numerical control machines and high precision equipment frequently require an expanded floor thickness, or in some instances special foundations. The experience of the vendor always should be sought, since wide differences in installation costs can easily arise. If special foundation hardware is needed, care should be taken to avoid duplicating any provisions included in the machine purchase price.

If estimates of the exact foundation costs are not readily available, Figure 7 may be used in the same manner as was described for Figure 6 in estimating the tooling investment.

The graph's line, the least squares linear regression line for the 13 data points, can be expressed by the equation $Y = (.027 \, X) − \$46$, where "Y" is the expected foundation cost in dollars, and "X" is the basic machine cost.

Support Equipment Cost

Programming and maintaining a computer or numerical control machine require certain support equipment that normally is not needed for conventional machinery. These investment costs should be included as part of the total investment and can be readily determined from vendor quotations once the specific needs are known.

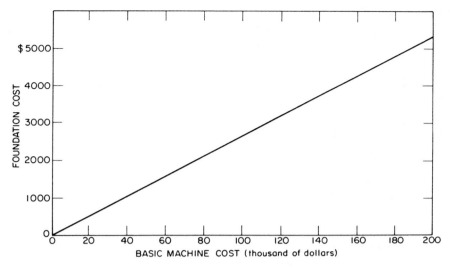

FIGURE 7

Foundation cost versus basic machine cost.

When a pro forma investment analysis is being made, it may be more expedient and acceptable to use the average support equipment cost experienced by other users—properly modified by specific application characteristics.

The major item required for manual programming and tape preparation is a tape punching "typewriter" costing approximately $5,000. The firms in the University of Michigan survey also spent an average of $500 for additional equipment needed for manual programming and tape preparation. Thus, the expected total cost of equipment for this function is approximately $5,500.

More advanced methods employ computers in part programming and require auxiliary equipment for producing the machine tapes. If a company is already using computers for other company functions, no additional equipment may be necessary. Compatibility of existing equipment for part-programming purposes, however, should be verified. When computer-aided programming is used, a computer often can be rented rather than purchased, thus giving rise to an operational expense, but no investment outlay.

A sizable investment for computer-aided programming may be required to obtain a postprocessor. The manufacturer of the computer or numerical control equipment usually provides the postprocessor as part of the machine price unless the machine tool-control

175

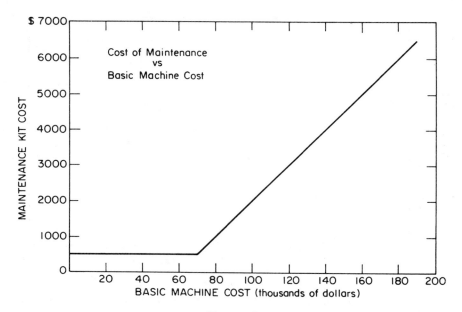

FIGURE 8
Cost of maintenance versus basic machine cost.

combination is unique—that is, one for which no postprocessor has been developed. If a postprocessor is not available, developmental costs can vary from less than a thousand to several thousand dollars. Because of wide price variations, it is unwise to estimate the cost of developing a postprocessor; specific proposals should be solicited to determine the exact cost.

Maintenance equipment for computer and numerical control generally fits one of two classifications. The first includes general-purpose electronic measuring devices. Firms that perform their own maintenance have at least an oscilloscope and volt, ohm, and amp meters. The average cost of such electronic maintenance devices among the survey firms was about $1,500.

The second classification includes special-purpose tools and an inventory of critical spare parts. Some manufacturers supply a maintenance kit that includes these items in the basic machine price. In such a case, care should be exercised to avoid a cost duplication during the investment evaluation.

The cost of the recommended maintenance kits should be readily obtainable from the equipment manufacturer. If for some reason this information is not available, the survey data may be a useful reference. The cost of the maintenance kits used by the survey companies is plotted against the basic machine cost in Figure 8. A maintenance kit cost of $500 was common for each numerical control machine with a basic cost of $70,000 or less. The cost of maintenance kits for more expensive machines increased linearly with higher equipment prices. The experience of the survey companies leads to a simple guideline for estimating the cost of a computer or numerical control maintenance kit: (1) If the basic cost of a machine is $70,000 or less, Kit Cost = $500; (2) if the basic cost of a machine is more than $70,000, Kit Cost = .05 × (Basic Machine Cost − $60,000).

The cost of the spare parts kit should be obtained from the manufacturer whenever possible; the use of the "average" information should be restricted to situations where it is absolutely necessary. The less the standard experience of other users is used, the more confidence financial analysts will have in the results of the investment evaluation study. For some preliminary studies where the exact machine configuration is not designated, however, the rule-of-thumb may be used to advantage; it may be a surprisingly accurate estimate.

Once the total amount of the investment is ascertained, the prospective operational savings and greater profit potential should be evaluated to determine if they are adequate to warrant the investment outlay.

Appendix A

The present worth "P" of a future amount of money "F" may be calculated by the formula

$$P = F \left[\frac{1}{(1 + i)^n}\right]$$

where "i" is the relevant interest rate per interest period and "n" is the number of interest periods "F" is away from "P."

In the discounted cash flow example, the rate of return of each option is the interest rate "i" that would make the sum of the present worths of the future profits equal to the amount of the original investment.

For Option A, we have

$$\$300{,}000 = \$200{,}000 \left[\frac{1}{(1+i)^1}\right] + \$100{,}000 \left[\frac{1}{(1+i)^2}\right] +$$

$$\ldots + 0 \left[\frac{1}{(1+i)^{10}}\right]$$

and we want to solve for an "i" that would make the equation an identity. A similar equation may be constructed for Option B.

The factor $\left[\frac{1}{(1+i)^n}\right]$ may be obtained from compound interest tables.

It is tabulated for different values of "i" and "n." The most convenient approach to solving for "i" in the equation given above would be to choose two sufficiently close interest rates by trial and error and look up the corresponding table values for $\left[\frac{1}{(1+i)^n}\right]$. After calculating two net present values based on the two interest rates, the true rate of return may be approximated by linear interpolation.

TABLE A.1

PRESENT WORTH CALCULATIONS FOR OPTION A

Year	Profit (thousands of $)	Present Worth Factor @ 20%	Present Worth @ 20%	Present Worth Factor @ 25%	Present Worth @ 25%
1	200	0.8333	166.66	0.8000	160.00
2	100	0.6944	69.44	0.6400	64.00
3	50	0.5787	28.935	0.5120	25.60
4	30	0.4823	14.469	0.4096	12.288
5	20	0.4019	8.038	0.3277	6.554
6	20	0.3349	6.698	0.2621	5.242
7	20	0.2791	5.582	0.2097	4.194
8	10	0.2326	2.326	0.1678	1.678
9	0	0.1938	0	0.1342	0
10	0	0.1615	0	0.1074	0
	TOTAL		302.148		279.556

$$i = 20\% \quad \text{yields} \quad 302.148$$
$$i = ? \quad \text{yields} \quad 300$$

$$i = 25\% \text{ yields } 279.556$$

Therefore, $\dfrac{302.148 - 300}{302.148 - 279.556} = \dfrac{i - 20\%}{25\% - 20\%}$

Solving for i,

$$i = 20\% + 0.095\ (25\% - 20\%) = 20.475\%$$

Note: $\dfrac{302.148 - 300}{302.148 - 279.556} = \dfrac{2.148}{22.592} = 0.095$

Another procedure might also help illustrate the concepts:

$$i = 20\% + P \text{ (where P equals the extrapolated amount between 20\% and 25\%)}$$

$$P = \frac{302.148 - 300}{302.148 - 279.556}\ (25\% - 20\%)$$

$$P = \frac{2.148}{22.592}\ (25\% - 20\%)$$

$$P = (.095)\ (5\%)$$
$$P = 0.475\%$$

Therefore, $\quad i = 20\% + 0.475\%$
$$i = 20.475\%$$

TABLE A.2
PRESENT WORTH CALCULATIONS FOR OPTION B

Year	Profit (thousands of $)	Present Worth Factor @ 6%	Present Worth @ 6%	Present Worth Factor @ 8%	Present Worth @ 8%
1	0	0.5584	0	0.9259	0
2	0	0.8900	0	0.8573	0
3	10	0.8396	8.396	0.7938	7.938
4	10	0.7921	7.921	0.7350	7.350
5	20	0.7473	14.946	0.6806	13.612
6	20	0.7050	14.100	0.6302	12.604
7	40	0.6651	26.604	0.5835	23.340
8	50	0.6274	31.370	0.5403	27.015
9	125	0.5919	73.988	0.5002	62.525
10	225	0.5584	125.640	0.4632	104.220
	TOTAL		302.965		258.604

$$i = 6\% \text{ yields } 302.965$$
$$i = \text{ ? } \text{ yields } 300$$
$$i = 8\% \text{ yields } 258.604$$

Therefore, $\dfrac{302.965 - 300}{302.965 - 258.604} = \dfrac{i - 6\%}{8\% - 6\%}$

Solving for i,

$$i = 6\% + 0.067 \ (8\% - 6\%) = 6.134\%$$

Note: $\dfrac{302.965 - 300}{302.965 - 258.604} = \dfrac{2.965}{44.361} = 0.067$

A second procedure to illustrate the concepts follows:

$i = 6\% + P$ (where P equals the extrapolated amount between 6% and 8%)

$$P = \frac{302.965 - 300}{302.965 - 258.604} \ (8\% - 6\%)$$

$$P = \frac{2.965}{44.361} \ (8\% - 6\%)$$

$$P = 0.067 \ (2\%)$$
$$P = .134\%$$

Therefore, $\quad i = 6\% + .134\%$
$$i = 6.134\%$$

Appendix B

The discounted cash flow technique will determine the interest rate at which a cash inflow of \$7,000 per year for ten years will be provided from the "annuity" investment of \$30,000 today.

$$P = F \frac{1}{(1 + i)^n}$$

$$30,000 = 7,000 \ \frac{1}{(1 + i)^n}$$

TABLE B.1
PRESENT WORTH CALCULATIONS

Year	Profit	Cumulative Profit	Present Worth Factor @ 19%	Present Worth @ 19%	Present Worth Factor @ 21%	Present Worth @ 21%
1	7000	7000	.8403	5882.1	.8264	5784.8
2	7000	14000	.7062	4943.4	.6830	4781.0
3	7000	21000	.5934	4153.8	.5645	3951.5
4	7000	28000	.4987	3490.9	.4665	3265.5
5	7000	35000	.4190	2933.0	.3855	2698.5
6	7000	42000	.3521	2464.7	.3186	2230.2
7	7000	49000	.2959	2071.3	.2633	1843.1
8	7000	56000	.2487	1740.9	.2176	1523.2
9	7000	63000	.2090	1463.0	.1799	1259.3
10	7000	70000	.1756	1229.2	.1486	1040.2
	70000			30372.3		28377.3

$$i = 19\% \text{ yields } 30372.3$$
$$i = \text{ ? } \text{ yields } 30000$$
$$i = 21\% \text{ yields } 28377.3$$

$$\frac{30372.3 - 30000}{30372.3 - 28377.3} = \frac{i - 19\%}{21\% - 19\%}$$

$$\frac{372.3}{1995.0} = .187$$

$$i = 19\% + .187 \, (21\% - 19\%) = 19\% + .374\% = 19.4\%$$

Chapter VI

Economic Justification: Computing the Savings

Phase II of the investment evaluation may be subdivided into two separate activities: Phase II–A, determining the direct labor savings, and Phase II–B, computing the savings derived from indirect factors. Because the analysis of direct labor savings is also required for conventional equipment, traditional investment evaluation principles are readily adaptable for computer or numerical control proposals.

DETERMINING THE DIRECT LABOR SAVINGS— PHASE II–A

A fundamental objective of Phase II–A is to determine the part floor-to-floor production time for computer or numerical controls so it may be compared to the cycle time on the competing conventional equipment. The production time advantage or disadvantage disclosed by this comparison can then be converted to annual direct savings by multiplying the machine-operator hours saved by the appropriate labor rate plus variable overhead expense items such as labor fringe benefits.

Methods for Determining the Computer or Numerical Control Machine-Time Ratio

Determining the computer or numerical control machine-time ratio, that is, the ratio of computer or numerical control part floor-to-floor production time to the conventional part floor-to-floor production time, is the most important activity of the entire investment analysis. As used in this investment analysis methodology, the expression, *computer or numerical control machine-time ratio,* is synonymous with *part floor-to-floor production time relationships.*

Machine time covers all activities, both productive and nonproductive, that are performed on the machine. Thus, the computer or numerical control machine-time ratio is a comprehensive measure of the effect of computer or numerical control on the rate of production. Since several investment conclusions are ascertained by applying this ratio, the care and effort devoted to measuring it accurately will have a direct bearing on the quality of the analysis.

Three alternatives are suggested for determining the computer or numerical control machine-time ratio. They vary widely, however, in the amount of effort that is required. Method I, which makes use of a compilation of the numerical control productivity experiences obtained in a survey of over 350 companies, is the simplest to apply. The resulting ratio is merely a general solution because this technique is useful only for a preliminary or limited pro forma analysis of a proposed investment. If the preliminary analysis shows that a satisfactory profit may be earned by the productivity improvement indicated by Method I, either Method II or III should be used for a more rigorous evelation.

Method I: Application of Average Machine
Cycle Times of Survey Companies

This method makes use of computer or numerical control machine-time ratios which have already been determined and illustrates how the direct savings can be estimated.

Average numerical control machine-time ratios for six types of numerical control equipment that were reported in one University of Michigan survey are shown in Table I. After identifying the type of computer or numerical control equipment being considered, the analyst selects a ratio from Table I which reflects the production experience of the survey companies with that type of equipment.

Numerical control justification requires knowledge and experience that, more often than not, is obtainable only after the purchase is made. All too often, a company facing its first plunge into the world of computer or numerical control has little or no guidance except for the information provided by the equipment's manufacturer. Even companies who already possess numerical control equipment have difficulty estimating savings for anything but the specific class of machines they now own.

For several years, the authors were involved in surveys at The University of Michigan to collect data from numerical control users for alleviating such problems in the justification of numerical control equipment. The survey material contained in this and the previous chapter has been largely derived from these investigations.

184

For example, if a company wanted to evaluate an investment in a five-axis numerical control milling machine, the appropriate data in Table I would show that this type of numerical control has produced parts for the survey companies in 37 percent of the time required for their conventional machines. If the equivalent of 10,000 hours of conventional machine time could be replaced by a five-axis numerical control milling machine, it is reasonable to expect that the automatic equipment could achieve approximately the same output in only 3,700 hours. The savings of 6,300 hours could be converted to direct savings in dollars by multiplying the hours saved by the appropriate machine operator labor rate and the variable portions of overhead.

TABLE I

TYPICAL NUMERICAL CONTROL MACHINE-TIME RATIOS
(COMPARISON OF NC CYCLE TIMES TO CONVENTIONAL TIMES)

Type of Equipment	NC Time as Percentage of Conventional*
Drilling	
2–axis NC system	50
3–axis NC system	52
3–axis with tool changer	57
Boring	52
Punching	65
Turning	
Between centers	46
Chucking	48
Milling	
2–axis NC system	51
3–axis NC system	55
Multioperational Machining Center With Automatic Tool Changer	
3–axis NC system with tool changer and work shuttle system	46
4–axis NC system	48
5–axis NC system	37

* Average processing times are subject to variations depending upon application characteristics.
Source: University of Michigan survey.

Method I can be quite effective for providing a speedy approximation of the expected direct savings. However, part distinctions can cause significant savings differences in particular applications. Therefore, the results of this method should be checked by either Method II or III before making a final investment decision.

Method II: Comparative Time Studies

The most commonly used method for determining the computer or numerical control machine-time ratio—or ascertaining the effect of computer or numerical control on productivity—consists of collecting comparable cycle times on a sample of typical workpieces. Five to twenty typical workpieces should be selected, each of which belongs to a separate family of parts expected to be produced by the new equipment. Time studies are then made of these sample parts as they are produced; first, on the present conventional equipment; then, on the proposed computer or numerical control machine. The ratio of the total computer or numerical control cycle time to total conventional cycle time for the sample workpieces may be used to estimate the machine-time ratio for all generally similar work to be performed on the proposed machine.

There are two obstacles which limit the effectiveness of Method II. Firms which have neither the services of a part programmer nor access to the proposed computer or numerical control machine will obviously have difficulty determining the computer or numerical control cycle times for the sample workpieces. Some computer or numerical control equipment manufacturers are minimizing the difficulty by furnishing prospective buyers with computerized machine-time studies and tooling cost estimates on a representative sample of parts. Some also furnish programming services and allow access to their equipment to determine computer or numerical control cycle times for the customer's sample parts. Many independent contract jobs with computer or numerical controls also will produce the sample parts so that time comparisons can be made.

Method III: Machine Activity Sampling Technique

Another technique, which is based on adaptations of work sampling procedures, may be used to determine the machine-time ratio if Method II is impractical. This technique, identified as Method III, determines the machine activities which affect the machine-time ratio and then evaluates their relative importance so that their impact can be accurately time studied. It essentially consists of two parts:

1. The technique of work sampling is used to determine the proportion of time a machine is occupied in each of its operational activities.

2. These proportions are weighted by the pertinent time advantage fractions (numerical control time compared to conventional machining time) to obtain the weighted comprehensive computer or numerical control machine-time ratio.

The resulting ratio can then be used for estimating the annual direct labor savings. This ratio will be low for those parts for which the majority of processing time is spent on activities especially suited for computer or numerical controls. Obviously, the machine-time ratio will be less favorable for parts dominated by activities that computer or numerical controls do not handle rapidly.

Intermittent, randomly spaced observations are used to obtain accurate estimates of the proportion of the overall production time devoted to each type of machine operational activity. A person responsible for the work sampling enters the shop and records a random sampling of the observed machine activities. At the end of the study, the number of times each machine activity was observed is tabulated, and a relative percentage for each activity is computed. If the study has been conducted carefully, these percentages should closely resemble the actual distribution of time spent on the various machine operations. Obviously, caution must be exercised to assure that the parts produced during the sampling activities are generally similar to the parts planned for the proposed computer or numerical control equipment.

Steps to Obtain the Ratio

When Method III is used, there are four steps necessary to obtain the computer or numerical control machine-time ratio:

Step 1. Defining Machine Operational Activities

All the operational activities which have an impact on the machine-time ratio must be determined and defined. Among the operational activities commonly encountered are the following:

Setup consists of preparing the machine for the next batch of parts. This activity begins when the machine becomes idle and the operator starts gathering material, supplies, tools, and other equipment for a job, and it ends when the cutting tool enters the first workpiece of the lot.

Load-unload consists of securing and releasing each piece in a batch to and from the worktable. This activity begins when the fixture is loosened to remove a machined piece and ends when the cutting tool enters the next piece in a batch. The act of loading the first piece in a batch is included in the setup activity.

Positioning consists of moving the cutting tool to the next machining location. The beginning and end points of this activity are, respectively, the termination of tool contact with a workpiece and initiation of contact with a new one.

Cutting consists of removing metal from the workpiece. This activity includes the period during which the tool is in contact with the workpiece.

Tool change consists of the changing of cutting tools in the spindle. This activity begins when the last cut of a tool is terminated and ends when the first cut of the next tool is initiated. The tool change activity may occur simultaneously with the positioning operation.

Planning occurs while a workpiece is on the machine but none of the above activities is being performed. During this time the operator reviews his instructions and plans his next activity.

Downtime consists of all time not covered by the above six elements. It includes the time during which the machine is idle.

This list may need to be revised to reflect the special features of the proposed equipment or unique manufacturing conditions at a specific plant.

Step 2. Designing a Plan for Observing the Activities

Before conducting the work sampling study, such factors as the length of the study, the number and scheduling of observations, the route through the shop area for the observer to follow, etc. must be determined. Too detailed a study requires unnecessary expenditures of effort and money; however, sufficient attention should be given to details to insure accurate results. The length of time during which the machine operational activities are studied may vary, but a one-week period is usually satisfactory. It should be long enough to eliminate errors due to daily variations in work schedules, but short enough to avoid unreasonable expense.

Step 3. Implementation of the Sampling Plan

Step 3 consists of collecting and tabulating the data planned in Step 2. After the observations specified in Step 2 have been made, the total number of observations for each operational activity should be calculated. The percentage of time that each activity occurs during the entire study can then be computed as follows:

$$\% \text{ Time} = \frac{\text{Number of Times Activity was Observed}}{\text{Total Number of Observations}}$$

Step 4. Computation of the Numerical Control Machine-Time Ratio

When a frequency distribution of the machine operational activities has been calculated in Step 3, the relative time advantage or disadvantage from using computer or numerical control for each activity can be found by determining the time spent for each operational activity by computer or numerical controls compared to the time spent by conventional machines. These comparative times therefore determine the relative time advantages or disadvantages. In the absence of actual data, the data in Table II, developed during a survey conducted by The University of Michigan, might be used for this purpose.

TABLE II

TYPICAL MACHINE ACTIVITY TIME ADVANTAGE PERCENTAGES

Machine Activity	Numerical Control Time as a % of Conventional Time
Load-Unload	95
Positioning	75
Cutting	90
Tool Change	
Single toolholders	95
Turret toolholders	6
Automatic tool changer	3
Planning	5
Downtime	65

Source: University of Michigan survey.

Table II gives a quick approximation of the time advantage percentages for different types of machine activities.

However, for results more attuned to unique applications, each firm should develop its own time comparisons by following the guidelines outlined in Method II.

A weighted numerical control percentage for each activity may then be calculated by multiplying the activity frequency percentage by the computer or numerical control time advantage percentage. Finally, the overall numerical control machine-time ratio is found by adding the weighted values for all operational activities.

As an example of Step 4, assume that a work sampling study was conducted on three machine operations—setup, cutting, and positioning. The machine operations were observed 50 times during the study period (10 observations for setup and 20 observations each for cutting and positioning). Therefore, the frequency observation percentages are setup —20 percent, cutting—40 percent, and positioning—40 percent. The cycle times, for computer or numerical control machines as a percent of conventional time obtained from Table II are cutting—90 percent and positioning—75 percent. (The setup percentage is assumed to be 30 percent.) By multiplying the frequency observation percentage by the computer or numerical control time advantage percentage for each of the three operational activities, and adding the resulting weighted values, the computer or numerical control machine-time ratio is 72 percent. This procedure is demonstrated below:

Activity	Frequency Observation		Computer or NC Cycle Relative Time Percentage		Weighted Value
Setup	20%	×	30%	=	6%
Cutting	40	×	90	=	36
Positioning	40	×	75	=	30
Computer or Numerical Control Machine-Time Ratio					72%

Results of Applying the Ratio

Whichever method for determining the machine-time ratio is used, the direct labor savings can be determined by subtracting (from the total conventional machine hours capable of being replaced) the product obtained by multiplying the total conventional hours by the numerical control machine-time ratio. This result should then be multiplied by the hourly direct labor cost and the variable portion of overhead expenses to determine the amount of the direct savings.

For example, if the total hours of the conventional machines equivalent to computer or numerical control's capacity were 10,000 hours, then the labor effort necessary to maintain the same production on a computer or numerical control machine having the machine-time ratio of .72 should be:

$$10,000 \times 72\% = 7,200 \text{ hours.}$$

This productivity improvement would create a direct annual savings of 2,800 hours. At the combined labor and variable overhead rate of $5.00 per hour the net savings would be $14,000 per year.

Since the investment evaluation should project the impact of the proposed acquisition over several future years, normally the projected economic life, the effects of increasing labor costs also should be reflected. If labor costs are expected to average an annual increase of 4 percent per year, a $10,000 labor savings projected for the first year grows to $11,700 in the fifth year; it will be $14,200 by the tenth year.

COMPUTING THE INDIRECT SAVINGS—PHASE II–B

In addition to the direct savings, several types of indirect economies may result. Among these are handling of work-in-process, maintenance, tooling, inspection, assembly, scrap, and programming savings—the latter sometimes is a negative savings or increased expense. Certain applications produce many other indirect economies, which will be defined and quantified as they are reached in this description of Phase II–B.

The lack of accurate cost data to serve as a base for estimating the economies has made the quantification of indirect savings for computer and numerical control equipment particularly difficult for new users. Historical cost information obviously should be used when it is available; however, uninitiated companies are virtually forced to rely on the experiences of other companies or data developed from industry-wide surveys if their estimates of indirect savings are to be more than guesswork. While the use of survey information may be questioned by traditional accountants, this method nevertheless

191

is preferred where real savings—even though of indefinite value—otherwise would be ignored in the investment evelation simply because in-house quantified experience does not exist.

Annual Programming Savings

Because part programming seldom is required for traditional equipment, this indirect expense nearly always must be estimated initially from the experience of others. If the processing of a part has been planned and the tooling designed, programming expenses normally consist of labor costs of the part programmer and the expenses for tape preparation and computer support.

Even though programming is not required for conventional manufacture, part programming for computer and numerical control equipment does not always increase overall costs. In estimating the cost impact, a comparison must be made between the expenses incurred for processing comparable parts across conventional machines and the costs of process planning and programming for computer or numerical control. Routing parts, composing job setup instruction cards, making operational drawings, setting incentive standards, and resolving incentive disputes are examples of the process planning functions. When all programming and processing costs were compared for conventional and numerical control operations, 190 of 356 participating companies in one University of Michigan survey found that the total process planning costs for numerical control—including part programming—were the same as or less than comparable costs for conventional equipment. Of the 190 companies, 86 said their numerical control costs were the same, and 104 said these costs actually were less. When numerical control favorably affected overall costs, it often resulted from reductions in process planning and tool designing made possible by operations being consolidated and fewer intermachine part transfers.

Since labor is the major programming cost, the size of the required staff should be determined as a first step in appraising the annual expense. A first approximation of the labor needs may be estimated by obtaining the experience of other companies or by referring to the University of Michigan survey data. Although investment decisions based on relationships between an "average" part and "typical" expenses may seem especially controversial for programming, referring to such data nevertheless has improved the quality of these decisions when the gross averages are adjusted for variable factors such as the part complexity, the batch size, the frequency of rerunning a batch and its tape, the use of computer-aided programming, etc.

Stripped of the many factors that indeed do affect the programming staff size, the bare statistics from the survey show that .73 of a programmer was utilized for each point-to-point machine, and almost one programmer (.94) for each continuous-path machine. These gross averages can be interpreted to some extent by reviewing the prevailing conditions affecting the two averages. The "average" point-to-point programmer programmed 269 parts per year, which was sufficient to keep 1.37 point-to-point machines supplied with tapes. Operating an average of 107 hours per week, these machines typically processed parts in batches of 65 units. A tape for a typical batch was reused an average of 6.3 times per year. The "average" programmer devoted 34.6 percent of his work period to tool designing, process planning, or other nonprogramming functions. Half of the survey parts were programmed through computer-aided techniques, and the general complexity of the part is suggested by the average tape length of 30 feet.

An "average" continous-path programmer in the survey programmed 113 parts per year, which was sufficient to provide tapes for 1.06 continuous-path machines operating an average of 97 hours per week. Parts were produced in average batch sizes of 52 units, and the batches were typically repeated 6.1 times per year. The "average" continuous-path programmer spent 31.2 percent of his time on nonprogramming functions such as tool designing or process planning. The complexity of these programmed parts is suggested by the tape length of 143 feet.[1] Computers were utilized to program 82 percent of the continuous-path parts.

Depending upon the desired accuracy of the cost estimate, the decision maker's needs may be satisfied by using one of the two gross programming averages or he may want to modify these ratios of programmers per machine to reflect his particular situation. Key questions to be answered are: Which factors will affect his program-

---

[1] Because there was a sufficiently large number of continuous-path machines included in the survey, no attempt was made to differentiate between tapes for controls with linear or circular interpolation. The increased tape length resulting from the use of controls with linear rather than circular interpolation was thought to have an inconsequential effect on the complexity averages for the full survey population where both types of controls were adequately represented.

ming? What will be the extent of the impact? In summary, costs for part programming mainly are affected by these factors:

1. Part shape and complexity of the operation;
2. Method of manufacture;
3. Capability and sophistication of the machine and control;
4. Division of functions between programming and process planning personnel;
5. Batch size and the frequency that each batch is repeated;
6. Number of hours per week that the proposed machine will be operated;
7. Extent to which computer support is available to the programmer; and
8. Number of machines to be procured.

Investigations conducted at the Technical University in Aachen, Germany, suggest that for many applications the part's shape and the associated complexity of the machining operations exert a major influence on programming costs. This inference is reinforced by the University of Michigan survey, wherein the ratio of programmers per point-to-point machine (.73) was considerably less than the ratio (.94) required to program tapes for relatively complex continuous-path parts. Figure 1 displays relative programming costs in the German study for parts manufactured by drilling, by boring and milling, and by turning. Their programming activities included writing the program, cataloging standardized tools, preparing the manuscript, tape punching, and testing the tape on the machine.

The Aachen study examined 42 point-to-point parts that were machined by the relatively simple drilling operation. Programming costs of more than 50 percent of these parts were less than $25 each; the highest amounted to $275. It can be seen that programming for boring and for continuous-path milling was considerably more expensive—primarily because of greater precision demands and the increased volume of tool path computations.

Programming costs for the simpler turned parts which could be machined by straight-line operations exceeded those of the drilled parts, but were far lower than those for parts involving boring and milling. Problems of manufacture by turning simple rotational parts could be solved more easily than milling operations since the tool path was relatively simple to calculate. The technology of turning

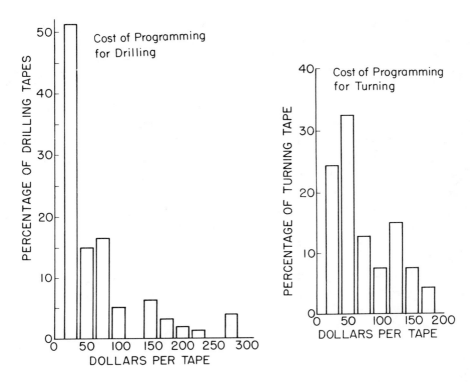

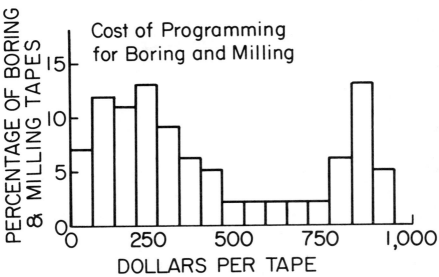

FIGURE 1
Comparative programming costs.

also is relatively well developed since the machinability data more often can be obtained from conventional manufacturing handbooks.

It is fairly obvious that the batch size and the frequency of re-running each batch and its tape affect the level of programmers necessary to supply tapes for a machine. High-volume applications, such as drilling printed circuit boards, permit a relatively low level of programmer support because one tape, which may direct a drilling machine for several hours or shifts, might be reused several times. By contrast, several days or weeks often are required to program a tape for a one-of-a-kind tool or die that may be completely machined in a single shift. Moreover, a tape for the machining of tooling in single units is seldom reused. Upon completion of the tool or die machining operation, another new tape is required to keep the machine productive. The level of programmers for single units or small batches with little chance of tape reuse is therefore relatively great. The influence of the batch size and the frequency of rerunning a batch is illustrated in Figures 2 through 5 for the companies in the University of Michigan survey.

The ratio of part programmers required to support a computer or numerical control machine also varies inversely with the number

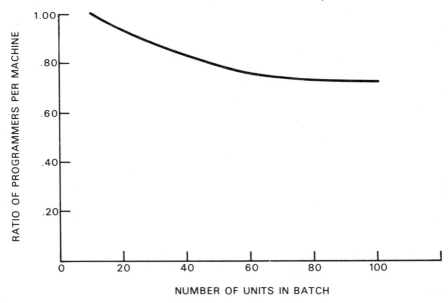

NUMBER OF UNITS IN BATCH

FIGURE 2

Relationship between size of programming staff and batch size: continuous-path equipment.

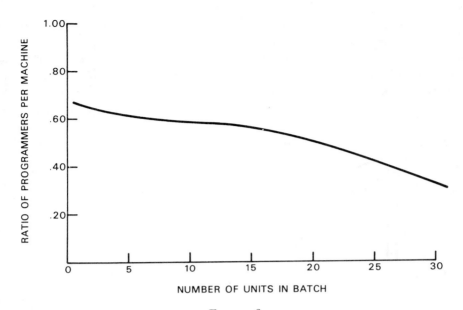

FIGURE 3

Relationship between size of programming staff and batch size:
point-to-point equipment.

of machines. From Figures 6 and 7, it can be seen that a typical survey company with a single point-to-point machine used slightly more than 1.0 programmer per machine; similarly a company with one continuous-path machine had a comparable rate. These programmer levels contrast sharply with the rate of programmers per machine for companies having 20 machines of the same type. The specialization of labor possible with a large complement of programmers and machines and the more extensive utilization of efficient computer-aided part-programming techniques primarily account for the greater programmer productivity.

Another factor affecting the ratio of programmers per machine is the amount of time part programmers spend on tool designing and process planning. As can be seen from Figures 8 and 9, the ratio of programmers per machine increases with the proportion of time devoted to such activities. In the 1970 survey, 34.6 percent of the "average" point-to-point programmer's time and 31.2 percent of the continuous-path programmer's time was devoted to tool designing and process planning. The latter two functions actually are not additional expense activities arising from the introduction of com-

197

puter or numerical control equipment. Since these activities also must be performed for conventional manufacture, approximately one-third of the average survey programmer's effort in reality was not a cost increase. As an example, because 31 percent of the work period of an average continuous-path programmer (.94 per machine) is devoted to tool designing or process planning, in reality only .65 (.94 − [31% × .94] = .65) of a full-time part programmer was required for each continuous-path machine.

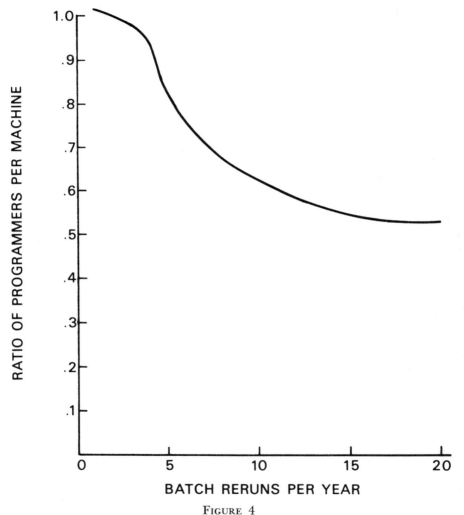

FIGURE 4
Relationship between size of programming staff and batch reruns/year: continuous-path equipment.

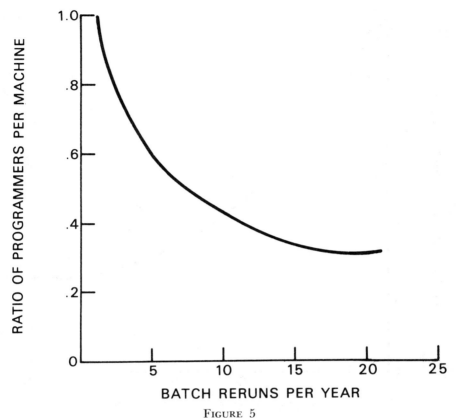

FIGURE 5

Relationship between size of programming staff and batch reruns/year: point-to-point equipment.

When a computer is to be used to assist the part programmer, computer use charges also must be estimated. These costs are affected by several factors, e.g., the computer type (whether it is a batch or remote access system), the programming language, and the influence of the part complexity on the number of calculations and other computer operations. Where a highly accurate cost estimate is demanded, sample programs should be computer-processed so that actual costs can be determined. If time does not permit or the expense of computer processing for cost estimation purposes is not justified, computer expenses may be estimated on the basis of tape length as reported by the survey companies. Tape length was assumed to be an approximate indicator of part complexity and is therefore roughly related to the volume of mathematical operations required. The

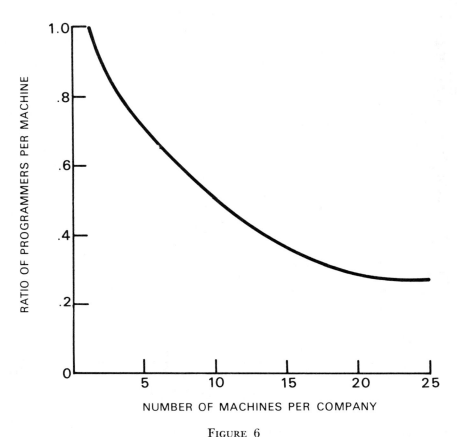

FIGURE 6
Relationship between size of programming staff and number of machines: continuous-path equipment.

average computer cost for a "typical" continuous-path tape was $69 compared to $31 for a point-to-point tape. Because many simple point-to-point tapes are programmed manually, this average computer cost may be somewhat inflated. The effect of part complexity and tape length on computer costs is shown in Figures 10 and 11 where it is apparent that computer costs for point-to-point tapes greater than about 50 feet and for continuous-path tapes longer than 200 feet exceeded the average survey costs.

Finally, programming staff requirements are significantly affected by the number of hours the proposed equipment will be operated. Obviously, around-the-clock machine operation requires more programmed tapes than single-shift operation.

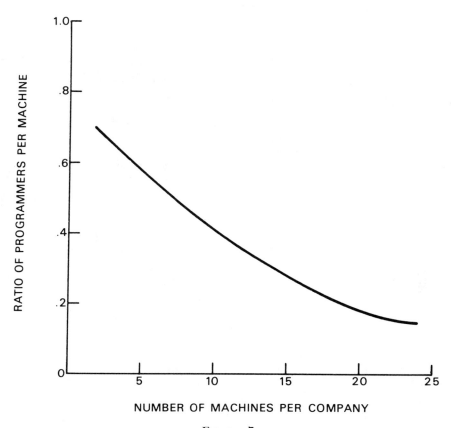

FIGURE 7

Relationship between size of programming staff and number of machines:
point-to-point equipment.

By considering the impact of the characteristics of his own application—part complexity, batch size, hours of operation, etc.—the investment decision maker can ascertain if the survey's average ratios of programmers per machine seem reasonable for his company. If not, the average ratios may simply be adjusted upward or downward, depending upon how the specific application characteristics measure up to the survey norms. Additionally, if a final check is desired, it might be worthwhile to utilize the quantitative procedure demonstrated below that was developed in an earlier University of Michigan justification survey. The size of the programming staff for a new user of numerical control machines can be estimated by the following procedure:

$$Y = 1.05x_1 - .009x_2 - .493$$

where

Y = Number of programmers (may be fractional, which would indicate that only a portion of a worker's time is spent on programming),

x_1 = Number of numerical control machines being considered, and

x_2 = Total dollar cost of the proposed numerical control machines in thousands of dollars.

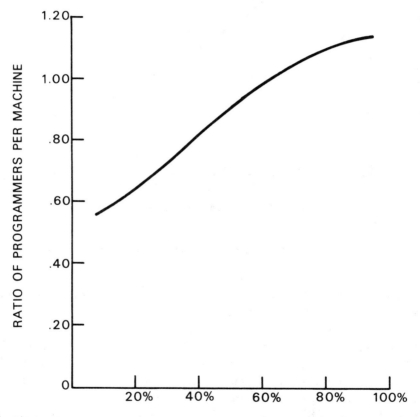

PROGRAMMER EFFORT ON TOOL DESIGN OR PROCESS PLANNING

FIGURE 8

Relationship between size of programming staff and tool design or process planning effort: continuous-path equipment.

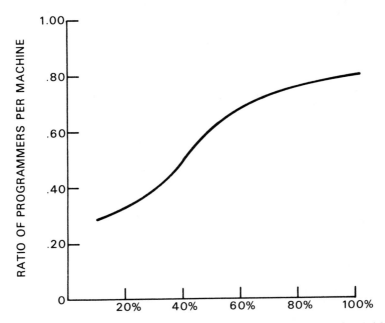

PROGRAMMER EFFORT ON TOOL DESIGN OR PROCESS PLANNING

FIGURE 9

Relationship between size of programming staff and tool design or process planning effort: point-to-point equipment.

A brief example illustrates the use of this procedure:

Assume:

$$x_1 = 3 \text{ machines, and}$$

$$x_2 = \$100 \text{ (i.e., the 3 machines cost } \$100,000);$$

then

$$Y = (1.05) \times (3) - (.009) \times (100) - (.493)$$

$$Y = 1.757 \text{ programmers.}$$

Since 1.7 programmers should be able to program the three machines, only 50 percent of a full-time programmer is needed for a single machine. If the prevailing pay rate for a programmer were $10,000 per year, the labor cost for programming one machine would be:

$$\frac{1}{3} \times 1.757 \times \$10,000 = \$5,857$$

203

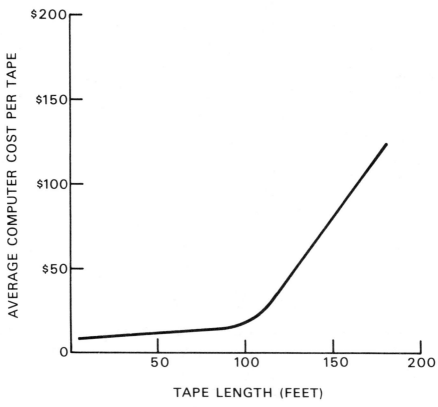

FIGURE 10
Relationship between computer costs and tape length:
point-to-point equipment.

When these guidelines are modified by the specific circumstances
of a given application, the investment decision maker should be in
a good position to estimate part-programming costs.

Annual Maintenance Savings

The electronic challenges of computer and numerical control
maintenance make maintenance expenses the second most difficult
indirect savings factor to estimate. Companies in a University of
Michigan justification survey reported that numerical control maintenance costs were about four times as great as those encountered
with equivalent conventional equipment. Thus, unless the early
numerical control machines were more than four times as productive,
maintenance expenses per unit of output in the survey firms in-

creased. Higher maintenance costs resulted mainly from the difficulty in isolating the fault and, to a less extent, from the time required for repair. Of the time the numerical control equipment was down in the survey companies, 73 percent was consumed searching for the cause and only 27 percent fixing it. This troubleshoot/repair time relationship was virtually the converse of the survey companies' maintenance experience with conventional equipment.

From data in a later survey, it is evident that better maintenance efforts and technological advancements have enhanced reliability. Of the 356 companies responding, 34 actually reported that it cost less to maintain numerical control than their conventional machines. Overall, the second survey companies generally reported that numerical control maintenance costs still exceeded conventional equipment

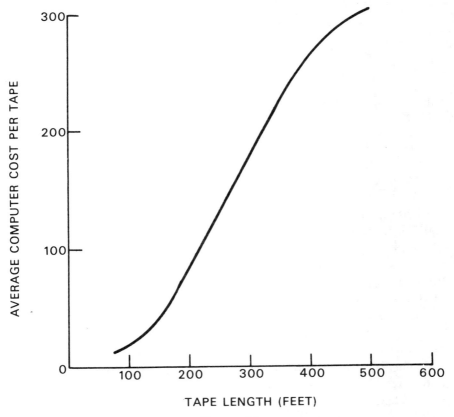

FIGURE 11

Relationship between computer costs and tape length: continuous-path equipment.

expenses in absolute terms; of greater importance, however, was the finding that the mean increase for all types of numerical control was only about 55 percent—some 345 percentage points below the 400 percent reported earlier. Over half of the second survey companies stated that the increase in numerical control maintenance costs was under 30 percent.

Equipment complexity has a significant impact on conventional-numerical control maintenance cost differentials. The greatest average cost increase among the survey companies was for machining centers, with a mean of 63 percent, followed in descending order by turning, punching, boring, drilling, and milling equipment (see Table III).

TABLE III

NUMERICAL CONTROL MAINTENANCE COST INCREASES
BY EQUIPMENT TYPE

Equipment Type	Average Percentage Increase Over Conventional Equipment
Milling	48
Drilling	50
Boring	56
Punching	59
Turning	61
Machining Centers	63

Although absolute costs for maintaining computer or numerical control equipment are likely to exceed conventional expenses, relative equipment productivities must be considered to ascertain the net impact on profits. To weigh absolute maintenance costs against productivity, it is necessary first to determine the annual cost for maintaining a comparable conventional machine.

For ease of discussion, conventional maintenance costs may be designated by "M." Next, the equivalent number of conventional machines that may be replaced by the computer or numerical control machine under consideration should be ascertained and designated by "N." If the new machine is being purchased for expansion rather than for replacement of existing machines, it is reasonable to let "N" equal the number of conventional machines that would be purchased to attain the same computer or numerical control capacity. In such a case, "N" is the reciprocal of the machine-time ratio calculated in Phase II–A. An estimate of the net Annual Maintenance Savings (AMS), or additional expense, may then be calculated from this equation:

$$AMS = [M \times N] - [(1 + NCMD) \times M]$$

where

$N =$ Number of conventional machines equivalent to computer or numerical control's capacity,

$NCMD =$ Factor representing Numerical Control Maintenance cost Differential, and

$M =$ Annual Maintenance cost of conventional machine.

An example will demonstrate the operation of the maintenance savings estimating procedure. If the machine-time ratio is .33 (i.e., $N = 1/.33$, or 3), the average annual maintenance cost (M) is \$600, and the absolute cost of maintaining the computer or numerical control equipment is 40 percent greater than that required for the conventional machinery, then:

$$AMS = [(\$600) \times (3)] - [(1 + .40) \times (\$600)]$$

$$AMS = \$1800 - \$840$$

$$AMS = \$960.$$

Therefore, for this example, the adjusted estimate of the net annual maintenance savings for computer or numerical control's greater productivity is \$960.

When the conventional-Numerical Control Maintenance cost Differential (NCMD) is not ascertainable from company records or such experience is lacking, appropriate survey information might be used. The conventional-numerical control maintenance cost differentials reported by survey companies shown in Table IV permit the selection of a NCMD estimate consistent with equipment type and product orientation.

Perishable Tooling Savings

The average numerical control impact on perishable tooling costs (cutting tool costs) of 327 survey companies amounted to an absolute increase of 11 percent. However, the greatest number of companies

TABLE IV

NUMERICAL CONTROL MAINTENANCE COST INCREASES BY INDUSTRY AND EQUIPMENT TYPE

Industry Classification	Percent Increase Over Conventional Equipment					
	Drilling	Boring	Turning	Punching	Milling	Mach. Center
Primary Metal Industry	26	n.a.	11	5	15	17
Fabricated Metal Products	43	22	144	46	5	351
Engines & Turbines; Farm Machinery & Equipment	9	-28	12	59	-27	-45
Construction, Mining & Material Handling Machinery & Equipment	30	35	29	177	49	74
Machine Tools, Metal Cutting Types	28	33	40	n.a.	50	47
Metalworking Machinery, Except Machine Tools; & Power Driven Hand Tools	74	167	137	17	200	117
Machinery, Except Electrical	55	60	39	74	61	67
Special Industry Machinery, Except Metalworking Machinery	70	157	62	n.a.	94	145
General Industrial Machinery & Equipment	42	27	22	31	50	121
Service Industry Machines	91	3	10	101	n.a.	25
Miscellaneous Machinery, Except Electrical	110	21	13	10	51	21
Electrical Machinery, Equipment & Supplies	55	76	124	78	24	28
Electronic Components & Accessories	73	150	46	170	47	48
Transportation	51	62	83	32	48	62
Aircraft Parts & Auxiliary Equipment	64	89	73	39	48	72
Professional, Scientific & Controlling Equipment	31	72	22	35	12	51

n.a.: Not available.

(140) experienced no difference, and the experience of the remaining 203 companies ranged from a 90 percent cost reduction to a 500 percent increase. About a third of all reporting companies experienced greater expenses, and a decrease was indicated by about one reporting company in four. A detailed range of the replies is shown in Table V.

TABLE V

COMPARISON OF PERISHABLE TOOLING COSTS FOR
NUMERICAL CONTROL AND CONVENTIONAL MACHINES

Numerical Control Cost Impact	Number of Companies	Percent
50 – 90% Reduction	13	4.0
1 – 49% Reduction	62	19.0
No Change	136	41.6
0 – 49% Increase	79	24.2
50 – 99% Increase	31	9.5
100% and Over Increase	6	1.8

Computer or numerical control perishable tooling costs are strongly affected by the equipment type and by the nature of the manufactured product. When the absence of experience or inadequate company records do not permit the determination of actual perishable tooling cost differentials, an appropriate value might be selected from Table VI and used for the investment evaluation.

A suggested procedure for estimating the Annual Perishable Tooling Savings (APTS) is:

$$APTS = T \times PTSF$$

where

T = Annual perishable Tooling costs for the number of conventional machines equivalent to computer or numerical control's capacity, and

$PTSF$ = Computer or numerical control Perishable Tooling Savings Factor (either positive or negative) as determined from company experience or Tables V and VI.

Tool presetting practices should also be considered during the investment evaluation. If tools are to be preset, capital required for

209

TABLE VI

COMPARISON OF PERISHABLE TOOLING COSTS FOR NUMERICAL CONTROL
AND CONVENTIONAL MACHINE COSTS BY INDUSTRY CLASSIFICATION

Industry Classification	Percentage Decrease (−) or Increase (+)
Primary Metal Industry	−5
Fabricated Metal Products	+7
Engines & Turbines; Farm Machinery & Equipment	+38
Construction, Mining & Material Handling Machinery & Equipment	−7
Machine Tools, Metal Cutting Types	+4
Metalworking Machinery, Except Machine Tools; & Power Driven Hand Tools	+49
Machinery, Except Electrical	+12
Special Industry Machinery, Except Metalworking Machinery	+9
General Industrial Machinery & Equipment	+4
Service Industry Machines	+43
Miscellaneous Machinery, Except Electrical	−3
Electrical Machinery, Equipment & Supplies	+7
Electronic Components & Accessories	+11
Transportation	+18
Aircraft Parts & Auxiliary Equipment	+16
Professional, Scientific & Controlling Instruments	+9
All Companies	+9

the presetting instruments and toolholders should be included as part of the investment cost in Phase I. These costs are then amortized through yearly depreciation charges.

Actual tool presetting costs are not, however, included in this phase (II–B) of the evaluation study. Whether or not tools are preset is an operational analysis question rather than an investment decision. Indeed, if tool presetting does not produce cost or technical advantages, then tools should not be preset.

As a general rule, the more expensive the machine tool, the greater is the likelihood that presetting tools will produce a cost savings. Often the improved machine utilization accruing from having preset tools ready to install for uninterrupted machine operation will alone more than offset the attendant expense. In many instances the machine operator presets his own tools during normal machine operation, thereby avoiding any additional labor cost whatsoever.

The wisdom of having tools preset and ready for machine installation is demonstrated by the fact that 69 percent of the 356 reporting survey companies did preset tools. Companies having expensive and sophisticated equipment tended to use preset tools more often. The relative use of preset tools for numerical control according to equipment complexity, and thus indirectly according to equipment cost, is summarized in Table VII.

TABLE VII

USE OF PRESET TOOLING FOR NUMERICAL CONTROL BY
EQUIPMENT CHARACTERISTICS

Equipment Characteristics	Number of Companies	Percentage Using Preset Tooling
Companies with only point-to-point machines	141	46
Companies with only contouring machines	25	82

Companies having relatively more numerical control machines also demonstrated a strong propensity to preset tools. Of the 248 survey companies having less than ten numerical control machines, 63 percent preset tools in contrast to 88 percent of the 91 companies that had more than nine machines.

Annual Scrap Savings

Where scrap is caused by conventional equipment deficiencies or operator errors, computer or numerical controls likely will reduce part rejections. This greater accuracy not only reduces scrap but it also lessens the labor for subsequent part inspection and assembly.

In one University of Michigan survey, three-quarters of the survey companies indicated that their numerical control equipment did indeed produce demonstrable scrap reductions. These numerical control users were asked to estimate the percentage of parts passing inspection before and after numerical control's introduction. The average rejection rate of parts produced by conventional machines was 3.5 percent compared to 1.9 percent after these companies switched to numerical control. The greater accuracy produced a net savings of 1.6 percentage points; that is to say, part rejections dropped by about 50 percent.

Scrap reductions reported by companies in a later survey were of about the same magnitude. The reported scrap savings, summarized in Table VIII, ranged from 31 percent for drilling and turning machines to 44 percent for machining centers.

Table VIII

NUMERICAL CONTROL SCRAP SAVINGS BY EQUIPMENT TYPE

Equipment Type	Percent of Scrap Decrease
Drilling	31
Boring	33
Punching	33
Turning	34
Milling	36
Machining Centers	44

In estimating computer or numerical control's scrap savings, actual company scrap reduction rates should be used where possible. If such information is not readily available, appropriate survey experiences should be helpful. Because scrap reductions are influenced by equipment complexity and the type of parts produced, a scrap reduction factor compatible with each application should be selected from Table IX.

Computing the value of the scrap reduction requires an appraisal of the total cost of one year's computer or numerical control output. This cost may be approximated by adding yearly wages for the equipment operator plus overhead (including equipment operational costs) to an estimate of the yearly computer or numerical control material and previous part-processing costs. Next, an appropriate salvage factor, the value of a rejected part that is recoverable, is considered. If rejected parts are thrown away, the salvage factor is obviously zero. An estimate of the Annual Savings In Scrap loss (ASIS) can then be determined as follows:

$$\text{ASIS} = (\text{Cost of one year's computer or NC output} \times \text{SSF}) \times (1 - \text{salvage factor})$$

where

$\text{SSF} = $ Scrap Savings Factor determined from company experience or Tables VIII and IX.

Annual Inspection Savings

Once the "bugs" have been removed from a new computer or numerical control machine, 100 percent inspection of the output is seldom employed beyond the first acceptable unit of each batch.

TABLE IX

NUMERICAL CONTROL SCRAP COST SAVINGS BY INDUSTRY AND EQUIPMENT TYPE

Industry Classification	Percent Decrease Over Conventional Equipment					
	Drilling	Boring	Turning	Punching	Milling	Mach. Center
Primary Metal Industry	42	n.a.	28	80	42	25
Fabricated Metal Products	27	20	16	31	10	27
Engines & Turbines; Farm Machinery & Equipment	20	66	23	25	35	40
Construction, Mining & Material Handling Machinery & Equipment	26	36	36	19	36	30
Machine Tools, Metal Cutting Types	32	30	50	85	34	46
Metalworking Machinery, Except Machine Tools; & Power Driven Hand Tools	30	42	18	75	26	29
Machinery, Except Electrical	30	34	33	33	37	41
Special Industry Machinery, Except Metalworking Machinery	41	44	35	45	52	71
General Industrial Machinery & Equipment	26	29	40	25	17	29
Service Industry Machines	29	n.a.	n.a.	33	60	43
Miscellaneous Machinery, Except Electrical	43	41	18	18	26	56
Electrical Machinery, Equipment & Supplies	38	48	56	39	45	65
Electronic Components & Accessories	40	38	74	44	50	127
Transportation	32	27	33	29	36	46
Aircraft Parts & Auxiliary Equipment	37	36	43	29	40	52
Professional, Scientific & Controlling Equipment	32	40	45	28	31	34

n.a.: Not available.

Inspection costs therefore vary with the volume of batches. Of the numerical control users in an early survey, half terminated detailed inspection after the first acceptable part. Both computer and numerical control inspection savings, like so many other indirect factors, are strongly influenced by equipment complexity. Table X shows that the average inspection reduction for relatively complex machining centers was 44 percent among the companies in a later survey compared to 32 to 38 percent for less sophisticated equipment.

TABLE X

ANNUAL INSPECTION COST SAVINGS RESULTING FROM THE VARIOUS
TYPES OF NUMERICAL CONTROL EQUIPMENT

Equipment Type	Numerical Control Inspection Reductions
Turning	32%
Boring	33
Drilling	37
Milling	38
Punching	43
Machining Centers	44

In assessing the quantitative effect of computer or numerical controls upon inspection, annual costs associated with checking the output of comparable conventional equipment must be determined. If inspection is performed by a separate department, such as a quality control group, that department's annual cost for examining the conventional output can usually be determined from existing departmental quality control or labor records. The annual cost of inspecting the conventional output that is equivalent to computer or numerical control's capacity can be calculated by multiplying the average inspection expenses for a comparable conventional machine by the reciprocal of the machine-time ratio determined in Phase II–A.

If finished parts are checked by the machine operator, the annual conventional machining inspection cost can be estimated by multiplying the operator's annual wages and overhead by the percentage of his time devoted to inspection. Sampling techniques, such as those described in Phase II–A, can be used to determine the percentage of time the conventional machine operator spends on inspection. Ob-

214

viously, inspection effort expended by the operator without idling the conventional machine would not allow for computer or numerical control savings beyond those possibly accruing from a less thorough inspection procedure.

The final step is to determine the portion of the annual conventional inspection cost that may be eliminated by computer or numerical controls. At issue here is how much inspection is necessary for the output of a computer or numerical control machine compared to that required for conventional equipment. Subtracting the computer or numerical control inspection costs from the annual conventional inspection costs provides an estimate of the annual inspection savings.

An optional procedure may be useful for applications where computer or numerical control inspection costs are difficult to determine. A practical guideline developed from company experience in one University of Michigan survey indicates that numerical control inspection costs are reduced by approximately 32 to 44 percent. A specific amount appropriate for a given application can be selected from Tables X and XI. Survey inspection reduction factors, classified by equipment type and product orientation are presented in the latter table.

The optional procedure for estimating the Annual Inspection Savings (AIS) follows:

$$AIS = ICM \times \frac{1}{\text{Machine-Time Ratio}} \times (IRF)$$

where

$$ICM = \text{Inspection Costs for a comparable conventional Machine, and}$$

$$IRF = \text{Inspection Reduction Factor from using computer or numerical controls.}$$

For example, if the annual inspection costs for a competing conventional machine were \$1,000, the machine-time ratio were .50, and the appropriate annual Inspection Reduction Factor as determined from company experience or from Tables X or XI were .40, then the Annual Inspection Savings could be calculated as follows:

$$AIS = \$1,000 \times \frac{1}{.50} \times .40$$

215

Table XI

Numerical Control Inspection Cost Savings by Industry and Equipment Type

Industry Classifcation	Percent Decrease Over Conventional Equipment					
	Drilling	Boring	Turning	Punching	Milling	Mach. Center
Primary Metal Industry	38	n.a.	34	75	43	80
Fabricated Metal Products	32	30	24	43	40	50
Engines & Turbines; Farm Machinery & Equipment	25	56	32	29	35	34
Construction, Mining & Material Handling Machinery & Equipment	40	34	51	43	46	47
Machine Tools, Metal Cutting Types	33	35	29	75	39	43
Metalworking Machinery, Except Machine Tools; & Power Driven Hand Tools	51	55	44	87	50	49
Machinery, Except Electrical	36	33	30	39	35	45
Special Industry Machinery, Except Metalworking Machinery	34	25	27	24	30	43
General Industrial Machinery & Equipment	34	10	29	40	n.a.	36
Service Industry Machines	40	n.a.	75	58	n.a.	73
Miscellaneous Machinery, Except Electrical	39	43	23	20	46	60
Electrical Machinery, Equipment & Supplies	48	30	44	51	46	43
Electronic Components & Accessories	45	16	50	54	33	50
Transportation	29	31	26	33	37	36
Aircraft Parts & Auxiliary Equipment	34	45	43	52	41	49
Professional, Scientific & Controlling Equipment	63	78	58	56	62	56

n.a.: Not available.

$$AIS = \$1,000 \times 2 \times .40$$

$$AIS = \$800.$$

Assembly Labor Savings

The enhanced accuracy and repeatability of computer and numerical controls often provide other less tangible, but definite benefits. Because the exact savings values are difficult to quantify, most justification studies simply include qualitative remarks about improved precision and its favorable impact on competitive advantages and business prospects. Beyond qualitative implications, better precision often shrinks part assembly time and labor costs. Unlike the relatively nebulous advantages such as enhanced business opportunities, it definitely is possible to estimate the quantitative impact on assembly labor.

A suggested procedure for estimating assembly labor savings starts with an appraisal of the annual average labor cost for assembling the output of a comparable conventional machine. Since most cost accounting systems routinely provide assembly labor costs for management control, in many applications it will be possible to equate this value for conventional equipment to computer or numerical control's capacity by multiplying it by the reciprocal of the machine-time ratio. Then, the computer or numerical control's Assembly Labor Savings factor can be applied according to the following procedure:

$$ALS = [CAL \times \frac{1}{\text{Machine-Time Ratio}}] \times RAL$$

where

ALS = Annual Assembly Labor Savings,

CAL = Annual Assembly Labor Costs for a comparable conventional machine, and

RAL = Reduction of Assembly Labor—from company experience or Tables XII and XIII.

Because assembly labor economies vary between applications, related experiences of other companies should be used with caution. However, the consistency in the savings reported by survey companies suggests that survey data may provide a savings approximation that is reasonably representative. Notice that the average assembly labor savings summarized from the survey data in Table XII vary only from about 12 to 20 percent for all equipment types except machining centers, where they understandably are somewhat greater.

Variations in the range of savings are somewhat greater when the effects of product orientation are considered, as shown in Table XIII.

TABLE XII

ASSEMBLY LABOR SAVINGS BY NUMERICAL CONTROL
EQUIPMENT TYPE

Equipment Type	Percent Assembly Labor Reduced
Punching	12
Boring	13
Turning	13
Drilling	16
Milling	17
Machining Centers	20

Floor Space Savings

Although computer and numerical control equipment typically requires more floor space than a comparable conventional machine, the resulting higher productivity tends to provide a more efficient shop utilization. When a firm's business capacity is constrained by space limitations, a computer or numerical control space benefit may prove profitable.

To determine if an actual saving is possible, it is necessary to ascertain first whether the floor space utilization is significantly improved. In an early survey, the companies indicated that the ratio of numerical control floor space requirements to that of conventional equipment was 1.8:1. By stating this ratio as a percentage value, the conventional machines required only 55 percent of the space numerical control needed. If their numerical control equipment had a machine-time ratio lower than $\dfrac{1}{.55}$, a more effective utilization of floor space resulted. Profits could be increased therefore by those companies that utilized the freed space for greater business volume.

An encouraging numerical control floor space trend became evident in a later survey. Although the early survey companies reported that numerical control required almost twice the space

TABLE XIII

NUMERICAL CONTROL ASSEMBLY LABOR COST BY INDUSTRY AND EQUIPMENT TYPE

Industry Classification	Percent Decrease Over Conventional Equipment					
	Drilling	Boring	Turning	Punching	Milling	Mach. Center
Primary Metal Industry	20	n.a.	12	n.a.	18	35
Fabricated Metal Products	12	5	5	13	5	13
Engines & Turbines; Farm Machinery & Equipment	9	11	1	8	10	n.a.
Construction, Mining & Material Handling Machinery & Equipment	19	33	42	5	21	42
Machine Tools, Metal Cutting Types	23	13	11	45	11	24
Metalworking Machinery, Except Machine Tools; & Power Driven Hand Tools	16	17	10	n.a.	16	13
Machinery, Except Electrical	18	16	14	18	17	24
Special Industry Machinery, Except Metalworking Machinery	12	9	9	32	9	29
General Industrial Machinery & Equipment	19	15	33	50	13	33
Service Industry Machines	20	n.a.	n.a.	12	70	45
Miscellaneous Machinery, Except Electrical	20	20	8	15	18	38
Electrical Machinery, Equipment & Supplies	10	5	7	9	17	8
Electronic Components & Accessories	14	3	11	13	10	6
Transportation	14	9	19	7	18	20
Aircraft Parts & Auxiliary Equipment	18	14	37	13	24	30
Professional, Scientific & Controlling Equipment	18	25	33	18	25	25

n.a.: Not available.

of comparable conventional equipment, because of integrated circuits and general miniaturization advancements the companies in the second survey found that numerical control required only 32 percent more space. The numerical control equipment owned by one-eighth (44) of the 356 companies in the 1970 survey actually required less space than conventional equipment. About one-sixth of the companies (57) reported no appreciable difference.

Unlike most other savings factors, conventional-numerical control space differentials appeared to be only partially affected by equipment type. For example, there were no substantial variations between the relative space differences for a conventional lathe and a numerical control lathe, or for a numerical control drill versus a conventional drill. If the company's products required a sophisticated conventional lathe, then a sophisticated numerical control lathe requiring about the same proportional space was also necessary.

Summarized in Table XIV are the combined floor space effects of the product characteristics of the major survey industries. The narrow range within which the floor space differentials vary between industries tends to support the concept of using a survey parameter for estimating numerical control's impact on the floor space requirements of a particular company. Floor space increases reported by half of the industries fell within 20 percentage points of the survey average of 32 percent. Thus, in the absence of actual floor space requirements for proposed equipment, a survey parameter from Table XIV corresponding to the appropriate industry affiliation may be selected with confidence that the data are reasonably close to what may occur.

To estimate the floor space impact of computer or numerical controls the annual value of a square foot of shop floor area should be ascertained. The next step is to determine the average floor space (in square feet) required for a comparable conventional machine. An estimate of the Annual Floor Space Savings (AFSS) can then be computed as follows:

$$\text{AFSS} = [\text{CMS} \times \frac{1}{\text{Machine-Time Ratio}}] -$$

$$[\text{CMS} \times (1 + \text{FSDF})] \times \text{Space Cost}$$

where

$\quad\quad\quad$ CMS = Space required by Conventional Machine, and

FSDF = Computer or numerical control Floor Space Differential Factor from company experience or Table XIV.

TABLE XIV

FLOOR SPACE INCREASES FOR NUMERICAL CONTROL
BY INDUSTRY CLASSIFICATION

Industry Classification	Increase Percentage
Primary Metal Industry	18
Fabricated Metal Products	14
Engines & Turbines; Farm Machinery & Equipment	−1
Construction, Mining & Material Handling Machinery & Equipment	33
Machine Tools, Metal Cutting Types	33
Metalworking Machinery, Except Machine Tools; & Power Driven Hand Tools	31
Machinery, Except Electrical	30
Special Industry Machinery, Except Metalworking Machinery	12
General Industrial Machinery & Equipment	24
Service Industry Machines	34
Miscellaneous Machinery, Except Electrical	17
Electrical Machinery, Equipment & Supplies	36
Electronic Components & Accessories	27
Transportation	48
Aircraft Parts & Auxiliary Equipment	52
Professional, Scientific & Controlling Equipment	29

Material Handling Savings

With multiple machining operations possible at one workpiece setting, fewer computer or numerical control intermachine part transfers are common. In the first University of Michigan survey the companies indicated that the average ratio of the number of intermachine part transfers after numerical control to the number of comparable conventional machine transfers was .49.

The second survey disclosed that equipment characteristics made a significant impact on material handling savings. Not surprisingly, unifunctional boring equipment showed a relatively low 18 percent reduction compared to 51 percent for multioperational machining centers. See Table XV.

A first step in estimating the annual material handling savings is to determine the workpiece transfer costs associated with the number

TABLE XV

NUMERICAL CONTROL MATERIAL HANDLING SAVINGS

Type of Equipment	Percent Cost Reduction
Boring	20
Turning	22
Drilling	25
Milling	27
Punching	39
Machining Centers	51

of conventional machines required to match computer or numerical control's output. Cost accounting records in many shops will readily disclose the expenses involved in transferring workpieces between specified machines. In the absence of such information, departmentalized material handling costs might be prorated over associated machines to determine an average annual material handling cost for a comparable conventional machine. When this result is multiplied by the reciprocal of the machine-time ratio, the productivity advantage of computer or numerical control is taken into account. Therefore, the annual Material Handling Savings (MHS) is estimated as follows:

$$MHS = [MHC \times \frac{1}{\text{Machine-Time Ratio}}] \times MHSF$$

where

MHC = Annual Material Handling Cost per comparable conventional machine, and

$MHSF$ = Material Handling Savings Factor, i.e., the reduction in material handling costs from using computer or numerical control.

Where plant experience provides cost data for the Material Handling Savings Factor, it obviously should be used. When such historical expense information is lacking or is expensive to garner, it may be helpful to use an appropriate figure from Table XVI, which possesses fairly sensitive information classified by both equipment type and product orientation.

Table XVI

Numerical Control Material Handling Cost Decreases by Industry and Equipment Type

Industry Classification	Percent Decrease Over Conventional Equipment					
	Drilling	Boring	Turning	Punching	Milling	Mach. Center
Primary Metal Industry	7	n.a.	10	49	18	40
Fabricated Metal Products	13	7	22	52	10	76
Engines & Turbines; Farm Machinery & Equipment	34	49	22	52	28	48
Construction, Mining & Material Handling Machinery & Equipment	24	25	28	35	25	44
Machine Tools, Metal Cutting Types	26	23	44	80	29	48
Metalworking Machinery, Except Machine Tools; & Power Driven Hand Tools	35	22	25	40	n.a.	49
Machinery, Except Electrical	24	23	22	38	27	49
Special Industry Machinery, Except Metalworking Machinery	13	18	22	5	29	54
General Industrial Machinery & Equipment	18	5	8	n.a.	40	54
Service Industry Machines	25	10	15	37	n.a.	89
Miscellaneous Machinery, Except Electrical	36	37	15	25	34	45
Electrical Machinery, Equipment & Supplies	34	19	22	42	31	50
Electronic Components & Accessories	33	24	23	34	32	64
Transportation	23	15	22	20	28	53
Aircraft Parts & Auxiliary Equipment	24	16	20	24	34	59
Professional, Scientific & Controlling Equipment	31	20	28	62	19	68

n.a.: Not available.

Annual Inventory Savings

Computer and numerical control may reduce inventories for jigs and fixtures, work-in-process, and finished goods. Savings derived from the latter two factors are considered in this section of the evaluation process, while the pervasive impact upon tooling inventories is treated in a later section.

Work-in-Process

Cost savings from reduced work-in-process inventories, amounting to the carrying costs on the inventory reduction, are estimated by using inventory values, the machine-time ratio, an appropriate computer or numerical control inventory reduction factor, and the inventory holding costs. First, an estimate is made of the value of the average work-in-process inventory applicable to the type of machine being considered. Since inventories are closely valued for accounting and tax purposes, plant records usually will disclose the appropriate inventory amount, at least to the departmental level. Averaging techniques may be needed to prorate departmental values over individual machines.

Once the inventory amount has been estimated, it is relatively simple to apply the reciprocal of the machine-time ratio and the inventory savings factor experienced by a particular plant. If actual inventory reduction factors are not available, it may be acceptable to use appropriate experience data from the survey.

As can be observed from Table XVII, the numerical control reductions of the work-in-process inventories ranged in the survey from 17 percent for drilling to 32 percent for machining centers. Of special significance is the clustering of percentage reductions for all types of equipment except machining centers. Drilling, boring, turning, punching, and milling work-in-process inventory reductions in the survey companies all were grouped rather closely between 17 and 22 percent.

When the effects of product characteristics are to be considered, a work-in-process reduction factor should be selected from Table XVIII, where survey data are classified by equipment type and product orientation. A value for the savings from the work-in-process inventory reduction (ASWPI) can be estimated as follows:

$$\text{ASWPI} = (\text{CAWPI} \times \frac{1}{\text{Machine-Time Ratio}}) \times (\text{WIPR}) \times$$

(Inventory Carrying Costs)

TABLE XVII

Equipment Type	Percent Reduction
Drilling	17
Boring	19
Milling	20
Punching	21
Turning	22
Machining Centers	32

where

CAWPI = Conventional Annual Work-in-Process Inventory, and

WIPR = Percentage Work-in-Process Reduction from computer or numerical control as determined from company experience or Tables XVII and XVIII.

Inventory carrying costs include storage and security expenses plus the interest on capital invested. A holding rate ranging between 10 and 15 percent of the work-in-process inventory value is common, although if the parts are valuable, fragile, or susceptible to theft, carrying costs as high as 25 percent can be encountered. If it is difficult to ascertain a specific holding rate for a particular company, a rate reported by the survey companies for finished goods inventory might be adapted and utilized (see Table XIX).

Finished Goods Inventory

Because of computer and numerical control's setup and lead-time efficiencies, parts are often made-to-order rather than supplied via finished inventories. Where total elimination of a part from finished inventory is not feasible, frequently there is at least a significant quantity reduction.

Greatest finished inventory reductions are experienced by companies with semi-standardized products. Job shops producing to a customer's order rather than for finished inventory have found these benefits valuable, but difficult to quantify. Since numerical control is not used typically for standardized high-volume applications, reductions in finished inventories are more common in medium-volume production applications.

TABLE XVIII

NUMERICAL CONTROL WORK-IN-PROCESS INVENTORY REDUCTIONS BY INDUSTRY AND EQUIPMENT TYPE

Industry Classification	Percent Decrease Over Conventional Equipment						
	Drilling	Boring	Turning	Punching	Milling	Mach. Center
Primary Metal Industry	13	n.a.	13	n.a.	n.a.	25
Fabricated Metal Products	13	18	16	40	15	42
Engines & Turbines; Farm Machinery & Equipment	13	4	5	45	5	28
Construction, Mining & Material Handling Machinery & Equipment	16	23	30	16	20	16
Machine Tools, Metal Cutting Types	21	12	22	14	22	30
Metalworking Machinery, Except Machine Tools; & Power Driven Hand Tools	9	9	19	n.a.	n.a.	26
Machinery, Except Electrical	15	17	18	17	14	30
Special Industry Machinery, Except Metalworking Machinery	10	33	11	16	13	28
General Industrial Machinery & Equipment	2	48	10	5	n.a.	37
Service Industry Machines	25	n.a.	n.a.	25	30	60
Miscellaneous Machinery, Except Electrical	27	38	12	18	15	50
Electrical Machinery, Equipment & Supplies	24	25	38	23	26	35
Electronic Components & Accessories	29	25	75	25	40	46
Transportation	18	17	24	14	22	32
Aircraft Parts & Auxiliary Equipment	14	8	21	9	25	37
Professional, Scientific & Controlling Equipment	32	35	28	31	30	38

n.a.: Not available.

Table XIX

Carrying Costs for Finished Goods Inventories by Industry Classification

Industry Classification	Average Inventory Carrying Costs (Inventory Holding Rate)
Primary Metal Industry	23%
Fabricated Metal Products	22
Engines & Turbines; Farm Machinery & Equipment	18
Construction, Mining & Material Handling Machinery & Equipment	18
Machine Tools, Metal Cutting Types	19
Metalworking Machinery, Except Machine Tools; & Power Driven Hand Tools	19
Machinery, Except Electrical	17
Special Industry Machinery, Except Metalworking Machinery	19
General Industrial Machinery & Equipment	18
Service Industry Machines	16
Miscellaneous Machinery, Except Electrical	16
Electrical Machinery, Equipment & Supplies	17
Electronic Components & Accessories	11
Transportation	15
Aircraft Parts & Auxiliary Equipment	12
Professional, Scientific & Controlling Equipment	20

Where computer or numerical control finished inventory reductions are expected, the procedure and appropriate holding rates described below can be used to estimate the savings. The value of finished goods inventory, an asset that is closely accounted for, should be readily obtainable from existing plant records. As with the work-in-process calculations, the finished goods inventory value should be computed by multiplying the reciprocal of the machine-time ratio by the inventory value of a comparable conventional machine.

Experienced computer or numerical control users can ascertain the inventory savings from existing records. Others may need to rely on the experiences of the survey companies summarized in Tables XX and XXI. Finished inventory reductions reported in the survey are generally clustered in a reasonably narrow range of 13 to 20 percent for drilling, boring, turning, punching, and milling. Reductions created by multi-functional machining centers are again substantially greater at 25 percent.

227

TABLE XX

NUMERICAL CONTROL FINISHED GOODS INVENTORY REDUCTIONS

Type of Equipment	Percent of Inventory Value
Boring	13
Drilling	14
Punching	17
Milling	17
Turning	20
Machining Centers	25

As was true for work-in-process inventories, the annual savings in finished inventories amounts to the saved carrying costs applicable to the inventory reduction. A procedure for estimating this savings value (AFGIS) follows:

$$\text{AFGIS} = (\text{CFGI} \times \frac{1}{\text{Machine-Time Ratio}})$$

$\times \text{ (FGIS)} \times \text{(ICC)}$

where

$\quad$ CFGI = Conventional machine Finished Goods Inventory,

$\quad$ FGIS = Finished Goods Inventory Savings Factor, and

$\quad$ ICC = Inventory Carrying Costs.

Included in the finished goods inventory holding rate are many of those items described earlier in the work-in-process section, e.g., storage and security costs, interest expense on the investment, etc. If an appropriate rate cannot be ascertained from accounting records, it may be desirable to use a parameter from Table XIX, where the reported holding rates range between 11 and 23 percent.

Annual Tooling Savings

Even more common than the computer or numerical control perishable tooling economies are nonperishable tooling savings, which include the expense of designing and building or purchasing jigs and fixtures. *Standard* nonperishable tooling costs need not be considered in this Phase II–B since they are capitalized in Phase I and the associated expenses are amortized by the capital recovery

TABLE XXI

NUMERICAL CONTROL FINISHED GOODS INVENTORY REDUCTION BY INDUSTRY AND EQUIPMENT TYPE

Industry Classification	Percent Reduction Over Conventional Equipment					
	Drilling	Boring	Turning	Punching	Milling	Mach. Center
Primary Metal Industry	5	n.a.	5	n.a.	n.a.	10
Fabricated Metal Products	9	9	18	37	10	25
Engines & Turbines; Farm Machinery & Equipment	15	7	n.a.	33	10	28
Construction, Mining & Material Handling Machinery & Equipment	11	10	39	18	20	20
Machine Tools, Metal Cutting Types	17	12	18	12	28	28
Metalworking Machinery, Except Machine Tools; & Power Driven Hand Tools	11	8	15	n.a.	n.a.	31
Machinery, Except Electrical	15	14	22	14	18	27
Special Industry Machinery, Except Metalworking Machinery	4	30	20	n.a.	15	16
General Industrial Machinery & Equipment	21	n.a.	30	n.a.	n.a.	28
Service Industry Machines	25	n.a.	n.a.	30	n.a.	45
Miscellaneous Machinery, Except Electrical	35	35	25	27	40	50
Electrical Machinery, Equipment & Supplies	15	20	35	23	23	27
Electronic Components & Accessories	25	25	50	40	50	38
Transportation	13	8	14	4	15	20
Aircraft Parts & Auxiliary Equipment	12	2	15	n.a.	18	22
Professional, Scientific & Controlling Equipment	28	18	25	22	18	28

n.a.: Not available.

accounting process. The annual savings in computer or numerical control *special* nonperishable tools, however, should now be evaluted.

In the Phase I discussion it was shown that the companies in the early survey required special jigs and fixtures on only 7.3 percent of their numerical control jobs. On the remaining 92.7 percent, special nonperishable tooling costs were avoided because standard workholders were substituted. The companies in the second survey reported their nonperishable tooling experiences according to equipment type. As expected, less capable numerical control equipment, generally producing simpler parts, required fewer special jigs and fixtures. Drilling, boring, punching, and turning machines needed special tooling on less than 40 percent of the numerical control jobs. By contrast, it was economically prudent to equip sophisticated machining centers with special tooling on 65 to 71 percent of their work (see Table XXII).

TABLE XXII

NUMERICAL CONTROL JOBS REQUIRING SPECIAL TOOLING
(NONPERISHABLE TOOLING)

Equipment Type	Percentage of Jobs Needing Special Tooling
Drilling	
2–axis, NC	27
3–axis, NC	36
3–axis, NC with tool changer	38
Boring	40
Punching	7
Turning	
Single turret	20
Double turret	21
Milling	
2–axis	40
3–axis	63
Machining Centers	
3–axis	65
4–axis	71
5–axis	71

Before the savings can be calculated, the relative complexity of special tooling for conventional and computer or numerical controls also should be evaluated. As part of the first survey, the companies were asked the following question: "Of the numerical control jobs requiring specially built jigs and fixtures, it is maintained that the jigs and fixtures required are less complex and less expensive than those required on conventional machining—is this statement true in your case?" Nine of the ten numerical control users answered yes, and they estimated that the ratio of numerical control tooling costs to conventional tooling costs on jobs requiring custom-built jigs and fixtures was about .50. Therefore, costs for tooling the remaining numerical control jobs that required special jigs should average about half the conventional tooling expense.

More specific information about the complexity of special tooling for numerical control was obtained in the second survey. While the findings displayed in Table XXIII show variations over the full range of simple to complex equipment, the general average is closer to a one-third savings rather than the one-half reduction.

TABLE XXIII

SPECIAL TOOLING COMPLEXITY REDUCTIONS CREATED
BY NUMERICAL CONTROL

Equipment Type	Percent Less Complex
Drilling	
2–axis, NC	33
3–axis, NC	38
3–axis, NC with tool changer	38
Boring	25
Punching	19
Turning	
Single turret	9
Double turret	16
Milling	
2–axis	21
3–axis	38
Machining Centers	
3–axis	35
4–axis	39
5–axis	32

In estimating the annual savings in special nonperishable tools, the yearly jig and fixture expenses for the conventional equipment equivalent to the computer or numerical control capacity must first be estimated. To simplify the discussion, this cost may be designated as "T." If the computer or numerically controlled machine is being considered for expansion, "T" is equal to the annual jig and fixture cost for the conventional machines which would be needed to obtain an equivalent capacity. "T" can be calculated as follows: an estimate is made of the average annual jig and fixture cost for a conventional machine functionally comparable to the proposed computer or numerical control machine. This average cost, represented by "t," is then multiplied by the reciprocal of the machine-time ratio to reflect the higher productivity made possible by using numerical control. That is,

$$T = t \times \frac{1}{\text{Machine-Time Ratio}}$$

For equipment that processes simple parts, for example, the drills, lathes, and punching machines which require special tooling for only 7 to 38 percent of the survey jobs, it is likely that the value of "T" in actuality approximates the annual savings in nonperishable tools. As a practical matter, when 80 to 90 percent of the computer or numerical control jobs are completed without special jigs and fixtures and the tooling complexity of the remaining 10 to 20 percent of the jobs is reduced by one-third to one-half, practically all the conventional nonperishable tooling costs are avoided. Such a relationship occurs in this methodology because the expenditures for standard holding fixtures were previously included as an investment cost in Phase I. However, to assure the confidence of financial analysts who will review the investment evaluation, it is advisable to compute the estimated tooling savings for each investment by using a formalized procedure such as the one described below.

When the value of "T" is known and an approximate proportion of computer or numerical control jobs needing special tooling is available, together with its complexity, then the two formulas below may be used to estimate the Annual Nonperishable Tooling Savings (ANTS).

$$\text{ANTS} = T \times \text{STRF}$$

where

$$T = t \times \frac{1}{\text{Machine-Time Ratio}}$$

(t = Annual tooling cost for a functionally similar conventional machine), and

$$STRF = \text{Special nonperishable Tooling Reduction afforded by computer or numerical controls.}$$

$$ANTCS = (T - ANTS) \times STCR$$

where

$ANTCS$ = Annual Nonperishable special Tooling Complexity Savings, and

$ANTS$ = Annual Nonperishable special Tooling Savings (from preceding formula), and

$STCR$ = Special nonperishable Tooling Complexity Reduction factor afforded by computer or numerical controls.

Information from the survey data or actual in-plant experience data from accounting records may be used in the above procedures.

The introduction of computer or numerical controls does not automatically produce a tooling savings. If the acquiring company plans to reroute parts of an existing design from an operable conventional machine to computer or numerical controls and has already invested in the tooling, then the savings will be limited to inventory costs and the salvage receipts. If the numerical control machine is being purchased for expansion or for newly designed parts, then annual tooling savings should approximate the combined values produced by the two formulas. This is true when production runs are of a short-to-medium volume and require about the same level of retooling each year. If such is not the case, it will be necessary to adjust the savings for future years upward or downward, depending upon the actual yearly level of retooling.

When jigs and fixtures are reduced by computer or numerical controls, another important economy results from less tool storage and lower maintenance expenses. Tooling carrying costs include these cost components: repair and alterations expense, interest on capital invested, physical deterioration or its prevention, handling, transportation, taxes, insurance, and storage. Although some companies lack adequate accounting records to identify the expense for each carrying cost factor, incomplete cost records should not preclude computing the full impact of this substantial nonperishable tooling savings.

The survey companies reported carrying cost experiences for five distinct expense factors stated as a percentage of the original tooling

233

cost. These factors and the associated percentage averages reported by the survey companies are depicted in Table XXIV. Here it can be seen that the average total carrying cost was 21 percent.

TABLE XXIV

TOOLING INVENTORY CARRYING COSTS

Expense Factor	Average Percent of Original Tooling Cost
Taxes, insurance, storage space	1
Handling and transportation	2
Physical deterioration or its prevention	3
Interest on investment	6
Repair and alteration	9
TOTAL	21

Carrying costs tend to be greater for tooling of contouring than for tooling of point-to-point equipment. This relationship is especially evident for the two factors shown in Table XXV.

TABLE XXV

TOOLING INVENTORY CARRYING COSTS
(Contouring versus point-to-point)

Carrying Cost Factor	Percentage Reported for	
	Contouring Equipment	Point-to-Point Equipment
Physical deterioration	4.0	2.8
Handling and transportation	2.8	1.7

Miscellaneous Benefits

Beyond the previously described savings which are relatively tangible, less obvious expense elements also may be affected. While a multitude of computer and numerical control characteristics may create additional indirect savings, those permitting fewer inter-machine part transfers typically are the most consequential. Cost accounting and production control activities are two commonly overlooked factors favorably influenced by reduced part handling and shorter routing. Combining previously discrete operations on one computer or numerical control machine reduces the administrative effort necessary for cost records, route sheets, job instruction cards, move tickets, etc.

Since fewer part transfers mean fewer cost records, accounting information from computer or numerical control operations also tends to be more faithful. Time standards are more dependable and subject to less dispute because a machine-controlled cycle is less variable than changeable human operations. Standard rates for cost centers also are more precise because expenses of a single or a few computer or numerical control machines are accounted for rather than several discrete units of varying capabilities, depreciation rates, and operator idiosyncrasies. Combining discrete operations, therefore, cuts both the mountains of paperwork and the cost estimation and accounting inaccuracies that pyramid in conventional operations.

Measurable production control and cost accounting savings do not instantly appear with the implementation of the first computer or numerical control machine. Although the savings potential exists when only a single machine is installed, more than one machine may be required to produce a full increment of employee savings. As can be seen from Tables XXVI and XXVII, production control and accounting economies generally were more common among survey companies having relatively more numerical control machines. Greater economies also were usually reported by companies having equipment with superior capabilities.

TABLE XXVI

COST ACCOUNTING SAVINGS FROM NUMERICAL CONTROL
BY EQUIPMENT CHARACTERISTICS

Equipment Characteristics	Present Experience		Future Potential	
	Yes	No	Yes	No
1–9 total NC machines	49	97	53	23
10 or more NC machines	35	29	33	11
Companies with contouring machines only	2	9	3	1
Companies with point-to-point machines only	25	56	23	14

Only 49 (34 percent) of the 146 reporting survey firms with less than ten machines experienced numerical control cost accounting savings compared to 35 (55 percent) of 64 companies with ten or more

TABLE XXVII

Equipment Characteristics	Present Experience		Future Potential	
	Yes	No	Yes	No
1–9 total NC machines	114	60	73	13
10 or more NC machines	50	22	43	5
Companies with contouring machines only	9	8	4	1
Companies with point-to-point machines only	61	34	38	8

machines. Similarly, 50 (69 percent) of 91 companies with ten or more numerical control machines experienced production control savings compared to only 114 (65 percent) of 174 companies having less than ten machines.

Examples of the production control and accounting benefits are illustrated by selected comments from survey respondents.

"Allows accurate formulation of cost estimates; process changes are more economical to incorporate."

"Eliminates handling for shipping and receiving of parts previously sent to outside vendors."

"Better control over the work flow and the quality of finished product."

"Better ability to break job down for cost control."

"Time to set incentive standards cut 50 percent."

"Better forecasting for cost control and delivery."

Savings in product development and design engineering effort are also common with computer or numerical controls. When restricted to conventional equipment, designers must create shapes producible by equipment having a much narrower range of capability. Now, with the ability to define the entire machine operation in as many as five axes of simultaneous machine motion, dramatically more complex shapes are produced accurately without prohibitive cost penalties. The designer, therefore, is in a better position to exercise a previously unattainable freedom of choice in meeting product requirements.

An even greater contributor to cost reduction programs is the ability to implement changes numerically. Inasmuch as standard or simple special holding fixtures commonly suffice, engineering changes may be effected by easy tape modification without tooling revisions. Formerly, expensive penalties were inherent in most changes once the tooling was set.

Computer and numerical controls lessen costs during the design engineering phase in at least two other ways:

1. The casting stage may be avoided more frequently by using raw stock since special shapes are easily attainable by contouring in five simultaneous axes.

2. Since the prototype lead time is less, a more thorough design evaluation is feasible before the production commitment must be released.

The advantages accruing in product development and design engineering are demonstrated by the comments of survey respondents quoted below.

"The usage of NC in research and development has opened many doors in respect to design and production of complex components."

"The design-manufacturing-engineering interface and communication process has been greatly improved; i.e., there is finally a common technological language."

"In fabricating prototypes for research and development, a significant savings is derived from the ease of modifying control tapes to reflect a prescribed engineering change without altering the valid sections of the part."

"Numerical control has permitted new design concepts whereby large machined parts are used for structural members in lieu of assemblies which result in significant labor savings."

About one-third (35 percent) of the 224 reporting firms enjoyed design engineering savings, and 44 percent benefitted in product design functions. Tables XXVIII through XXX summarize the design engineering and new product development savings reported by the survey companies. As was true for both production control and cost accounting activities, design engineering and product development savings increased as the numerical control machine complement became larger.

Table XXVIII
Design Engineering Savings from Numerical Control by Equipment Characteristics

Equipment Characteristics	Present Experience		Future Potential	
	Yes	No	Yes	No
1–9 total NC machines	82	74	76	12
10 or more NC machines	41	24	40	7
Companies with contouring machines only	3	10	5	1
Companies with point-to-point machines only	54	35	37	8

Table XXIX
Design Engineering Savings from Numerical Control by Industry Classification

Industry Classification	Present Experience		Future Potential	
	Yes	No	Yes	No
Primary Metal Industry	7	2	2	1
Fabricated Metal Products	11	4	12	0
Engines & Turbines; Farm Machinery & Equipment	5	1	7	0
Construction, Mining & Material Handling Machinery & Equipment	5	4	4	0
Machine Tools, Metal Cutting Type	10	10	10	2
Metalworking Machinery, Except Machine Tools, & Power Driven Hand Tools	3	3	2	1
Machinery, Except Electrical	56	60	57	13
Special Industry Machinery, Except Metalworking Machinery	10	5	8	0
General Industrial Machinery & Equipment	1	7	5	4
Service Industry Machines	8	4	5	1
Miscellaneous Machinery, Except Electrical	6	6	6	0
Electrical Machinery, Equipment & Supplies	19	10	15	1
Electronic Components & Accessories	6	3	4	0
Transportation	18	16	18	3
Aircraft Parts & Auxiliary Equipment	12	7	12	1
Professional, Scientific & Controlling Equipment	5	3	6	0

Reduced lead time and better quality create profitable benefits for the sales departments of many companies. The newly achieved quick reaction capability of engineering and manufacturing depart-

Table XXX

NEW PRODUCT DEVELOPMENT SAVINGS FROM NUMERICAL CONTROL BY EQUIPMENT CHARACTERISTICS

Equipment Characteristics	Present Experience		Future Potential	
	Yes	No	Yes	No
1–9 total NC machines	105	64	91	6
10 or more NC machines	48	20	39	8
Companies with point-to-point machines only	61	32	47	3
Companies with contouring machines only	6	8	6	0

ments helps sustain a competitive edge, particularly in their ability to create fresh designs rapidly. An important contribution to profits stems from increased sales margins on products selling at more favorable prices in the marketplace before the competition intensifies. Other profitable advantages are: (1) more accurate delivery estimates due to improved management control, (2) less time spent on scrap and rework, and (3) greater accuracy in pricing and making sales forecasts.

Contouring machines produce marketing benefits more frequently than do point-to-point machines, and these improvements tend to be more significant (see Table XXXI). Sales benefits are most likely to occur in companies in service, job shop, special products, and aircraft industries.

Table XXXI

MARKETING SAVINGS FROM NUMERICAL CONTROL BY EQUIPMENT CHARACTERISTICS

Equipment Characteristics	Present Experience		Future Potential	
	Yes	No	Yes	No
1–9 total NC machines	31	98	47	24
10 or more NC machines	16	41	19	20
Companies with contouring machines only	1	8	1	1
Companies with point-to-point machines only	16	56	24	12

Typical comments describing the numerical control advantages flowing to company sales departments are quoted below:

"Much broader range of customers."

"Lead-time reduction—small order handling improved."

"We find we get more things through the shop on time."

"Quick response for replacement items on an emergency basis."

"Accurate control by management of production activities, resulting in better sales relations and market potential."

"Image of precision, growth, pride of leadership in our industry."

"Lead-time savings; newly designed systems are introduced faster in the marketplace."

"Sales promotion, e.g., product improvement, interchangeability for replacement parts. Without numerical control we could not compete with those who have it."

Electrical power consumption is another of the less obvious savings factors which merits consideration during computer or numerical control investment evaluations. Generally, automated equipment's power consumption exceeds that of conventional machines; however, computer and numerical control's productivity is also increased. The combined effect is that power consumption per unit of computer or numerical control output generally does not significantly differ from that of conventional machinery. When the survey companies were asked to estimate the ratio of power consumption between conventional and numerical control equipment, their average response was 1.1:1. Compared to the relative magnitude of the other costs and savings considered in the investment study, a possible 5 to 10 percent increase in electrical power expenses is not significant enough to affect the evalution results materially. This factor, therefore, usually does not need to be included in the summary data unless inordinate conditions are present in a particular application.

Finally, the benefits flowing from a fast reaction capability, although very difficult to quantify, were nevertheless reported by over 100 survey companies. Lead-time reductions generally improve with equipment complexity and the extent to which multi-operations are possible or a special tooling activity can be avoided (see Table XXXII).

Product characteristics also heavily influence lead-time reductions.

240

Shortened the most are the lead times of aircraft parts and auxiliary equipment; electronic components and accessories; special industry machinery; metalworking machinery; and electrical machinery, equipment and supplies (see Table XXXIII).

TABLE XXXII

NUMERICAL CONTROL LEAD-TIME REDUCTIONS

Equipment Type	Average Lead-Time Reduction
Boring	26%
Turning	31
Drilling	33
Milling	34
Punching	39
Machining Centers	44

Overview of Investment Decision Making

Because traditional investment evaluation techniques for less versatile and pervasive conventional equipment have paid little attention to many of the previously described indirect expense factors, historical costs too often are buried in shop overhead. It should not be surprising, therefore, that computer and numerical control investment decision makers often are frustrated by a lack of accurate cost records. Moreover, they frequently experience great difficulty in obtaining advice about procedures to use in quantitatively assessing automatic control's full impact. This series of formalized procedures for estimating indirect savings values, together with the related survey standards, should help mitigate such investment evaluation problems. Most importantly, a logical set of procedures is now available for approximating the value of definite, but sometimes obscure, computer and numerical control cost factors.

There is yet a vital question that must be settled before a final computer and numerical control investment decision is determined. It is more elusive than all the others and in many instances is far more crucial: What new opportunities for improved business management, operational control, and profits does the proposed equipment provide which do not now exist with conventional equipment?

Answers to this vital and wide-ranging question are usually more qualitative than quantitative and, therefore, serve to supplement

241

TABLE XXXIII

NUMERICAL CONTROL LEAD-TIME DECREASES BY INDUSTRY AND EQUIPMENT TYPE

Industry Classification	Percent Decrease Over Conventional Equipment					
	Drilling	Boring	Turning	Punching	Milling	Mach. Center
Primary Metal Industry	37	n.a.	15	25	33	50
Fabricated Metal Products	28	25	33	36	25	37
Engines & Turbines; Farm Machinery & Equipment	39	41	22	37	30	54
Construction, Mining & Material Handling Machinery & Equipment	32	25	33	10	34	35
Machine Tools, Metal Cutting Types	26	16	24	15	23	41
Metalworking Machinery, Except Machine Tools; & Power Driven Hand Tools	29	23	10	47	35	42
Machinery, Except Electrical	28	23	27	35	30	44
Special Industry Machinery, Except Metalworking Machinery	21	32	35	35	35	50
General Industrial Machinery & Equipment	31	23	26	43	n.a.	64
Service Industry Machines	30	n.a.	n.a.	47	n.a.	50
Miscellaneous Machinery, Except Electrical	33	26	20	32	26	29
Electrical Machinery, Equipment & Supplies	47	26	50	48	47	44
Electronic Components & Accessories	44	28	58	53	41	56
Transportation	31	27	29	35	33	44
Aircraft Parts & Auxiliary Equipment	39	30	35	38	42	47
Professional, Scientific & Controlling Equipment	38	63	37	31	37	48

n.a.: Not available.

the quantitative answers provided by this methodology. Making the proper inclusive assessment of computer and numerical controls requires searching beyond cost relationships inherent in traditional production methods. This demands opening one's mind to new profit-making capabilities based on entirely new management strategies for marketing, manufacturing, and new product development. Through such broadened decision-making approaches, the manager is not restricted to dealing with single machine justification comparisons or with existing production methods; he is dealing with a totally modernized manufacturing system composed eventually of several computer or numerical control machines. Such a manufacturing system promises to include integrated material handling and a computer-based management information system.

Only through comprehensive long-range planning can the investment analyst evaluate the actual capability and economic impact of computer and numerical controls. Procurement of the total system may proceed on a piecemeal basis over a period of years, with each investment decision bringing the company closer to the full realization of the profit-making potential of the master plan. The failure to take this broader view, or conversely, to demand that each individual machine fully justify itself in the light of business practices that are being outmoded, may shortsightedly rule against vital and proper initial investments.

Chapter VII

Part-programming Procedures and Alternatives

Part programming which creates instructions that regulate a machine's motions and auxiliary operations is the heart of computer and numerically controlled operations. It must be carried out at minimum cost and yet provide the means for directing the machine to produce a part in the shortest possible time.

Four methods for developing a programmed control tape are in common usage. Two of the techniques produce the tape codes by mechanical processes, while the other two create tape instructions from words and numbers recorded on a planning manuscript. One mechanical process develops a control tape as a by-product of a manually controlled machining operation. Identical parts can then be manufactured from the tape with very little human intervention. Another mechanical process uses a sensor attached to a coordinate measuring machine that determines the desired dimensions. As the sensor follows the contour of a model or line drawing, the related dimensions are encoded on tape. The tape can then be used to control a machine, enabling the path recorded by the sensor to be duplicated.

Instructions composed of alphanumeric characters are recorded on a planning manuscript when the nonmechanical programming techniques are used. The manuscript information is either manually punched into the control tape by means of an electric typewriter having a tape-punching device, or automatically converted through computer assistance. The nonmechanical programming methods, referred to as manual and computer-aided part programming, are the most widely used of the four techniques.

THE PROGRAMMING PROCESS

Information for the control tape is usually assimilated by a part programmer who coordinates his efforts with several other workers throughout the organization, e.g., the product designer—to assure that the design intent and specifications are properly interpreted;

the machine operator—to assure that process plans are fully understood; the fixture designers and tool setters; and the quality control and maintenance personnel. The programming process begins when the part characteristics are analyzed to determine the type of equipment needed. Subsequent programming decisions define the fixturing procedure, the type, form, and sequence of cutting tools, the tool's path, and the machine's feed and speed rates. At least ten distinct levels of activity are directly involved with, or closely related to, part programming: (1) selecting parts, (2) making design interpretations, (3) planning the process, (4) specifying workholder and fixture provisions, (5) preparing dimensional and machine management data, (6) selecting cutting tools and machinability rates, (7) preparing the program manuscript, (8) converting the manuscript to coded tape information, (9) verifying the encoded information, and (10) proving the tape.

Depending upon the application and organizational practices, the part programmer may perform all, or only a few, of these ten activities. The programmer will usually, however, have major responsibility for the design interpretation, data preparation, and completion of the manuscript. Because of the close interdependence of these ten activities—as described in the discussion to follow—a programmer requires a thorough knowledge of all the factors affecting every activity. Special training and skills in mathematics, tooling, and machining practices are especially important.

Selecting Parts for Computer or Numerical Control

Except in large computer or numerical control operations, the part programmer plays a central role in choosing the jobs best suited for equipment with automatic controls. Process planners or a programming supervisor often select the parts in large operations. The process planner may also define the process plan, including the fixturing and tooling provisions. In smaller operations, where specialization of labor is difficult, the part programmer selects the part and carries out all the other functions required to create and verify the control tape.

Design Interpretation

Before the part can be programmed, a detailed and thorough design analysis is necessary. To help the programmer interpret the design parameters and to identify potential troublesome areas, an outline sketch of the part is often prepared. The programmer's sketch serves many additional functions such as helping to define the cutter path and determine the appropriate cutting tools and fixtures.

Computer and numerical controls allow great latitude for conveying the design intent to the part programmer. Often a crude sketch is adequate for the programmer to complete his task. In some point-to-point applications, a simple table listing the coordinate locations of the holes suffices, thereby entirely avoiding costly drawings. For large diemaking applications, the configuration may be presented as a model or a mock-up, from which the control tape is programmed by a mechanical process using a coordinate measuring machine. In an aircraft plant, tables of master dimension data and engineering drafts may be acceptable.

Process Planning

With few exceptions, process planning for computer or numerically controlled manufacturing generally is similar to the procedures used in conventional production. Traditional engineering principles forming the basis of sound process planning are hardly changed. First, the part drawing and sketches made during design interpretation are analyzed. In addition to determining the major fabrication steps and necessary equipment, the preliminary fixturing and setup provisions as well as the tentative cutting tools are recorded on a form similar to a routing sheet or step procedure. Regardless of the form used, the programmer or process planner defines in specific terms every major function required to manufacture the part.

The use of computer or numerical controls has, however, changed the nature and location of process decisions. For conventional operations, the level of detail included in the process plan varies with the application's complexity and management's organizational philosophy. A telling difference between conventional and computer or numerical control process planning must be emphasized: regardless of the organization's size or management policies, every computer or numerical control production activity must be preselected and completely defined. This requirement sharply contrasts with conventional methods in which the operator is often relied upon to complete sketchy plans and improvise missing steps.

To a great extent, computer and numerical controls were designed to minimize the number of processing decisions made on the shop floor. Such decisions, whether they are good or bad, are nearly

247

always suboptimal. Since the machine operator is largely outside of the machine control loop, manufacturing by automatic controls makes tighter management control both possible and imperative. Profitable benefits can result, but only if the choice of all work materials, tooling methods, process sequences, and machinability provisions are completely and correctly settled before the part is ever placed on the machine. With virtually no margin for error, greater demands are obviously placed on the process planner and the programmer. Nothing can be left to chance, and very little to the discretion of the machine operator. Incomplete instructions or errors causing revisions to the tape are not only delaying, but pyramid cost penalties if production is interrupted partway through the processing of a part program.

Specifying Workholder and Fixture Provisions

A major difference between computer or numerical control and conventional jig and fixture requirements is that with instructions on the control tape, the need for, and complexity of, nonperishable special tooling is greatly reduced. As noted in Chapter V, jigs and specially designed tooling are required for less than 10 percent of the computer or numerical control jobs.

Workholding methods and procedures are recorded on a sketch or process sheet to aid in determining cutter path definition, as well as to guide the operator in machine setup. A major concern for the programmer is to achieve the shortest possible machine cycle time for a tool path that provides adequate, but not sloppy and time-consuming cutter-fixture clearances. Unlike the situation in conventional processing, the programmer cannot rely on the operator to make in-process adjustments which allow the cutter to clear the workholders.

Workholders attached to a subplate and risers are used whenever possible to guard against machine damage if a programming error or equipment malfunction causes too deep a tool penetration. Where families of parts are produced, a subplate with milled slots or tapped holes simplifies workholding and speeds part setup. If the subplate's holes for threaded studs are arranged in a convenient pattern, such as in two- or three-inch grids, then the programmer can define the programmed set point as a specific hole center. Obviously, clamps or other workholders must be precisely located on the machine as specified by the programmer, since the program fixes the path of the cutter relative to a set point. These locational requirements are especially critical for machines without a floating zero or zero offset capabilities. The operator's failure to place the fixture at the proper location can cause collisions, broken cutters, improperly cut parts, and serious machine damage.

To take advantage of the high revenue-generating capacities of computer and numerical controls, programmers maximize the use of fixtures providing quick workpiece loading and unloading. To handle large-volume parts requiring multi-sided processing and to minimize the number of relocations, special indexing fixtures or machining centers are often quite profitable.

Data Preparation

Making the arithmetic and geometric calculations for cutter paths, tool offsets, feed and speed rates; deciding on tool sequences; and assigning the miscellaneous and preparatory function codes are the major activities of the data preparation phase. All these tasks must be coordinated to avoid cutter dwells and improper accelerations and decelerations which might create under- or over-cuts during cornering and other motion changes.

The extensiveness of the data preparation task is determined not only by whether the application is point-to-point or continuous path, but also by the control's interpolating capabilities. For point-to-point applications, the data points are usually the hole centers; while the entire course of each slide movement may need to be completely dimensioned for parts on certain continuous-path controls. In performing the data preparation activity, the programmer must be able to visualize mentally the relationship of the part and each machine motion. The data processing and calculations required for translating these parameters to coded program information can be divided into two major tasks.

1. For each tool motion a programmed starting and ending point is defined. Intermediate points defining the entire path may need to be calculated depending upon the path's shape and whether the control unit has linear, circular, or parabolic interpolation. Mathematical computations are also required for redimensioning certain parameters such as tool offsets and rounding-off vectors, and for determining proper speeds and feeds that allow the tool to travel between points within acceptable tolerances.

2. The codes for auxiliary and miscellaneous functions must be determined and arranged in a very precise order. These include spindle speed and direction, the mist or flood method of applying coolant, tool changes, etc.

Draftsmen can help minimize the calculations needed by showing all dimensions in decimals rather than fractions, and by using a dimensioning system compatible with the characteristics of the control. Once the required data have been prepared, the programmer checks his work by asking such questions as these:

1. Have all tool paths been mathematically defined?
2. Is the machine tool physically capable of carrying out all the defined operations?
3. Will the feedrates, under automatic control, achieve the specified dimensional precision standards?
4. Are there any potential collisions between the cutter and the fixtures or machine structures?

The results of the data preparation phase are recorded on working papers or directly on a programming manuscript in a format compatible with the equipment.

Selecting Cutting Tools and Machinability Rates

As each machining motion is established, the programmer specifies, in addition to the feeds and speeds, the proper type, length, degree of taper, and shape of the cutting tool. Machinability decisions are influenced by the type of work material, the part's size and shape, the machine's power, and the nature of the machining process—all governed by quality and cost constraints.

Management policies and organizational procedures must assure that programmed tooling specifications are precisely adhered to during subsequent operations. Otherwise, broken tools and unacceptable tolerances are inevitable. The pressure to maximize productivity in the face of such strict tooling requirements may dictate the use of preset tools.

The importance of precisely following the programmed tool dimensions has greatly reduced the use of resharpened tools. When resharpened tools are used, they must be ground to predetermined standard sizes, and to much closer tolerances than are required for conventional equipment. Computer and numerical control tools are usually programmed from standard sizes, and this may require costly removal of more tool material during resharpening than would otherwise be necessary. The use of nonstandard tools having dimensions different from those programmed can require redoing the tape or interrupting the machine operation to enter cutter compensation information into the controller. For many applications, it is cheaper to restrict the use of nonstandard resharpened tools to conventional machines.

For tool changing equipment, the tool changes and sequence of operations, such as center drilling, drilling, reaming, and tapping, must be strategically programmed to assure the shortest overall cycle time. Although many sequence variations are possible for parts with multioperations involving several tools, only one set is the most efficient. When a batch consists of several parts with many operations, the difference between a marginal tape and a tape that optimally interleaves tool changes and sequences can amount to a costly time penalty of 20 to 25 percent.

Automatic tool changers require the programmer to enter on the tape an appropriate code number for the tool to be used during each operation. Depending upon the equipment design, one of several methods is used to program these codes. For example, in a turret machine each turret is assigned a number, and the programmer assigns a specific tool to each turret position; he then calls out the desired turret number when a specific tool is required. The setup instructions accompanying the tape inform the operator which tools are to be installed in the respective turret stations, and when a tool in a turret should be replaced by another tool.

Having relocated the machining decisions from the shop floor to the programmer's office, processing errors now more frequently result from improper tooling or machinability decisions than from inaccurate cutting configurations. Because automatic controls operate in a closed-loop system without human intervention, the programmer even more than a conventional machinist must have a sound basic knowledge of machinability principles such as the interrelationship of material hardness and the ductile, tensile, and sheer strengths. In achieving maximum productivity, programmers keep the cutting rates within a critical narrow band, one boundary being high feedrates and the other a machine overload condition. Automatic controls, being particularly vulnerable to machinability practices that overload the equipment's capacity, can cause dwells or stalls, producing unacceptable surface finishes and dimensional variations before the operator can intervene.

When the programmer has selected and coded the cutting tools and the machinability rates, he searches for problems by asking such questions as the following:

1. Are the sizes and shapes of the cutting tools adequate?
2. Are the feed and speed rates suitable for the workpiece, fixturing, cutter materials, and the capabilities of the machine?
3. Does the workpiece need to be reset to machine any areas blocked by the initial fixture placement?
4. Are all tools properly coded and of standard dimensions?
5. Are the programmed feedrates as high as possible without overloading the machine?

Preparing the Program Manuscript

Upon completion of all the preliminary work, the part programmer begins extracting the relevant information from the working papers and writes an ordered listing of machine instruction codes on the manuscript. Each line of manuscript information defines a single machine operation. Coordinate points for each cutter path segment are entered along with appropriate feedrates, coolant flow, tool selections, etc. The manuscript, from which the control tape codes will be taken, must be filled out in strict compliance with the conventions established by both machine tool and control manufacturers. If a diversified array of equipment is the responsibility of a single programmer, the different requirements may be confusing until he has acquired a thorough familiarity with them all. Word forms, address forms, punctuation conventions, and the methods for computing movement dimensions and feedrate limitations are commonly different for various machines.

If the tape format requires six rows of information, and should the programmer provide any other number on the manuscript, the tape reader will not be able to interpret the words correctly. On equipment using letters for operation codes or word addresses, only the correct use of the letters authorized by the control's design will produce an acceptable tape. Should the tape reader process an incorrectly programmed word, costly damage to the part or machine may result. If a programmer is responsible for both absolute and incremental equipment, a common source of error is the failure to compute the dimensions according to the proper convention—be it incremental or absolute. An extra verification step is recommended to guard against such a pitfall.

The type of information entered on the manuscript by the programmer is indicated by the column headings:

Sequence Number
Preparatory Function
X Position
Y Position
Z Position
Tool Function
Miscellaneous Function
Comments

The Sequence Number column identifies the order in which each line or block of information is to be positioned on the control tape. The Preparatory Function column designates the type of operation to be performed. Examples of Preparatory Functions, commonly called G Functions and numbered from zero through 99 include mill cycle, mill-cycle stop, drill cycle, tap cycle, and bore cycle. The number of digits that identify a Preparatory Function is an explicit number determined by the machine and control builders.

Data in the X- and Y-Position columns, and the Z-Position column for a three-axis control, record the cutter path dimensions. Equipment manufacturers also specify the length of the number and the location of the decimal point for recording the coordinate dimensions. Decimal points are not punched into the tape; on a format specifying five digits with three decimal places, a coordinate of 15.250 inches would appear simply as 15250. The control's circuitry interprets the location of the decimal point. If six digits and four decimals were called for, the same coordinate would be punched as 152500. The dimensional information usually consists of five, six, or seven digits. Depending on the equipment's design, dimensional numbers may need to be preceded by negative or positive signs. Similarly, leading zeros may, or may not be necessary. If the spindle travel is less than ten inches, the Z-Position column may specify one less digit than the X- and Y-Position columns. Because the number lengths and decimal point locations vary, the programmer is faced with another pitfall if he is responsible for several types of equipment.

The information in the Tool column identifies the code numbers of the tools to be used. These coding decisions are carefully communicated to the tool-setting personnel and machine operator to make sure that all understand and follow the programmer's specifications.

The tool codes often are selected from the preset tool-coding system established by the user within the limitations of the controller and the machine. On some equipment only the number codes specified by the manufacturer may be used, such as the turret numbers on a lathe or drilling machine. Special tool-coding schemes have been developed that use rings and binary coded keys attached to the holders of the appropriate tools. Machines with this feature automatically search the tool drum or magazine when a particular tool code appears on the tape. Some tool-coding techniques allow the operator limited freedom for randomly loading the coded tools in the machine's tool storage device.

The Miscellaneous Function column provides information for machine management functions such as speed and feedrate codes, program stops for part inspection and changes of tools and depth cams.

Remarks are entered in the Comments column to record significant assumptions that were used to program the information for each line. These notes are especially helpful in verifying the tape or locating programming problems. In simple applications, the remarks in the Comments column may serve as the formal instructions to the operator for part setup and program operation. However, the remarks in the Comments column normally are not part of the instructions.

The format and content of the information to be entered on the manuscript are also influenced by whether manual or computer-aided programming is to be used. A manual manuscript is written so that coded data can be punched directly into the tape and therefore must conform to the particular equipment tape format requirements. Computer-aided part programming permits greater manuscript flexibility by allowing the programmer to write less complete information and statements consisting of abbreviated English-like words. The computer then interprets these, executes the calculations, and converts the results into a tape with proper formats and complete codes. Not only does the computer-aided method avoid many of the manual calculations, it also eases the programmer's task by reducing his need for learning special tape coding requirements and the dynamic response peculiarities of each machine.

When the programmer has finished the manuscript, he examines the written instructions by asking such questions as these:

1. Are the word and address forms and punctuation proper?
2. Are all machine operations properly activated and recorded in the right columns?
3. Are the dimensional words of proper length?
4. Are the decimal points in correct position?

Programming procedures must contain adequate accuracy checks, since even the smallest of errors, such as the misplacement of a comma, may cause a collision or fail to activate a speed or feedrate change. As another example, an inverted dimensional value or an inaccurately recorded decimal point can cause the cutter to collide with the table. Many manuscript errors can be avoided by having a second programmer review the work or prepare another copy of the manuscript for comparison. This practice of course must be used only where it is cost-effective.

Converting the Manuscript to Coded Tape Information

Information from the manuscript is encoded on punched paper tape or on data processing cards if computer-aided programming is to be used. Tape preparation for manual programming is a clerical procedure in which a clerk typist, using an electric typewriter equipped with a tape punch, produces the tape. With computer-aided part programming, the data processing cards containing the encoded manuscript information are computer-processed, and the paper tape is produced by the computer or by a tape-punching device from information on computer-produced magnetic tape or data processing cards.

In both manual and computer-aided programming a listing of the encoded manuscript information is printed so that the programmer can review a typed record of the exact information that was punched into the control tape. A typed copy can be compared to the programmer's handwritten manuscript to check for errors. The computer prints out a listing of the results of the data processing and calculations it performed, showing the X, Y, and Z data points and the auxiliary code information. Both types of print-out are extremely useful for program and tape verification procedures.

Verifying the Encoded Information

Before the tape is released to production, it should be thoroughly checked to eliminate any punching errors. In addition to visually checking the accuracy of the typed manuscript, the mechanical process of encoding the information on cards can be verified by repeating the typing operation. For computer applications a key-punch verifier is usually used to check the coded information. The verifier operator retypes each data processing card from the source information, and the keyboard locks if a discrepancy is distinguished between a character coded on the card and the related information being typed for that card. After the verifier operator determines the source of the error and corrects it, the remaining cards are checked in the same manner. Because it is highly improbable that a character will be typed erroneously in the same way during both the original and verification typing, this procedure has proved quite effective for checking the mechanical encoding of computer input data. Punched paper tapes may be verified in the same manner, and some tape-verifying equipment produces a second tape during the process. One of the verified tape copies then becomes a master and is stored for future use.

A second method of tape checking, parity checking, is performed automatically as each character is encoded. The punching equipment counts the number of holes used to encode each character. Depending upon the controller to be used, the characters for control tapes must consist of either an odd number or an even number of holes, but never both; otherwise the punching machine senses a coding error. Parity checking is done automatically, but it only detects the presence of a character with missing or extra holes. Improperly punched characters having an acceptable number of holes cannot be detected by parity checking.

The channel and row alignment of the tape holes should also be inspected while the punching accuracy is being checked. After hours of high-speed operations, tape punches may perforate holes of irregular shape, and with improper spacing. Hole punches also lose their sharpness, which might lead to incomplete perforations, causing the punched material to stick in some parts of the tape. With punched chad sticking to the tape, the tape reader may not sense a hole where one should be located. Many of these problems can be avoided by proper equipment maintenance to make sure that the hole punches are kept sharp and the feed mechanism is supplying the tape to the punches with perfect alignment and timing. Special attention should be given to the sprocket hole punch, because these smaller holes are usually the first to have chad that is not completely removed.

The hole's shape and alignment are suitably checked visually unless the tape is long, or the work material exceptionally valuable. Normally, spot-checks of the tape at three- to five-foot intervals is adequate, since tape-punching errors are seldom limited to one or a few rows of holes. Equipment malfunctions usually produce long sections of tape with several consecutive rows of imperfect holes. Intermittent errors do occur, however, and to guard against such contingencies, some companies use a checking gauge or photoelectric tape scanner with error-detection capabilities to check all the characters on tapes for valuable parts.

Proving the Tape

Having satisfied himself that the manuscript information has been properly coded, the programmer then tests the tape and all the programmed dimensions and machine management instructions. During tape verification every task performed throughout the manufacturing organization connected with part programming is checked. Tape prove-out can be time-consuming and tedious, especially if the part is to be produced by a complex, continuous-path machine. The thoroughness of the testing is determined by part complexity and the consequence of an error. Popular methods of proving control tapes include:

— Processing the tape on a block-by-block basis, under dry run or actual machining conditions.
— Drawing the programmed cutter path on a drafting machine or a computer-driven plotting device.
— Machining a sample part from Styrofoam, wood, or some easily machined material.
— Machining a test part out of a scrap casting or forging.
— Checking dimensions of the first part on a numerically controlled inspection machine.

The programmer, or someone from the programming group, usually supervises tape verification regardless of the technique used. To detect problems or inefficient sequences, every motion of the machine slides and cutting tool, as well as the dimensional data on the position readouts and the information displays is closely studied, and the clearances between the cutter, part, and fixtures are carefully inspected. When the machine is the testing device, the operator helps the programmer observe the nature of the problems and note the tape sequence numbers which have errors. Common changes required during the tape prove-out are recomputing feeds and speeds and adjusting acceleration and deceleration commands.

On complex parts, the tape trial may be performed in a machine dry-run mode without a cutting tool in the spindle. If the cutting tool is installed, the critical sections of the tape are cautiously processed by using the feedrate override and by having the operator remain in constant touch with the emergency stop button. A smaller nonmetal stylus to simulate the cutting tool may also be used for an approximate dimensional check, but this method does not determine the correctness of the feeds and speeds, the effects of cutter deflection, or the dynamic response of the machine's drives under loaded conditions.

The cutter path may also be checked by installing a ball-point pen in the spindle or its equivalent in place of a cutting tool. After locating a piece of stiff paper or mylar on the machine's table, processing the tape causes the ball-point pen to record the profile of two-axis movements of the spindle. All dimensional errors except possibly those less than a few thousandths of an inch become apparent when the profile line is inspected. This technique is not useful for proving tapes of more than two axes, unless all but two axes of control can be locked out while the tape is being checked.

Three other techniques that also plot the programmed cutter path are used to check tapes. The most popular of these method uses a computer or numerically controlled drafting machine. On some equipment, the control tape for the drafting machine is modified by a computer to adjust the commands for the instructional differences between a machine tool and a drafting machine. On other equipment such adjustments are handled by the control. Center lines of a cutter path can be plotted by a drafting machine to an accuracy of 0.001 to 0.004 of an inch.

A second plotting method produces a two-axis plot of the cutter path on the face of a cathode-ray tube, and a third plots a line drawing of the path on strip paper. Because these plotting areas are smaller than the drafting machine's, both of these techniques require a substantial scaling down of dimensions for large parts.

Depending upon the equipment's capabilities, computer or numerically controlled drafting machines, cathode-ray tube displays, and plotters can draw cutter paths in any combination of two axes. If needed, some drafting machines and cathode-ray tube devices can also sketch three-dimensional views. Despite the inherent drawbacks of the plotting techniques, which may include their accuracy limitations and inability to test machinability instructions, they are effective for many tape tests, and their popularity is growing. Just as important, the cost of such equipment is declining rapidly.

For parts to be produced from costly, hard-to-machine alloys, many companies first cut a test part out of aluminum, low-carbon steel, wood, or Styrofoam. One inherent problem of machining Styrofoam is that it creates a light, fluffy dust which may aggravate the machine's slideways and block filters on the controls. Testing control tapes by cutting easily machined material adequately checks dimensions, but is still deficient in fully checking feeds and speeds under actual cutter loads. The complete checkout of feeds and speeds can only be achieved by machining the actual workpiece or a material of equal strength. Scrap castings are sometimes effectively used for this purpose.

The use of computer or numerically controlled inspection machines for tape verification is also increasing. Inspection machines operate like a machine tool, except that they position a stylus according to the tape information. The stylus position for each checkpoint is sensed and the coordinate dimensions are shown in a numerical readout display or printed as a manuscript. The correctness of the control tape can be verified by comparing the recorded dimensions to those specified in the part drawing, planning sketch, or program manuscript.

A general indication of the relative popularity of the various tape-proving techniques is shown in Table I. The proportion of users employing the machine dry-run mode indicates its effectiveness for both point-to-point and continuous-path applications. A significant disadvantage, however, of proving tapes on a machine is that equipment that is capable of generating a high rate of revenue is unproductive during tape check-out. The machine may also be heavily loaded with parts having critical delivery times, making it especially difficult to remove the machine from production for the slow process of tape verification. Another apparent trend indicates that nearly one-third of the companies with continuous-path applications verify some of their tapes with automatic drafting machines. A relatively high proportion of the users check their tapes simply by inspecting the results of the first production part. The popularity of this practice, especially for point-to-point applications and simple continuous-path parts, indicates that if adequate checks are exercised throughout the various programming phases, a high degree of accuracy can be expected.

TABLE I

COMMON METHODS OF VERIFYING CONTROL TAPES
PERCENTAGE OF COMPANIES USING METHODS SHOWN

	Type of Application	
Verification Method	Point-to- Point	Continuous Path
Machine tool dry run	83%	64%
Drafting machine	11	30
Cutting scrap or other inexpensive material	3	9
Other—including inspection of first part	46	18

Source: University of Michigan Survey.

Note: Totals add to more than 100 percent due to the use of multiple methods by reporting companies.

A combination of two or more verification methods may also be used; for example, a tape for a contouring application may be tested on a drafting machine; it may then be checked again by cutting a sample part out of a scrap casting. Obviously the tape-proving method selected must satisfy the complexity of the application, the availability of tape-proving equipment, the loading of the machine, and the consequence of a tape error.

After all economically feasible checks have been made, the programmer analyzes the problems and determines what corrective action may be required. If the problems are inconsequential and only one or a few parts are to be produced, the control tape may be released to the operator with the necessary supplemental instructions that will permit the marginal tape to be used. Slight dimensional and machinability adjustments to modify marginal tape instructions can sometimes be entered through the control's cutter compensation or feedrate override devices. Machine economics or quality requirements, however, may rule out any of the foregoing possibilities and dictate redoing the tape.

Transferring the Tape to Production

Once the tape is proven, the tool setting, machine setup, and operation become the vital links to quality production. Except for very simple point-to-point applications, detailed instructions should supplement the tape when it is forwarded by the programmer. For drilling a few holes, the instructions contained in the Comments column of the programming manuscript may be complete enough, or they may only need to be supplemented by the programmer's sketch. Progressively more detailed instructions, however, are needed as the complexity of the part increases.

In the production of multi-axis continuous-path parts, the programmer, or a programmer liaison representative, often accompanies the tape to interpret the instructions and assist the operator during initial setup. Many companies have found that this procedure results in better quality and avoids delays that arise from ambiguities in the sketch or instructions.

The programmer's instructions must provide complete tooling information so the operator can inspect the cutting tools to ensure that the diameter, length, flute characteristics, and radii of the tools supplied are the same as those specified in the program. Other instructions, but especially the fixture alignment and part setup information, will vary between equipment types. For equipment with zero offset or a floating zero reference point, the programmer is relatively free to choose the position for the part on the table; in this case the operator concerns himself mainly with positioning the fixture parallel to the X and Y slides; he then electronically synchronizes the machine by using the zero shift device.

Equipment without the flexible zero shift capabilities, however, demand much stricter setup procedures and correspondingly more definite operator instructions. These instructions must precisely specify to the operator the required positions of the slides and the exact distance that the fixture and part are to be located from the machine's fixed reference point along each axis.

Quick machine setup is also enhanced by sending a proven tape and the instructions directly to a make-ready crib where everything the operator needs can be prepared and assembled in a job container. Besides the tape, the fixture, preset tooling, sketches, and the instructions are included in the package when the crib releases the job. Some companies also include the print-out of the coordinate data points in the cutter path as an aid to the operator or maintenance personnel when troubleshooting. A side benefit seems to be that when the operator is able to relate the computer print-out with the punched tape, he is more likely to consider himself a professional member of a team that uses modern methods, rather than a subordinate to a programmed tape.

Complete instructions not only speed the setup, but also permit management to pinpoint the responsibility for unacceptable parts. The operator, since he is the last person to scrutinize all the process elements before the tape is actuated, should be instructed as part of the setup procedure—and be held accountable—to review the fixturing, preset tools, and work material provisions, and to ensure that all conform to the programmer's requirements.

Although all steps in the part-programming process have a high degree of interdependency, no single interrelationship is more vital than the interface between the operator and the programmer. If the operator fails to understand even a trivial program assumption, the most perfectly conceived tape will likely end up producing scrap. Carefully selected organizational procedures will ensure the effective two-way flow of complete information between the operator and the programmer.

PROGRAMMING ALTERNATIVES

Part programming has created an entirely new technology for which the evolving skills have continued to be scarce. As a result, operational costs have remained high and are, at best, only decreasing at a modest pace. In the search for programming expediencies, four tape-preparation techniques have evolved to a general level of common usage, and a fifth—computer graphics—is in limited use.

Selecting the best part-programming method from the alternatives is primarily influenced by the part configuration and operations required, the skills of the programmer, and the availability of a computer and supporting software. Normally, it is the programmer who weighs the relevant factors and selects the best from at least two feasible methods.

Tape Preparation as a Machining By-Product

A review of the five tape-preparation alternatives can logically start with the relatively simple technique wherein a control tape is generated as the machinist manually produces the first part. This tape by-product method uses a machine-control combination that has position transducers and an automatic tape punch to capture and encode the commands on tape during the machine operation. To minimize the chance of errors, the location dimensions for each operation are usually entered into the control through an operation location tape which is punched and verified before the first part is actually machined.

Typical procedures used to produce a tape on a machine equipped with a position encoder and an automatic tape punch are summarized below:

1. The machine operator manually enters the X- and Y-axis dimensions for each operation by using the control's manual dials. The control reads the commands for each operation and punches the information on a location tape. When all dimensions have been entered, the location tape is read by the tape reader and the machine's actions are observed for accuracy.

2. A part is then machined as the operator adds the machine management commands for each location on the tape. Not only is the part produced, but a final control tape is punched containing all necessary commands which will completely and automatically regulate subsequent production of that part.

Producing a tape as a by-product avoids the detailed work required for manual programming in which all dimensions, feedrates, etc., must be completely specified on a program manuscript. Because every machine action can readily be associated with each manually entered command, this mechanical programming technique allows machine operators to program their own tapes. Since duplicate tapes for other machines may be produced as the original copy is being run, engineering changes and tape corrections are easily made by the operator by interrupting the automatic tape-duplicating process and manually entering corrected or new data.

Because the need for specially trained programming personnel is reduced, small shops with limited supporting personnel are the main users of the by-product method. This technique, however, has definite limitations: the capabilities of available equipment restrict its use to point-to-point and limited straight-line milling work and, secondly, when the operator programs the machine, management relinquishes control over productivity.

FIGURE 1
The Mark Century Autoprogrammer.

Tape Preparation by Scanning-Digitizing Techniques

A second part-programming alternative uses various types of electromechanical and optical sensors to transcribe coordinate dimensions for control tapes. Drawings, templates, and three-dimensional models are the media commonly scanned. Coordinate dimensions of the measured points usually are recorded as a printed manuscript or punched into data processing cards or paper tape. The recorded data may be used directly as a machine control tape or as basic information for subsequent computer processing in such applications as automotive or aircraft surface development.

To satisfy the diversified needs of the various types of equipment now having computer or numerical controls, three distinct levels of transcriber-digitizing techniques have evolved. The least sophisticated process simply measures and records in digital form the coordinate locations of point-to-point operations for drilling, boring, or hole punching. Since these transcribing devices are limited to sensing two-axis coordinate measurements, the dimensions of the third axis and the auxiliary and miscellaneous machine commands are usually entered manually through an electric keyboard.

Transcribing Point-to-Point Operations

The two-axis transcriber-digitizer shown in Figure 1 is typical of the equipment used to measure and digitize dimensional information for point-to-point control tapes. After an accurately scaled drawing or template is placed on the scanner's layout table, the transcriber's stylus is manually positioned over each point whose X- and Y-axis locations are to be sensed. At each location, the operator also manually enters the miscellaneous and auxiliary machine commands so that the resulting control tape will be complete.

The major components of the transcriber-digitizer shown in the illustration include a precision layout table fitted with X- and Y-position transducers, a coordinatograph, and a microscope with a cross-hair reticle for precisely sighting the stylus over the desired drawing positions. A coordinate position readout display which shows the X, Y location of the coordinatograph, an electric keyboard, and a cabinet containing the digital logic circuits, power supplies, and tape punch are also included. Two-axis transcriber-digitizers are usually capable of electronically expanding the drawing's dimensions by at least 2:1 to 4:1 factors.

Printed circuit boards, cabinet panels, electronic sheet metal chassis, and air-frame structures are examples of parts efficiently programmed with a transcriber-digitizer. The latter application is particularly attractive where full-scale structural drawings are available from aircraft surface development activities. These drawings are normally accurate enough to be used on the transcriber with little additional processing.

Relatively unskilled workers learn to prepare tapes with transcribers in 25 to 50 percent of the time required to train experienced workers for conventional part programming. Another important savings results because draftsmen need not record the hole placement dimensions on drawings that will be scanned. Some transcriber-digitizer users have experienced a one-fifth savings in drafting time by eliminating the dimensions on part drawings which have several holes.

Complex Digitizing Techniques

Combination drafting-digitizing machines like the one shown in Figure 2, being considerably more capable than position transcribers, permit the preparation of both point-to-point and continuous-path

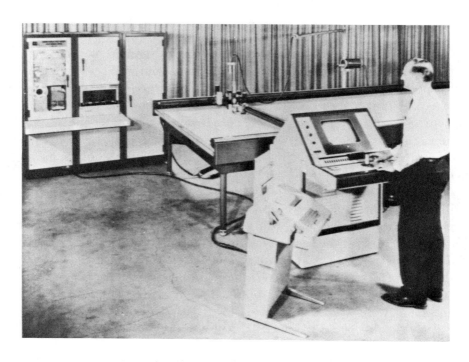

FIGURE 2

An Orthomat Mark II, combination drafting digitizing machine model.

control tapes. The equipment's flexibility has led to a variety of applications, including tapes for template machining, contouring and drilling of metal parts, automotive toolmaking and die sinking, drilling of printed circuit boards, and ship bulkhead contouring.

Typical drafting-digitizing machines employ an optical follower operating on X, Y slides and rails which are stationed on a large table. Some tables are as large as 8 by 24 feet. Since the optical system magnifies the line being measured several times, very precise measurements are possible. Although there are variations in equipment complexity and capabilities, the components commonly used are a drafting table with position transducers, an optical scanner and automatic line follower, a stored program computer, an operator's console with controls, an electric keyboard, coordinate position readout displays, a television monitor, a tape punch, and a printer.

Once the machine is set up, the operator only monitors the scanning-digitizing process and directs the tracer head at line branches or intersections where it cannot differentiate among the alternatives.

266

FIGURE 3
The Tridea electronics ALTAPE system.

The tracer head is also capable of following an edge of a template, either a dark background containing white lines or a white background with dark lines.

The automatic tracing function of a typical system shown in Figure 3 is facilitated by a continuous null-balancing closed loop in which light on each side of the line is continually compared in order to ascertain the local direction vector that will describe the line tangent. A rotating photosensor automatically seeks the line-tangent direction. The sensor servo resolves the operator-regulated tracer velocity into the X- and Y-axis components; these velocity signals are then supplied to the velocity servo drives of the respective axes to make the tracer head follow the line. The tracer head thus provides a continuous-direction angle output which guides the boresite center precisely along the line center.

During the tracing of a drawing, the X and Y coordinates of points along a line are continuously measured. For the equipment shown, the measurement subsystem includes a reference grating which extends the full length of each axis; it has bidirectional counters that continually accumulate the X- and Y-coordinate values. The system's

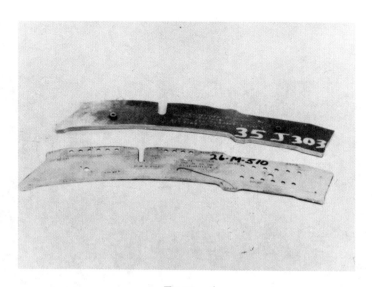

FIGURE 4

Developed Template (DT) and Router Block used to rout part
from stock material.

small computer is programmed to process the resulting coordinate
dimensions completely into a tool path description.

The tracer's velocity is controlled by the operator's foot pedal and
is independent of the specified machining feedrate. Instead, the
operator controls the tracing rate as a function of drawing complexity. Maximum tracing speed on typical equipment is 100 to 200
inches per minute (ipm) on straight lines; typical rates on a contour
line such as a 1-inch radius range from 15 to 75 ipm.

The procedures for tape preparation with the combination drafting-digitizing machine can be illustrated by reviewing the methods
utilized by the McDonnell Douglas Corporation for the template
shown in Figure 4. Upon receipt of an order to make a template,
a layout man secures the appropriate drawing and prepares the instructions for the digitizer operator. The operator locates the drawing on the table and enters through the electric keyboard the cutter
radius, the scanning feedrate at 40 ipm, and the turret number of
the machine tool that should contain the specified cutting tool.
As the tracing begins the computer activates the tape punch, punches
the necessary blank tape leader, and starts producing tape. While the
tracer head is automatically following the line, coordinate dimensions are simultaneously displayed on the readout panel and fed to

the computer, which continually receives every 0.001 inch of data change in either axis. The computer's software program directs it to sample the incoming data to determine its significance, to discard the insignificant data, and to maintain an up-to-date buffer of input points for use in the correction routine.

The first step of the data selection process is to define mathematically the line segment formed by the current point and the previous point. This line segment is then offset by the cutter radius, and the slope of the new line is tested for deviation from the slope of the previous line. Points which lie on the same straight line are rejected as insignificant. However, when a new point is discovered that does lie more than 0.001 of an inch from the straight line, the point of intersection is determined; this distance becomes the value of the next X, and Y increment. Since the computer handles the cutter offset computations, the output data on the tape describe the tool center path rather than the line on the drawing.

Having determined the required X and Y move, further calculations based on the specific machine tool characteristics are made to determine if any changes in the machining velocity are required. When a change is necessary, as in the case of a high feedrate block approaching a 90-degree corner, the output block is separated into several small blocks with diminishing feedrates so that over-or-under cuts at the part corner will be avoided. When all calculations are completed, an output block is assembled, and a high-speed tape punch is used to encode the tape commands.

After the periphery of the template has been fully traced, the operator depresses the digitizer's TOOL UP control push button, causing all stored data in the buffer to be processed, and the instructions required to raise the cutting tool are punched on the tape. The tracer head is then manually directed to the template center for an internal cutout operation. After recording an entry point, the operator depresses the TOOL DOWN push button. Tracing is then resumed within the cutout until the entry point has been reached again, at which point the operator depresses the TOOL UP push button. Since there is also a hole pattern on the template, the DRILL ROUTINE push button is depressed and hole centers are recorded as single point entries. When all operations are complete, the operator depresses the END PROGAM push button and the system then computes the path back to the set point, outputs a stop code, punches the trailer tape, and finally, turns the tape punch off.

FIGURE 5
A Sheffield Three-Axis Cordax Coordinate Measuring Machine
interfaced to a computer.

McDonnell Douglas has found that similar templates are programmed by such digitizing techniques in approximately 15 minutes and at about one-third the cost of conventional programming. Since the tape produced is fully postprocessed by the system's computer, the template can be immediately machined. Programming time savings are even more impressive: at McDonnell Douglas, as at many other companies, an average of 84 hours elapses from the time a part program is written to the time it is debugged and a postprocessed tape is satisfactorily computed and ready for production.

Although the normal operational capabilities of the type of equipment illustrated in Figure 2 are limited to two-dimensional parts, a combination tape can be made for certain three-dimensional contours by integrating in a suitable computer the data of two tapes prepared from related orthogonal drawing views. A three-axis tape can also be created by entering the third-axis dimensions through the computer's keyboard. Because the latter method can be time-consuming if changes in the third axis are frequent, it is not a widely used production method.

Three-Dimensional Model-Scanning Techniques

When a physical model of the part is available, the three-dimensional scanner provides still another programming alternative. One of the earliest three-dimensional scanners, shown in Figure 5, was originally designed as a coordinate measuring machine that provided a printed dimensional record for inspection purposes. As new requirements for producing difficult-to-program parts arose, the inspection device was modified to generate two- and three-axis control tapes by the addition of a tape punch and additional software for the computer. Scanners typified by Figure 5 are used most commonly in automotive and aerospace applications and hold overall accuracies of ±0.0005 of an inch.

Common procedures for using a three-dimensional scanner are summarized below:

1. The scanner's probe, which usually corresponds in physical shape and dimensions to the actual cutting tool, is moved to the start point, and is manually traversed across the surface of the three-dimensional model. The probe's path is thus identical to the desired cutter path.

2. A computer automatically stores the sensed coordinate measurements, computes any required modifications, and punches the dimensions on a tape. By comparing the contour's rate of change, the computer determines what curvature data are significant and punches only the coordinate dimensions needed to maintain specified tool path tolerances.

Model-scanning equipment having a minimum degree of sophistication requires the operator to index the probe manually to the next path as each scanning pass is completed. More refined equipment, capable of a completely automatic model-scanning cycle is shown in Figure 6 digitizing an automotive fender die model. Parts with a volume of 60 inches by 36 inches by 24 inches can be digitized on

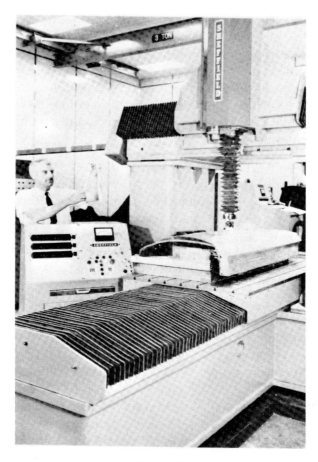

FIGURE 6
A contact probe-sensor.

such equipment to accuracies of ±0.005 of an inch. Somewhat larger and more accurate digitizing machines have also been built for similar applications.

For many jobs, it is not feasible for the probe to contact the model surface. The automotive clay model, for example, can be easily damaged by the probe's pressure. Consequently, a noncontact, or a very low pressure contact, null-seeking probe must be used. Contact probes capable of operating at a two-to-five gram pressure are now available for scanning sensitive models.

Photogrammetric and electronic measuring methods have also been developed for noncontact model scanning. For example, the laser beam scanner, located on X, Y slides for two-dimensional measurements, determines the third spatial dimension by measuring the time required for light wave travel between the light source and the model. A typical laser scanner shown in Figure 7 has an optical, null-seeking probe, with a sensitivity of ±0.0005 of an inch. The laser beam has a spot diameter less than 0.020 of an inch. The optical system effectively integrates the center of this spot, even when its angle of incidence is up to 45 degrees off normal, thereby creating a sharp point of examination of the surface. Dimensions produced by a laser must, however, be adjusted for cutter diameter, a simple task in two dimensions, but requiring extensive calculations on three-dimensional surfaces.

Stereophotographic model mapping is also utilized to lift contour

FIGURE 7
A Sheffield null-seeking probe. This is a
laser-powered noncontact sensor.

dimensions where contact sensors cannot be used. The potential of photogrammetry has been greatly improved through advancements in holography which captures three-dimensional information on a two-dimensional storage surface. Holography has several useful characteristics for transforming contour dimensions into a computer-processable form. The hologram reconstructs an object quickly and in three dimensions with contour lines superimposed. The lines can be used, for example, to recreate plane-model intersections comparable to the template signatures used in conventional manual methods. Contour signatures can then be recorded on film and scanned by an optical line-follower to digitize the coordinate values. Because the laser and photogrammetric scanning-digitizing methods are usually employed in preliminary surface development activities, the output of both techniques is commonly fed into a computer for further processing rather than punched directly into a control tape.

The various types of scanners capable of digitizing drawing and model coordinate dimensions not only offer varied alternatives for difficult-to-program parts, but avoid many of the computational and clerical procedures of manual programming. Major benefits are:

1. Necessary part-programming skills are reduced.
2. Precise measurements for undimensioned drawings can be obtained easily.
3. Repeated scalings of undimensioned drawings are avoided.
4. Tape-preparation time is shortened.
5. Total cost is reduced for appropriate applications.
6. Number of dimensions and amount of drafting time on drawings to be digitized are reduced.

The high relative cost of digitizing equipment has tended to restrict its use to large companies having adequate capital and control tape workload. A single digitizer can quickly create all the tapes required for several computer or numerically controlled machines. Medium-sized and small companies, therefore, find it economically difficult to justify owning an expensive digitizer solely for tape preparation, unless it is one of the less sophisticated, point-to-point transcriber-digitizers.

A scanner-digitizer achieves higher productivity because its scan rate is considerably greater than machine tool feedrates. Moreover, on parts having opposite but symmetrical elements, the digitized dimensions from a single scan may be used for both elements simply by reversing certain positive and negative coordinate values. This capability is particularly beneficial in automotive die work when the dimensions obtained by scanning a single fender model can be modified to serve as the numerical definition of both the left and right panels. Additionally, with minor adjustment of the dimensional data to compensate for metal thicknesses of the material to be formed by the die set, the coordinate values sometimes can define the mating surfaces of both the die and the punch elements. Similar principles apply to scanning for molds. The scanning of a single model may, therefore, provide the basic dimensions for the control tapes of four related, but distinct surfaces, and since metal cutting feedrates are considerably slower than scanning rates, a single scanner-digitizer may supply tapes for several machines.

Tape Preparation by Computer Graphics

Several large aerospace, automotive, and computer manufacturers initiated the development of a third part-programming technique which uses computer-graphics equipment. Computer graphics, a synthesis of computer technology and the graphic arts, greatly shortens part-programming time by permitting the immediate and dynamic representation of computer-stored or generated information. As illustrated in Figure 8, the part programmer sits at a computer-driven display, consisting of a cathode-ray tube (CRT) and function keys, and creates a control tape by using a light-sensing pen to draw the part and the tool path electronically on the face of the display.

The display serves as a window through which the part programmer communicates and interacts with the computer. Among the major advantages is the programmer's ability to inspect his and the computer's work immediately and to modify the results instantaneously. The computer-graphics system thus performs as a dynamic, interactive tool with response time measured in hundredths of a second. Programmers who previously had to create and write detailed manuscript instructions and who were generally frustrated by keypunching or data processing delays—delays which often were measured in hours or days—are understandably the greatest supporters of computer-graphics part programming. Other savings arise because the programmer can translate, rotate, and change the part orientation and scale of the display as required.

Although the detailed operational principles vary between different computer-graphics systems, normally the outline of the part

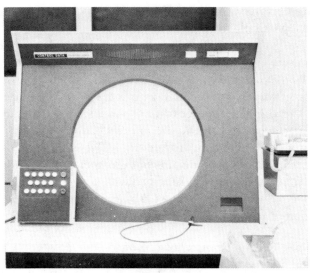

FIGURE 8
Graphic console.

to be programmed is first portrayed on the display CRT. With a "light pen" the programmer then traces the desired cutter path on the CRT. As the coordinate locations of the pen are tracked across the CRT by the computer, the cutter path's X- and Y-coordinate dimensions are recorded. Although the displayed and tracked information may contain graphical errors, once it is corrected by mathematical representations in the computer, it is highly accurate.

Detailed computer-graphics part-programming techniques are demonstrated by reviewing the operation of a typical system. Equipment similar to that in Figure 9, uses a medium-sized digital computer, CRT display, electric keyboard, light pen, and push button function box. Serving as a point-sensing device, the light pen transmits the coordinate location data to the computer. Computer routines to set machining rates, turn on coolant, and generate other machine management commands such as bore, drill, or pocket mill cycles are initiated by special function push buttons. The programmer uses the electric keyboard and typewriter to enter other commands not included in the function buttons and to receive printed messages from the computer. Systems similar to the one shown in Figure 9 are capable of defining point, line, and circle geometry and are essentially two-and-one-half-axis continuous-path programming devices since third-axis dimensions are entered through the electric keyboard.

FIGURE 9
Basic equipment for a graphic part-programming system.

The process begins as the programmer transfers the part geometry onto the display CRT to record in the computer the mathematical model of the part. Lines defined by coordinate values are entered through the keyboard; an arc tangent to two displayed lines may be created by depressing the "circle" push button, pointing the light pen to the two lines, and typing the arc radius. As these elements are entered, they are also displayed.

After lines, circles, and points are used to portray the part, the programmer creates the cutter path by moving the light pen over the appropriate displayed part surfaces on the CRT. The computer calculates the coordinate values in the cutter path, complete with tool offsets which are then stored on magnetic tape for postprocessing.

The majority of computer-graphics part-programming applications have been parts with a two-axis profile, although three-axis continuous-path parts have also been handled. Application results have been quite encouraging, with users experiencing an average labor productivity improvement of five to one over conventional computer-aided part-programming methods and a lead-time reduction of eight to one. Higher quality output from tapes prepared by computer graphics is demonstrated by a 50 percent reduction in scrap parts. Many users find that their better part programmers virtually eliminate geometry and tool path errors when they make use of computer graphics. Relative ease of revising tapes is another advantage. Because most computer-graphics systems store the mathematical model of the part and the computed cutter path on magnetic tape, the programmer can readily retrieve and display the tape information and quickly edit the cutter path section needing revision. Minutes or hours, rather than days, are all that is needed by computer-graphics programmers to revise tapes.

Most computer-graphics part-programming systems require the availability of a very large computer which simultaneously services many different types of remote computer input-output devices on a time-shared basis.[1] Smaller computers primarily dedicated to a few graphics terminals are rapidly gaining in popularity. Depending upon the core storage requirements of the computer-graphics part-programming applications, both the large time-shared systems and the dedicated smaller computers have their places.

A major problem with large time-shared systems has been the difficulty in allocating adequate computer core memory that is required for each part-programming graphics terminal, without harmfully restricting the amount of core memory available to other simultaneous computer users. With large multi-programmed time-shared computer systems which dynamically allocate core memory to simultaneous users as they move through the processing queue, part programmers hooked to the computer through graphics terminals sometimes wait impatiently for assignment of adequate core memory space. The effect of the delay is aggravated if the computer then encounters a problem and aborts the part-programming computation. During such delays neither the programmer nor the graphics terminals are productive.

To maximize both programmer output and computer usage, several companies have selected computer-graphics programming systems with a smaller computer completely dedicated to the graphics terminals. The economic justification of such a setup obviously requires a substantial part program or other computer-graphics work load. Although the hourly equipment cost per graphics terminal can be about one-fifth greater than the expense associated with large

---

[1] A time-shared computer system provides multiple use of the central processor via terminals stationed at remote locations. The terminals may be of several configurations; the most common are teleprinter or other electric keyboard devices and input-output devices having a CRT.

multi-programmed time-shared computer systems, increased programmer effectiveness can result in an overall lower operating cost.

Because computer-graphics technology is relatively new, there is no ready-made solution that universally fits every part-programming application for all size operations. Some useful guidelines are, nevertheless, apparent. Small and medium-sized companies that experience difficulty in justifying large-scale, time-shared computer systems will find the dedicated computer-graphics approach the most economical for many years. However, the core utilization problems encountered in the early multi-programmed, time-shared computer-graphics part-gramming systems will surely, though gradually, be resolved. As refinements are implemented, the price and cost-effectiveness of these large-scale systems will become more favorable, thereby making the dedicated computer approach relatively less competitive. Companies relying on the dedicated computer technique may then encounter additional software developmental expenses in order to convert to the more efficient large multi-programmed system. Deciding upon a long-term optimal computer-graphics part-programming system can be accomplished by carefully matching existing computer capabilities and predicted equipment cost and technological trends with present and future part-programming needs. Selecting dedicated equipment that may be compatible with future large multi-programmed computers will often be the safest policy.

Major limitations of computer graphics include the high equipment costs, the shortage of proven universal software, and the lack of personnel qualified in both computer and manufacturing practices. As a result, development and operational costs and the degree of risk have been high. However, the resolution of these barriers appears to be inevitable. All new computer and numerical control users, therefore, should monitor the status of this dynamic and powerful technology before computer equipment is selected for part programming.

Tape Preparation by Manual and Computer-Aided Programming

Manual and computer-aided part programming, the fourth and fifth methods of preparing control tapes, are the most widely used of all the alternatives. The process of converting manufacturing information into machine commands without the aid of a scanner, a transcriber, or a computer is known as manual programming. Up to the phase of writing the program information on the manuscript, manual and computer-aided part programmers perform generally similar operations. Both methods require that the process be planned, tooling and machinability parameters be set, the program manuscript be prepared, and, finally, that the tape commands be encoded and proofed. Major differences lie in the type, format, and completeness of the information that goes on the manuscript, and in the avoidance of extensive manual calculations if a computer is used.

Programmers supported by a computer are not only freed of repetitive calculations and arduous clerical activities, they also can leave to the computer many of the special tape coding and format requirements. The computer does nearly all the remembering and the calculating, and then generates a properly coded control tape—a tape which is in no way different from the manually programmed tape.

Information for the manuscript used in computer-aided part-programming is written in abbreviated English code words and numbers that are compatible with the requirements of each part-programming language and the computer. Among other standards, these language conventions delineate the syntax rules for describing the part so the computer can understand the programmer's instructions. The manuscript words and numbers for a computer-aided part program are keypunched into data processing cards and then compiled on magnetic tape for rapid computer entry. After reading the magnetic tape, the computer performs the necessary calculations, creates the proper code and format, and punches the control tape information into a deck of data processing cards or a magnetic tape which is subsequently converted to the control tape. The computer also prints a listing of the calculated program information as it will appear on the tape. If computing is aborted because of erroneous manuscript information, the computer prints diagnostic interpretations of its analysis of the problem. The computer's checking for errors not only improves accuracy, but the diagnostic comments guide the programmer to the problem source.

Structure of Computer-Aided Part-Programming Languages

A computer-aided part-programming language provides the directions for a computer to carry out three major activities. A path is calculated and completely defined by coordinate dimensions. It is also separated into segments of appropriate lengths, and then necessary auxiliary and miscellaneous commands are properly interleaved. Most part-programming computer languages have separate sections to perform each of these activities. The first section, known as the general processor, handles the cutter path calculations which define the intersections of the cutter center line with the cutter-end. Since the general processor determines the cutter path without regard to the peculiarities of the specific machining equipment, a second computer program, the postprocessor, adapts the cutter path data to the special conditions and demands of each machine and control combination. The postprocessor produces the correctly formatted cutter location data coordinated with the proper feedrates and auxiliary commands in order to produce the part within tolerances and without undercuts or overshoots. To write a program for producing identical parts on different machine-controller combinations, the part programmer uses the general processor only once, but will use several postprocessors; each accommodating the peculiarities of individual machine-control combinations.

Reading the manuscript statements and checking each to see if they are in an acceptable format and order are the first operations of the general processor. If unacceptable statements are encountered, the computer aborts the processing and prints a description of its interpretation of the problem. When all statements are acceptable, the computer begins the calculations under the guidance of the general processor's instruction element. It ascertains the shape of the part as defined in the manuscript and then calculates the cutter path coordinates. A magnetic tape of all calculated cutter path locations and associated statements for controlling the feeds and speeds, tool changes, etc. is subsequently produced by the general processor. However, the noncutter path parameters—i.e., auxiliary function statements such as feeds and speeds, tool changes, etc. are not handled computationally or logically by the general processor.

A second distinct computer program, the postprocessor, takes the information from the magnetic tape, creates appropriately modified cutter locations, and converts the auxiliary function statements to set the safe feeds and speeds and other auxiliary commands which meet the specific equipment requirements. There are five major elements in a typical postprocessor: input, motion, auxiliary, output, and control.

The input element reads the magnetic tape containing the calculated cutter path data and the machine management codes; it then performs a series of inspections to determine their acceptability. Diagnostic comments are produced if any problems are encountered. If the general processor's output is in an acceptable form, the input element transfers the incoming data to the proper elements of the postprocessor.

The motion element handles the geometry and machine dynamics aspects and performs all coordinate transformations required to convert the cutter path data into the appropriate coordinate system of the machine tool involved. The coordinate transformations are comparatively simple for two- and three-axis machines; however, calculations for four- and five-axis machines are considerably more complex.

The cutter location information for multi-axis parts includes direction cosines—these are cosines of the angles the cutter makes with the parts' X, Y and Z axes—that define the desired cutter motion. Since machine tools normally do not have rotary axes controlled by direction cosines, the postprocessor must convert these cutter direction cosines from the part coordinate system to the appropriate machine coordinate system. The geometry section also identifies any commands that exceed the machine's physical limits and checks to see that the cutting tool path will not collide with a machine component. The geometry section performs another important task. When a combination of linear and rotary motions is to be executed, it assures the part programmer that the resulting path is geometrically accurate within his specified tolerance.

The dynamics section of the postprocessor determines feedrate changes necessitated by the interrelationship of the equipment's dynamic response and the programmed geometry and feedrate. This section also establishes permissible cornering velocities so that the resulting part will be machined without undercut or overshoot and within the tolerance specified.

The auxiliary element contains logical procedures for properly coordinating and coding the programmer's miscellaneous and preparatory statements with correct associated functions. When such functions are called out for the part program, the auxiliary element searches the computer memory to find the appropriate control tape codes for the function specified. Properly coded commands are transferred to the postprocessor's output element. The auxiliary element also interprets and evaluates other manuscript statements, such as machine tolerances, feedrates, spindle speeds and directions, and tool or turret selection information, all of which establish modal conditions within the postprocessor.

The output element converts the information from the motion element into the proper motion data and coded feedrates, which are then output in an acceptabe order and format. The output element also accepts miscellaneous preparatory function data and other non-motion information produced by the auxiliary element and merges this information into the postprocessor's output in a properly coded form at the appropriate time. In addition, the output element maintains and generates a printed listing of all the control tape information together with explanatory comments and diagnostic information which may have been transferred from another post-processor element.

The control element orchestrates the flow of information between all postprocessor elements. It controls the timing of the information transfer and insures that diagnostic comments appear in the proper sequence.

In summary, postprocessors may be described as serving as an interface between the part-program computer-processed output—the cutter location data—and the input tape for the machine controller. In fulfilling the interface role, eleven postprocessing tasks are performed. Specifically, the postprocessor:

1. Generates the tape leader, including the part identification punched in man-readable characters.

2. Truncates the coordinate location values so that the number of digits to the right and left of the decimal point is correct and converts the absolute values to incremental data if required.

3. Converts feedrate to the required coding system for the machine, e.g., Inverse Time, Magic 3, Direct IPM, etc.

4. Outputs the correct Preparatory (G) and Miscellaneous (M) codes as they apply to a specific machine.

5. Provides an output listing for the machine operator's use.

6. Controls acceleration and deceleration factors as they apply to the specific machine dynamics, including overshoot and undershoot tolerances.

7. Ensures that the expected travel distance does not exceed the slide travel limits of the machine.

8. Calculates machining time based on distance and rate of move.

9. Outputs the proper format for circular or parabolic interpolation if applicable.

10. Controls the generation and frequency of sequence numbers on the tape along with tool change and other directives for the operator on the output listing.

11. Ensures that point-to-point operations such as drilling, boring, tapping, and reaming are processed as programmed macros in the postprocessor.

As will be seen in the next chapter, some part-programming languages integrate the general and postprocessing sections to obtain compactness, thereby permitting use of minimal computer memory space, as well as other economies. There are some sacrifices for these benefits, however, since limited capabilities are inherent in languages with integrated general and postprocessors. Their application may be restricted as a result.

Postprocessors and their related documentation are commonly obtained from machine tool builders or from computer and control manufacturers. To meet their own special requirements some companies, especially the early computer or numerical control users, were forced to write their own. Computer user organizations have also developed postprocessors and disseminate them to their members. Despite the many organizations involved, postprocessors remain one of the most vexing and costly problems faced by users of computer or numerical controls. With the relatively wide use of specially designed machines and controls and the continued advance of technology, full standardization in computer or numerical controls is many years away. Postprocessor problems will, therefore, remain for sometime.

Before equipment is purchased, the wise buyer determines the availability and reliability of suitable postprocessors for the machines being considered and the extent to which they are implemented on his computer. Not only are separate postprocessors required for each machine control combination, a postprocessor must be written in the special language of a given computer. The computer or numerical control user may therefore be limited to using those postprocessors that have been written for the type of computer in his plant.

The Roles of Manual and Computer-Aided Programming

The volume of calculations is obviously a major factor determining the profitability of computer-aided part programming. Complex parts can easily require thousands of tape commands derived from complicated mathematical procedures. The innumerable co-ordinate locations required to define a contour path of a ball-end cutter, for example, may quickly exceed a person's ability to calculate the points manually—even with the assistance of a fast desk calculator. A computer, on the other hand, can generate all the necessary data points for most contouring applications in a few seconds. Computers not only reduce programmer labor but often turn a marginal computer or numerical control application into a highly profitable one.

Manual programming, however, can be efficient for simple applications. Parts requiring only a half dozen drilled or tapped holes or a few boring operations commonly are programmed economically by hand. Neither the complexity of the calculations nor the number of operations dictate using a computer. Even for such point-to-point jobs, however, it may be profitable to use a computer, especially if there are hole patterns or if the work requires repetitive machining cycles. Computer routines, such as those described in the next chapter greatly reduce the manual calculations and manuscript statements required for recurrent operations.

The more common benefits of using computer-aided rather than manual part programing include:

1. Reduced lead time.
2. Easier handling of complex parts and design changes.
3. Reduced labor costs.
4. Improved programming accuracy and reliability.
5. Increased productivity of part programmers.
6. Simplified control tape optimization.

The computer has proven to be an especially valuable tool for tape optimization. By relying on the computer for high-speed calculations, the programmer is free to concentrate on the more creative tasks of selecting the best tooling, machinability, and process alternatives. Having the time to review the computer instructions and the ability to make tape revisions by simply changing a few manuscript words, the programmer enjoys a practical technique for upgrading his work several times before the tape need be released. The payoff of computerized tape-optimization was demonstrated dramatically in a typical lathe application where 41 minutes were required to machine a manually programmed part; later, the same part was computer programmed, and by using the path and sequence optimization power of the computer it was machined in 9 minutes.

Companies switching to computer-aided part programming commonly reduce their manual tape errors by a third to a quarter. A major contributor to better accuracy is the computer's ability to check each instruction to assure that mathematical boundaries defining dimensional envelopes composed of part, fixture, and machine limits are not violated. As each command is processed, the computer tests to see if the programmed tool erroneously penetrates any occupied space within a protective envelope. If unacceptable penetrations are detected, the computer prints a diagnostic statement. Many manual tape errors go unchecked and undetected because hand program verification is arduous and must be more thorough than it is for computer-prepared programs. By contrast the logical and computational accuracy of the latter tapes can be checked simply by verifying the correctness of the computer input data. Only in very rare instances do computer errors escape the verification process.

The productivity of programmers supported by a computer is commonly doubled. One company's programmers, handling 52 point-to-point machines, increased their productivity 2.4 times after the firm introduced computer-aided part programming. Another company with 105 numerically controlled machines found that their tape preparation costs dropped by two-thirds after they had fully converted to computer programming.

Lead-time reductions typically exceed 50 percent when computer-aided rather than manual methods are used. Some time savings have been as high as 25 to 1.

As in most management decisions, the choice between manual and computer-aided programming is determined by economic advantages unless special factors take precedence. However, since part programming permeates several manufacturing functions, a true cost picture is often obscured. One obvious advantage of computer-aided part programming, less programmer effort, is usually a significant savings in itself. Additionally, shorter lead times also produce secondary economies by reducing raw materials, work-in-process, and finished parts inventories. A similar pyramiding of indirect savings is also inherent in greater accuracy and reduced scrap which make possible smaller lot sizes, and less inspection and rework costs. Although the many facets of improved efficiency sometimes may be difficult to measure, once completely identified, total direct and indirect savings quickly compensate for the computer cost.

Which Computer-Aided Programming Language?

Neither manual programming nor any one of the approximately 75 computer-aided part-programming languages is a universal panacea. Part-programming languages must be compatible with the firm's computer, skills, and manufacturing operations. Compatibility is largely dependent on part configurations, the numerically controlled equipment owned and planned for the future, and the type of a computer that is available. As discussed in Chapter II, computers have critical distinguishing characteristics such as information format requirements, precision and storage capacities, and types of languages they can understand. Some computers are less efficient and considerably more costly to use on part-programming problems. Moreover, some computers simply do not process part-programming languages, at all, or if they do, the storage capacity may restrict the computer's use to point-to-point or very simple continuous-path applications. As will be seen in the next chapter, these are only a few of the many factors that must be considered in the complex process of identifying the best part-programming language for each application.

Appendix A

Sample Part Program

Figure A.1 shows an engineering drawing of a part of a nozzle assembly to be made on a numerically controlled turret lathe out of commercial brass stock. The turret has six possible tool positions. Figure A.2 shows the layout for the necessary tooling. The part programmer is generally responsible for informing the operator and the tool crib of the tooling required so that when the tape is mounted the tooling will be ready and in place. This part shows the necessity of preset tooling for certain numerically controlled machines. The tolerance requirements of the part can only be met if the tooling is ground to specification and mounted in the turret so that the geometrical relationships from the tool tip to the center of the turret are precisely known to the programmer. Once this has been accomplished, the programmer can write his manuscript. Using simple arithmetic and trigonometry the programmer determines where the

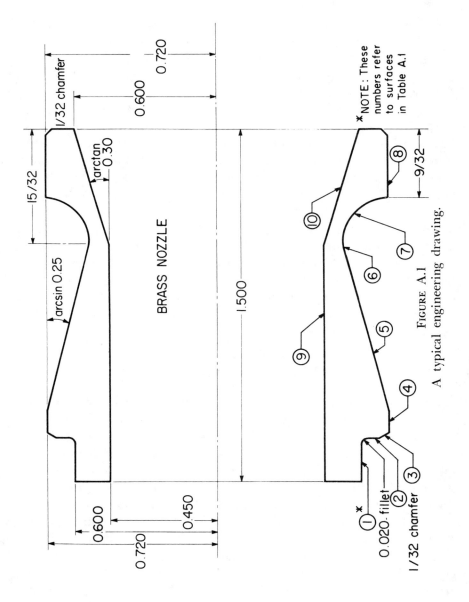

FIGURE A.1

A typical engineering drawing.

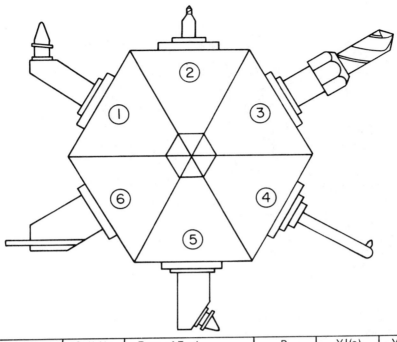

Station No.	Call No.	Type of Tool	R	X'(a)	Y'(a)
1	T1	Left Hand Turning	8. 375	4. 437	7. 685
2	T3	Center Drill	11. 500	11. 125	0. 218
3	T4	51/64" Dia. Drill	13. 450	13. 300	.3984
4	T5	Boring Tool	9. 600	9. 534	.3175
5	T5	Right Hand Turning	8.. 875	4. 437.	7. 658
6	T6	Cut-Off Block	12. 000	5. 527	10. 000

(a) X' and Y' are dimensions from turret center line

FIGURE A.2

Turret setup and dimensions.

center of the turret must be in order to machine the part. After the absolute coordinates of each move are determined (i.e., the coordinates of the center of the turret in relationship to the spindle center line and the front face of the spindle center line and the front face of the collet), the part programmer begins to calculate the incremental moves necessary for machining the part. Each move will be programmed into one block of tape.

The initial position location for the turret is as shown in Figure A.3. Since the machine operator must set his initial position switches

289

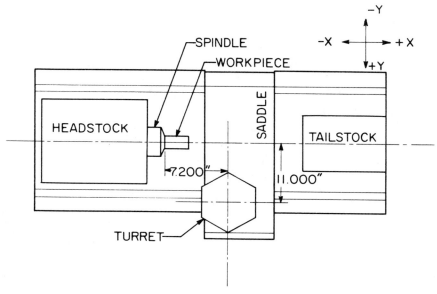

FIGURE A.3
Axis nomenclature and setup location.

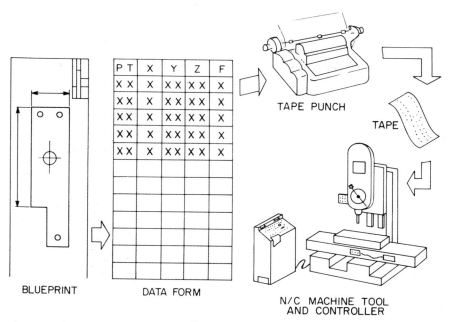

FIGURE A.4
Manual tape preparation.

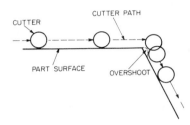

FIGURE A.5
Dynamic overshoot.

accurately according to these coordinates, data must be expressed in clear, specific terms. The part programmer is also responsible for providing information regarding the loading of the turret.

Table A.1 is an outline of the part program manuscript as the programmer might write it. The surface elements E1, E2, etc., as referred to in the "Remarks" columns, are symbolic names for the surfaces shown in the part drawings, Figure A.4. Table A.2 gives a brief description of the code[1] used in programming the lathe-controller unit to be used for this job. The tape format is word-address. Although this program does not directly provide for acceleration and deceleration, the programmer has inserted dwell commands so that the mechanical inertia of the machine elements can catch up with the electronic speed of the controller. Figure A.5 shows what a cutter path might be like if a dwell was not programmed in after the Y-approach in block (4) of the manuscript. Note that the programmer has made the first plunge cut so that it serves as a chamfering cut on the next piece. This, of course, means that the first part is not chamfered in each bar; however, this could be done manually at the beginning of each new bar as it is loaded.

After the data have been carefully calculated, coded, and put into

---

[1] This is not a standard code; it is an older version of the EIA code.

Card No.	Coordinates of Turret X'	Center After Move Y'	Instruction Block	Remarks
1	7.2000	11.0000	P4X05S30TIM−3	
2	7.2000	11.0000	P4X03S37	
3	7.2000	8.4550	P1XY−2545KL1F02	Y-Approach
4	7.2000	8.4550	P4X01	Dwell, .1 sec.
5	7.5000	8.3050	P1X+03Y−015K003L0015F06	Plunge Cut
6	7.6875	8.3050	P1X+01875YK1LF002	Element (E)-1
7	7.6875	8.4050	P1XY+01KL1	E2
8	7.7075	8.4250	P1X+002Y+002K0707L0707	E3
9	7.7813	8.4250	P1X+00738YK1L	E4
10	8.4883	8.2435	P1X+0707Y−01815K00707L001815F03	E5
11	8.5313	8.2380	P2X+0043Y−00055K001665L00043F1	E6
12	8.7033	8.4100	P2X+0172Y+0172K00172L	E7
13	8.7033	8.4250	P1XY+0015KL1F002	E7
14	9.1033	8.4250	P1X+04YK1L	E8, Goes to 0.1033 beyond part
15	9.1033	8.4350	P1XY+001KL1	Feed Out
16	7.2000	8.4350	P1X−19033YK1LF019	Return
17	7.2000	8.4350	P4X01	Dwell, 0.1 sec.
18	7.5000	8.2850	P1X+03Y+015K003L0015F06	2nd initial cut
19	7.6875	8.2850	P1X+01875YK1LF002	E1
20	7.6875	8.3850	P1XY+01KL1	E2
21	7.7075	8.4050	P1X+002Y+002K0707L0707	E3
22	7.7813	8.4050	P1X+00738YK1L	E4
23	8.4883	8.2235	P1X+0707Y−01815K00707L001815F03	E5
24	8.5313	8.2180	P2X+0043Y−00055K001665L00043F1	E6
25	8.7033	8.3900	P2X+0172Y+0172K00172L	E7
26	8.7033	8.4050	P1XY+0015KL1F002	E7
27	9.1033	8.4050	P1X+04YK1L	E8, Goes to 0.1033 beyond part
27a	9.1033	8.4050	P4X02M+3F01	
28	9.5000	8.4050	P1X+03967YK1L	
29	10.5000	8.4050	P1X+1F03	
30	11.5000	8.4050	P1F06	
31	12.5000	8.4050	P1F09	
32	15.5000	8.4050	P1X+3	
33	16.5000	8.4050	P1X+1F06	
34	17.5000	8.4050	P1F03	
35	18.5000	8.4050	P1F01	
36	18.5000	8.4050	P4X02T3M−3	Index to center drill
37	18.5000	0.0000	P1XY−84050KL1F02	
38	16.2500	0.0000	P1X−2.25YK1LF019	
39	15.7500	0.0000	P1X−05F01	Center drill
40	18.5000	0.0000	P1X+2.750F019	
41	18.5000	0.0000	P4X02T4	Index to drill
42	18.0750	0.0000	P1X−0425YK1LF01	
43	16.2500	0.0000	P1X−1825F007	Drill
44	18.5000	0.0000	P1X+2250F019	
45	18.5000	0.0000	P4X02T5	Index to Boring tool
46	14.3000	0.0000	P1X−42YK1LF019	
47	14.3000	0.1325	P1XY+01325KL1F01	
48	12.5750	0.1325	P1X−1725YK1LF002	Bore 0.900 Dia. E9
49	12.5750	0.0000	P1XY−01325KL1	
50	14.2470	0.0000	P1X+1672YK1LF019	
51	14.2470	0.2375	P1XY+02375KL1	
52	13.8970	0.1325	P1X−035Y−0105K0035L00105F06	E10-1, rough
53	14.2470	0.1325	P1X+035YK1LF019	
54	14.2470	0.1325	P1XY+018KL1	
55	13.5470	0.1025	P1X−07Y−021K007L0021F03	E10-2, finish

Card No.	Coordinates of Turret X'	Center After Move Y'	Instruction Block	Remarks
56	14.1470	0.1025	P1X+06YK1LF019	
57	14.1470	0.4325	P1XY+033KL1F002	E11
58	18.5000	0.4325	P1X+4353YK1LF019	
59	18.5000	8.4350	P1XY+80025KL1F02	
60	18.5000	10.7000	P1XY+2265	
61	18.5000	10.7000	P4X02T6	Index to cut off tool
62	9.5900	10.7000	P1X−8910YK1LF019	
63	9.5900	9.8900	P1XY−081KL1F002	E13
64	9.5900	11.0000	P1XY+111F02	
65	18.5000	11.0000	P1X+8910YK1LF019	
66	18.5000	11.0000	P4X02S30T1	Index turret
67	12.8500	11.0000	P1X−565YK1LF019	Return to initial position
68	7.2000	11.0000	P1S20	Reduce spindle speed
69	7.2000	11.0000	P4X01S10M0	Shut Down

TABLE A.2

Tape code of example part.[1]

Prep. Codes
    P1—initiates linear moves
    P2—initiates clockwise circular move
    P3—causes a dwell, whose length of duraction is specified by following X instruction

Misc. Codes
    M0—program stop
    M+3—rapid traverse
    M−3—regular feed

Speed Codes
    Sab—Spindle speed code, followed by two numbers: "a" indicates clutch range for gear box, "b" indicates speed within that range.

Tool Codes
    Ta—tool station call ups to index turret to proper position. NOTE: the call-up code and station number do not always coincide because of tool configurations.

X+Y Codes
    X—distance of X-axis motion in either + or − direction
    Y—distance of Y-axis motion in either + or − direction

Departure Codes
    K—cosine of angle of departure between start and end points of a move, and the X-axis, for *angular and circular cuts*
    L—cosine of angle of departure between start and end points of a move, and the Y-axis, for *angular and circular cuts*

[1]See footnote 1, page 291.

manuscript form, they are ready for punching. This is done by a key punch operator who produces a tape on an electric typewriter that punches tape at the same time that it produces a "hard-copy" manuscript showing exactly what code has been punched. After the programmer reviews and accepts this manuscript, he packages the tapes and the operator's instructions to be sent to the shop.

FIGURE A.6
Approved sample part.

FIGURE A.7
Approved sample part.

In most cases the part programmer is present for the machining of the first part regardless of which tape checkout methods have been used. Part tryout is usually done on a block-by-block basis so that each move can be observed critically by the programmer and the operator. Often a piece of scrap stock is used, or the machine is left empty for the first pass to check for gross clearance errors. When the first part has been cut and approved, the programmer's task is finished.

Figures A.6 and A.7 show the approved sample part.

A close study of the sample program indicates that manual part programming requires:

- a variety of mathematical calculations (depending upon the part configuration) that must be done meticulously and accurately
- a working knowledge of the machine-controller characteristics
- that the EIA code and the necessary tape formats for each machine be memorized by the programmer so that he is not constantly looking up codes and formats
- a great deal of tedious, highly error-prone "busy-work."

294

Chapter VIII

Computer-aided Part-programming Systems

Part-programming systems for computer and numerical controls are composed of a set of computer procedures and a group of special words used to delineate the required operations. For example, a representative programming system, APT, includes the APT computer routines which comprise a series of instructions to regulate computer operations, and the APT language which consists of special words the part programmer uses to describe the location, type, and sequence of the desired machine functions. The words of the language are recorded on the part-program manuscript and supplied to a computer operating under the guidance of the APT program. As the words are read by the computer, they cause the appropriate APT routines to be executed and the necessary calculations to be performed. A set of machine commands coded on a control tape is the visual result.

General-purpose part-programming systems and machine-oriented systems are two distinct types of part-programming languages. The machine-oriented languages create tool paths by doing all the necessary calculations in one computer processing stage. General-purpose languages break the computer processing into two stages—a processing stage and a postprocessing stage. The output of the first stage is an intermediate set of data points called the cutter location data, or CL DATA. These intermediate data are commonly output by the computer onto a magnetic tape or a disk memory for subsequent use in the postprocessing stage.

Machine-oriented languages do not produce an intermediate listing of cutter location information, but rather compute directly the special coordinate-data format and the coding for speed and feed requirements of the automatically controlled equipment. Although general-purpose systems provide greater flexibility, they require larger core storage and more computer time than do machine-oriented languages which use the integrated computer processing method.

Functional relationships and process flows for a typical general-

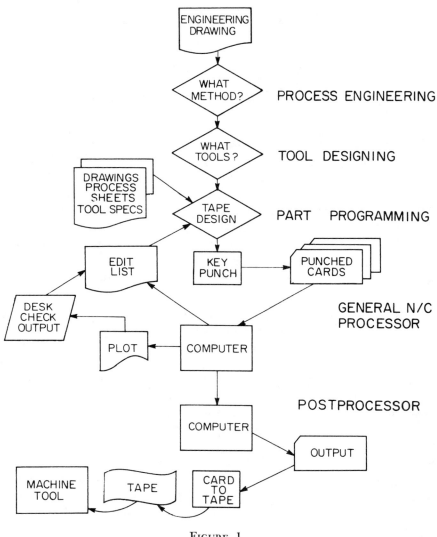

FIGURE 1

Computer control tape preparation.

purpose language are shown in Figures 1 and 2. Although the characteristics and the computational approaches of the languages vary depending on the part-programming system and computer implementation, these diagrams illustrate generally applicable concepts. Note that for one general-purpose language in one particular computer implementation (Figure 2), a part program is fully processed in each section before the subsequent element begins its activity. As will

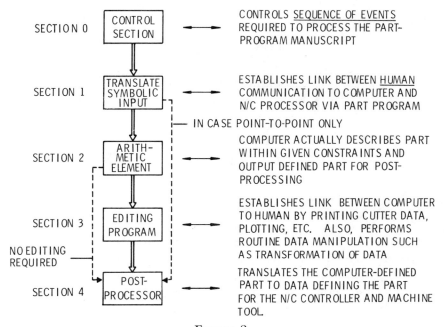

FIGURE 2

Design of a numerical control computer program.

be demonstrated later, this practice contrasts sharply with the process flow used in machine-oriented languages.

LEVELS OF CAPABILITY

Beyond the distinction between machine-oriented and general-purpose systems, part-programming languages can be further differentiated by their control capabilities, i.e., point-to-point, continuous-path, etc. Table I lists the programming system capabilities by the degree of equipment sophistication that can be controlled by the tapes produced. Few languages are restricted to a single category on Table I and most systems can create tapes for equipment of several different levels.

A more meaningful distinction between part-programming systems would separate languages according to whether they have point-to-point or continuous-path capabilities. Continuous-path languages could be further subdivided into those capable of controlling less than three axes and those controlling three or more. Levels (a) through (c) in the table are commonly associated with point-to-point equipment, and levels (d) and (e) with continuous-path machines.

Table I

CAPABILITY LEVELS OF PART-PROGRAMMING
LANGUAGES

a. Simple positioning
b. Two-axis
c. Partial three-axis
d. Full three- or four-axis
e. Multi-axis (five or more)

SPECIAL FEATURES

Part-programming systems can also be distinguished by their special features. Some point-to-point languages have computer routines which allow the part programmer to use a form of shorthand to instruct the computer to create several instructions for hole patterns. Some languages may also have computer routines to make limited machinability decisions, while others have process optimizing capabilities. Common special features of part-programming languages are introduced below; more detailed examples are included later when specific types of languages are described.

Hole-Pattern Manipulation

Virtually every part-programming language accepts coordinate locations as a means of specifying holes, but not all languages have hole-pattern manipulation routines. Over 50 separate machine instruction statements are required to program the part in Figure 3 using hole coordinates, but only about a dozen statements are needed when a language is used with the pattern manipulation capability. A part programmer working with this computer aid might first have defined the holes in the lower left-hand pattern of Figure 3 by a group of coordinate statements in the part-program manuscript as follows:

DPT 1,	1XB,	5YB,	ZB
DPT 2,	2XB,	5YB,	ZB
DPT 3,	1XB,	6YB,	ZB
•			
•			
•			
DPT 9,	4XB,	7YB,	ZB

where DPT 1, DPT 2 become symbolic names for defined point 1, defined point 2, etc., and where 1XB, 5YB, and ZB indicate that the hole is located at a point one inch in the positive direction of the X axis from the defined base, five inches in the positive Y-axis direction, and at the previously defined Z-base height. By using a language with pattern routines, this set of nine point locations can be defined and stored in the computer as a pattern by the statement:

$$\text{STGRP1, 1, 2, 3, 4, 5, 6, 7, 8, 9}$$

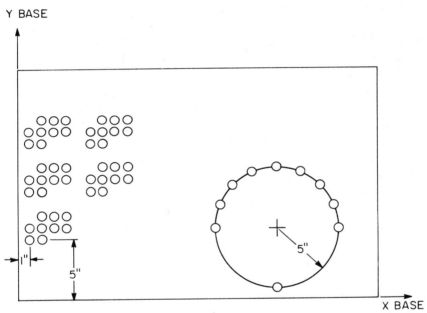

Number of coordinate statements
to define hole locations = 55

Number of statements using a language with
hole-pattern manipulation facilities to define
hole locations = 17

FIGURE 3
A point-to-point part.

299

where each number represents a previously defined point, and the symbolic word STGRP1 tells the computer to "store Group 1." After this grouping of points has been defined as a pattern, it can be manipulated in a variety of ways including translation, rotation, and inversion. For example, the pattern of points directly above the initial pattern could be specified and drilled with the simple command:

DRL, X, 4Y, PTGRP1

which will translate the pattern Group 1 (GRP1) upward along the Y axis four inches. This can be repeated again and again for each of the other hole patterns.

Another useful routine is the manipulation of bolt-circle patterns. Notice that the part in Figure 3 has a bolt circle containing ten holes, one of which is not evenly spaced. By using a language with hole-pattern manipulation capabilities the complete bolt circle could be specified in only three statements.

To calculate the X–Y coordinates and develop the code manually for the 55 holes in the part in Figure 3 would be time-consuming, and the chance of part programmer error would be fairly high. A manual programmer might take hours to define and code these points, check for errors, and correct them. A programmer using computer-aided pattern manipulation methods could specify the points, and the computer could generate the appropriate instructions in a few minutes with much less chance of error.

Minimum-Path Routines

Minimum-path or traveling salesman routines allow the computer rather than the part programmer to determine the "best" route for the cutter to follow from location to location as an automatically controlled machine executes a series of positioning operations for processes such as drilling, boring, or punching. Minimum-path routines derive their name from the problem faced by a traveling salesman who must visit several locations and wishes to conserve time. The mathematical procedures used to determine the optimal tool path in manufacturing operations are more complex than those needed simply to identify the fastest route because some holes require multiple tools, and the machine's travel motion may take place in more than one axis simultaneously, causing variations in the time required for individual movements. Because the mathematical procedures required to ascertain the truly optimal tool route consume

300

more computer time than is economically justified, approximations of the best path are determined. Such estimates, however, can be quite profitable. Companies using path optimization methods for point-to-point jobs, typically have experienced savings in production time of one-fifth to one-fourth.

An application of the traveling salesman routine is demonstrated in Figure 4. The sample part has two bolt circles which require drilling and tapping. The first tool path requiring 31.8 seconds to complete is typical of what a part programmer might intuitively specify. The second path has been computer optimized with a production time savings of approximately 50 percent. No additional part-programming time or effort is required to have the computer calculate the "best" path, but the difference in production time can represent hundreds of dollars in savings when several parts are produced.

Although traveling salesman routines depend on sophisticated mathematical procedures, once the mathematical routines are written for the computer, lesser-skilled part programmers can easily instruct the computer to execute the routines to arrive at an efficient tool path. In addition to drilling and boring, the minimum-path computer routines also have been effectively applied in punching operations.

Macros and Canned Cycles

Macros and canned cycles are special computer routines that in general create a series of instructions from a single command. A macro instruction is formally defined as a source language instruction which is equivalent to a specified series of machine instructions. It follows then that a macro program or a macro routine is a group of instructions that can be stored in a computer and recalled as a group to solve a recurring problem. The formal definition for a canned cycle is a preset sequence of events initiated by a single command.

An example of a canned cycle would be the command, DRILL PATERN[1] X, where pattern X might consists of several hole locations. The several instructions required to carry out all the activities, including drilling, reaming, and tapping of all holes, would be previously defined and stored in the computer. The single command, DRILL PATERN X, would then be sufficient to activate computer

---

[1] The spelling form is used to meet language requirements for word length.

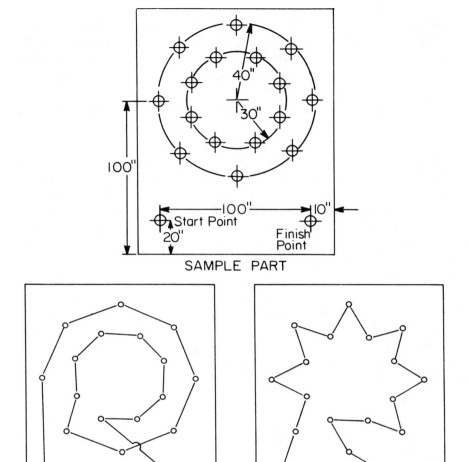

SAMPLE PART

Unoptimized Tool Movement
Time = 31.8 seconds

Computer Optimized Tool
Movement Time = 16.2 seconds

FIGURE 4
A computerized routine for finding shortest machine tool time.

production of all the tape codes for the entire drilling operation.
Reaming and tapping the holes in the pattern can be accomplished
by recalling PATERN X and changing the DRILL command to
REAM and then to TAP.

Like the minimum-path routines, the computer procedures comprising the macros or canned cycles are created and written only once by a computer programmer. The part programmer then writes the proper code words on the manuscript which causes the computer to execute the macro or canned cycle routines. Once created, canned cycles allow the computer, rather than the part programmer, to determine how the operations should be carried out; the computer also performs the clerical task of generating the code for all instructions.

Machinability Routines

To reduce both programming drudgery and the detailed knowledge of machining practices that a part programmer must have, machinability routines are increasingly being added to part-programming languages. These computer routines allow the part programmer to specify certain basic information about the machine, the cutting tool, the workpiece, and the desired surface finish. The computer then calculates the appropriate machining feeds and speeds. Languages with machinability facilities alleviate to various degrees the need for programmers to refer to cutting feed and speed tables, and promote more consistent machining practices. Some of the advanced machinability routines, for example, those contained in the EXAPT language, are capable not only of calculating the proper feeds and speeds but also of selecting the roughing and finishing cuts.

Several other special features available in part-programming systems are delineated in the language descriptions that follow. As programming languages are futher developed, the range of special capabilities will continuously broaden. While a special feature may not be the major consideration in choosing a particular programming system, each should be evaluated to determine if it will produce significant programming or production savings.

COMMONLY USED PART-PROGRAMMING SYSTEMS

To illustrate characteristics that differentiate one type of part-programming system from another, the capabilities of several major classes are summarized below. Rather than describing the 50 to 75 systems that have been developed, languages have been selected that show the evolution of important features as the technology matured. The application of significant concepts is also demonstrated. The discussion is limited to concepts which are expected to endure as future part-programming developments occur. With language refinements continuing, up-to-date information about the systems, their costs, the advent of new special features, and the continuity of technical support should be obtained before making the final selection of a programming system.

APT

The most powerful general-purpose part-programming system has been APT, an acronym derived from the words Automatically Programmed Tools. Following the 1952 numerical control feasibility demonstration at MIT, the need for computer-assisted part programming became painfully evident and the development of the APT language was initiated. Supported initially by the Air Force, MIT completed the development of the APT I version by the mid-1950's. In 1957 American aerospace companies recognized the vital role of computer-assisted part programming and pooled their resources to continue the Air Force work at MIT. Soon the APT system had evolved into a third version and the Illinois Institute of Technology Research Institute (IITRI) assumed the development and administrative responsibility. A fourth APT version was developed and distributed by 1970. Over 100 international and domestic companies and organizations, including many competitors, cooperated in the financial and technical support of the APT development project.

A working familiarity with APT can be achieved by reviewing IITRI's *APT Encyclopedia*. Because APT is the most powerful general-purpose part-programming system, the complete encyclopedia should be studied before any management decision is made regarding the selection of a part-programming language. Once APT is generally understood, other systems can be compared and evaluated to determine performance differences and cost relationships. Summarized from the *APT Encyclopedia* are these APT characteristics:

1. Three-dimensional unbounded surfaces and points are defined to represent the part to be made.
2. Surfaces are defined in an X–Y–Z coordinate system chosen by the part programmer.
3. In programming, the tool does all of the moving; the part (geometry) is stationary.
4. The tool path is controlled by pairs of three-dimensional surfaces; other motions, not controlled by surfaces, are also possible.
5. A series of short straight-line motions is calculated to represent curved tool paths (linear interpolation).

6. The tool path is calculated so as to be within specified tolerances of the controlling surfaces.

7. The X, Y, and Z coordinates of successive tool-end positions along the desired tool path are recorded as the general solution to the programming problem.

8. Additional processing (postprocessing) of the tool-end coordinates generates the exact tape codes and format for a particular machine.

The three-dimensional structure permits the use of APT on machines with three or more axes of control, as well as on two-dimensional machines with continuous-path or point-to-point control systems.

As a first step, the part programmer prepares a manuscript using APT words to describe all the geometry, motions, and machine functions to produce the part. Since the APT system is continuously being refined, its language of approximately 300 words continues to expand. The manuscript information is then punched into data processing cards. Before the computer is ready to accept and operate on the manuscript words, the APT computer program routines must be read into its memory. The computer can then process the manuscript words by translating the APT statements and calculating the cutter positions. The manuscript words call out and activate one or more of the 100,000 computer instructions contained in the APT computer program.

APT may be viewed as consisting of three, four, or five separate sections depending upon status given to the control and editing elements (see Figure 5). As can be inferred from Figure 2, most of the work occurs in the translator, arithmetic, and postprocessor sections. The control section—designated as Section 0 in Figure 2—generally controls the sequence of events required to process the part program. The editing program—Section 3 of Figure 2—establishes the link between the computer and the programmer by printing cutter data, plotting information, etc.

The translator-compiler reads the source information coded in the manuscript words, translates them into computer language, separates the statements into statement classes, verifies the correctness of the statements, and prepares diagnostic comments when required. It then compiles a sequence of numerically coded instructions acceptable to the APT program control. The control element interprets and regu-

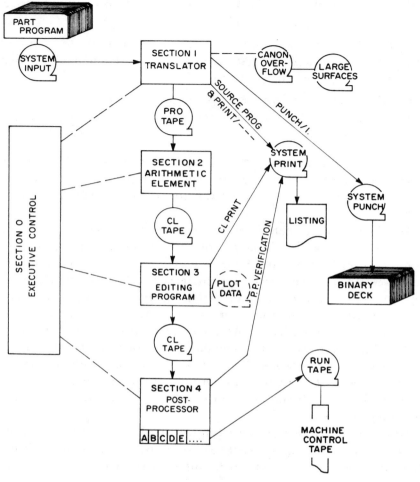

FIGURE 5

APT III system structure.

lates the order of cutting commands, and activates the arithmetic section at the proper time. The arithmetic section computes all the coordinate positions the tool must pass through to create the desired part shape. Tool path computations consider the cutter shape, the part geometry, and the tolerances specified.

The last APT section is the postprocessor. Figure 6 shows a modified diagram of the functional relationships of the sections in the APT language as implemented on one IBM computer. The several postprocessor examples imply that the output of this general-purpose

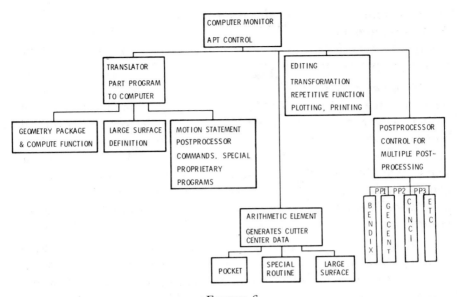

FIGURE 6

The APT operating system. (Courtesy of IBM, White Plains, New York)

language can be modified to meet the requirements of a variety of machines and control systems.

The APT system's ability to check the validity of the programming statements being processed helps greatly to promote accuracy. When a manuscript error is recognized, whether a simple case of a misspelled word, wrong punctuation, or a more complex logic problem, the system will print a diagnostic notation, identifying the statement being processed when the error was recognized. For some errors, only a diagnostic number is printed. In other cases, both the number and a suggestion about the correction of the error is included.

APT accuracy checks determine whether any of the following types of errors are present in the program manuscript:

1. Spelling and format errors,
2. Impossible mathematical situations,
3. Cutter-position errors,
4. Machine control errors, and
5. System faults.

Machine control errors refer to improper program statments that specify a situation which physically cannot be executed by the ma-

307

chine; system faults are errors resulting from malfunctions in the APT computer programs.

Certain other APT facilities further aid the understanding of the language's power and utilization.

1. *Geometric Definitions.* Geometric definitions are used to describe the part to be produced. The part programmer can think of riding on the tool and "driving" it in the desired directions of motion. Seven parameters are available for defining tool shapes. Both positive and negative tolerances may be specified. The geometric shapes available in APT for defining a part include planes, cylinders, conic cylinders, tabulated cylinders, general quadrics, ruled surfaces, generalized parametric surfaces, and surfaces defined by a mesh of points.

2. *Tool Position Relative to Controlling Surfaces.* The three basic types of surfaces to be considered are shown in Figure 7. In general, the *part surface* is commonly engaged by the end of the cutter; the *drive surface* is normally engaged by the side of the cutter; and the *check surfaces* define spatial positions at which decisions are made by APT relative to changes in tool motion. A universally valid distinction between the drive surface and the part surface is that the former changes with each new tool motion, while the part surface serves as a continuous-control surface throughout a series of tool motions.

3. *Computation.* APT computational routines include addition, subtraction, multiplication, division, exponentiation, and a number of functions such as sine, cosine, arc tangent, dot product,[2] square root, absolute value, logarithmic function, and vector length.

4. *Auxiliary Commands.* Auxiliary commands, such as feedrate, spindle speeds, start, coolant, etc., for a number of different machines are included.

5. *Macros.* Individual macros can be written for any part program, or system macros can be added to the APT computer program routines. The latter capability allows the part programmer, who generally is not a computer programmer, to write his own canned cycles, and in effect permits a part-programming department to create its own library of special macros for frequently used routines and definition statements. Effective utilization of APT macros has re-

---

[2] Dot product is the scalar product of two vectors.

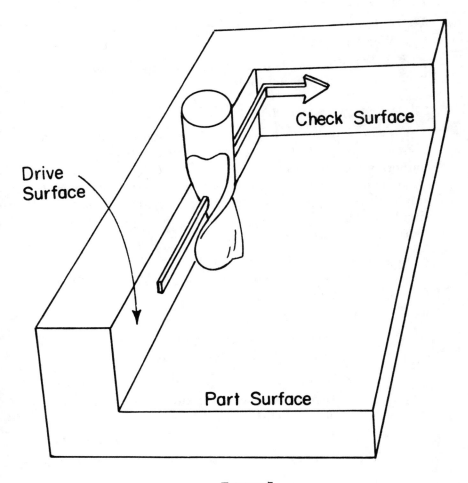

Check Surface

Drive
Surface

Part Surface

FIGURE 7

duced the part programmer's work by about half; in some cases by
as much as 90 percent.

6. *Loops.* APT's looping capability,[3] together with such features
as computation and macros, enables the construction of extremely
sophisticated and efficient part programs for complex parts.

---

[3] A loop is a program section which repeats itself until a specified result is obtained.

The application of the preceding APT concepts and facilities is demonstrated in the following basic types of APT statements.

1. *To Define Tool Shape*

   A tool shape can be defined using up to seven parameters. Example: CUTTER/1, .25

   > Defines a flat-end cutter of 1-inch diameter and ¼-inch corner radius.

2. *To Define Part Geometry*

   A part can be defined using some 90 different definition forms. Even though some of the definitions have a two-dimensional connotation such as "line" or "circle," the APT system stores these geometric elements as three-dimensional forms. For example, lines and circles are stored in the system as planes and circular cylinders perpendicular to the X–Y plane. Cartesian coordinates are assumed.

   Examples: a) P1 = POINT/2, 3, 0

   > Defines a point at coordinates X = 2, Y = 3, Z = 0, and names it "P1."

   b) L2 = LINE/P1, ATANGL, 30

   > Defines a line through P1 at an angle of 30 degrees with the X axis.

   c) C3 = CIRCLE/CENTER, P1, RADIUS, 3.5

   > Defines a circle with center at P1, with a radius of 3.5 inches.

   d) SP4 = SPHERE/CENTER, P1, RADIUS, 6

   > Defines a sphere with center at P1, with a radius of 6 inches.

   e) PL5 = PLANE/0, 0, 1, 3

   > Defines a plane by its equation $0.X + 0.Y + 1.Z = 3$, i.e., the plane 3 inches above the X–Y plane.

3. *To Specify Tolerance*

   Both negative and positive tolerances can be specified and are used by the computer in calculating cutter offsets and in generating cut vectors on curved surfaces. (There is no tolerance associated with the definition of a surface.)

Example: OUTTOL/.001

> Means that when calculating cutter offsets of the tool from the surfaces, no more than .001 inch of material may be left on the tool side of a part (see Figure 8).

4. *To Command Cutter Motion and Specify Cutter Position Relative to Controlling Geometric Surfaces*

Examples: a) TLRGT, GORGT/L2, PAST, L3

> With the tool on the right side of the surface relative to the motion of the tool, go right along the surface L1 until the tool has just passed the surface L3.

b) GOFWD/C1, TO, PL2

> Go forward along the surface C1 until the tool just touches the surface PL2.

Given these commands, the system calculates the series of straight-line motions necessary to move the specified tool along the defined surface, always keeping within the indicated tolerance.

5. *To Indicate Machine Functions*

Examples: a) COOLNT/ON

> Turn the coolant on.

b) FEDRAT/50

> Feedrate: 50 inches per minute.

c) SPINDL/2400

> Spindle speed: 2400 revolutions per minute.

6. *To Perform In-Line Computations*

A FORTRAN subset is available for computations.

7. *To Execute Program Logic and Specify Geometric Transformations*

The APT system provides the part programmer with methods of branching in his program when specified arithmetic or

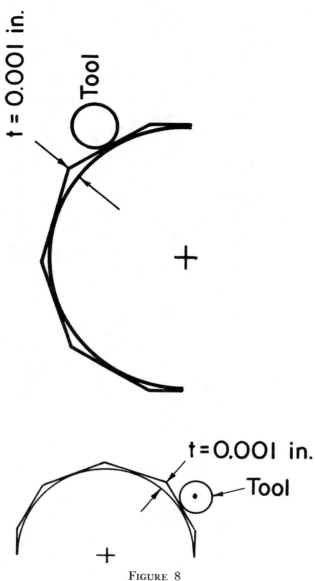

FIGURE 8
Example of tolerance specification.

geometric conditions have been met. This permits him to perform a series of definitions or motions under control of an arithmetic index, or permits him, during a given motion, to perform alternative sets of operations based upon the intersection of the tool with one or another of the controlling surfaces. The system allows for transformation of coordinates so that patterns of geometry or cut vectors can be translated or rotated. This facilitates the repetition of patterns in programming of parts with symmetry.

APT is similar to most other programming languages in its use of abbreviated English words which allow the part programmer to communicate with the computer in a language relatively similar to his own. The similarity between APT and the other languages ends here—with the exception of the APT derivatives such as ADAPT or UNIAPT. Other languages have varying input forms, require somewhat different data, and in many cases are processed by smaller computers.

A significant APT advantage is that its computer routines can handle complex elliptical, cylindrical, or ruled configurations. To process these complex shapes, however, APT requires a large and expensive digital computer. Since many companies produce parts that do not have elliptical or ruled surfaces, they may not need the full capability of all the APT routines. Less powerful languages using smaller computers were developed that often prove effective and economical. Also to be considered are languages based on modifications to the APT system that permit their use on certain small computers.

ADAPT

The ADAPT language was one of the first attempts to adapt some of the more commonly used APT routines to smaller computers. In this case, a small computer was defined as one with 40,000 decimal digits of storage and a 600 millisecond adding time. One significant objective of the ADAPT development project—to circumvent the need for the large computer required to handle the full APT system —was selected after a survey of users disclosed that two-thirds of all numerical control jobs consisted of drilling, straight-line milling, or the contouring of circles. None of these operations demanded the APT three-dimensional contouring capabilities that are mainly responsible for requiring a large computer.

ADAPT was designed to have great flexibility: the program has a modular construction that allows both the addition and deletion of routines whenever the user desires. Flexibility was deemed necessary to compensate for the relative speed and storage deficiencies inherent in using a small computer to process a relatively complex numerical control part program.

Another design objective specified that ADAPT be compatible with existing APT postprocessors so that they could be used with little or no modification. The Air Force, which funded the initial project, also required that the original ADAPT be written in FORTRAN, a language acceptable to a wide variety of computers.

ADAPT has full two-dimensional and some limited three-axis capabilities. Newer versions allow points to be defined 12 ways, lines 10 ways, circles 10, and planes 2, 3, or 4 ways. Ellipses, general conics, and tabulated cylinders can also be defined. ADAPT has routines for curve fitting, inclined planes, polygonal pockets, vectors, and macro (canned cycle) definitions. The program can also handle basic arithmetic operations and the functions of sine, cosine, tangent, arc tangent, square root, exponentiation, and logarithms.

The original ADAPT system consists of three major sections: the input translator, the arithmetic phase, and the postprocessor. Like APT, it also has control and editing elements. The input translator accepts the original part-program manuscript, checks for language violations, and creates a numerical output. The arithmetic phase calculates the points through which the cutter will pass, and outputs these data along with postprocessor information. As in the other general-purpose languages, the third section or the postprocessor produces the codes for satisfactorily directing the actual cutting of the part on a specific machine and control.

So that small computers can be used, only one section of the ADAPT computer program is in the computer memory at a time. Further, the modularized translation and arithmetic phases are composed of discrete subsections for the various geometric configurations which can be specified in the ADAPT system.

Part programmer language violations and incorrect part definitions can be detected during the translation phase. Typical language violations are the use of a word not in the dictionary or an incorrect definition format. Motion statement errors often mean that the computer cannot calculate the check surface for the part because of the inability to compute an intersection. Errors may also result from exceeding the computer storage allotted for the dictionary and macro definitions.

As an ADAPT program is processed, each statement is read and translated into a numerical form by the computer as it encounters

314

the statement and looks up the word definitions in the dictionary. The word definitions are stored in the computer for immediate access until the statement is completely translated. Next, the class of the statement is identified, and the control is transferred to that segment of the ADAPT computer program which will complete the translation. The necessary data will then be stored or sent to the output section for the arithmetic phase. This arithmetic phase, since it is primarily designed for two-dimensional work, is completely analytic. Each type of curve has a separate cutter offset routine. When cutter center locations are to be calculated, the type of curve is determined, and control is transferred by means of a communication routine to that segment of the computer program which will calculate the cutter offset. The information describing the curve and the cutter center locations is then sent to the computer output section.

The information entering the postprocessing phase may come from the arithmetic phase, or directly from the translation phase as in point-to-point applications. If circular or parabolic interpolation is used by the machine's control, the postprocessor will apply the specific interpolation, since the arithmetic phase performs the calculations with respect to linear interpolation only.

Most statements in the ADAPT system are compatible with APT and can be written in a free form consisting of key words and their parameters which may be symbolic or numerical. An acceptable symbol contains up to six alphanumeric characters, at least one of which must be a letter. A number may have a decimal point and a mathematical sign. Elements of statements are separated by the following special characters:

$$, + - * / \$ ( ) .$$

There are three basic types of statements:

1. Definition statements, geometric or scalar:

A geometric definition takes the form
symbol = major section/minor section, e.g.,

$$\text{CIR } 1 = \text{CIRCLE}/5,5,3.5$$

where the major section defines the type of geometry, and the minor section gives numerical data pertinent to the actual size and form of the geometry.

A scalar definition takes the form:

symbol = minor section, e.g.,

$$SCOORD = 3*CO5F(60)$$

Geometric definitions may be used in nested parenthetic phrases such as

LIN 1 = LINE / (POINT/ (3*COSF(60)), (−3*SINF (60)$)), RIGHT, TANTO, (CIRCLE / 5,5,3.5).

2. Instructions:

Instruction statements are used to specify motion, part surface definition, Z−surface definition, machine function, postprocessor instructions, or tool definition.

Instructions take the form:

Major section/minor section, e.g.,
GODLTA/0,0,2 where GODLTA describes an incremental move of 0 inches in the X and Y directions and 2 inches in the +Z direction

3. Special statements:

These consist of one word and are of the form:
major section, e.g.,

CUT

TERMAC

FINI

ADAPT includes macro instruction definitions which the part programmer can use to define a series of instructions that can be called whenever the macro is specified. A series of statements may be used more than once with a slight variation of the parameters of the statements. New geometric definition modules or macros may be created by the programmer to handle his own needs provided the new words are added to the dictionary for computer translation.

UNIAPT

The development of UNIAPT is especially significant because it was one of the first successful attempts to handle the *full* power of APT on a small computer. Completely compatible with APT, UNIAPT has similar syntax structure, processing features, and variable field formats. Differences in the two systems exist mainly in the internal designs of their processors which are not evident in

UNIAPT's external form. Some users have actually run a deck of APT part-program data cards through a UNIAPT computer without any modifications.

One APT version required about 262K of core storage—approximately half the total memory capacity of a typical APT computer, such as the IBM 360 Model 50. UNIAPT can be processed by a computer having as little as 12K of core memory. The list of small computers for which UNIAPT was initially designed implies the relative compactability of the language.

DEC PDP–8/I, 8/L, 8/E

DEC PDP–10 (Multi-processed, time-shared version)

IBM 1130

GA 18/30

GE GEPAC 4020

CDC 1700

Hewlett Packard 2100 and 2116

Because UNIAPT is built around a minicomputer, the investment and operational costs can be greatly reduced. A minimal hardware configuration includes the minicomputer equipped with 12K memory, an internal input-output interface, a data break, a hardware multiply and divide unit, a disk storage memory, a paper tape reader and punch, and a teletype.

A minimal system initially could be purchased for about $30,000, or about one month's rent of a typical APT computer. Expanded UNIAPT systems usually contain more core memory (from 16 to 32K), a larger disk, a line printer and card reader—all priced around $75,000. The basic purchase price of UNIAPT software is $15,000 with increased cost for certain additional features such as five-axis capability and a lathe module. Postprocessors cost an additional $500 to $2,000 each. A complete hardware-software system can be leased for about $1,000 per month for the larger system on a three-year lease basis. When analyzed on an hourly basis, a rented system costs between $1 and $7 an hour—depending upon the number of days per week and the shifts per day over which it is amortized.

Although minicomputers may be slower than much larger computers normally used for APT, elapsed times for completed program tapes can often be shorter—due to instant turn-around time. Because minicomputers are cheap and do not require special environmental considerations, they can be located in the shop or right in the part programmer's office. When a computer is easily accessible and dedicated to part programming, the total tape preparation cycle is greatly shortened. Processing of UNIAPT part programs average 10 to 20 minutes of computer time; total elapsed time—including preparations and scheduling delays—seldom exceeds an hour. When lead time is critical, UNIAPT's short turnaround time contrasts sharply with the 12- to 24-hour delays often encountered in typical centralized computer facilities. The time advantage is even more pronounced if several computer runs are necessary to purge errors from the part program to obtain an acceptable tape. Total elapsed time in such instances have ranged from a day to a week. On a UNIAPT system as many as six reruns of a part program have been made through the computer in one day.

With direct accessibility and short turnarounds, programmers more often make additional computer runs needed to optimize tapes resulting in higher productivity, better quality, and increased machine utilization. Just as important, easy access encourages programmer experimentation leading to new and more efficient methods, techniques, and programs.

UNIAPT Operation

Part programs may be loaded into the UNIAPT computer from cards, paper tape, typewriter keyboard, or disk memory. Program statements can be retained in the disk memory for subsequent editing during tape check-out.

As described earlier, APT processes part programs in three to five phases. UNIAPT has been simplified into two phases, plus postprocessing. The first phases of APT and UNIAPT are similar. From this point, however, the internal structure of the two systems differs significantly. UNIAPT combines the equivalent of APT's second, third, and fourth passes into a compacted second pass which facilitates the execution of the part-programming statements in a logically sequential manner similar to that used in FORTRAN. For example, only those surface definitions made logically prior to a given motion command are executed before the tool motion calculations are made. This allows the part programmer to obtain the coordinates at the end of a given motion sequence (Obtain Tool End is a special UNIAPT command) and use these coordinates to define future geometry for future motion commands. In other words, UNIAPT provides the capability to use motion statements to define geometry.

Other advantages gained from UNIAPT's internal structure are easy surface redefinition, dynamic table size allocation (also available in APT), avoidance of loop start and loop end statements, and improved main program-macro-nest communications.

The UNIAPT processor and associated postprocessors reside on the computer's disk storage. By using the disk memory to supplement the computer's core storage and by applying memory overlay techniques, UNIAPT is able to operate without having all APT segments in its primary memory at any one time. UNIAPT actually divides the APT line processor into slices which are selectively called in from the disk as needed in the minicomputer.

All processing operations are automatic once UNIAPT starts to read the part-program source data. Postprocessors are specified by a machine statement in the part program and activated by the UNIAPT processor. Multiple postprocessors can be called from the UNIAPT source program.

The output of a UNIAPT run—fully processed data for the machine control tape—can be left on disk or punched directly on tape. A tape can be copied on disk or duplicated by punching on another tape. It can also be reread against its disk image for verification.

UNIAPT detects certain errors during operating system control, part-program decoding, system setup, motion section processing, and postprocessing. Error statements are printed on the computer output listing the point they are encountered and are also communicated to the programmer via the computer's teletype. Error codes defined in the system documentation are printed which not only classify the error, but also suggest its possible cause.

During source deck decoding and system setup, error detection occurs without preventing the completion of this processing phase. Errors encountered during the tool path calculation are also identified and processing is similarly allowed to continue by the transfer to a point at which a valid position can be established and the path calculations continued. Accuracy is also promoted by special postprocessors which facilitate the drawing of the tool path for inspection on a connected or off-line plotter. The tool path can also appear on a CRT display.

UNIAPT II, a refined and augmented version which offers additional capabilities, allows the use of system macros, CRT editing of both source program and object statements, and, most importantly, a tie-in to DNC. By having direct communication with a DNC computer, the programmer can go directly from the APT source program to properly coded machine commands without the medium of tape. Moreover, when UNIAPT operates in tandem with DNC, program editing at the source level is available at the machine—this is in addition to the ability to edit tape level data.

When UNIAPT is implemented in a DNC system, a second but smaller minicomputer having only 4K of core storage is added. With the necessary interface and communication devices, the second computer shares the same disk memory as the primary UNIAPT computer and provides the link between the part-program data stored on disk and the machine control.

UNIAPT solves several dilemmas previously encountered in operations that require the power of APT, but lack adequate computing facilities. It permits the manufacturing department to operate independently of the hardships so often encountered with "computer utilities" under the direction of financial or accounting departments. These constraints frequently cause part programmer inefficiency and dissatisfaction. Moreover, UNIAPT-type languages can serve as a learning tool that manufacturing personnel can use to experiment with more sophisticated computer applications. Thus, while new management attitudes are being formed and necessary management and production control procedures refined, the manufacturing staff can be gaining valuable computer experience in preparation for the advance into large-scale computer-aided manufacturing systems.

EXAPT

The EXAPT part-programming system was an important development in the evolution of part-programming technology because it gave impetus to the application of computerized machinability decisions. It is a product of a study group formed in the mid-1960's by personnel from several German technical universities. The project specified the requirements and initiated the development of a part-programming system appropriate to European conditions. Of special interest was the need for an APT-like system that could operate on smaller computers because of the relative scarcity of large computers in Europe. But more importantly, EXAPT represented a significant attempt to add computer machinability calculations to part-programming languages.

The resulting system, EXAPT (an acronym for the words EXtended APT), actually consists of five separate components:

BASIC EXAPT — for programming machines with either straight-line or continuous-path controls;

EXAPT 1 — for programming drilling and milling machines with point-to-point and simple straight-line controls;

EXAPT 1.1 — for programming drilling and milling machines, and machining centers having no more than $2\frac{1}{2}$ axes[4] of automatic control;

EXAPT 2 — for programming lathes with straight-line or continuous-path controls.

EXAPT 3 — for programming $2\frac{1}{2}$-axis continuous-path operations on milling machines.

The following features characterize EXAPT: the vocabulary is user-oriented and is readily understood by manufacturing personnel; instructions that describe the geometry and the machining processes have a relatively flexible format; tool movements, feeds, and speeds can be determined by the computer; and the computer selection of feeds and speeds can be adapted to individual firms' special requirements.

The computer processing of an EXAPT part program is done in three sections: first, in a geometrical processor; secondly, in a technological processor; and finally, in a postprocessor. EXAPT is one of the few part-programming systems having a technological processor for performing machinability calculations.

Language Structure

EXAPT uses both the grammar and the syntax of APT. All letters of the alphabet (upper case), all ten digits, and the following special signs may be used: . , / + − ( ) * = $. The special signs are known as syntax elements and are used to separate language units. Spaces have no significance, but they are used to improve the readability of the manuscript.

---

[4] The term "$2\frac{1}{2}$ axes of control" refers to the ability to position the tool in the third plane under automatic control and then carry out normal two-axis operations. The third axis of motion is not simultaneous with the other axes.

Words may contain no more than six characters, the first of which must be a letter, e.g.,

POINT
PAT 2
P 1.

In addition to regular vocabulary words, special word symbols may be created which call up an entire sequence of operations.

Numbers are formed from the digits and, if necessary, a mathematical sign. Numbers without signs are positive. Decimal fractions are separated by a decimal point. Leading zeros may be omitted. The EXAPT system utilizes either the metric or the American (inch) dimensional systems. If metric conventions are used, the following dimensional references apply:

length	millimeter
angle	degrees
feeds	millimeter per revolution
rotational speed	revolution per minute
cutting speed	meter per minute

Instructions

Instructions are built up from words, numbers, and syntax elements. An instruction contains a principal part and, if necessary, an auxiliary part. Principal and auxiliary parts are separated by a slash, elements of the auxiliary part are separated by commas, e.g.,

SPINDL/n,CLW

There are three types of instructions: definition statements, executive statements, and technological statements. Definition statements may be divided into instructions with and without symbolic references. Those containing symbolic references have the form:

Symbol = defined expression

Defined expression denotes details of the coordinates of a point, the parameter of an operation, or an arithmetic expression. Generally, each symbol need be defined only once in a part program, e.g.,

Symbol = POINT/X, Y, Z

Executive statements are movement and work instructions. Movement instructions determine the end position of a machining motion, e.g., GOTO/40,0,12 would direct the machine to the absolute coordinates of 40 mm. in the X axis, 0 mm. in Y, and 12 mm. in Z. Work instructions call up a previously determined machining definition, e.g., WORK/DRILL 1, SINK 1,X,Y,Z which would cause drilling and countersinking operations to occur at a defined location. "Nested" instructions can occur with a work statement, i.e., a series of operations can be programmed with one statement, e.g., pre-drilling, counterboring, and tapping.

Technological statements can be divided into instructions that describe the workpiece and instructions which indicate all other information necessary for machinability decisions. From this information tool paths, feedrates, cutting speeds, spindle reversals, and feed decreases, as well as tool and operational sequences can be determined by the computer operating under EXAPT control.

The EXAPT programmer has two important aids for creating the technological statements, the tool card index and a raw material card index. The data in the tool card index include: a number system describing the type of tool, the dimensions necessary for calculating cutter paths, the technological data necessary to determine whether these tools can achieve the desired surface finish and machining standards, and an identifying number for each tool. The material data may apply to a single type, or groups of materials with the same machinability characteristics. Information from the two index sources are used as input information to the computer so it can generate the machinability commands.

Fundamental characteristics of the various EXAPT levels are delineated below.

BASIC-EXAPT.   BASIC-EXAPT provides the following facilities for the user:

— creation and use of the computerized Tool File (possible but not required);

— definition of tool motions similar to APT, including calculation of cutter offsets;

— simplified statements for the machining of edge chamfers and radii;

— simplified statements for axis-parallel lines;

— geometric definition facilities as in EXAPT 2; and

— facilities designed for small-sized computers.

Because BASIC-EXAPT has a modular architecture, individual

323

modules of new technological capabilities can be incorporated over time to extend the system's power. The minimum core storage capacity on IBM computers was originally 128,000 bytes, and after reorganization, it fits in a computer with 64,000 bytes (1 byte equals 8 binary digits).

EXAPT 1. A programmer using EXAPT 1 for drilling operations can define both points and point patterns. Limited line and circle geometry capabilities are also available. Drilling, center drilling, counterboring, reaming, tapping, and milling are admissible machining operations. The technological processor in EXAPT 1 offers both the determination of cutting speeds, feeds, and the generation of complete machining sequences.

EXAPT 1.1. As the acronym suggests, EXAPT 1.1 extends the power of EXAPT 1. The following facilities were added:

a. Computerized determination of work cycles is implemented through decision tables. Besides standard work cycles supplied with the system's decision tables, company-specified cycles also may be added. This flexibility permits the optimal adaptation of machining sequences tailored to the experiences and preferences of each company.

b. Programming of boring bar problems is simplified by means of single statements based on a separate description of boring bars and boring bar bits in the system's Tool File.

c. Programming of continuous-path machines is achieved by the addition of motion statements.

d. Computerized tool selection is available based on optimization criteria such as the minimum number of tools, optimal diameters for predrilling operations, the selection of shortest possible tools, etc.

EXAPT 2. EXAPT 2, developed principally for turning operations, handles points, lines, and circles. The part to be machined is defined by blank and finished part characteristics. It is possible to designate specific elements of the finished part contour so that a selected area later can be easily called up for machining.

Definitions for straight-line turning operations, contour parallel turning operations, and grooving and thread-cutting operations are provided. Distribution of the cuts and cutting values need not be indicated by the progammer since these data can be determined by EXAPT's technological processor. Workpiece elements can be assigned qualities of surface finish for the technological processor's consideration.

This third level of EXAPT has a similar structure and generally operates by the same conventions as EXAPT 1. Technological instructions of EXAPT 1 for drilling in the direction of the axis of rotation also are usable in EXAPT 2.

While EXAPT 2 was developed primarily for turning applications, it is also used for programming other two-dimensional continuous-path operations, such as flamecutting and plotting. A major advantage of EXAPT 2 is its advanced computerized machinability decision-making facility. Using the programmer-prepared technological statements describing the type of machining required and the areas of the workpiece to be machined, the computer generates:

1. Cut distribution,

2. Tool motions, and

3. Cutting values.

The cutting values are calculated using programmer-specified tool application conditions, material, and machine characteristics. All required data for the calculations are entered just once into the EXAPT computer files. These files, containing the geometrical and technological values of the tools as well as the machinability criteria of the material and machine characteristics, are used by the computer during EXAPT part-program processing. In the part program, therefore, only identification numbers for material and tools are required.

Another important asset for the part programmer is the EXAPT facility which automatically calculates machining offsets. For example, when a desired surface finish cannot be achieved with a single machining operation, the EXAPT program automatically allows for an oversized cut. Thus, when a part area needs a "fine finishing operation," the computer-selected roughing operation leaves sufficient material for finishing and fine finishing cuts.

Like APT and certain other languages, EXAPT 2 has macro and looping facilities. Specially dimensioned engineering drawings are not required, as the coordinate system used for the description is arbitrarily selectable. And it is not necessary to convert coordinates, as the computer automatically calculates all motion statements based on the coordinate system of the machine.

EXAPT 3. EXAPT 3 contains instructions for point, line, and circle definitions, and point patterns which facilitate the description of milling and drilling operations. This fourth level permits taper cuts and tabulated function definitions. EXAPT 3 includes the language part of EXAPT 1, further expanded to describe milling operations. The capability of describing contours is based on the contouring facilities in EXAPT 2, but extended so that contours can be designated by symbols. The further convenience of a transformation definition has been added.

As in other levels of EXAPT, cutting speeds, feeds, and the distribution of milling cuts are determined by the computer. The computer selection of tools as well as the determination of the work cycle for conditions described in EXAPT 1 are also available in EXAPT 3.

AUTOSPOT

The acronym, AUTOSPOT, constructed from the words AUTOmatic System for POsitioning Tools, is the name of a three-axis, point-to-point language with limited fourth-axis and contouring capabilities. It holds an important position in the evolution of part programming because it answered the needs of many companies that had only a small computer and used primarily point-to-point machines. Also, it was subsequently combined with ADAPT to provide an effective language for both point-to-point and continuous-path applications. Because the language's output information is cutter location data, a postprocessor is required. AUTOSPOT was developed for the IBM 1620 computer—a computer used extensively by smaller operations. A subsequent version (AUTOSPOT/360) was written for the IBM 360 series computers. There are four types of AUTOSPOT III statements:

1. Tool specifications,
2. Vocabulary words,
3. Geometric definitions, and
4. Machining statements.

Tool specifications statements define tool parameters such as drillbit lengths and diameters, tap sizes, and end-mill diameters. A cutter is related to each machining operation by specifying its tool number. Cutter parameters are used in any required calculations such as offsets, depths, clearances, etc.

Vocabulary words are used to assign some value to a given word. An example would be:

$$R1 = 5$$

where a programmer may have a series of bolt circles with five-inch radii and may wish to specify the radius once as R1. Thereafter he can use R1 to insert a five-inch value in the program whenever he wants it.

Geometric definitions allow the specification of the geometric features of the part drawing. AUTOSPOT III allows a point to be defined several different ways, a line eight, a circle five, and a pattern nine ways. With these statements, most point-to-point and some simple milling configurations can be readily defined. The general format for geometric statements is:

NAME = GEOMETRIC TYPE/parameters

where NAME is a symbol, GEOMETRIC TYPE is one of the allowable vocabulary words (POINT, LINE, CIRCLE, PATERN, or MATRIX), and the parameters are those values used to specify the geometry.

Machining statements describe the operations necessary to produce the part. There are two basic types of machining statements in AUTOSPOT: point-to-point and milling. In a point-to-point statement the cutting tool is positioned above each point and fed at the proper speed to the specified depth of cut. The tool then retracts to the clearance level where it is ready to move on to the next point. In the milling mode, the tool drops from a starting point to the proper depth and proceeds along the prescribed path.

Machining statements are composed of three basic sections: the type of operation (e.g., drill, tap, mill) and the cutter identification number of the tool to be used, the coordinates of the machining location(s), and the operating specifications such as depth, speeds, and feedrates.

AUTOSPOT/360 has a computing feature in its general processor which allows the programmer to take advantage of certain computer arithmetic operations that he would otherwise have to do by hand. For instance, a programmer may wish to place 13 equally spaced holes along a line of 27.437 inches. Rather than manually calculating the incremental lengths he may use a statement such as:

$$I1 = 27.437/13$$

The computer would then calculate the size of the equal increments and the programmer could specify I1 wherever he needed it in the program. This feature allows the use of numbers, scalars, arithmetic operators, and arithmetic expressions. The allowable operations are addition, subtraction, multiplication, and division.

The AUTOSPOT language has a number of other operating conventions that are designed to increase programmer productivity. Many of these routines originated during AUTOSPOT's early use for electronics jobs. AUTOSPOT's effective pattern manipulation routines evolved primarily for drilling circuit boards. These pattern routines specify, translate, and rotate point groups. Patterns can be quickly defined as linear or circular arrays, with explicit point data, or any combination of these. Once a group of points is defined as a pattern, the group can be recalled at any time in the program simply by specifying its name. The most common form of a pattern statement is:

$$NPAT = PATERN/\text{point specification}$$

where NPAT is some arbitrary name for the group of points. PATERN defines the statement type, and the point specification is the means of constructing the pattern.

Once the pattern has been defined, it may be inverted, translated, or rotated. The first illustration in Figure 9 shows a pattern defined and then rotated; the second example illustrates pattern translation; and the lower figure shows four possible inversion methods, up/down or left/right.

When the same tool is used, it is possible to combine operations into one statement because all coordinate data are reusable. Such a combination feature allows the continuous machining of a number of patterns without reprogramming each time a new pattern is encountered.

Other routines associated with point-to-point work are a deep-hole drilling routine, a chip-breaking sequence, reaming and boring sequences, and internal groove and pull-bore routines.

AUTOSPOT also has three limited milling routines: standard, face, and pocket milling. Standard milling is an operation where the cutter is directed along some defined path. Minor sections of milling statements may be labeled and retained as are patterns in point-to-point operations. Face milling is an operation where a rectangular surface is to be cleaned off to a specific depth. Pocket milling is used

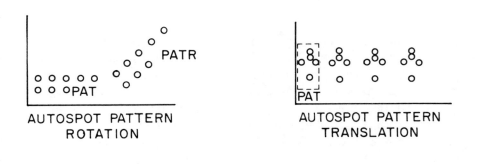

AUTOSPOT PATTERN
ROTATION

AUTOSPOT PATTERN
TRANSLATION

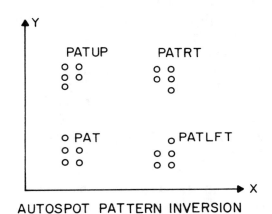

AUTOSPOT PATTERN INVERSION

FIGURE 9

Example of point-to-point pattern manipulations.

to cut out the inside of a polygonal cavity. In AUTOSPOT/360 a generalized pocket milling routine can handle any triangle, any four-sided figure whose opposite sides are parallel, or any shape whose sides are of equal length and form interior angles less than 180 degrees.

For other AUTOSPOT routines, the IBM programming manual for the computer on which the part program will be run should be checked. Since some routines apply only to certain computers or versions of the AUTOSPOT language, it is important to review all the appropriate manuals.

One of the advantages of AUTOSPOT is the extensive number of postprocessors available. Many numerical control users with IBM computers have obtained several postprocessors at little or no charge through IBM's library service.

COMPACT

As computers increased in size and speed, it became apparent during the early 1960's that multiple users could be serviced simultaneously. Existing telecommunication technology also permitted the economical access to computers remotely located from potential users. All this gave rise to the development of part-programming languages that extended the power of a relatively large computer directly into the part programmer's office via conventional telephone lines. COMPACT was one of these languages and it has grown steadily to become a widely used language for programming parts for simple point-to-point drilling machines as well as complex three-, four-, and five-axis machines.

The COMPACT system converts its language statements to machine control codes in a single computer iteration. In contrast to languages requiring additional postprocessing to complete the tape coding, COMPACT's Machine Tool Link (MTL) automatically performs the postprocessing as each statement is computer-processed. The MTL, acting as an integrated postprocessor, shortens the computational time and greatly facilitates the prompt discovery of detectable statement errors.

COMPACT has many useful pattern manipulation routines. Linear, circular, and random hole patterns as well as arrays of points can be defined, translated, inverted, or rotated. A powerful rotation routine was developed to extend COMPACT's capability to a fourth axis. In the four-axis mode a part definition can be rotated around the X, Y, or Z axis, depending on the configuration of the machine tool, so that the plane being worked will be perpendicular to the tool. This capability offers substantial programming time reductions on parts that have point-to-point operations on many sides or on oblique planes. Also, a single COMPACT statement can initiate several commands to control a sequence of drilling, tapping, and reaming operations or a complex series of cuts.

An important characteristic of time-shared languages is that they are unusually receptive to program revisions, either of simple statements or of whole blocks of information. Program changing and editing can be done rapidly with an interactive computer editing subsystem. Through the editor, the part programmer can instantly insert, create, or delete characters and complete lines of manuscript information; alternatively, he can copy or modify all or portions of an existing line. Direct access to any line of typed manuscript information can be gained simply by specifying a set of characters or digits contained in the line.

If a statement cannot be processed because it is incomplete or has a grammatical error, or because the data values are beyond allowable limits, a diagnostic comment is promptly returned by the computer explaining the error to the part programmer. Once the source of the error is identified, the programmer corrects the statements and proceeds. If he fails to see the problem, he can have the computer type the processed statements up to that point. He can also inspect the computed X, Y, Z coordinates of his tool tip locations in order to visualize the location of the tool to pinpoint whatever geometric error may be present. The instant responsiveness of the computer to the part programmer contrasts vividly with the delays experienced when similar problems are encountered in a batch-processing type of computer operation. After a part program has been processed and approved by the programmer, the control tape is immediately punched at his terminal.

A COMPACT program comprises statements having a major word and a set of associated minor words. The major words describe *what* operation is to be performed, and the minor words describe *where* and *how* the operation is to be executed. A typical program consists of five logical parts; initialization, part definition, tool specification, tool path specification, and termination (Figure 10).

Initialization

The program's initialization section establishes certain system parameters and identifies the machine being used. The MACHIN statement identifies the Machine Tool Link (MTL) to be used. The MTL is loaded into computer core along with the system's general processor, thus allowing each input statement to be both processed and postprocessed before the next statement is handled. This incremental processing permits the user to completely debug a program in a single computer pass.

The IDENT statement identifies each set of output data generated by the program. Information contained in the IDENT statement is printed on each output listing and also punched in visually readable characters in the tape leaders. The INIT statement specifies the input and output mode for dimensional data.

Example: INIT,METRIC/IN,INCH/OUT

331

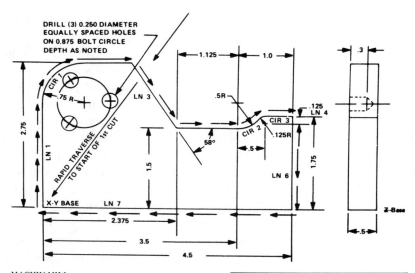

```
MACHIN,MILL
IDENT,DEMO PROGRAM
INIT,INCH/IN,INCH/OUT
SETUP          $ USE THE ASSUMED PARAMETERS
BASE,3XA,8YA,6ZA
DCIR1,.75XB,2YB,.75R
DLN1,CIR1,90CW,XS
DLN3,2.375XB,1.5YB,58CW
DCIR2,3.5XB,1.5+.5YB,.5R
DLN4,1.75YB
DCIR3,CIR2/.125,LN4/.125YS,XL,.125R
DLN6,4.5XB
DLN7,YB
ATCHG,TOOL1,.5TD,6GL,250FPM,.01IPR
MOVE,PASTLN1,PASTLN7,.6ZB
CUT,-.03ZB
OCON,CIR1,CW,S180,F270
CUT,PARX,PASTLN3;PARLN3,TOLN(1.5YB )
ICON,CIR2,S270,F(TANCIR3),CCW
OCON,CIR3,S(LOC),F(270),CW
CUT,PASTLN6;PASTLN7;PASTLN1
ATCHG,TOOL2,.25TD,6GL,800RPM,.01IPR,118TPA
DRL3,CIR1/.875D1A,SO,CW,.5ZB,.3DP
END
```

MACHIN IDENT INIT SETUP	**INITIALIZATION**
BASE DPT DLN DCIR DPB DPAT DSET	**PART DESCRIPTION**
ATCHG MTCHG TOOL GL GLX GLZ TLR TD FPM RPM IPR IPM MPM MMPM	**TOOL SPECIFICATION**
MOVE CUT BORE DRL FLT CONT ICON OCON	**MOTION DESCRIPTION**
END NORWD	**TERMINATION**

FIGURE 10

A COMPACT part program illustrating the five
logical elements of the program.

The SETUP statement contains information describing certain machine and control options, work limits of the machine, and the starting position of the machine slides (tool gage length reference point) at the beginning of the tape cycle.

Part Definition

The coordinate system used for programming in COMPACT is established by a set of mutually perpendicular axes (planes). The intersection of these axes defines Absolute Zero and is the origin of the primary coordinate system. The relationship between the primary coordinate system and the machine tool coordinate system is specified in the SETUP statement as the travel limits allowed relative to Absolute Zero.

A secondary coordinate system may be defined through the use of a BASE statement. Each BASE statement defines a secondary coordinate system parallel to, and at some distance from, the primary coordinate system. This capability allows the programmer to establish a local programming reference system suited to the dimensional requirements of the workpiece. The parameters specified in the BASE statement identify the zero (BASE) position of the secondary coordinate system. This position may be redefined in the program as many times as desired.

Part shapes are defined by describing a series of points, lines, circles, and part boundaries. Definition of the part shape is accomplished by specifying dimensional data and symbolic instructions conforming to a set of conventions understood by the computer. These data and the instructions define the points, lines, and circles. Segments of the lines and circles represent surfaces of the actual part.

An important COMPACT convention is that, except for arithmetic expressions, all numeric values are specified with a vocabulary word which provides the meaning of the number. The sequence of data in any statement is therefore not important. This "free format" reduces the pressure on the programmer to memorize fixed formats, and reduces errors.

Examples: DPT1,LN1,CIR1,XL
             DPT1,XL,CIR1,LN1

In addition to the two points of reference previously defined, a third—the location specified in a particular statement—can also be used. This allows dimensional specifications from one fixed location

(Absolute Zero), one movable location (BASE), and incrementally from any other known location. Coordinate dimensions are specified along an axis of the coordinate system from a point of reference in the following manner:

nXA	(X dimension from Absolute Zero)	
nXB	(X dimension from BASE)	(xdim)
nX	(Incremental X dimension)	
nYA	(Y dimension from Absolute Zero)	
nYB	(Y dimension from BASE)	(ydim)
nY	(Incremental Y dimension)	
nZA	(Z dimension from Absolute Zero)	
nZB	(Z dimension from BASE)	(zdim)
nZ	(Incremental Z dimension)	

Angular dimensions are specified as decimal degrees measured from the primary axis (X for mills and Z for lathes), in a clockwise (CW) or counterclockwise (CCW) direction.

Example: nCW
         nCCW   Angle

Radial dimensions are identified by the vocabulary words R (Radius and DIA (DIAmeter).

Example: nR
         nDIA   (This is equivalent to two times the radius.)

Each vocabulary word used to define a geometry element begins with the letter "D" (define). The vocabulary words for point, line, and circle definition are DPTn, DLNn, and DCIRn. The following illustrates the basic definition for each of these elements.

Point: DPTn,xdim,ydim,zdim
Line: DLNn,xdim,ydim,angle
Circle: DCIRn,xdim,ydim,radius

Some basic geometry definitions are shown in Figure 11.

A location may be specified as the intersection of two geometry elements (LN–LN, LN–CIR, CIR–CIR). The LN–CIR and the CIR–CIR specifications produce two points of intersection, and the programmer selects one of these intersections by specifying the larger

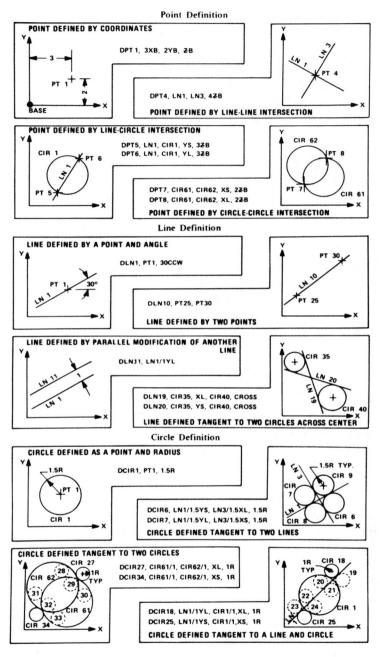

FIGURE 11

Some simple point, line, and circle definitions.

or smaller X, Y, or Z value. This is done by including one of the vocabulary words (XL,XS,YL,YS,ZL,ZS) in the statement.

Example: DPT1,LN1,CIR1,XL

There obviously are many variations of these definition statements since COMPACT allows substitution of any valid definition of a point, line, or circle for that element in a definition statement.

Tool Description

COMPACT recognizes two tooling statements: the automatic tool change (ATCHG) and the manual tool change (MTCHG). Minor words are programmed which describe the physical tool dimensions and the feed-speed specifications. The minor words used to describe the tool shape are GL (gage length for mills), GLX (gage length in X for lathes), GLZ (gage length in Z for lathes), TD (tool diameter), TLR (tool radius), and TPA (tool point angle).

The minor words used to specify speeds and feeds are FPM (surface feet per minute) or RPM (revolutions per minute), and IPR (inches per revolution) or IPM (inches per minute). Metric feed and speed may be specified.

Example: ATCHG,TOOL1,GL6,.75TD,118TPA,680RPM,
.01IPR (Mills)
ATCHG,TOOL1,GLX4,GLZ5,350FPM,.008IPR,
.032TLR (Lathes)

A Tool and Material Library capability enables the user to store and retrieve dimensional descriptions of cutting tools and holders and machinability parameters of both tool and work materials.

Machining Specifications

There are two types of tool motion: straight-line and circular.

The two COMPACT words which specify straight-line motion are MOVE and CUT (BORE may be used in place of CUT for internal operations on a lathe). The difference between the two words is that MOVE specifies rapid traverse motion and CUT specifies feed controlled motion. The information that specifies *where* and *how* the motion is made is the same for each word and may be specified:

1. As incremental in one or more axes.

Example: MOVE
CUT ,2X,3Y

2. As an absolute end point of the motion.

Example: MOVE
        CUT   ,PT1

3. As a direction for the motion and a termination relative to some defined geometric element.

Example: MOVE
        CUT   ,30CCW,TOLN3

The direction of the motion may be specified in one of three ways:

1. At an angle to the primary axis.

   Example: nCW or nCCW

2. Parallel or perpendicular to a defined line.

   Example: PARLNn or PERLNn

3. Parallel or perpendicular to an axis.

   Example: PARX or PERX or PARY or PERY
           (PARZ or PERZ for lathes)

The termination may be specified relative to a defined line or circle.

	TOLn	(To the line)
Line	LNn	(On the line)
	PASTLNn	(Past the line)
	OUTCIR	(Outside the circle)
Circle	CIRn	(On the circle)
	INCIRn	(Inside the circle)

Figure 12 illustrates some of the more basic straight-line tool motion specifications.

There are three COMPACT words which specify circular motion. OCON is used to specify tool radius offset outside the specified circle, and ICON is used to specify tool radius offset inside the specified circle. CONT specifies that the tool center path be on the circle.

A COMPACT contouring statement must specify:

1. The center of the arc.
2. The radius of the arc.
3. The start angle on the arc.

337

Linear Motion

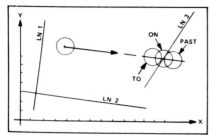

CUT,PERLN1,LN3 ⎤
CUT,PARLN2,ONLN3 ⎦ Equivalent

CUT,PARLN2,PASTLN3,5ZB
CUT,PERLN1,TOLN3

Motion parallel or perpendicular to an axis may be specified as a direction. In the third statement, the Z-value of the termination location is specified as 5 positive units from Z-base.

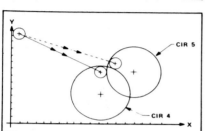

CUT,INCIR4,OUTCIR5,YL,5ZB

CUT,OUTCIR4,INCIR5,YL (Dotted Line)

In the first statement, the Z-value of the termination location lies at 5 positive units from Z-base.

Circular Motion

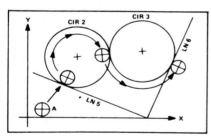

ICON,CIR2,CW,S(TANLN5),F(TANCIR3)
OCON,CIR3,CCW,S(TANCIR2),F(TANLN6)

The tool moves at feed rate from its present location (A) to the position inside circle 2 tangent to line 5. An inside contour is then made to the location tangent to circle 3. Following this an outside contour is performed around circle 3 beginning at the position tangent to circle 2 and finishing at the location tangent to line 6.

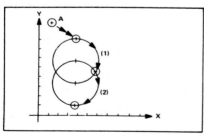

(1) CONT,CIR1,CW,S(270),
F(ONCIR2,XL)

(2) CONT,CIR2,CW,S(LOC),F(90)

(1) A cut is made from location (A) to a position on circle 1 at the 270 degree position as measured clockwise from the X-axis. A contour is made to a position on circle 2 at the XL intersection of circle 1 and circle 2. (2) A contour is then made from the present tool position to a location 90 degrees in the clockwise direction around circle 2.

FIGURE 12

Examples of motion specification in COMPACT.

4. The finish angle on the arc.

5. The direction of the circular motion (CW or CCW).

The start and finish angles are specified by the vocabulary words S and F.

Example: CONT,2XB,3YB,1R,S45,F60,CCW

The center of the arc may be specified by a defined point.

Example: CONT,PT1,1R,S45,F60,CCW

The center of the arc and its radius may be specified by a defined circle.

Example: CONT,CIR1,S45,F60,CCW

When the start and finish angles are unknown, sufficient symbolic information may be enclosed in parentheses to allow the system to compute the angles.

Example: CONT,CIR1,S(TANLN3),F(TANCIR2),CCW

In this example LN3 and CIR2 are tangent to CIR1. As can be observed in Figure 12, there are a number of methods available to symbolically define the start and finish angles for contouring motions.

Point-to-point Programming

Holes may be drilled, reamed, bored, counterbored, or tapped. All such operations can be separated into three basic tool motion cycles. The vocabulary words DRL (drill), BORE (bore), and FLT (float tap) specify these cycles. The tool motion produced is as follows:

1. The tool moves to the specified location at rapid traverse rate.
2. The tool feeds to the depth specified.
3. DRL Motion: The tool retracts to the start of the feed stroke at rapid traverse.
4. BORE Motion: The tool retracts to the start of the feed stroke at feed rate.
5. FLT Motion: The spindle and feed stop simultaneously and the spindle is reversed. The tool is then retracted to the starting position at feed rate.

These cycles may be invoked at a single location or a group of locations with a single statement as delineated later in the Repetitive Programming section.

Termination

The END statement is used to terminate a COMPACT program. The system will return the tool to its starting position (or other specified position) and reset all machine and control functions to their starting condition.

Additional System Features

A threading routine enables the programmer to specify a complete threading operation using a single input statement. This routine can be used for cutting both straight and tapered internal and external threads, face (scroll) threads, and multiple start threads. The programmer may control the depth of cut or allow the system to calculate the depth of cut, which decreases as the tool cuts deeper into the thread.

The path of the tool can be described as a box. The sides of the box approximate the major (MAD) and minor (MID) thread diameters and the start (S) and finish (F) path of the thread. The cycle consists of four elements: position, chase, retract, and return. Figure 13 shows a sample threading statement and the resultant tool path produced.

Lathe Stock Removal Cycle (fasTurn). The fasTurn cycle provides a simplified method for performing roughing and finishing lathe operations. When using fasTurn, the programmer defines boundaries representing the shape of the raw stock and the finished part profile. Together they enclose the work area from which the material is to be removed. The part in Figure 14 and the part program and center path plot in Figure 15 illustrate the power of this capability.

Definition and Use of Variables. The programmer can define and store variables within his program for subsequent recall and use during program processing. A variable may be defined as a specified number, the value associated with an arithmetic expression, the value associated with a trigonometric or geometric function, the distance between geometric elements, or the result of a bend allowance computation.

Some of the functions available for variable definitions are as follows:

ABSn	Absolute value of n.
IPn	Integer part of n.

340

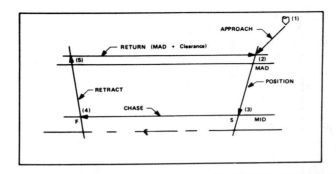

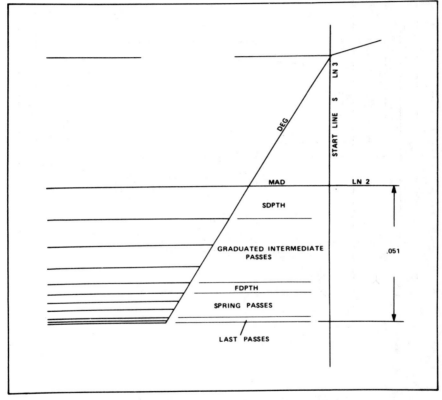

THRD12,CX,MAD(LN2),MID(LN2/.051XS),S(LN3),F(LN4),
.012SDPTH,.004FDPTH,3SP/.003,2LP/.001,DEG30

FIGURE 13
Thread programming in COMPACT.

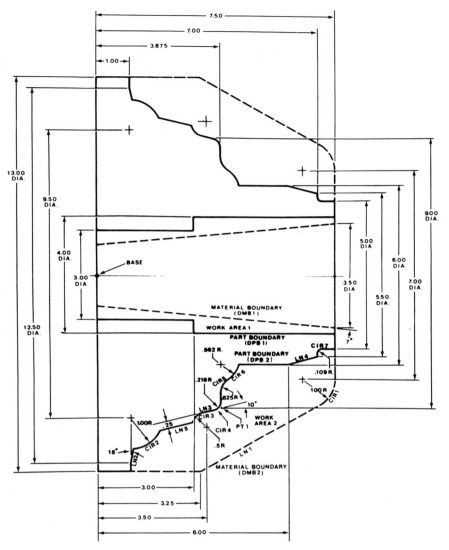

FIGURE 14

Complex part configuration to illustrate
the use of fasTurn (see Figure 15).

FPn	Fractional part of n.
PI	Sets variable equal to PI.
SQRTn	Square root of n.
SINn	Sine function of n.
COSn	Cosine function of n.

TANn	Tangent function of n.
ASINn	Angle whose sine is n.
ACOSn	Angle whose cosine is n.
ATANn	Angle whose tangent is n.

XV, YV, ZV, HV, TV, RV, and AV obtain the axis value stored for a point, line, or circle as applicable.

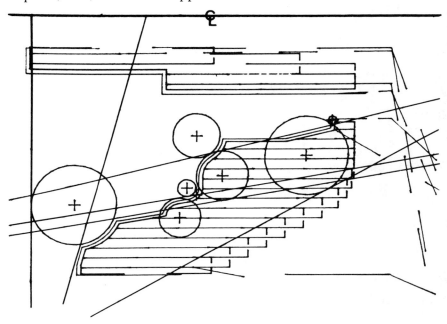

MACHIN,LATHE
IDENT,FASTURN SAMPLE PART PROGRAM
SETUP,14X,22Z
$ DEFINING BOUNDARIES
DMB1,7.5ZB;LN(7.5ZB,3.5D,7CW),NOMORE
DPB1,4D;3ZB;3D;-.2ZB,NOMORE
DCIR1,7.5-iZB,7D,1R
DLN1,PT(13D,3.25ZB),CIR1,XL
DCIR7,5+.218D,7+.109ZB,.109R
DLN4,PT(5.5D,7ZB),PT(6D,6ZB)
DCIR6,6D,3.875ZB,.562R
DCIR5,CIR6/.625,3.875+.625ZB,XL,.625R
DLN3,9D,3.875ZB,10CCW
DCIR4,3.875-.218ZB,LN3/.218XS,.218R
DLN5,LN3/.25XL
DCIR2,9.5D,1ZB,1R
DLN2,1ZB,12.5D,75CCW
DMB2,7.5ZB;CIR1,F(TANLN1);LN1;13D,NOMORE
DPB2,5D;CIR7,F180;7ZB;LN4;6D;CIR6,S(ZL),

F(TANCIR5);CIR5,F180;3.875ZB;CIR4,F(TANLN3)
;LN3;CIR3(3.5ZB,LN3/.5XL,.5R),F(LN5,ZS)
;LN5;CIR2,S(ZL),F(LN2,XL);LN2;1ZB,NOMORE
$ ROUGH BORE
ATCHG,TOOL1,GLX4,GLZ12,.093TLR,OFFSET1
MOVEB,2D,8.5ZB,400FPM
BOREL1,.063STK,.25SDPTH,.015IPR,NOX
$ROUGH TURN
ATCHG,TOOL2,GLX5,GLZ5.8,.093TLR,OFFSET2
TURNL2,.25SDPTH
$ FINISH BORE
ATCHG,TOOL3,GLX6,GLZ11,.062TLR,OFFSET3
MOVEB,4D,8.5ZB,0STK
BOREL1,FINISH,450FPM,.011PR,NOX
$FINISH TURN
ATCHG,TOOL4,GLX4,GLZ6,.062TLR,OFFSET4
MOVEC,5D,8.5ZB
TURNL2,FINISH,NOX
END

FIGURE 15

Part program for part in Figure 14. Also a plot
of the cutter path and defined geometry.

Example: DVR1,SIN35
DVR2,ATAN1/2

XVEC   A signed number indicating the distance between two geometric elements along the X axis.

YVEC   Same as XVEC, for Y axis.

ZVEC   Same as XVEC, for Z axis.

DIST   True distance between two geometric elements. This is always a positive number.

Example: DVR1,DIST,LN1,LN2
DVR2,XVEC,PT1,CIR2,XS

Looping and Macro Capabilities. Statements may be labeled for future reference by GOTO or DO by enclosing the identification number between the "less than" (<) and "greater than" (>) symbols. The statement may then be referenced by that label.

Example: GOTO 65 (would transfer processing to statement 65)

DO 65   (would execute statement 65 and return)

The COMPACT word DO allows the programmer to execute a statement or sequence of statements at any location in the program.

Example: DO 1/4,3TMS

In the above example, statements between the statement labeled 1 and the statement labeled 4 would be executed three times. One of the statements executed could increment a variable that would alter one or more of the statements during execution.

COMPACT also allows conditional testing to control the processing of the program. The vocabulary word IF is used to test certain conditions and bypass or execute portions of the program based on the result of the test. IF compares the relation of two values based on the operator used and will process the remainder of the statement only if the test is true.

A significant benefit of the program process control statements DO, IF, and GOTO occurs in "family of parts" programming. Thoughtful application of these statements enables the programmer to accommodate a number of similar parts to be produced within a single program.

344

Repetitive Programming. Various capabilities for programming a repetitive operation cycle at a number of different locations are available. DPATn (define pattern n) allows the programmer to group a number of defined points into a pattern for later reference.

Example: DPATn, 1/8 (defines pattern as points 1 through 8)

The programmer would then substitute the word PATn (pattern) for PT in a statement to specify where the operation is to be performed.

Example: DRL,PAT1,1DP

The preceding statement would cause a hole one-inch deep to be drilled at every point location in the pattern. Also, statements describing a machining sequence may be specified in relation to a reference point (PTO), and when those statements are executed by a DO statement containing a PAT reference, the machining operations will be performed with the reference point of the sequence being placed at each point in the pattern (see Figure 16).

Another method for defining a group of locations for subsequent reference is DSET (define set). Sets may be defined as random locations or as linear or circular arrays and as other sets propagated in some random pattern or in a linear or circular array. Figure 17 illustrates these principles.

Any definition or motion statement may be translated and/or rotated by specifying the translation along each axis as an increment from the position at which it is defined and a rotation (ROTXY, ROTYZ, or ROTXZ) around BASE. Using BASE as the center of rotation allows the programmer to change the center of rotation at his discretion. Figure 18 illustrates this capability.

Programming Four- and Five-Axis Machining Centers

COMPACT allows designation of head and table positions in point definition and tool motion statements. Head and table positions may be specified either incrementally (H or T) or as locations in the absolute or BASE coordinate system (HA or HB and TA or TB). The system provides for automatic retract to a clearance plane for table indexing when the locations in a pattern or set are on different faces of the part. Also, a tool axis (TLAX) may be specified which provides control of the spindle orientation. TLAX is specified by a head angle and table angle in a point definition or motion statement.

345

```
DPAT1,1/4
GOTO3
<1>MOVE,PT,.1Z
CUT,-.75Z
MOVE,PT,-.5-1.3+.1Z
CUT,-.75Z
<2>MOVE,PT,.1Z
<3>DO1/2,PAT1
```

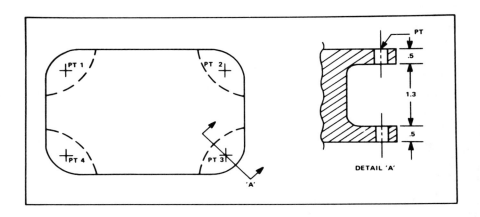

```
DPAT1,1/4
GOTO3
<1>MOVE,PT,1X,.1ZB
CUT,-.1ZB
CONT360,PT,1R,OCCW
<2>MOVE,.1ZB
<3>DO1/2,PAT1
```

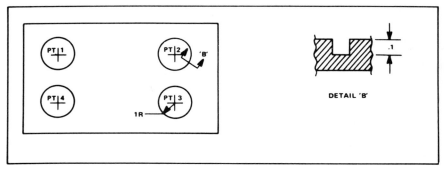

FIGURE 16
Programming of special cycles at multiple locations.

346

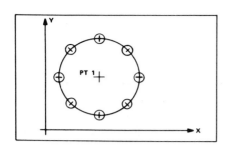

DSET1,PT1,8BC,8EQSP,0CW,NOMORE
DRL,SET1,1DP

This pair of statements is equivalent to:

DSET1,8BC,8EQSP,0CW,NOMORE
DRL,PT1,SET1,1DP

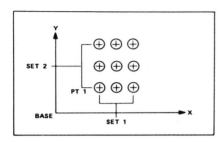

DSET1,3EQSP,2LX,NOMORE
DSET2,3EQSP,3LY,SET1,NOMORE
DRL,PT1,SET2,1A

This group of statements is equivalent to:

DSET1,3EQSP,2LX,NOMORE
DRL,SET1,PT1,3EQSP,3LY,1A

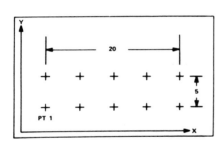

DSET1,RECT(20LX/5EQSP,5LY/2EQSP),NOMORE
DRL,PT1,SET1,1A

These two statements are equivalent to the statement:

DRL,PT1,RECT(20LX/5EQSP,5LY/2EQSP),1A

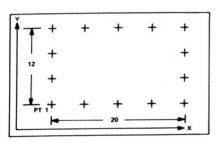

DSET1,RECT(20LX/5EQSP,12LY/4EQSP,PERIM),
NOMORE
DRL,PT1,SET1,1A

These two statements are equivalent to the statement:

DRL,PT1,RECT(20LX/5EQSP,12LY/4EQSP,PERIM),
1A

FIGURE 17
Defining linear, circular, and rectangular arrays as sets.

```
<1>MOVE,OFFLN1/XL,OFFLN2/X5,.5ZB
CUT,-.5ZB,NOX,NOY
OCON,CIR1,CW,S(OFFLN2/XS,YL),F(OFFLN1/XL,YL)
CUT,PARLN1,PASTLN2
<2>MOVE,.5ZB,NOX,NOY
<3>DO1/2,4X,2Y
```

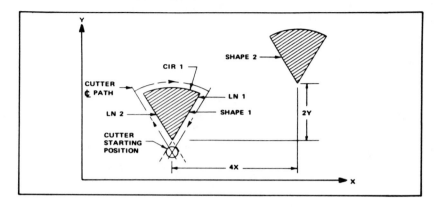

Same initial motion sequences as above. Statement <3> changed
to cause rotation.

```
<3>DO1/2,ROTXY90
```

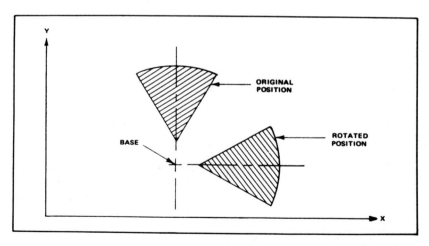

FIGURE 18
Examples of rotation and translation in COMPACT.

Example: DPT1,4XB,3YB,6ZB,TLAX(48HB,53TB)

TLAX is also used to compute the location of the point in the machine coordinate system when all axes are rotated to present the spindle center line along the tool axis.

Machining on canted planes is accomplished by describing a point which lies on the plane and a tool axis (TLAX) which is perpendicular to the plane. All part description and motion commands are then specified using conventional COMPACT statements.

The system performs "swarf" cutting motions by linearizing the motion between two points which have a different TLAX designation. The tool tip is maintained on a straight line between the points within a specified tolerance.

Program Processing

If a part program error is encountered, processing is interrupted and an appropriate diagnostic is printed at the time-sharing terminal. The user is placed in the edit mode where the error can be corrected from the terminal keyboard, and processing may proceed immediately with that statement. These errors may range from simple syntax errors to omitted definitions or to machine limit over-travel. Additional statements may be inserted into the program as required to provide a solution.

When the END statement is processed, the programmer is assured that his program is completely debugged from the standpoint of computer acceptability. The user may then verify his program graphically by plotting the cutter center path and the defined geometry used to describe the part shape (see Figure 19). Interactive processing allows the programmer to debug and plot his program simultaneously, if desired.

The user concludes the programming session by issuing the commands to punch the machine control tape and print a listing containing the input statements, the computed cutter locations, and the actual tape codes generated.

Figure 20 summarizes the flow of a COMPACT program from original manuscript preparation to machine control tape generation.

TRENDS IN THE USE OF PART-PROGRAMMING SYSTEMS

One programming trend is particularly clear: companies having large-scale computers and multi-axis machines are likely to use APT,

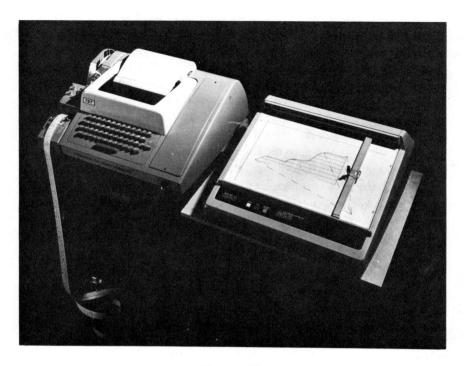

FIGURE 19

Visual presentation of the part program provides a powerful assist to
program debugging. On-line editing can be performed whenever
an error is observed in the plot of the program being processed.

while companies with smaller computers and less complex machines
will generally employ more limited systems. The latter companies
are also more likely to be using one of the machine-oriented part-
programming systems.

The most obvious reason for APT's popularity is that many
hundreds of man-years of development effort has made it the most
advanced, refined, and powerful part-programming system. If a company needs the full capability of APT, there is no practical alternative. Companies that must use APT for their complex parts are
likely to program all their jobs with it. The desire to use only one
language to ease logistic and part programmer training problems
is indicated by the fact that only about one plant in four utilizes two
or more programming systems. New numerical control users are
also attracted to APT because more postprocessors are available for
it than for any other language.

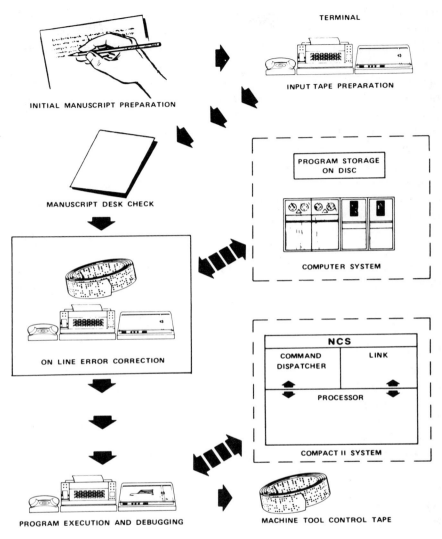

INITIAL MANUSCRIPT PREPARATION

TERMINAL

INPUT TAPE PREPARATION

MANUSCRIPT DESK CHECK

PROGRAM STORAGE ON DISC

COMPUTER SYSTEM

ON LINE ERROR CORRECTION

NCS

COMMAND DISPATCHER

LINK

PROCESSOR

COMPACT II SYSTEM

PROGRAM EXECUTION AND DEBUGGING

MACHINE TOOL CONTROL TAPE

FIGURE 20

Schematic diagram showing the flow of the COMPACT program from blueprint to punched tape.

Nevertheless, several factors restrict a still wider usage: the need for a large computer, the greater efficiency of other languages for certain point-to-point jobs, and the concern that APT's highly mathematical character increases part programmer training problems. Finally, as confirmed by a survey leading to the development of the

351

ADAPT specifications, machining jobs, requiring relatively simple operations far outnumber those requiring the full APT capability.

Most of the factors restricting the wider use of APT seem to suggest the utilization of ADAPT. However, despite the merits of the original ADAPT objectives, the language has yet to fulfill its expectations. One serious obstacle ADAPT has encountered is the inability to make the system operate effectively within the computer size for which it was originally designed. Companies that tried to implement the original ADAPT version on computers like the IBM 1620 experienced hours of computer time for processing a part that took only minutes on a large computer. ADAPT became far more effective after being modified to operate on medium-sized, time-shared computers, and its popularity increased significantly when it was implemented in combination with efficient point-to-point languages.

The popularity of AUTOSPOT was attributable mainly to its being implemented on a small, widely used computer; furthermore, it is an easily understood system whose vocabulary is manufacturing-oriented. Although the initial version of AUTOSPOT was limited to positioning jobs, the addition of certain milling routines made the language usable for a surprisingly large proportion of numerical control applications. Combining AUTOSPOT with ADAPT further extended both the language's utility and popularity.

One should also recall that IBM developed the system first for its own use, then released it on a no-charge basis to their computer users. Since IBM accounted for approximately three-fourths of all the computers sold up to that time, many companies considering computer-aided part programming preferred the acquisition of AUTOSPOT to paying several thousand dollars for APT. However, restricting AUTOSPOT's implementation to IBM computers has also somewhat limited its use.

Other constraining factors enter the picture: companies requiring part-programming capabilities which exceed those of AUTOSPOT must use an additional language; moreover, because it is not a subset of APT, separate AUTOSPOT postprocessors must be written. Normally, the cost of writing a new AUTOSPOT postprocessor is borne by the language user.

The rapid development and implementation of EXAPT warrants special consideration. Despite the exceptional promise that the many EXAPT strengths afford, there are certain areas of concern. Like

ADAPT, EXAPT was designed for a small computer, but failed to operate effectively within the computer size specified in the original design goals. EXAPT 1 soon expanded to the point that the equivalent of an IBM 360–40 was required, and EXAPT 2 needs the facilities of a 360–50 or its equal. Another obstacle confronting the prospective EXAPT user is the current lack of uniformity in machinability practices among companies and manufacturing engineers. The fundamental principles of the EXAPT technological processor, however, are sound, and as the language develops, the inherent economies that can be derived from computerized machinability decisions will encourage consistent workshop technology practices among plants and industries. Eventually, most general-purpose and many machine-oriented part-programming systems will incorporate a technological processor.

The rapid acceptance and application of UNIAPT and the time shared computer languages such as COMPACT seem to suggest that they are attracting many of the potential users that previously may have selected languages like AUTOSPOT and ADAPT. Both of the former languages resolve the need for a large in-house computer, and UNIAPT in particular competes effectively with the power of APT. Perhaps of greater importance for the future is the fact that both the UNIAPT and COMPACT systems are being continually refined by their profit-oriented developers. Clearly this competitive struggle to capture an ever larger share of the computer-assisted part-programming market is producing dramatic improvements in these two languages—especially when compared to the developmental effort applied to AUTOSPOT and ADAPT.

CHOOSING A COMPUTER-AIDED PART-PROGRAMMING SYSTEM

The earlier synopsis of only the more popular programming systems may threaten to overwhelm some who face the task of selecting the optimum language. However, when computer availability and desired part configurations are considered, the list of usable programming systems quickly narrows.

The types of application for which the more popular languages can be used are summarized in Table II. Notice that of the 22 distinct systems, a user would have to select from only 8 if five-axis equipment were involved. The list of usable languages may be reduced even further by ascertaining the availability of postprocessors and then

TABLE II

COMMON PART-PROGRAMMING LANGUAGES AND THEIR CAPABILITIES

Languages	Machine-Oriented	General-Purpose	Positioning	2-Axis	Partial 3-Axis	3- & 4-Axis	Multi-Axis
APT		*	X	X	X	X	X
APT/360		*	X	X	X	X	X
ADAPT		*	X	X	X		
AUTOSPOT I, II		*	X	X			
AUTOSPOT III		*	X	X	X		
ADAPT/AUTOSPOT		*	X	X	X		
AUTOMAP		*		X	X	X	X
COMPACT	*	*	X	X	X	X	X
REMAPT		*	X	X	X		
EXAPT I		*	X				
EXAPT II		*		X			
EXAPT III		*	X	X	X		
SNAP	*		X				
SPLIT	*		X	X	X	X	X
ACTION	*	*	X	X	X	X	X
AUTOPROPS		*	X				
CAMP III, IV		*					
COMPOINT		*					
AUTOPROMPT		*				X	X
NCPPTS		*	X	X			
SHOP		*	X	X	X		
UNIAPT		*	X	X	X	X	X

determining which programming systems can be handled by the available computer.

Selecting the best programming system is commonly accomplished by determining the answers to these questions:

1. (a) Are the present and future parts point-to-point or continuous-path types?

   (b) Do they require simple or complex operations?

2. How many machines will be required?

3. (a) What are the characteristics of the computer that is available?

   (b) What numerical control programming languages can it process?

4. Is there a time-shared computer service center nearby which offers a programming system capable of handling the part requirements?
5. What postprocessors are available for the machines and languages being considered?
6. (a) What programmer training schools are available?
   (b) Is the existing staff capable of learning how to use the selected programming system?
7. Who will maintain the program language and keep its development current with advancing technology?
8. What system will do the programming at the lowest cost?

Delineated below are the major considerations to be weighed when reviewing these questions.

Matching the System's Power with Part Requirements

The selection of an appropriate part-programming system can begin by matching language capabilities with production needs. Running a five-axis machine with a language capable of handling only two axes of motion is an obvious waste of resources. Likewise, using a two-axis machine with tape prepared by a fixe-axis language may result in excessive training and computer costs.

Companies should be wary, however, of eliminating a powerful language from their consideration just because their present machines do not perform all of the operations the language can handle. A plant that starts out with a few point-to-point machines will likely add continuous-path equipment. If a general-purpose point-to-point language with contouring capabilities was originally selected, the conversion to continuous-path programming can be done smoothly with a minimum of personnel training and reorientation. Another reason to select languages that may seem too powerful at first glance is that the more powerful language may have profitable point-to-point routines that facilitate the programming of bolt circles, hole matrices, patterns, etc.

Impact of the Computer Characteristics

Computer considerations are likely to be the most influential factors affecting the choice of a part-programming language. Despite the work that has been done to make programming systems less computer-dependent, virtually all numerical control languages still de-

355

pend in some way on a particular type of computer. Some computers simply do not process numerical control languages at all, or if they do, the storage capacity may restrict the computer's use to point-to-point or very simple continuous-path languages. Also, some computers are considerably more costly to use when processing part-programming languages.

By the time many firms reach the phase of selecting a part-programming system, they are already committed to the computer their accounting or financial staffs have selected earlier. The manufacturing personnel are, therefore, faced with the task of finding a part-programming system that can be run on the existing computer. Because manufacturing personnel are often not sufficiently represented when a computer is chosen, the available computer frequently is incapable of handling the optimum language. When faced with such a condition, it is worthwhile considering a language that uses a time-shared remote access computer. As the outside computing bill builds, consideration should be given to the justification of buying a computer, even a minicomputer, for in-house manufacturing operations.

Availability of Postprocessors

Before a general-purpose language is selected, and even prior to ordering numerical and computer controls, the user should know exactly where he can obtain postprocessors for his machines and the language-computer combinations with which they can be used. Information on available postprocessors can be obtained from the Numerical Control Society or the Society of Manufacturing Engineers, as well as from the machine tool builders and the computer and control manufacturers. Computer manufacturers, however, have frequently taken the position that postprocessors are the responsibility of the machine tool and control builders.

Although improving slowly, the postprocessor question remains aggravated by a lack of program standardization. Market pressures are building to force machine tool builders to furnish these programs as part of the equipment acceptance process. However, they too are reluctant to supply postprocessors for all but the most common computer-controller combinations. The numerical control user is frequently the man in the middle and is forced to write or contract for the development of a postprocessor. Too often he has discovered that his equipment purchase agreement quietly leaves the responsibility for obtaining postprocessors on his own shoulders.

Maintenance of Programming Systems

A computer-aided programming language, like any other manufacturing tool, must go through an installation and shakedown period, and then be maintained as operating problems are encountered. Even the APT system that has a full-time staff constantly working on its maintenance has occasional problems in its computer routines. Part-programming systems will also require modernization as technology advances. Usually the language supplier will assume these responsibilities—either for a charge or as part of the original selling price. If a user intends to do the language maintenance and modernization work himself, he must have a staff well trained in writing computer programs. Computer software personnel are mathematically-oriented and, therefore, are not likely to be the same people interested in part programming.

Some computer manufacturers and computer service firms offer software writing services as part of their numerical control packages. Although these services may be available from several sources in many industrialized areas, it is important that the user know exactly where he will get the qualified personnel. Whatever the source, a cost for the services is nearly always involved, and this expense should be considered during the process of selecting the part-programming system.

Training Sources

It is important to know what training is necessary to qualify programmers to use the language, and where training programs are conducted for each programming system under consideration. Manual part programmers usually can readily adapt to computer-aided part programming because they already have a good understanding of the required mathematics and the overall part-programming process. Depending upon the language selected, new users going directly into computer-aided programming are faced with a greater training problem. Some of the interactive computer part-programming systems, however, are easier to learn than certain manual part-programming methods. These considerations should be translated into training cost estimates.

Unless a company selects APT, problems can arise in finding a language general enough for all of the machines that eventually may be purchased. It is seldom desirable to equip a plant with machines of the same type or manufacturer. A company using a machine-oriented language, therefore, may encounter problems in acquiring other numerical control equipment that can be programmed by the special language. Either it must revise or supplement the old language to handle the new machines, use other languages, program manually, or use a new language to cover all of the equipment through a series of postprocessors, including a new one for the old machine.

OBTAINING PART-PROGRAMMING SYSTEMS

Once the alternatives have been considered and a programming system has been chosen, the manager is faced with the question of identifying the sources of the selected language. Most computer manufacturers offer numerical control programming systems to help support their equipment sales. Major computer manufacturers have been active in part programming almost since its inception, both as suppliers of computer-aided programming systems and as users. Generally, the local sales representative for these firms is a good person to contact with questions about part-programming software.

Associations will be another programming system source for many companies. One of the earliest developments in numerical control was the formation of a group of aircraft manufacturers who undertook the task of continuing the development of APT. For a variety of reasons the aircraft group decided that APT should be made available outside the represented companies.

The Illinois Institute of Technology Research Institute (IITRI) was chosen to administer and further the development of APT under the guidance of the APT Long-Range Planning Committee—the group formed at the outset largely by representatives of the aircraft companies. Later a new association was formed, known as Computer Aided Manufacturing-International, Inc. (CAM–I), to administer APT and extend its development. New versions of APT can now be obtained by joining CAM–I at a fee ranging from approximately $5,000 to $10,000. However, after APT developments are about two years old, they are placed in the public domain and released to nonparticipants. One of IBM's part-programming languages (APT 360) was based on such a release.

Computer service organizations have been previously discussed as a source of outside computational work. Many of these companies, particularly those in industrialized regions, also serve as a source of numerical control languages. Some offer no more than the standard languages available from computer manufacturers, while others offer special languages that they have developed for the general market or for a certain customer. New independent software companies seem to spring up continuously. As these firms mature, they will be an increasingly important source of part-programming languages. In addition, they also can aid users through their consulting services for system maintenance and modernization.

Since some part-programming languages can be obtained from computer manufacturers, user associations, or computer service companies, each should be contacted to determine the source with the most favorable terms. The selling price of the language, its efficiency, training resources and charges, and the availability and terms of future maintenance and modernization support should all be considered in selecting the best proposal.

Chapter IX

Maintenance Practices and Policies

Traditional maintenance practice and organization often must be refined to keep computer and numerically controlled equipment operating at profitable utilization levels. A maintenance program that is both effective and economical must be based upon qualified personnel having a thorough understanding of electronics, hydraulics and mechanics, and a good working knowledge of the equipment to be maintained. Effective maintenance also requires proper test equipment and readily available spare parts.

Of the many factors affecting the complexity of a maintenance program, the control's sophistication is the major consideration. Many simple drills and lathes with modular solid-state electronic controls in easily replaceable circuit modules actually demand less on-the-floor maintenance knowledge than traditional tracer or pneumatic controls. As computer or numerical control's complexity grows, however, the skill required by shop maintenance men changes and increases sharply.

Devising an effective maintenance program begins before the purchase order is written for the new equipment. Maintenance personnel should be called upon early in the procurement process to thoroughly evaluate the reliability characteristics of all competing equipment. The equipment design, the construction methods, and the materials are major factors affecting reliability. Since yearly maintenance costs for well-designed equipment can easily average 1 to 2 percent of the investment, in just a few years a poorly conceived or cheaply constructed machine can easily consume the price differential between the cheapest and most expensive equipment. When the value of lost production and sales is added in, unreliable equipment is seldom a bargain at any price.

EQUIPMENT RELIABILITY AND MAINTAINABILITY

A first step in evaluating the reliability and maintainability of proposed equipment involves the maintenance supervisor's ascertaining the operating performance of similar machines in other companies. If an effective maintenance program is followed, lost production time due to emergency machine breakdowns should not exceed 4 to 7 percent. Equipment that has a higher emergency downtime profile and is receiving proper preventive maintenance should be analyzed carefully before being selected.

A detailed comparison of the design and construction of the competing equipment is a second step in evaluating equipment reliability. The following mechanical features should be investigated: slide-way materials, spindle construction and rigidity, horsepower capacity of drive motors, rigidity and precision of the lead screws, and design of lubricating systems. Specific questions to be investigated in evaluating the electrical features include:

1. Is the computer or control of a rugged industrial design?
2. Does the design incorporate a modular concept with plug-in components?
3. Are integrated, solid-state circuits used?
4. Are the printed circuit cards adequately braced and supported?
5. Do circuits cards, component assemblies, and cables have rugged connectors?
6. Are the electronic circuits and assemblies arranged functionally for simple troubleshooting?
7. Are circuit cards of a standard design that will be readily available from one or more manufacturers?
8. Is the computer or control cabinet sealed from factory air, dust, dirt, oil mist, etc.?
9. Does the heat generated by the electronic components threaten their reliability?
10. If the control system requires its own air conditioning system, does it have adequate capacity, and is it properly located in the cabinet to avoid dropping potential condensation on the control electronics?

Maintenance personnel should also determine what information is needed from the equipment manufacturer to help keep the machine operating efficiently. Information commitments should be obtained while all the proposals are being evaluated. The types of maintenance information that must be specified in the purchase order and their associated costs included in the quoted purchase price, are listed below:

362

1. Spare parts list
2. Preventive maintenance schedules
3. Specially programmed tapes to cycle the equipment during tests
4. Manuals describing theory of operation and troubleshooting procedures
5. Complete electrical and mechanical drawings including parts lists
6. Manufacturer-conducted maintenance training schools.

Because of organizational and psychological considerations, maintenance personnel supervisors should be involved early in the project; they perform both the reliability evaluations and generate the maintenance information requirements. Many automation projects fall disappointingly short of reasonable productivity goals because maintenance personnel lack the necessary motivation that could have been assured had they been included in the procurement evaluations. Involving maintenance supervision at the outset is vital to instilling confidence in themselves as important team members. Moreover, their training, experience, and interest make them especially well qualified to evaluate equipment reliability and maintainability characteristics.

MAINTENANCE SKILLS

As soon as the equipment has been selected, the changes required in the existing maintenance program should be ascertained and promptly initiated. Of the more common changes, teaching maintenance personnel new skills requires the longest lead time. Retraining and changing attitudes consumes as much time as that needed for the equipment manufacture and delivery. Failure to recognize these demands results in lengthy equipment check-out periods and high downtime.

The extent of retraining is measured by the difference between available skills and those required to maintain the new equipment. Workers qualified to repair conventional equipment having some form of a nonmanual control apparatus can usually be trained to cope with the electromechanical aspects of computer and numerically controlled equipment. Mechanical and hydraulic systems in particular can be handled by tradesmen capable of maintaining conventional equipment after minor retraining.

Computer and numerical control systems maintenance, however, requires considerably more specialized skills. The necessary qualifications can be gleaned from an abbreviated version of a U.S. Department of Labor description of the duties such tradesmen perform:

Discusses events immediately preceding machine error or stoppage with machine operator and machine maintenance personnel to eliminate the possibilities of operator or part program error and machine failure, and to determine the general nature of the malfunctions. Localizes, isolates, and repairs or replaces faulty modules and components by following schematics, diagrams, and handbook instructions, using such aids as a dual-trace oscilloscope, test probes, and electrician's hand tools, to restore control system to operating conditions. Tests system by using system and trouble-localization test tape to simplify diagnostic tasks, whenever such tape is available. Inserts replacements for defective modules when control is of modular design, and repairs defects later, at workbench, or returns modules to manufacturer for replacement.

Follows preventive maintenance schedules to reduce breakdowns and machine errors by such means as replacing components before they become defective or marginally functional. Keeps written records of downtime and nature of malfunctions to provide statistical base for modifying these maintenance schedules. Repairs associated machine tool electrical and electromechanical components, or guides shop electrical maintenance personnel who perform this function. Maintains spare parts inventory.

May repair machine tool hydraulic and mechanical defects, depending on breadth of training and experience. May also repair electronic control systems that monitor and control continuous-flow industrial processes and machines other than machine tools. May originate testing procedures. May devise and construct module test equipment. May assist on installation, check-out, and maintenance of numerical controls at customers' establishments as manufacturer's representative.

In only a few companies are traditional maintenance tradesmen prepared to troubleshoot electronic equipment successfully without supplemental training. Personnel who maintain conventional electromechanical relays and standard electric circuits are often bewildered by problems concerning the photoelectric tape and card readers, the power supplies, the transistorized control logic, or other solid-state circuitry. Extensive damage has resulted when maintenance personnel *thought* they knew what they were doing.

Maintenance training must start long before the equipment is received. Prior to starting any sort of training program a company must select its candidates. Some sort of screening program should be established to determine who is eligible for consideration and what criteria for selection will be used. The machinery maintenance training tree shown in Figure 1 provides a conception of the kinds of skills that would be valuable in various areas of maintenance even before the formal training program begins.

Prior to the advent of computer and numerical controls, the typical maintenance tradesman acquired his skills by serving as apprentice to a journeyman. Although this form of instruction may be effective for training building construction and maintenance tradesmen, a more thorough training in the physics of electronics is necessary for computer and numerical controls. Personnel lacking a sound academic background overly rely on experience that affords too few stock solutions to the varied problems they encounter.

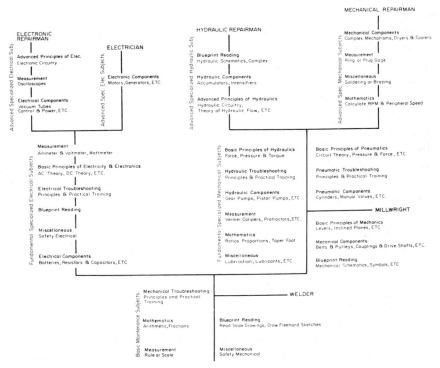

FIGURE 1

Machinery maintenance training "tree."

Due to the dynamic interaction of the electronic, hydraulic, and mechanical subsystems, the symptom of a system malfunction, regardless of its source, may be evident in any of the three subsystems. At least one maintenance tradesman qualified to isolate the location of a system problem is therefore essential. Often, companies that experience high equipment downtime do so not so much because their craftsmen are incapable of repairing the system, but because they have difficulty in isolating the trouble. Identifying the cause takes about two-thirds of the time required to return electronically controlled equipment to operational status. However, if a major mechanical problem occurs, it sometimes may take days to correct the malfunction, even when the problem is detected immediately.

In a plant with several electronic controls, a system diagnostician usually restricts his work to locating the problem; then a tradesman is assigned who specializes in repairing the malfunctioning subsystem—be it hydraulic, mechanical, or electronic. This split maintenance concept, however, is shunned by some companies because it fails to develop the confidence of many of the technicians. They become inclined to avoid analytical work altogether and call on specialists for work they should be performing themselves. These companies argue that no maintenance group can grow effectively until individuals are charged with responsibility and required to achieve satisfactory results.

Qualified system diagnosticians make it possible to avoid costly situations where a mechanic or an electrician alternately watches while the other troubleshoots the subsystem in which he is specialized. To meet the new skill requirements, many companies have turned to a new crop of younger maintenance technicians because seasoned tradesmen often refuse to wrestle with the retraining challenges. One company that had to train new employees recruited a team whose members had experience in the following areas: office equipment repair, electronics, test equipment mechanics, automotive mechanics, and radar.

TRAINEE SELECTION

A maintenance tradesman qualified to diagnose and isolate a malfunction in complex systems often possesses specialized post-high school education, and is thoroughly familiar with the basic principles of mechanics, hydraulics, and electronics. If possible, it is often more economic to select craftsmen with sound electronic backgrounds and teach them the hydraulic and mechanical aspects.

Personnel with the following minimum qualifications should be sought for training: four years of high school or the equivalent, e.g., a special technical certificate. Graduation from a two-year post-high school technical institute with an electronics major is preferred for candidates expected to maintain complex equipment. Military service school training and experience in repair of complex, specialized electronic systems is also worthwhile, because these programs normally (1) provide a background in servomechanism theory; (2) train students in nondecimal number systems; and (3) introduce the concepts of higher mathematics essential to understanding how typical control systems operate.

Intangible personal characteristics, including adaptability, stability, social-status satisfaction, and an appetite for new challenges, are also important. A motivation to learn new skills is especially helpful. A well-motivated, though less-qualified trainee may be preferred over an uninterested person, since the former may learn at a slow pace, while the poorly motivated trainee may choose to learn very little. Persistence is also important. In addition to weeks of classroom training and night study, a system malfunction occasionally defies detection by one person. To minimize delays, a maintenance man must be willing to swallow his pride and seek assistance.

Good vision and color discrimination are necessary as circuitry becomes miniaturized and color-coding techniques become more widespread. As in other maintenance jobs, manual dexterity is demanded as is the physical strength to transport test equipment and replacement assemblies.

A complete summary of the characteristics required by workers who maintain equipment with electronic controls has been prepared by the U.S. Department of Labor for counseling and placement activities of the various State Employment Services. Their compendium of maintenance worker traits includes many helpful guidelines for industrial recruiting and training:

APTITUDES:

Verbal ability to discuss reasons for machine and control malfunctions and stoppages, read and assimilate technical materials, and suggest changes in standards and procedures that might reduce downtime.

367

Numerical ability to level of decimal and binary arithmetic and Boolean algebra (logic) to comprehend functions of numerical control switching circuitry, perform diagnostic tests, interpret display lights, read punched paper control tapes, and keep written downtime and inventory records. A course in introductory differential and integral calculus is very helpful in providing a background for understanding how complex machine and control systems operate, and successful completion is an indicator of fairly high numerical aptitude; however, such a course is not regarded as absolutely necessary for successful on-the-job performance.

Spatial ability to interpret wave form displays, and to comprehend schematics and diagrams and relate physical components to them.

Form perception to check circuitry for such defects as loose or corroded connectors, and for presence of dust or other foreign matter.

Clerical perception to perceive pertinent detail in written material, as when comparing test displays to handbook values.

Manual dexterity to use test probes and hand tools.

Finger dexterity to move small objects in confined work spaces.

Color perception to recognize and work with colorcoded components.

INTERESTS:

An interest in working with machines and techniques for repairing them.

A preference for activities resulting in tangible satisfaction to repair, and perform preventive maintenance services on electronic control systems.

TEMPERAMENT:

Must adjust to a variety of tasks, such as initiating a series of tests to localize and diagnose equipment failure, and carrying out preventive maintenance duties.

Must be able to make decisions concerning performance of equipment based on factual information such as test data, manufacturers' manuals, and predetermined test routines, to isolate and identify marginal or faulty components.

Must adjust to working with precise and established standards of accuracy indicated by written specifications, and at speed sufficient to hold machine downtime and production rescheduling to a minimum.

PHYSICAL DEMANDS AND WORKING CONDITIONS:

Work is light, involving lifting and carrying equipment seldom exceeding 10 pounds, occasional pushing and pulling of heavier dolly-mounted test equipment, and infrequent stooping and crouching.

Reaching, handling, fingering, and feeling to work with delicate, miniaturized printed circuit modules and components.

Near visual acuity and accommodation to read handbooks, schematics, diagrams and tabular data, to operate precision test instruments, and repair complex miniaturized equipment. Color vision to distinguish among colored wires and interpret color codes.

Work is performed inside.

Computer and control manufacturers, who frequently are responsible for maintenance training programs, find that inadequately prepared trainees too often are selected for retraining. To aid in selecting the better prospects, tests obtained from the organizations listed in Table I have been used. The readily available Wonderlic test has proven quite effective for measuring general intelligence levels. Some control builders also furnish valuable aptitude tests that are specially tailored to reveal a facility for working with computer and numerical control devices.

TABLE I
TESTING SERVICE ORGANIZATIONS

E. F. Wonderlic P.O. Box 7 Northfield, Illinois	Human Engineering Laboratory 161 E. Erie Street Chicago, Illinois
International Correspondence Schools Scranton, Pennsylvania	Purdue University Division of Applied Psychology Lafayette, Indiana
The Psychological Corp. 304 E. 45th Street New York, New York	Science Research Associates 57 W. Grand Avenue Chicago, Illinois

TRAINING PROGRAMS

Aside from meeting the existing skill levels and equipment complexity, the scope of a training program depends upon the number of machines being acquired. If only a few machines with simple electronic controls are planned, a company may minimize training by relying on an outside contractor for maintenance. Such service contracts permit a serviceman to respond to a trouble call within a given number of hours after notification. Unless the company locates in a city with a resident technician, however, this maintenance method is often impractical. A company generally must have in-plant maintenance capability to get the job done. Most companies meet their maintenance needs by building a qualified maintenance staff.

Hiring from the outside is another technique used by many companies to avoid retraining. Although a tradesman already qualified to handle the system maintenance can usually be hired, a "bought" worker tends to change jobs frequently. Companies who have tried to hire rather than train invariably find it necessary to upgrade loyal maintenance personnel by retraining.

Once the personnel are selected, they may be trained within the plant or more commonly at the equipment manufacturer's school. These latter courses are one to three weeks in duration, depending upon the subject matter covered and the equipment complexity. Mechanical and hydraulic maintenance procedures can be covered in one to two weeks, while electronics courses may take up to three. Since course fees are usually included in the equipment price, the only additional cost is for transportation and living expenses if travel to another city is required.

When the training courses offered by the several machine and control builders are analyzed, the following topics will be found to be weighted in emphasis as follows: electronics—45 percent, shop mathematics—10 percent, hydraulics and mechanics—20 percent, control and machine operation—15 percent, and programming—10 percent. The subjects normally included in maintenance training programs conducted by manufacturers are listed below.

1. Introduction to the basic concepts of computers and numerical control.
2. Conventions used for programming and tape coding.
3. Operation and capabilities of the machine tool and control system.

370

4. Servo systems.

5. Binary number system and binary logic.

6. Control system theory of design and operation.

7. Interpretation of electronic circuit drawings and schematics.

8. Step-by-step procedures for diagnosing malfunctions that are indicated by specific symptoms.

Companies acquiring their first computer or numerically controlled machine nearly always send the maintenance supervisor and/or a technician for training at the equipment manufacturer's plant. If the equipment is point-to-point, the trained craftsman can train his properly educated co-workers during equipment installation and any typical subsequent operation. When the equipment is more complex, however, this technique is rarely acceptable. In this case, more personnel must be trained and a separate maintenance unit eventually established for the electronically controlled equipment.

Companies not using the manufacturers' courses rely on their own programs because they do not want to lose their key maintenance tradesmen temporarily, or because they own several brands of equipment with electronic controls and fear that conflicting instruction from different manufacturers may create confusion. The duration of the in-house programs depends upon the education and skill levels of the trainees and the complexity of the equipment. One very effective training program used by a large aircraft manufacturer formally lasts ten weeks. Trainees spend four hours each day in the classroom and four hours in laboratory work. Informal training and learning continue for several months.

In another company the trainees are given 600 hours of classroom instruction covering basic mathematics, DC and AC circuits, electrostatics and electromagnetics, transients, motors, basic tube and transistor theory, and circuits, e.g., amplifiers, single-shot, free-running, and bi-stable multivibrators, power supplies, digital circuits, and hydraulics. The classroom training is conducted four hours per day, five days per week, for a period of seven months. The other half of the day the trainees work in the shop where they have the opportunity to work on the controls and to receive instruction from journeymen electronic specialists on troubleshooting the various controls. Part of this time is also spent on a 100-hour laboratory phase where the trainees build and test circuits discussed in class. The laboratory projects help the trainees become familiar with instru-

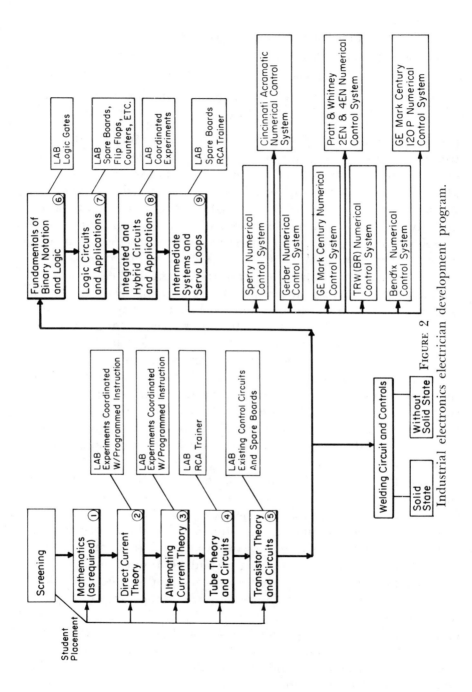

FIGURE 2 Industrial electronics electrician development program.

ments to be used on their job. Before completing their program the trainees are given advanced training on a specific control. This phase consists of 125 hours of instruction covering both the digital and analog portions of the control.

An excellent training tool is the Society of Manufacturing Engineers' programmed learning series, "Numerical Control—Its Application to Manufacturing," which includes the basic concepts of controlling a machine tool by numerically coded instructions. It covers principles of point-to-point and continuous-path systems; reading and writing a program manuscript; numerical control logic circuits and the basic electronics involved; two-valued logic systems used in numerical control; and the functioning of related servomechanisms. This programmed learning course involves 46 hours of instruction.

Figure 2 outlines an electronic electrician training course provided by Rockwell International Corp. The topical outline of an in-house course for training electronic maintenance personnel used by a large numerical control user is shown below.

Topic Outline for Electronics Training Program

1. Screening Examination

2. Direct Current Theory
    Magnetism
    Current voltage and resistance
    Ohm's law for dc
    Circuits—series, parallel, complex
    Electromagnetism
    Induced electromotive force
    Inductance

3. Alternating Current Theory
    ac theory
    Inductance
    Capacitance
    Resonance and tuned circuits
    Transformers

4. Tube Theory and Circuits
    Electron emission and diodes
    Basic triode action
    Multigrid tubes
    Amplifiers, power

Coupling methods
Wide-band amplifiers
Audio amplifiers
R.F. amplifiers
Oscillators

5. Transistor Theory and Circuits

Semiconductor fundamentals
Transistor fundamentals
Bias stabilization
Characteristic curves and charts
Audio amplifiers
Tuned amplifiers
Wide-band amplifiers
Oscillators
Measurements

6. Fundamentals of Binary Numbers and Logic

Binary system
Binary arithmetic
Boolean or logical algebra
"And" operation
"Nor" operation
Inverters
Boolean equations

7. Logic Circuits and Applications

Fundamentals of pulse circuits
Multivibrators
Logic gates
Flip-flops
Counters
Delay lines
Typical application of logic functions

8. Integrated and Hybrid Circuits

9. Intermediate Systems and Servo Loops

Feedback fundamentals
Resolvers
Synchros and servos
Applications
Detection

Command and error signal generation
Closed-loop system
Digital-to-analog conversion
Types of servo drives

10. Final Examination

The teaching staff for such a program would consist of the company's own personnel supplemented by instructors from a nearby college. While the companies operating such extensive training programs need unusually skilled tradesmen, others having only point-to-point machines or relatively simple contouring equipment achieve suitable equipment uptime with less ambitious in-house training. Those latter companies usually minimize the in-house training by relying almost totally on the equipment manufacturers' programs.

Because many personnel sent to factory training courses are not sufficiently grounded in electronics fundamentals, some companies find it worthwhile to sponsor a prefactory training course consisting of approximately 30 hours of instruction. The General Electric Company, Specialty Control Department, Waynesboro, Virginia, has developed an instruction course in binary notation and logic circuitry that can be purchased for $25. This programmed learning course is general enough that it is applicable to many different control systems. It consists of three separate manuals: "Binary Notations," "Fundamental Logic of Control Systems," and "Binary Counters." Completion of this course prior to the training at the factory ensures management that the technicians about to undergo training will be able to absorb and digest the highly concentrated content of the factory numerical control electronics courses.

MAINTENANCE STAFFING

Another question to be answered is the number of tradesmen that must be trained. The reliability of today's electronic controls is sufficiently advanced that only a few workers must undergo the more specialized training. Since computers and control systems with integrated circuits are several times more reliable than the earlier durable electronic controls, their mean time between failures is longer. Moreover, when a malfunction does occur, the faulty module is more easily identified and quickly replaced.

In addition to the equipment reliability and complexity, and the effectiveness of the repairman, the number of shifts per day and the

375

days per week the equipment is operated also influence the size of the maintenance staff. A general guideline on maintenance staffing can be inferred from the experience of others. Aerospace companies generally use approximately 0.5 of an electronic and 0.5 of a mechanical-hydraulic maintenance technician per machine. Typical aerospace machines are relatively large and complex and are often operated around-the-clock, six or seven days per week. Less ambitious operations will require considerably less maintenance, often in the range of 0.1 to 0.2 of a technician per machine.

Because of the higher productivity of automated equipment, the seemingly large maintenance staffing need not result in a higher overall maintenance cost per unit of output. "Real" maintenance costs must be viewed as including both troubleshooting and repair expenses, as well as the cost of equipment downtime and lost output. It is usually economical to invest in an effective maintenance program to minimize machine downtime expenses.

REPRESENTATIVE MAINTENANCE PROCEDURES

Both computer and numerically controlled equipment, operated around-the-clock to reduce hourly operational costs, may be in motion 15 to 20 hours per day. Because this high utilization contrasts sharply with the operation of conventional equipment, a breakdown of automated equipment creates a productivity loss equal to several conventional machines. The pressure to reduce downtime also builds because when parts are programmed for electronically controlled equipment, the necessary tooling is seldom available for emergency manufacture on conventional machines. Production of these parts is therefore delayed until the maintenance staff can repair the automated equipment.

Preventive maintenance programs, used somewhat randomly for conventional machines, are vital for complex numerical computer-controlled equipment. Rigid preventive procedures are established and carried out according to a fixed schedule. A machine, though operating satisfactorily, is temporarily removed from service for scheduled maintenance checks and adjustments. Preventive maintenance must be given the same high priority as a production job. Usually, the payoff is the discovery of an emerging problem that can be handled by a minor adjustment rather than a major repair.

Daily and weekly preventive procedures cover tape reader servicing, control circuitry and servo inspection and adjustment when needed, and checking the hydraulic and mechanical elements. The monthly, quarterly, semiannual, and annual schedules are devoted to system cleaning and calibration, lubricating mechanical parts, and the replacement of parts whose operational life exceeds predicted longevity, and such other procedures as subsystem overhaul and the installation of manufacturer change orders.

The schedule of recommended preventive maintenance procedures furnished by the equipment manufacturer is followed faithfully until deviations can be established, which are based on the experience gained from operating the equipment in a particular shop environment. An abnormally dirty or dusty shop or relatively severe temperature or moisture conditions are typical factors that cause modifications of the manufacturer's maintenance program.

Before modifying the manufacturer's recommendations, a complete record of the equipment's maintenance history should be developed and evaluated. Starting with the equipment installation, a log is maintained showing the chronology and nature of all malfunctions and the corrective action, including the procedures used for diagnosis and repair. The replacement parts used are also logged.

A detailed log embodies invaluable data which can be analyzed to uncover failure trends and help diagnose an elusive cause of a specific breakdown. Maintenance personnel should be taught to use this log as a troubleshooting tool. Repetitive problems identify equipment elements that require special precautions or special testing devices and spare parts. Patterns of a particular problem also may indicate the need for an equipment design change.

The machine operator and the maintenance technician are each responsible for completing certain sections of the log. A log entry may vary from a few key words to a paragraph describing an erratic performance or a catastrophic failure.

Maintenance programs that are compatible and interfaced with a total management system have been highly profitable. It is desirable for the system to be designed so that information from industrial engineering, maintenance, production, accounting, purchasing, etc., can be input in a computer with interface programs. (See Figure 3.) By this means management information may be quickly printed out or displayed in a format that is meaningful to those responsible in all areas of the plant. Figure 4 shows typical maintenance input into the data processing system. As part of the maintenance management system a CRT display unit may be used for constantly reviewing

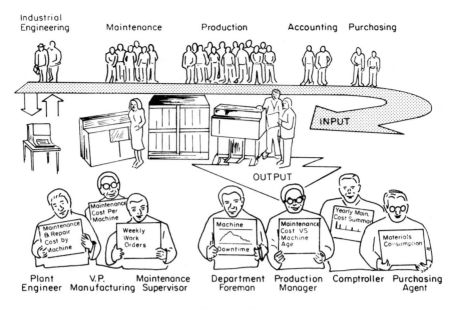

FIGURE 3
Maintenance data processing system.

and updating information. Locating this unit close to the maintenance office permits up-to-the-minute management surveillance and access to the entire factory maintenance system.

The computer outputs may also include programmed maintenance procedures. These programs may feature step-by-step instructions to the technician and a computerized lubrication schedule. Other computerized maintenance reports include a cost analysis by machine, labor expenditures, automatic time-keeping, and machine history files. These data are constantly surveyed and analyzed so that corrective action may be taken by management.

CONTROL MAINTENANCE

Maximum equipment uptime, the ultimate goal of electronic control maintenance, depends upon safe usage practices, faithful adherence to practical preventive maintenance schedules, and the utilization of efficient system test techniques. It also depends upon complete repairs, not just temporary corrections that get the machine running again.

Before any control adjustments are made, system tests should establish that a malfunction is definitely in the control. In applying such

378

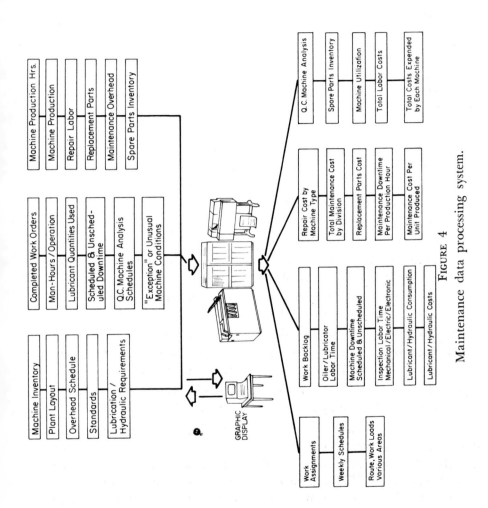

FIGURE 4

Maintenance data processing system.

tests maintenance workers must understand all normal operational input and output parameters for the major elements in each subsystem. Although system troubleshooting techniques vary and are determined by equipment characteristics and the skills and idiosyncrasies of individual workers, a representative sequence of checks for pinpointing a system malfunction follows:

1. Is the control tape information correct?
2. Does the tape reader read the input data correctly?
3. Are the control panel switches, operator console controls, and the test mode selector switch in the proper positions?
4. Are all power sources and the AC and DC power supply voltages normal?
5. Is the hydraulic pressure normal?
6. Are all the voltages and pulses in correct status at the various test points?
7. Is there backlash in the drive system?
8. Does the machine tool slide operate properly under manual control?
9. Does the machine tool slide move in the correct direction under automatic control?
10. Does the machine tool slide move approximately the desired speed when and where speed control is called for?
11. Does the machine tool slide stop at the correct position?
12. Is there a position error small enough to be a servo-following error, or so large to be an error in executing the command?
13. Does the malfunction start or coincide with an operation of a solenoid or relay in the control or machine?

When tests establish that the control is the source of the trouble, diagnostic tapes and built-in checking features on many controls greatly aid troubleshooting. As a diagnostic tape exercises the control according to a specified sequence, built-in test circuits carry out automatic checks. When certain malfunctions are encountered, these controls activate a warning indicator and stop reading the tape. After determining the diagnostic tape block number being processed when the malfunction occurred, the maintenance technician refers to the test sequence description in the maintenance manual and identifies the most likely faulty control element and, perhaps, the specific circuit. A still unlocated faulty circuit is then pursued by the technician with appropriate test instruments. Faulty circuits are usually replaced with a spare module so the control can return to work without delay. Circuit cards are usually sent back to the manufacturer for repair unless the user has the capability of repairing circuit boards.

The number of diagnostic test tapes used in preventive maintenance or troubleshooting increases with the complexity of the equipment. The test tapes listed below are considered to be a minimal set for a continuous-path control:

Linear interpolation
Circular interpolation
Square-cutting exercise
Diamond-cutting exercise
Rapid traverse
Miscellaneous functions
Sequence number
Rotary axes.

System elements tested by each of these eight tapes are indicated by the specific titles. When employed during preventive maintenance, the tapes are used for regularly scheduled inspection to determine necessary equipment adjustment and calibration. For troubleshooting a breakdown, the diagnostic tapes continuously test certain system elements while a series of checks and evaluations are made. If the source of the breakdown is not readily apparent, the tapes are sequentially processed until the test directed by one of the tapes discloses the fault. The utility of diagnostic tapes in system troubleshooting or preventive maintenance is demonstrated by a review of a specific tape that exercises the control's tape error detection device.

Tape errors, frequently resulting from improper tape punching, must be detected by the control to avoid damage to the part or equipment. Improperly punched characters and excessive data are two common types of tape errors. Since the former problem is revealed by an even number of holes representing a character, a tape parity error is present. An excessive data error occurs when the data in the control's active storage are processed by the control before the next block of tape information is fully read into intermediate storage. Frequently, this problem is the result of poor programming or a postprocessor output error in making the tape, as well as in tape

381

punching. On many controls, if the next block of data has not been read into the intermediate storage when an "end-of-cycle" pulse occurs, a tape error should be detected by the control. The "end-of-cycle" pulse is an internal control signal which indicates the end of an active cycle, i.e., the information in the active storage has been processed.

When either tape error is encountered, controls having this capability should detect it and immediately interrupt the process and activate the error indicator. In preparing an error detection diagnostic tape the manuscript data shown in Table II can be punched into a tape so that erroneous data will exist in blocks of six and nine.

TABLE II
TAPE ERROR DETECTION TEST MANUSCRIPT

n001	x+00001	y+00001		f0101		*
n002	x+00002	y+00002		f010		*
n003	x+00003	y+00003		f010		*
n004	x+00004	y+00004		f010		*
n005	x+00005	y+00005		f010		*
n006	x+00006	y+00006		f010	ø	*
n007	x+00007	y+00007		f010		*
n008	x+00008	y+00008		f999		*
n009	x+00009	y+00009	z+00009	f010	m01	*

Notes: All letters to be lower case.
     * denotes End of Block (EOB) code.
     ø denotes a 4 code punched over a zero code to create a parity error.

As the sixth block of data is read into intermediate storage, the control system should sense the parity error and stop as the tape error indicator light is activated. The test may be resumed by depressing the tape error reset and cycle start switches. By activating these buttons the operation of the "error reset" and "cycle starting" circuits are also checked.

As the ninth block of data is read from the tape the control should stop again. If it does, the tape error reset indicator will light when only part of the ninth block of data will have been read into intermediate storage, because there was not enough time allowed in Block 8 to completely read Block 9. This type of problem is also called a read-time error. If the control detects the error and reacts properly, the control logic is functioning reliably to detect an excessive data error. If the error is not detected, the diagnostic tape has successfully pinpointed a source of trouble.

382

The series of diagnostic tapes described below and used at a U.S. Atomic Energy Commission plant demonstrates how other control functions can be checked by specific test tape procedures.

One diagnostic tape has the shortest possible commands, the greatest feedrate, and the algebraic dimensional sign of each axis varied with each block of information. Since these tape commands place maximum stress on the tape reader and input circuitry, conditions are created that produce a high probability of a malfunction if any of the circuits being tested is marginal. This test tape also allows the observation and evaluation of a repetitive pulse pattern rather than a transient pulse.

A second tape repeatedly activates each miscellaneous machine function 20 times with a delay of five seconds between occurrences. Adequate time for the technician to observe the repetitive operation of each miscellaneous function relay is thereby provided.

The third AEC diagnostic tape checks servo loop response by exercising the slides at stepped inputs of one-inch movement at one inch per minute, two-inch movement at two inches per minute, and three-inch movement at six inches per minute. A fast and sensitive strip-chart voltage recorder or an oscilloscope is used to monitor servo-loop response. Problems in lag, overshoot, damping time, and quiescent point can be identified by comparing test tape performance profiles with similar previously recorded patterns that characterize normal conditions. Problems in mechanical linkages, servo gain, etc. also may be discovered by this testing procedure.

System testing techniques using the diagnostic and the built-in automatic checking features are equally valuable when troubleshooting a breakdown or during preventive maintenance. During preventive maintenance for the electronic control it is better to refrain from major adjustments to the circuits unless the processing of a diagnostic tape uncovers a problem that is likely to become critical before a major control adjustment or calibration is scheduled. Barring an emergency, control preventive maintenance is restricted to circuit inspection and the frequent check-out and lubrication of the tape reader.

Daily control preventive maintenance commonly takes about half an hour and includes a careful inspection of the turn-on and start-up procedures and, occasionally, the running of a short test tape. A review of the malfunctions and symptoms logged during operating hours but not requiring immediate correction is also an important phase of the control's daily preventive check. As well, the technician should check and clean the tape reader.

The monthly or semi-monthly maintenance check, an extension of the daily check-out, probes more deeply into circuit operation. Circuit balance and logic checks are typical preventive maintenance procedures. To inspect the balance of electronic circuits, the maintenance technician uses an oscilloscope or a special test device to display each circuit's wave form so that it can be compared to a wave form reproduction that characterizes the circuit in a normal operating condition. When a nonconforming wave form is encountered, the technician isolates the source by troubleshooting back through the circuit until a checkpoint is found with a proper wave form.

Two important usage practices that greatly affect maintenance are the avoidance of unnecessary control cool-downs and heat-ups and the keeping of foreign matter outside the control—especially outside the tape reader. In contrast to electronic controls which are turned off at the end of each day or shift, controls having power continuously applied require far less maintenance. It is evident that equipment downtime caused by malfunctions tends to decrease as continuous electronic control usage increases. The circuit component deterioration from the cool-down, heat-up process accounts for reduced reliability.

Careful handling of the tape and tape reader components also can greatly reduce control maintenance problems. A neglected or abused tape reader is almost always the greatest source of control system malfunctions. It is vital, therefore, to adhere faithfully to the manufacturer's recommendations regarding tape reader inspection, cleaning, and lubrication.

Daily usage practices should assure frequent cleaning of the tape reader's contact heads and the protection of the tape from all contamination. The operator can help by running a new tape backward and forward a few times to remove loose oxide.

Because tape reader failures may be frequent, and the repair can be time-consuming, it is wise to have a spare reader for rapid replacement. Once the spare reader has been installed, the troublesome tape reader can be repaired elsewhere on a test fixture in the maintenance area. Because a substantial investment would be required for the inventory of spare tape readers of several different models, it is desirable to standardize the type of readers used in a plant wherever feasible.

384

MECHANICAL MAINTENANCE

The mechanical maintenance practices required for computer and numerically controlled equipment are not markedly different from the techniques used generally for automated equipment. However, since the former equipment is typically high-performance machinery, the maintenance practices must be more thorough and adhere more closely to the manufacturer's recommendations. Conforming to them less often will only result in excessive equipment downtime.

Freedom from dirt and contamination is likewise a critical requisite for reliable high-performance mechanical systems. Servo systems are especially sensitive, and foreign matter as fine as lint from a maintenance rag can clog filters. Even if the shop environment is relatively clean, all equipment seals should be checked periodically so that dirt, lubricant, and cutting fluid are kept out of the servo and hydraulic systems. Hydraulic fluid is analyzed periodically to assure that there is no contamination or any change in viscosity beyond acceptable limits.

Contamination, the prime enemy of all hydraulic systems, causes premature wear in the system components and is the direct cause of many system malfunctions. Contamination can be controlled; to what extent, however, depends on how a decontamination program is implemented and maintained.

The two basic categories of system contamination are "built-in" and "externally introduced." Built-in contamination comes from system manufacture and wear of components within the system. This wear, a constant source that will always be present, can take place very rapidly or very slowly, depending on the actual amount of contamination in the system. External contaminants enter a system with new oil or through the breathers, usually as a result of careless workmanship. These contaminants consist of solids, liquids, and gases. Solids pose the greatest problem of the three, so any program of decontamination should be directed at these solids.

The solid particles that are most harmful to the hydraulic system are from one to ten microns in size; they are invisible to the unaided human eye. An average human hair, for example, is 74 microns in diameter.

These contaminants come from many different sources, for example:

1. Sealants (Teflon tape, thread seal, permatex, etc.)

2. Metal scraped off moving surfaces (pumps, valves, etc.)
3. Metal flakes from "B" nuts and threaded fittings
4. Particles from elastomer seals ("O" rings, packings, etc.)
5. Sand from castings (core sand)
6. Oxides (rust)
7. Lint from rags and clothing
8. Paint from interior and exterior of system
9. Metal dust from manufacture or repairs
10. Fiber particles from filters
11. Bacterial growth within the system
12. Carbon and varnish from overheated oil
13. Particles present in new oil as purchased
14. Particles added to system from improper work methods.

The problems that these solid particles cause within the hydraulic system include:

Erosion Wear. Closely related to sandblasting or vaporhoning, wear occurs when particles travel at high speeds through the system and erode more particles off of system components. This is a chain reaction or snowballing process and continues to generate more and more particles.

Abrasion Wear. A process that is analogous to placing sand between two mating surfaces that are in motion, abrasion wear also takes place in small passages or orifices where two or more particles pass each other and are jammed against the passage walls. Abrasion wear is also a chain reaction process.

Silting. Sometimes, fine particles tend to settle out and build up against an obstruction in the system, such as where fittings screw together or where diameters change size. At some point in time this silt bank breaks loose and a flood of particles hits the hydraulic system. Most servo valves can pass a considerable number of particles, but when the silt flood hits one, it will almost certainly jam or malfunction long enough to scrap a production part. Frequently, silting is responsible for a temporary malfunction.

Oil Oxidation. Ultra-fine metal particles can act as a catalyst to accelerate oxidation and shorten oil life. The solid contaminants in the system continue to multiply and if uncontrolled will, in turn, produce serious wear of system components, causing them to perform sluggishly, or at the extremes, causing loss of control or complete failure. Ideally, we would like to remove all of the solid contaminants from the system, but realistically, we know there is a direct relationship between a contaminated system, component life, performance, and dollars and cents.

CONTAMINATION CONTROL

To control contamination at reasonable costs, one needs to be able to determine the cleanliness levels of the hydraulic system. The levels or contamination classes are related to the particle count.

One method of collecting a sample and counting particles is known as SAE Method ARP–598. This consists of forcing a 100-milliliter oil sample through a five-micron membrane filter patch. This filter is marked with grid lines over its entire surface. The particles are counted by their micron size for a portion of the grid squares; the count is then increased in proportion to the number of uncounted squares, to give a representative count for the filter patch. These counts are then compared to the SAE contamination levels chart to determine the class number of the oil. Class 1 is least contaminated, while Class 6 is most contaminated.

Most companies choose Class 3 oil as that which can be maintained at realistic costs for satisfactory performance in a hydraulic system. One company listed the following reasons for choosing Class 3 oil:

1. Erosion wear increases rapidly between Class 4 and Class 5. At Class 3 it is still nominal.
2. Abrasion wear is at a minimum at Class 2 and Class 3. It becomes greatly accelerated between Class 4 and Class 5.
3. Silting is held to a reasonable minimum.
4. Oil oxidation is greatly reduced.
5. Maintenance of Class 3 oil can be done at minimum cost.

Using Class 3 oil in a hydraulic system means that (1) new oil must be filtered to this level; and (2) once it is in the system, it must be maintained at this level. To accomplish these goals one company took the following steps:

1. Arrangements were made with the supplier to have the hydraulic oils, D.T.E. 24 and D.T.E. 26 delivered in "jumbo," 500-gallon drums, so that large batches of oil could be filtered at one time.

The jumbo drums were stored and used in locations where temperature changes were not particularly severe, to avoid water-oil emulsification, which itself would constitute serious contamination.

2. Filter elements, the heart of any decontamination program, were designed. These depth-type elements had a five-micron rating; after 30 hours of operation, Class 6 oil could be improved to Class 3.

3. Getting the clean oil from the "jumbo" drum to the machine without contaminating it was accomplished by means of a transfer drum equipped with a pump, air filter, sight gage, by-pass valve, and filter.

4. All openings into the hydraulic system reservoirs were sealed off; then the reservoirs were fitted with a Hansen fitting and a special air filter capable of stopping 96 percent of all airborne particles. The air filter and fittings were also installed on the jumbo drum and transfer drum so that the oil was protected and contained from the time it was packaged by the supplier until it was used in the machine tool.

5. Ball-type sampling valves with no metal-to-metal contact were installed on the hydraulic system's return lines. Samples were taken every 30 days on each system and processed by the company's Production Development Laboratory. The results of the samples were sent to the firm's Plant Services Administration.

6. A running record was kept on each particle count for each machine. When a report sheet showed a system above Class 3, responsible personnel were notified so that a portable filtration unit could be tied into the system to clean it up.

7. All maintenance mechanics, oilers, and supervisory personnel underwent a training program, which emphasized work habits and proper procedures.

8. Specifications were written to provide a procedure for cleaning systems and checking system cleanliness on all new, used, retrofitted, and rebuilt automated machines. These specifications became part of all installation contracts.

All of the foregoing steps are essential for a decontamination program that really works. If these steps are followed, there should be a marked reduction in hydraulic system malfunctions and downtime.

The company that developed that program also worked up a list of "do's" and "don'ts," for maintaining a Class 3 hydraulic system. It is worth considering:

1. Remember: the particle you can't see does the damage.
2. Don't use flexible lines unless it is absolutely necessary; if it is necessary, use Teflon- or nylon-lined lines.
3. Remove paint and spray down components and fittings with Freon before opening any part of the system.
4. Have clean line plugs and cover plates on the job site before opening any part of the hydraulic system.
5. Clean all reservoir and hose fittings with Freon before adding oil.
6. Don't use any painted, aluminum-, brass-, or cadmium-plated fittings on numerical control hydraulic systems. Use steel fittings.
7. Keep reservoirs completely sealed and unpainted internally.
8. Thoroughly clean all components and parts before assembly. Watch blind holes and threaded holes particularly.
9. Place all parts in plastic bags if they are not to be used immediately.
10. Don't use rags anyplace around the hydraulic system; there is no such thing as a lint-free rag.
11. On a new hydraulic servo system or after major repairs, run system for 24 hours with flushing blocks installed. Change axis filters and run ten minutes before removing flushing blocks.
12. After minor repairs to a hydraulic servo system, run the system for a minimum of 15 minutes before releasing the machine to production. Servo valves should be bypassed for ten minutes of this time.
13. Don't add any oil to the equipment hydraulic systems unless you know that oil has been filtered and has been proven to be Class 3. Transport oil only in the clean transfer drums.
14. Work with clean hands, clean tools, in clean surroundings.
15. Remember: new parts are dirty parts; new filters are dirty filters; new oil is dirty oil.

BEARING MAINTENANCE

Bearing failures, long a frustrating problem among machine mal-

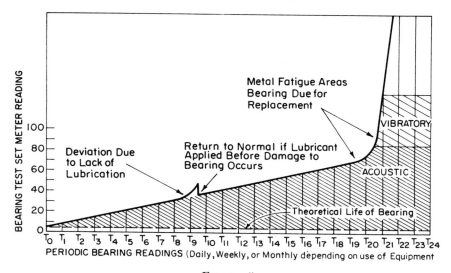

FIGURE 5

Predicting bearing failure by instrumentation checks.

functions, have been reduced by several companies with an imaginative acoustical test technique. Bearing noise is periodically and systematically recorded on tape and compared with noises under the same conditions in a previous six-month period. Figure 5 graphically indicates bearing life.

PREVENTIVE MECHANICAL MAINTENANCE

Preventive maintenance procedures recommended by a typical machine tool manufacturer provide an indication of the frequency of repeating checks that is required by high-performance mechanical systems operating under computer or numerical control.

Checks To Be Made During Each Shift

1. Refill the hydraulic unit oil if the sight gauge level is lower than 80 percent.
2. Check the oil level of the X–, Y–, and Z–axis gear boxes. If it is not above the sight bulb line, fill the unit.
3. Check the Y–axis lube tank pressure; 5 to 25 psi is normal.
4. Check to insure that the machine and power supply are free from oil leaks.

120-Hour Preventive Maintenance Schedule

1. Clean or replace the air line filters.
2. Clean and inspect the X– and Y–axis Accupin covers.
3. Check all exposed oil lines and repair any existing leaks.

480-Hour Preventive Maintenance Schedule

1. Check and record the pressure drop across the hydraulic filter on the power supply. If it exceeds 18 psi, replace the filter cartridge.
2. Clean the hydraulic heat exchanger's air passage.
3. Check and clean the air inlet filters on the hydraulic power supply.
4. Take an oil sample and send it for analysis.
5. Check the alignment of the drive motor and pump.
6. Measure and record the drain line leakage rate of the X, Y, Z table and the spindle drive motors, both when the motors are stationary and when they are operated in both directions.

1440-Hour Preventive Maintenance Schedule

1. Grease the hydraulic pump couplings.
2. Adjust the pressure switches.
3. Check the pump case:
   a. Drain pump case and remove the covers to inspect for evidence of flaked bearings or the presence of other foreign material in the bottom of the pump case.
   b. If any foreign material is found in the pump case, examine it carefully. If the material is metallic, do not operate the pump until it has been completely cleaned and the bearings inspected.
4. Check all axis accuracy with a Vernac.
5. Check all machine alignments.
6. Change all hydraulic line filters.

2800-Hour Preventive Maintenance Schedule

1. Remove way covers and check condition of way wipers, joint covers, and seals.
2. Turn the hydraulic pumps off. Discharge the accumulator and remove the gauge. Lower a dipstick through the opening until

it rests on the top of the piston. Remove the dipstick and record the level of oil above the piston (if the oil level is greater than two inches, the "O" ring must be replaced). Replace the gauge and recharge the accumulator.

3. Check the tightness of mounting bolts and screws of the following units:

   a. X–, Y–, and Z–axis drive motors
   b. X–, Y–, and Z–axis tachometer motors
   c. Spindle drive motor mounting bracket.

4. Check the tightness of the servo valve mounting bolts for the X–, Y–, and Z–axis feed and traverse with a 98-inch-pound torque. Check the spindle with a 175-inch-pound torque.

It is also important to establish a lubrication schedule delineating all parts that must be lubricated. The requirements for lubricating frequency and type of lubricant should be closely followed. The operation of automatic lubrication systems should also be inspected periodically. When one considers that about two-thirds of the malfunctions of a computer or numerically controlled system occur in the mechanical elements, the importance of proper preventive lubrication becomes readily apparent.

TEST EQUIPMENT

The time-honored axiom that a worker is no better than his tools has special relevance to maintenance for computer and numerical controls. Precision oscilloscopes and voltmeters, capable of measuring extremely short time periods and small voltage levels in pulse circuits, and other finely calibrated test instruments are major requirements. In addition to these and the traditional small hand tools needed for mechanical and hydraulic repairs, recorders, tube testers, tachometers, soldering and desoldering tools, wire unwrapping and wrapping tools, and wire nippers and cutters also may be required. Like the maintenance skill levels, test equipment requirements depend upon the equipment complexity.

A recommended list of test equipment and miscellaneous hand tools is specified by the equipment manufacturer. For less complex equipment, like most positioning machines, the required tools and equipment cost between $500 and $2,000. Here the major test equipment items are a voltmeter, an ammeter, and an oscilloscope. Complex machines demand a considerably greater investment. The test equipment enumerated below costing several thousands of dollars and used by an AEC facility, provides an indication of the requirements for a diverse array of complex machines.

Oscilloscopes

A portable, rugged, well-maintained oscilloscope is needed to display wave forms and pulse rates for testing digital control circuits. The rise time should be less than 0.1 microsecond for checking control pulses; sensitivity should be 50 millivolts per centimeter for checking electronic switch settings and servo-loop response. The horizontal base should have a calibrated time range adjustable from about one microsecond to 0.1 second per centimeter. The scope should also have triggering level controls for both positive and negative input signals. A fast rise time, dual-gun oscilloscope with delayed synchronization may also be needed to compare one pulse pattern with another for special circuit analysis.

Just as a well-maintained oscilloscope can be a maintenance worker's best friend, a defective scope can be his worst enemy. The cost of hours spent fruitlessly looking for transient faults with a marginal or faulty oscilloscope can offset severalfold the cost of a precise, high-speed instrument. As well, an improper oscilloscope test setup, particularly one having a faulty connection with the circuit being tested, can cause serious transistor and diode damage to the control circuit.

New maintenance equipment should include faster operating oscilloscopes. The speed at which integrated circuits operate is 100 to 1000 times faster than transistor circuits and a million or more times faster than relays. Industry will have to keep abreast of this need for better diagnostic equipment. No longer will a clip lead carry the signal to the oscilloscope. Proper test leads and grounding will be required to prevent the loss or masking of a nanosecond signal.

Voltmeter

A vacuum tube voltmeter is used for setting electronic switching levels and for checking certain analog voltages. The voltmeter is also used for making accurate DC low voltage or AC sinusoidal measurements. With integrated circuitry, however, a voltmeter is less useful, since it cannot detect a signal that only lasts for a millionth of a second.

Voltage Differential Transformer Gage Head

A linear voltage differential transformer gage head with amplifier is necessary for making some mechanical tests and for correlating the machine and control actions.

Strip-Chart Recorder Amplifier

A strip-chart recorder amplifier is useful, not only in conjunction with the gauge head for recording mechanical information, but also for recording voltage data in the servo loops. The response of the servo loops to commands may be recorded and used for comparison with analyzing future problems.

Oscilloscope Camera

Since some circuit activity occurs too fast for a strip-chart recorder, an oscilloscope camera can be valuable for high-speed circuit wave form recording. Just after a new system is installed and thought to be perfectly tuned, the correct wave form of each circuit is often recorded by the oscilloscope camera. Wave form records of the circuits in their tuned condition are then used to compare future circuit wave forms during preventive maintenance or trouble-shooting.

Volt-Ohm-Milliammeter

A volt-ohm-milliammeter is the most frequently used piece of test equipment. It should accommodate at least 20K ohms per volt (DC). In most controls, trouble can be isolated in a particular section by test tapes and built-in check features. Faulty components such as diodes and transistors in a section or logic board are then detected through the use of this instrument. Because of the usefulness and the relative low investment, every electronic technician should have a volt-ohm-milliammeter. Just as with an oscilloscope, a defective or improperly operated volt-ohm-milliammeter can quickly cause control circuit damage.

Pulse Generator

A pulse generator can be quite helpful for introducing test pulses into the control system. It is especially useful in maintaining controls which have pulses generated by a logical sequence of events, but do not have a built-in, constant digital clock.

Audio Oscillator

An audio oscillator can be especially useful to stimulate resolver inputs into electronic switching circuits while adjusting wave shapers.

The Interferometric Laser Calibrator

More and more companies are making effective use of the interferometric laser calibrator for numerically and computer controlled machine check-out. Machine accuracy and repeatability can be determined in hours instead of days with this device. Furthermore, the output of the interferometric laser calibrator can be tied into a remote time-shared computer to determine the relevant statistics and plot a histogram of the data taken for machine positioning capability study.

The first portion of the program calculates the statistics required for the capability study. The following statistics are generated from the input study:

the mean, variance, standard deviation, and three sigma values— X ± 3 sigma;

the range, including the largest and smallest data numbers;

the confidence interval of the mean, the standard deviation, and the process calculated at the 95 and 99 percent levels.

A table of values required for confidence estimates is stored in memory for use with the program. The program automatically selects the proper table values and interpolates when a table value does not exist for a particular sample size. The interpolation is linear, the distribution of the sample data is assumed to be normal, and the confidence intervals are at 95 and 99 percent.

The second part of the program plots a histogram of the input data. The cell size and cell midpoint are selected by the operator. The computer program handles both linear and rotary motion.

Other Equipment

Depending upon control reliability characteristics, special test equipment, such as a logic package and component testers, is often worth the investment. Most control manufacturers design and sell their own special units for easier and faster control troubleshooting. A good transistor tester has proved to be invaluable, since some faulty transistors cannot be detected with the volt-ohm-milliammeter.

Because controls with integrated circuits may operate at speeds up to 1000 times faster than transistor circuits, and also at lower voltages, an integrated circuit control requires somewhat different maintenance equipment. The traditional voltmeter is no longer useful to display a signal parameter that is only present for a millionth of a second.

System testing procedures for a control with integrated circuits are also different. It is no longer possible to check a discrete input and output signal. Rather, testing requires multiple input signals of a specified amplitude, width, and timing, as well as multi-point examination of output signals. Special procedures are also needed because integrated circuits are more sensitive to noise interference during testing and operation. They may require special isolated grounding.

The shift to integrated circuits should lead to faster and easier training of maintenance personnel because of simplified integrated circuit design. It is no longer necessary to study each transistor and diode; one need only study the general function performed by the functional modules.

SPARE PARTS

A computer and numerical control maintenance program that includes policies and practices to minimize equipment downtime is incomplete if it does not provide for readily available spare parts and assemblies. An adequate supply of spare parts should be close at hand so that component repair can be restricted to the maintenance area after a spare component has been installed quickly in the equipment. It is not unusual for the annual savings in reduced equipment downtime made possible by readily available parts to be as great as 50 percent of the spare parts inventory.

So that optimum machine tool utilization can be accomplished with a minimum investment, computerized spare parts inventories have been developed that furnish management information similar to the following data:

1. Part listing—mechanical or hydraulic; electronic or electrical.
2. Part number—machine brand; model number; control system; part description; replacement source.
3. Spare part sorting and print-outs by—machine; mechanical or

hydraulic; electronic or electric components and assemblies; and commonality between machines.

Once this program is in operation, print-outs or decks of cards may be distributed between other company divisions or other area companies with similar equipment. Such computer-aided management of spare parts inventories has assured an adequate supply with the minimum investment of capital.

Critical spare parts should not only be inventoried in the plant, they should be stored in the shop area near the associated equipment. Such immediate access not only speeds replacement, but also promotes quicker troubleshooting by facilitating the immediate insertion of a good part for one suspected of faulty operation.

The spare parts recommended by the equipment manufacturer are stocked until some operational experience suggests a change. Generally, the electromechanical and mechanical parts demonstrate the highest failure rates. Relays, switches, solenoids, and tape readers are examples of such items. Electronic component failures have their highest frequency during the first 200 operational hours. Beyond that period, these electronic components will have relatively low mortality rates. Expensive mechanical parts such as drive motors and hydraulic and servo components are stocked when the machine is critical to production, is extremely costly, or has a high hourly operational cost, or when the part cannot be flown in from the manufacturer or a distributor within 24 hours.

IMPACT OF THE COMPUTER-CONTROLLED SYSTEM ON MAINTENANCE

With the advent of the direct numerical control (DNC) and the inevitable growth of computer-controlled machine systems, the maintenance function faces a new challenge and expanded opportunities. The very computer that runs the system will be the best maintenance tool that can be used. Such utilization will involve a step-by-step troubleshooting approach, using the CRT device at the machine tool. This will further permit the computer to perform many system diagnostics. Also, the limits of each module and component can therefore be programmed and analyzed by means of software rather than hardware. The automatic equipment checking techniques developed in the NASA space exploration program clearly demonstrate the technical possibilities. Further application developments will surely create the necessary economical techniques for commercial production operations.

Significant maintenance cost reductions will accrue from attendant design changes; these include a reduction in overall system electronics, transfer of a large part of the electronics from the hostile shop environment, elimination of the troublesome tape reader, etc. Once system and machine control is transferred to a central computer, as much as two-thirds of the electronics previously located on the shop floor can be relocated in the controlled climate of the computer room where component reliability is much greater. Not only can the atmosphere be more friendly, but having the bulk of the electronics in one central location eases the problem of managing an otherwise dispersed maintenance staff and simplifies replacement-part logistics. Certain problem causes are also avoided since data are entered into the system at the central computer; the medium for entering computer information, be it cards, punched paper, or magnetic tape, is not contaminated by the grease, coolant, dust, chips, and magnetic fields so common in the plant environment.

Routine maintenance reports, computer-generated for each machine as a by-product of the control process, are not only invaluable in analyzing the effectiveness of the maintenance program, they also help in designing preventive maintenance schedules. Analyses of past equipment failures and repair expenses can be used to assess future maintenance cost probabilities when comparing refurbishment or replacement options.

Computerized performance monitoring and fault isolation can be accomplished through various techniques, but a general approach involves the continual computer monitoring of machine transducers. Standard machine performance characteristics are determined and stored for computer evaluation when a critical machine function is sensed. If the machine performance is marginal, a test program may be automatically executed to determine if the apparent problem is significant. Component monitoring can be accomplished on a go, no-go or a quantitative basis. When a sensed condition exceeds acceptable limits, an alert message is generated. In one typical system, parameters are programmed for the computer and if a transducer value exceeds an acceptable parameter, an alarm indicating a developing problem or an actual malfunction is signaled to the maintenance supervisor and the shop foreman. Examples of maintenance elements that can readily be computer monitored and reported are:

Spindle and axis-way lubrication

Hydraulic oil temperature and pressure

Spindle vibration and machine chatter

Control power supply voltages

Gear box backlash—each axis

Contamination of hydraulic filters

Hydraulic volume per established axis feedrate

Maximum rates of acceleration and deceleration

Loss of feedback signal—valve unbalance or servo amplifier

Line voltage fluctuations—emergency stop or auxiliary failure

Axis over-travel—limit switch function

Command counters phase with reference counters.

Synchronization circuits, spindle speeds (actual versus programmed)

Record number of maintenance calls per month coded by category, i.e., mechanical, hydraulic, electrical, etc.

Maintenance man-hours and accumulated replacement parts costs per machine.

The time-sharing capability of the central computer, in addition to controlling several machines, allows the various transducers to be monitored several times per second. Since enlarging deviations can be measured by the computer, it is possible to have the computer sense a worsening condition and signal for corrective action before a major breakdown occurs. The corrective action may involve stopping the process, sending a warning message to the maintenance department, instructing the operator to make an adjustment before proceeding—e.g., calling for a resupply of the hydraulic oil, or, if an adaptive control capability exists, recalculating modified machine commands that will allow the process to continue satisfactorily within the new constraints.

Depending upon the stored program sophistication, the central computer may have the capability of analyzing the malfunction symptoms and sending recommendations that guide the maintenance technician in which troubleshooting procedure to follow. In one system that employs a failure-checking program to monitor and diagnose the system's operations, an error message occurring in the event of malfunction is immediately displayed on CRT's at both the machine tool and the maintenance department. For many problems, the computer's checking program can diagnose the problem sufficiently to identify the particular circuit board to replace.

Some large-scale computers even make it feasible for much of the logic contained in equipment maintenance manuals to be called into computer memory. By sensing key information about the malfunction, the computer in effect associates the symptoms' characteristics with the possible causes programmed in its memory. Along with a list of possible faulty components, the computer might also list the testing procedure for checking the equipment to determine if the suspected fault is actually the trouble. An example of how such computer-aided troubleshooting concepts may be applied is illustrated in the following section.

When a malfunction is encountered, the operator or maintenance worker activates the computer program by depressing the "9" and "10" Operator Select buttons on the machine control; he then depresses the "SEND" button. The program is self-continuing after appropriate responses, which are transmitted by the worker through the use of four-digit thumbwheel switches on the control. When the maintenance worker depresses the Operator Select buttons "9" and "10," the following introductory information from the computer is displayed on the CRT at the machine tool.

0000—THIS PROGRAM IS DESIGNED TO PROVIDE THE USER WITH A CONVENIENT MEANS OF QUICKLY AND EASILY ISOLATING THE CAUSE OF A MALFUNCTION AND TO SUGGEST THE MOST LOGICAL STEPS FOR CORRECTION. IT ALSO CONTAINS SECTIONS DEVOTED TO ADJUSTMENT PROCEDURES, AND REFRESHER TRAINING COURSES. TO PROCEED WITH THE PROGRAM, DIAL THE SEQUENCE NUMBER THUMBWHEELS BELOW THE DISPLAY SCREEN TO 0002, ALSO PRESS THE INSERT BUTTON TO THE RIGHT OF THE THUMBWHEELS, AND THEN PRESS THE "SEND" BUTTON.

Then the following information is displayed:

0002—THE PROCEDURE YOU HAVE JUST FOLLOWED WILL ALLOW YOU TO BRANCH TO ANY DESIRED AREA OF THIS PROGRAM. AT EACH POINT IN THE TROUBLESHOOTING SECTION THE PROGRAM WILL ASK A QUESTION RELATED TO THE SPECIFIC PROBLEM. ANSWER THE QUESTION IN THE FORM OF A SELECTION OF THE FOUR-DIGIT SOURCE NUMBER THAT FITS YOUR SITUATION. ANSWERS ARE EITHER A YES-NO RESPONSE OR MULTIPLE CHOICE. FOR EXAMPLE, "DO YOU WISH TO CONTINUE WITH THIS PROGRAM?"

400

0003 — YES

7777 — NO

Assuming that the answer to the above question is affirmative, the following Master Program Library is displayed:

0003—MASTER LIBRARY SOURCE INFORMATION AVAILABLE

    0700—TROUBLESHOOTING GUIDE

    7000—TRAINING DATA—ELECTRICAL

    0200—CLEANING PROCEDURES

    0110—KEY AXIS SIGNALS

    0220—SETUP PROCEDURES—ELECTRICAL

    7000—MACHINE TEST PROGRAM INDEX

    0120—WIREWRAP AND PLUG LISTS

For illustrative purposes, a malfunction in the machine will be pursued. It is therefore necessary to enter the four-digit sequence number 0700. The following display would then appear:

0700—TROUBLESHOOTING GUIDE: INSERT AND SEND THE SOURCE NUM-
    BER WHICH IS ASSOCIATED WITH THE PROBLEM SUBSYSTEM

    1000—AXIS

    6200—TOOL CHANGER

    6100—SPINDLE SPEEDS

    6300—CRT

Since the problem being experienced is incorrect feedrates, the complete list of troubleshooting suggestions related to axis feedrates will be displayed by entering the code 1000 by using the four thumbwheels; then the following information is displayed:

1000—AXIS:FURTHER DEFINE YOUR AXIS PROBLEM

    4100—BIT LOSS

    4200—FEEDRATES NOT CORRECT

    4400—ROUGH AXES

    7001—JOGS INCORRECTLY

    7001—JOGS OVERHEAT

    7001—HIGH CURRENT, ALL AXES

    4500—BAD LEAD CHECK

    1002—MISPOSITIONING

4300—SERVO ERRORS

4700—AXES RUNAWAY

7000—AXIS OSCILLATION

7000—HIGH CURRENT, ONE AXIS

0200—AXES MOTORS DIRTY

4600—AXIS GOES WRONG WAY

From this the maintenance worker selects the "Feedrates not correct" category to further define the problem. After the code 4200 is entered through the thumbwheels, the following information is displayed:

4200—INCORRECT FEEDRATES

    ARE ALL FEEDRATES INCORRECT?

        4210—YES

        4220—NO

After an affirmative reply is given, the computer program displays the following troubleshooting instruction:

4210—CHECK FEEDRATE OVERRIDE VOLTAGE
        (MCU SLOT 16, PIN 8)

    IS THIS VOLTAGE HIGHER THAN 0.6 VOLTS D.C.?

        4211—YES

        4212—NO

Another affirmative answer prompts the following information:

4211—REPLACE SED BOARD. LOCATION MCU SLOT 16

        7777—YES

        4213—NO

When the computer has been told that this instruction was carried out and the malfunction still exists, it suggests the following action:

4213—CHECK WIRING TO FEEDRATE OVERRIDE POT

    PROBLEM SOLVED?

    7777—YES

    4200—NO

At this point, the maintenance worker locates the source of the problem and tells the computer that the malfunction is corrected. From such an example, it is apparent that the program recommends a logical sequence of steps to isolate the problem and its solution. Other similar computer programs define cleaning and setup procedures, and some make use of simulated wave forms displayed on the CRT screen to illustrate what should be appearing on the maintenance worker's oscilloscope.

The immediate accessibility of the information contained in these Diagnostic Programs not only aids in providing faster response to troubleshooting and ultimately more productive up-time on the machine tool, but it also has a marked influence on personnel staffing requirements. In total, the influence of all these computer aids when fully developed should reduce the number of maintenance workers required and, to some extent, the level of skills they must have.

SUMMARY

When the introduction of computer or numerically controlled equipment is contemplated, it must be recognized that a more sophisticated maintenance program will be required—particularly if no automated, high-performance equipment is owned. Efficient maintenance of electronically controlled equipment will undoubtedly defy the unprepared traditional maintenance tradesman. Maximum equipment uptime will therefore require skills, practical preventive maintenance, and the proper test equipment and spare parts. Without a total management commitment to fulfilling these needs, the investment in computer and numerically controlled equipment will probably fail to achieve its true potential.

Index

410